Gene Autry

Gene Autry

His Life and Career

Don Cusic

McFarland & Company, Inc., Publishers
Jefferson, North Carolina, and London

The present work is a reprint of the library bound edition of Gene Autry: His Life and Career, *first published in 2007 by McFarland.*

LIBRARY OF CONGRESS CATALOGUING-IN-PUBLICATION DATA

Cusic, Don.
Gene Autry : his life and career / Don Cusic.
p.   cm.
Includes bibliographical references and index.

ISBN 978-0-7864-5978-0
softcover : 50# alkaline paper ∞

1. Autry, Gene, 1907–1998.   2. Motion picture actors and actresses —
United States — Biography.   3. Singers — United States — Biography.
I. Title.
PN2287.A9C87   2010   791.4302'8092 — dc22   2007003814
[B]

British Library cataloguing data are available

Cover images: Gene Autry, c. mid-1940 (Photofest);
background guitar, ©2010 Shutterstock

Manufactured in the United States of America

*McFarland & Company, Inc., Publishers
Box 611, Jefferson, North Carolina 28640
www.mcfarlandpub.com*

ACKNOWLEDGMENTS

The first serious research I did on Gene Autry came when I wrote *Cowboys and the Wild West: An A to Z Guide from the Chisholm Trail to the Silver Screen* (New York: Facts on File, 1994). In addition to that encyclopedia, I also wrote biographies of Eddy Arnold, *Eddy Arnold: I'll Hold You in My Heart* (Nashville: Rutledge Hill, 1997) and Riders in the Sky, *The Cowboy Way: The Amazing True Adventures of Riders in the Sky* (Lexington: University Press of Kentucky, 2003), which added information about singing cowboys in general and Gene Autry in particular. The first serious treatment of Gene Autry that I remember reading was Douglas B. Green's chapter on Autry in *Stars of Country Music*, edited Bill C. Malone and Judith McCulloh. That chapter changed my thinking on Gene Autry when I first read it in the mid–1970s.

I have been writing this book — off and on — since 1999. I must admit that I stopped writing several times, convinced I should forget it, but discovered that I could not *not* write this book; it simply grabbed hold of me and would not let go. There were long periods of time when the manuscript was in a filing cabinet, but I was always drawn back to it. Sometimes subjects do that to you; in this case, I felt compelled to write this book on Gene Autry despite a number of obstacles and barriers along the way.

O. J. Sikes, who knows as much as any living person about western music, answered countless e-mail inquiries and provided names, facts and information that only he could locate. Elvin Sweetan from the Gene Autry Oklahoma Museum allowed me to go through a large number of scrapbooks that he had collected. Douglas B. Green, known to others as "Ranger Doug" of Riders in the Sky, is a friend and fellow Autry devotee whom I called on when I had questions that stumped me. Larry Hopper provided valuable feedback and a copy of his excellent work on Bob Nolan. Don Reeves at the Cowboy and Western Heritage Museum in Oklahoma City made me feel welcome there. Kevin Mulroy at the Autry Museum helped me in Los Angeles. Phillip Loy, Michael Duchemin and Gary Yoggy with the Popular Culture Association are always good critics for ideas.

I had conversations about Gene Autry with Eddy Arnold, Mike Curb, Charles Wolfe, Ivan Tribe, William Lightfoot, Johnny Western, Don Edwards, Fred LaBour ("Too Slim"), Wesley and Marilyn Tuttle, Ronnie Pugh, Packy Smith, and attendees at the International Conference on Country Music, organized by James Akenson and held at the end of May each year at Belmont University. This group can always be counted on to provide connections and insights about a variety of country performers.

Glenn White, in Oklahoma City, invited me over to his house one evening and provided me with interesting stories and rare press clippings. In Dover, England, I visited Dave Barnes several times, and he provided a number of old and rare CDs of Autry's recordings. Jon Guyot Smith and I exchanged numerous e-mails, and he sent me articles from *Gene Autry's Friends* (the newsletter which he edits) and corrected facts; I also corresponded via e-mail with Wayne Daniel, who found a number of articles buried in *Billboard* and *Variety* for me. The Country Music Hall of Fame and Museum's Oral History Project includes interviews with Johnny Bond, Frankie Marvin, Art Satherley and Ray Whitley, which I consulted, along with the museum's copy of the unpublished manuscript on Gene Autry by Johnny Bond.

I am indebted to the Mike Curb College of Entertainment and Music Business at Belmont University for providing travel funds for several research trips. Becky Williams, Page Carter and Barbara Goss at the Lila Bunch Library at Belmont always smiled while they provided needed help.

I am the editor of *The Western Way*, a quarterly magazine published by the Western Music Association, and am indebted to the many friends in western music and the WMA who provided insights and observations about Gene Autry from personal experiences with him.

At Autry's birthplace in Tioga, Texas, the folks at the local real estate office and local Chamber of Commerce were kind and helpful. I would also like to thank those working at the following libraries who provided help whenever I needed: the Autry Museum of the West, the Academy of Motion Pictures Arts and Sciences Margaret Herrick Library, the Museum of Television and Radio in Los Angeles, the libraries at UCLA and Southern California University in Los Angeles; the Chicago Historical Center and the Harold Washington Public Library in Chicago; the archive at the Baseball Hall of Fame in Cooperstown, New York; the Frist Library and Archives at the Country Music Hall of Fame and Museum in Nashville; the Cowboy and Western Heritage Museum in Oklahoma City; the Gene Autry Oklahoma Museum in Gene Autry, Oklahoma; the Will Rogers Museum and Archive in Claremore, Oklahoma; the downtown public libraries in Atlanta and Nashville.

For pictures I am indebted to Sherry Bond, Stan Corliss, Brenda Colladay at the Grand Ole Opry Archive, Elvin Sweeten with the Gene Autry Oklahoma Museum and Denny Adcock with the Country Music Hall of Fame and Museum. John Rumble was also a great help at the Country Music Hall of Fame and Museum.

The Autry office in Los Angeles did not provide information for this book; however, Maxine Hansen, Karla Buhlman and the late Alex Gordon were always kind, considerate and helpful when I visited their office and provided information to me for articles on Gene Autry prior to my working on this manuscript. (One day in the Autry offices I committed the ultimate faux pas: I asked about Jon Tuska. Tuska does not have a favorable opinion of Autry, and the two had clashed, with Autry at one time threatening a lawsuit against the writer; in Tuska's books of western film criticism he doesn't find much nice to say about Gene Autry.)

I would like to thank my wife, Jackie, for being supportive of someone immersed in writing to the point of sometimes being distracted at home. Jackie always provides a wonderful home no matter what book I'm working on. At the end of the day, we did not discuss Gene Autry or watch his movies together; that was a nice break for someone who spent much of the rest of his time living, eating and breathing Gene Autry. My sons Jesse, Eli and Alex, with my daughter, Delaney, and her husband, Scott, always remind me of the value of family and how lucky I am. Hopefully, some day they'll realize why I spent so many hours away from home to write a book about Gene Autry.

It is customary at this point for the author to accept the blame for all mistakes, errors, omissions and anything wrong in this book. I have never liked doing that; however, I must bow to the inevitable.

Finally, I loved every single day I spent working on this book on Gene Autry and hope the reader enjoys reading it as much as I enjoyed writing it.

TABLE OF CONTENTS

INTRODUCTION

Sitting in the 21st century, it is difficult to fathom just how popular, how famous, how *big* Gene Autry was during an approximately 20 year period during the 20th century. By and large, young people no longer have a fascination with cowboys and the West, so the music of Gene Autry is not on their iPods, and his movies seem hopelessly outdated. And, of course, the notion of wholesome entertainment with a good guy cowboy hero doesn't dominate the entertainment landscape as it used to.

During the period 1935 to 1955 Gene Autry influenced countless youngsters — most now over 50 years old. Grandparents of today's youth remember him because they wanted to *be* like the Gene Autry they saw on the silver screen.

That is the true, lasting legacy of Gene Autry: To have been a person that others wanted to emulate. Kids who grew up in the 1930s, 1940s and into the 1950s carry the memory of Gene Autry as a straight-shooting hero — honest, true and brave — with them their whole lives. He was a source of strength, an example of fairness and justice, and a model that kids used to guide the decisions made in their own lives. In that way, he profoundly touched the personal lives of millions of Americans.

On the professional side, he was one of the most important figures in the history of country music. Gene Autry was the second influential artist in country music, after Jimmie Rodgers. Rodgers paved the way for country singers to be superstars, and his "blue yodels" influenced countless singers, including Gene Autry. Autry's influence was taking country music to the nation; the singing cowboy movies were the first vehicle that carried country music to a national audience. Gene Autry also changed the look of country music. The mountaineer and hillbilly, both early images of country entertainers, were not positive images; the cowboy was. As Douglas B. Green once astutely observed, "No youngster in the thirties and forties ever wanted to grow up to be a hillbilly, but thousands upon thousands wanted to be cowboys."[1]

Some people have a talent for making a lot of money; most don't. Gene Autry was one of those rare individuals who had a talent for making, and keeping, a lot of money. This talent — and it is a talent — is especially rare for artists and musicians, who tend to devote their time and energies to making music, not money. Indeed, most have a disdain for money because, for the most part, the accumulation of money is not a driving force in their lives; the creation of something new, like a song or work of art, is the driving force. Money is either a by-product at best, or a barrier to creation at worst.

Gene Autry was fortunate to earn a great deal of money during his lifetime. His wealth came from record sales, movies, personal appearances and merchandising in show business. In fact, it was the merchandising that supplied the really big money for Autry. This did not happen by accident; if Autry had only relied on his record sales, movie income and personal appearances, he would not have attained the wealth that he did. In that way, he is a model for all the current artists who sell t-shirts, caps and other merchandise at their concerts.

It is rare for artists to have a business sense, a concern for the business side of their career, but Gene Autry certainly had a business sense and was as interested in the business side of his career as he was in the performing side. Johnny Western observed that Gene Autry "had two personas: a performing persona and a business persona."[2]

Autry realized the value of investing in his career, spending money to promote himself and his show, on publicity and hiring people to take care of the myriad aspects of his businesses and career. He also knew the value of investing in long-term businesses, like radio and real estate, that provided a return on the dollar which provided him a wealthy lifestyle later in life. Gene Autry viewed wealth as the just reward for his hard work and success in his movie and recording careers, and he pursued material wealth with no shame or inhibition.

Gene Autry's professional successes are well known and are documented in this book. But his basic decency as a person is also a success. Jon Guyot Smith, an Autry fan, collector and friend, notes: "When he was relaxed and among friends, Gene told fascinating stories. I have never known a more relaxing person to be around. He was so good natured and unpretentious in his demeanor that one felt at ease talking to him about anything."[3] There are literally countless stories — most untold — about Gene Autry's easygoing nature, his friendliness, his generosity, sincerity, lack of pretension, common decency and sense of loyalty to those close to him.

The singing cowboy movies have generally been overlooked by film historians and even historians of western movies; at best, the singing cowboy movies have been a footnote in the history of the movies. But there have been no other movie heroes as influential to young audiences as the singing cowboys, especially during the 1930s and 1940s. They were not "cutting edge" movies in the Hollywood sense, and they were not "classics" in terms of having an ongoing appeal to movie watchers, critics or historians. But for their day and time, no other movies reached a broader cross-section of Americans, especially in rural areas, or inspired youngsters to strive for something bigger than themselves than the singing cowboy films.

Proof of their importance is the fact that so many Americans today, now headed into their golden years, remember Gene Autry and the other singing cowboys with the fondest of memories. And they wish their children and grandchildren could have a hero like Gene Autry to look up to and help guide America toward its future.

1

BEGINNINGS

It seems appropriate that the "Cowboy President," Teddy Roosevelt, was in office in 1907, the year Gene Autry was born. Buffalo Bill Cody was still touring with his *Wild West Show*, and during this year an Ohio dentist named Zane Grey traveled to the West, where he gained the inspiration to write western novels when he returned to his home in Pennsylvania. In Chicago, Max Aronson formed Essanay Film Manufacturing Company with George K. Spoor; Aronson changed his name to Bronco Billy Anderson and became the first silent movie cowboy star.

But in Tioga, Texas, on September 29, 1907, when Orvon "Gene" Autry came into this world, things moved at a slower pace. People still got around by natural horse power in the small town in the North Central Texas Plain between Dallas and the Red River, which separated Texas from Indian Territory. On November 16, about six weeks after Orvon was born, Indian Territory became Oklahoma, the forty-sixth state in the Union.

There has been some controversy over Gene Autry's real name. His high school yearbook lists him as "Orvon Grover Autry," whereas some railroad records show him as "Orvon Gordon Autry." Jon Guyot Smith spent time with Kate Anderson in Tioga in 1970. Anderson was said to have been a childhood sweetheart of Autry and "the ultimate authority of Gene in Tioga."[1] Kate informed Smith that "she had never heard him called anything but 'Gene' since they were small children." She also told Smith how much Gene loved eating boiled peanuts and going fishing.[2]

The Autry family lineage in America has been traced back to Cornelius Autry, who settled at Autry's Creek in Edgecombe County, North Carolina, around 1756. James Autry, son of Cornelius, was born circa 1742 in Edgecombe County, North Carolina. James had three sons; the eldest, Elijah, was born in 1765. Elijah had one child, William A. Autry, born in North Carolina, but he moved to Tennessee and is buried in Benton County. William and his wife, Mary Campbell, had eleven children; their third, Elijah Henry Autry, was born on August 15, 1813.

"Elder Elijah" was known as "a sound Bible teacher and successful preacher."[3] He was married to Mary Parish on November 14, 1832. He first joined the Hopewell Baptist Church in Henderson County, Tennessee, then joined other congregants in forming a church at Mt. Comfort, Carroll County, Tennessee. Elijah Autry was ordained in May 1840 and became pastor at the Mt. Comfort Church before pastoring other churches in Tennessee.

Elder Autry died on September 22, 1858. He led a meeting at the Oak Grove Church in Tennessee, then returned home to discover some cattle destroying his crops. As he left his home to drive the cattle out, his nephew urged him to carry a small derringer pistol to help scare the cattle. Elder Autry refused, but the nephew slipped the pistol into his pocket. When Elder Autry tried to remove the pistol, the gun accidentally discharged and the bullet lodged under his ribs. A day later Elder Elijah Autry, a loyal member of the Free Masons, died and was buried with Masonic honors.

Elijah and Mary Autry had twelve children; their ninth child was William Elijah Autry (sometimes listed as Elijah William Autry), who was born December 16, 1848. He married Mary Elizabeth McCauley on November 29, 1868, in Carroll County, Tennessee. Sometime around 1885 they moved to Cooke County, Texas, where, from August 1894, William Elijah Autry served as the Baptist Minister at Indian Creek Baptist Church.

The tenth child of William and Mary Autry was Delbert, born June 11, 1886, and their first child born in Texas. Delbert's first wife was Margaret Maggie Patterson, and they had one child, Ray, born in 1904. Maggie died and Ray was raised by his maternal grandparents, taking the name Ray Patterson. Delbert's second wife was Myrtle Mae Gilbert, and they had a daughter, Bessie, born January 8, 1906.

Delbert's third wife was Elnora Ozment, who was born in 1882. Delbert and Nora (as she was known) had four children; the oldest was Orvon, known better as "Gene" who was born on September 29, 1907, followed by daughters Vida (born December 14, 1911) and Wilma (born April 14, 1913) and son Dudley Doug Autry, born in 1922.

There has long been some rumbling that Gene Autry actually took the name "Gene" from a cousin. If that rumor is true, then it most likely came from the thirteenth child of William and Mary Autry, Homer Ezra Autry, who had three children; their second, Homer Gene Autry was born April 23, 1921.

Delbert and Nora Ozment Autry lived outside Tioga; they raised cattle and vegetables on their rented farm but were not ranchers. Delbert Autry was a buyer and trader of livestock, a middleman who judged horseflesh and cattle and made a decision about whether he could turn a profit by brokering a transaction. He would go to Fort Worth or Dallas, buy some horses, then bring them to Tioga or Indian Territory and try to sell them to ranchers, settlers, or whoever wanted to buy a horse. On good days, he made a handsome profit; at other times, he was lucky to break even or not lose too much money on the deal.

Nora Ozment Autry was apparently well-liked by those who knew her; reminiscences of her indicate she was a sweet-tempered, easy going saint of a woman with a calm disposition. That easy-going, even-tempered disposition was apparently inherited by her first-born son. He also inherited her musical talent; Nora played organ in the church and guitar at home. Gene always gave her credit for teaching him to play the guitar.

In Grandpa William E. Autry's Indian Creek Baptist Church, young Gene Autry said he learned to sing in the church choir. Reverend Autry reportedly allowed the youngster to sing even though little Gene wanted to drown out the others. The Baptist church was small; it measured about 24 feet wide by 33 feet long and was a white, wooden structure with a single, open room inside. Young Gene Autry did not have the opportunity to sing for his grandfather for long. William Autry died on April 28, 1913, in Collinsville, Texas, when the youngster was five and a half years old.

After Oklahoma became a state, more settlers came in, which made it a land of opportunity, so Delbert moved his family into the new state, settling just across the Red River in Ravia. "I left Tioga when I was about five years old," remembered Autry. "We lived on a farm about four or five miles west of Tioga. I was probably there until I was ten or 12 years old and then we came back to Texas and I lived in Tioga until I was 17."[4] Robert Ozment, Nora's brother and his family, lived in southeastern Oklahoma, which is probably why the Autry family moved there for awhile. Gene's family also lived in Achille, Oklahoma.

When he was 12, Gene bought a guitar from Sears with money earned by helping his Uncle Cal bale and stack hay. The guitar in the Sears, Roebuck catalog that year was the "Pearletta," a flattop with a body made of imitation rosewood, a spruce top and poplar neck with mahogany finish. The fingerboard had four imitation pearl (Pearletta) position ornaments. Along with the guitar came an instruction book and fingerboard chart.[5]

Young Orvon Autry was an ambitious, energetic lad, growing up in a family with two sisters and a much younger brother. He performed around town and joined the Field Brothers Medicine show, a traveling show that sold tonics and elixirs and came through his hometown. The traveling group consisted of "Doc" Fields and his two younger brothers; Autry, probably 14 or 15 years old at the time, joined the show for several months one summer.

Gene Autry wanted to make something of himself, to be "somebody." There are generally two ways that a young man in America who grows up poor can achieve fame and fortune: sports or entertainment. Young Gene Autry had his eye on both; he was a lifelong baseball fan who claimed to have been a pretty good shortstop, although he was a "banjo hitter." He also loved to sing and play his guitar.

Callie Jane Autry, Gene's cousin, told an interviewer that when he was a youth Gene came to her father's ranch in Wetumka, Oklahoma, for a visit. The ranch had been established around the turn of the century, and land from the ranch was spread over three counties — Hughes, Seminole and Okfuskee. Callie's dad, Riley, invited Gene to go hunting, but Gene had no interest in hunting, in guns or in riding horses. "He just wanted to sit around and talk or play the guitar and sing," remembered Callie. The young lady related that her father did not care for Gene because he "wasn't a real westerner, the real he-man type. He was too 'soft.'"[6]

In 1925, when Gene Autry turned 18, the radio, recording and movie industries were in their infancy. Radio was the youngest of the three; in 1925 there were a number of crystal sets available — simple radios that used a "crystal" or diode, antenna and coil — but there were no networks, no NBC or CBS. On local stations, there was a hodgepodge of performers and programs — perhaps a pianist with a singer, maybe a country fiddler. WBAP in nearby Fort Worth held the first "barn dance" in January 1923, and this became the term used for variety programs aimed at a rural audience which featured country music and were broadcast live on radio.

Two of the most popular entertainers in America were Al Jolson and Will Rogers, and both were early heroes of young Autry. Rogers, known as "the cowboy philosopher," was a popular and influential newspaper columnist, humorist, speaker and movie star. He started in show business as a trick-rope performer and toured the vaudeville circuit, incorporating humorous political commentary into his act. By 1925 Rogers had starred in a number of silent movies.

Jolson billed himself as "the greatest showman on earth" and was certainly the biggest star of the musical stage by 1925. An energetic performer who usually did his act in black-face, Jolson had starred in a number of Broadway musicals by 1925 and toured the country a number of times.

Cowboys were also popular in American entertainment when Gene Autry dropped out of high school before his senior year. Otto Gray and his Oklahoma Cowboys was a popular touring act. Gray, born around 1890 in Ponca, Oklahoma, has been called "the first singing cowboy in American show business" because he performed western music before large audiences during the vaudeville era. Gray's career was launched in 1924 when William McGinty of Stillwater, a veteran of the Spanish-American War who served with Teddy Roosevelt's Rough Riders, organized a cowboy band and hired Gray to manage it. The reason McGinty formed a band was because he wanted to preserve the music of the Old West. The six-member string band was comprised of real Oklahoma cowboys, recruited from ranches. They first performed over KFRU in Bristow, Oklahoma. Gray was good at what he did and the group soon attracted large audiences on radio and the vaudeville circuit between 1928 and 1932. The group traveled in three custom-built automobiles and two custom trailers; Gray's auto reportedly cost $20,000 and included a radio transmission facility. The group made only a few recordings and eventually disbanded in 1936, although former members Zeke Clements and Whitey Ford (the Duke of Paducah) later achieved success in country music.[7]

In 1925 former Texas A & M college student Carl Sprague went to Camden, New Jersey, and recorded some cowboy songs for Victor Records. "When the Work's All Done This Fall" became a genuine hit for Sprague, selling almost a million copies. This was the first "cowboy" or "western" hit.

Gene Autry did not pursue a career as an entertainer when he left high school before graduating; instead he saw his future with the railroad. He was hired as a telegrapher by the St. Louis & San Francisco Railroad and began working for them on June 18, 1925. The railroad offered prestige in the 1920s; it represented a giant, national industry, linking the country. To be part of the railroad — even as a relief telegrapher — was a giant step forward for a young, poor Oklahoma boy in 1925 who grew up watching trains roll past as he dreamed of where they had come from and where they were going.

"I had worked at the depot there in Tioga and was unloading baggage and mail and express and all those kinds of things," said Autry. "So when I heard the Frisco Railroad up in Oklahoma was hiring telegraph operators I thought I was about ready to be an operator so I went up to Oklahoma and got a job on the Frisco Railroad as an operator and depot agent, yard master and train dispatcher."[8]

Autry had worked at the railway station in Ravia — hired by a Mr. Picket for $35 a month — before he landed a job with the St. Louis and San Francisco Railroad, commonly known as "the Frisco line." Two people — both from Ravia, Oklahoma — have claimed credit for teaching young Gene Autry the Morse Code and how to operate a telegraph. C. W. Webster, a Frisco agent, claimed he taught Autry ("a swell 16-year-old kid") telegraphy in 1923. In an interview in 1940 Webster stated that Autry "carried a guitar with him almost every place he went" and that, after serving a year of apprenticeship, Autry "got on at 70 cents an hour." Webster also noted that Autry "used to sit around the depot every night until midnight, playing that guitar and singing."[9] The other person who claimed he taught Autry was Authur Mayberry, who showed up at a Gene Autry Oklahoma Museum Festival one year with his story. Actually, there were probably several people who helped Autry while he was learning.

W. Rudd claimed to have given Autry his first job as a telegraph operator in Sapulpa, Oklahoma in 1927.[10] Autry lived in Sapulpa, a suburb of Tulsa, a division point for the railroad, after he was transferred from Ravia by the Frisco line.

While he was with the railroad, Autry took a correspondence course in accounting that he credited with later financial success. As Autry recalled later in life, "Even as a boy, I planned ahead."[11]

During his life, Autry often told a story of Will Rogers coming by the telegraph office one night while he was working. Although there were slight variations in Autry's recollections, the essence of the story was that he was in Chelsea, Oklahoma, one night (either at 7 or 11 o'clock) when someone came into the little Oklahoma depot and said he wanted to send a telegram. Autry's guitar was either sitting on a desk or Autry was playing it when the gentleman walked in. In some stories, Rogers asked Autry to sing some songs while, in other versions, Rogers sang some cowboy songs. At the end of this encounter the man tells Autry, "You've got mighty good stuff there. You belong somewhere else playing that guitar — maybe Hollywood. You'll never get anywhere playing that telegraph instrument. Your heart ain't in it."

At this point, Autry takes the telegram message and sees the name "Will Rogers" at the bottom, and that's when he recognizes the stranger.

There have been some questions raised about this story through the years. A newspaper reporter who retrieved some records from the Frisco railroad noted that Autry worked in Waleetka, south of Chelsea on the Oklahoma City–Fort Smith line at first, and his first official transfer came in September 1927 to Vinita, which is northeast of Chelsea.[12] However, at the end of September 1927, Autry was in Chicago, on his way to New York City.

In Jon Tuska's book, *The Vanishing Legion: A History of Mascot Pictures 1927–1935*, the author quotes Guinn "Big Boy" Williams, an actor and close friend of Will Rogers in Hollywood, who notes that Autry did not tell this story until after Rogers died in August 1935.[13]

According to the Will Rogers Memorial Museum in Claremore, Oklahoma, Will Rogers filed a daily telegram from Chelsea on Tuesday, May 1, 1928, which was published in newspapers on May 2.[14]

Callie Jean, Autry's cousin, related to Glenn White in an interview that she asked Gene about the Will Rogers story during a dinner one night with Gene and his wife, Ina. Autry told her the story "wasn't quite like what you heard." Autry related that he was in the back of the telegraph office, sweeping up and the office was dimly lit. A man came in and, since there were a number of telegram blanks on the front counter, Autry did not rush up to greet him. The man wrote hurriedly, and by the time he was finished Gene was there to take the telegram. The man handed it to Autry and said, "Son, can you get that off pretty quick?" Autry replied, "Yes, sir." Autry went to the telegraph and began transcribing the message and did not recognize the man who quickly left the telegraph office until he got to the bottom of the telegram where it said "Will Rogers."

There was no guitar playing, no swapping songs, no long conversation — just a hurried, quick meeting.[15]

****

The children born 1901 to 1924 are known as the "G.I. Generation" because so many of them — 75 percent of the men — served in World War II. This generation was certainly shaped by World War II as well as by the Great Depression. This group produced seven presidents: Lyndon Johnson, Ronald Reagan, Richard Nixon, Gerald Ford, John Kennedy, Jimmy Carter and George H. W. Bush.

There was little thirst for religion from this group, who generally believed that God spoke in deeds and events — not in spiritual awakenings. They valued the outer life over the inner and were, on the whole, not an introspective generation. Throughout his life, Gene Autry loved to tell stories from his life and career, but was seldom reflective about his life and career; he was rational but not analytical about the forces that shaped him and the success he achieved.

Overall, this was a male-fixated generation who disliked womanish influences; the men found it hard in later years to accept women as equals in business or public life. There was an exaggerated masculinity in this group that valued virility and manliness and disdained feminist influences.

Known for their enduring sense of civic duty, they were joiners of civic organizations such as the Elks, Lions, Moose and Eagle Clubs, American Legion and Veterans of Foreign Wars; during their lifetime organizations such as the Boy Scouts, Camp Fire Girls, Girl Scouts and 4-H Clubs were created. In political affiliation, they were heavily Democratic with 65 percent registered Democrats (although they might vote for a Republican candidate for president who came from their generation). In politics, most of their core beliefs were shaped during the years of Franklin D. Roosevelt and his New Deal.[16]

During the lifetime of those in this generation there was a march of technological progress so they were optimistic in their faith in progress and believed in the central role of Great Men. During their lifetime they saw the Wild West tamed as the cowboy became a rancher and cars replaced horses as modes of transportation. For many, the cowboy was a hero because movie cowboys presented him as a "Great Man." But the cowboy was also a regular fellow who could be a team player, and the group-enforced virtues of this generation embraced the idea that team players were wholesome. Gene Autry was part of this group.

Gene Autry was no cowboy by a long shot, but he took advantage of the fact that he was born among cowboys and his early life touched real cowboys. Later, he capitalized on his western roots to develop an image as a singing cowboy, but in the mid-'20s his dreams and ambition took him away from the cowboy life. Still, he remained connected to cowboys by virtue of the fact that he was born a westerner.

2

FIRST RECORDINGS

Early in 1927 Gene Autry was working as a telegraph operator in Madill, Oklahoma. He traveled over to Butler, in western Oklahoma, where Mr. and Mrs. Marvin had a cafe. Autry went to Butler either because he was assigned to be a relief telegrapher at their depot or as a special trip to Butler to meet the Marvins because he heard their sons were in show business in New York. On the wall of the restaurant were pictures of Mrs. Marvin's two sons, Johnny and Frankie Marvin, who were in New York making recordings and appearing on stage. Mrs. Marvin gave Gene Autry the address of her sons in New York.

Johnny Marvin was born in 1897; Frankie was born in 1904, both in Butler, Oklahoma. Johnny was bitten by the show biz bug early and left home to perform with traveling shows before making his way to New York, where he appeared in *Honeymoon Lane*, starring Eddie Dowling and Kate Smith (it was her first show). He sang "A Little White House" and "Half a Moon's Better Than No Moon" in the show, and Victor talent scouts were impressed enough to have him make recordings. Known as "the ukulele ace," Johnny Marvin was a successful band singer; his biggest hit was "Breezing Along with the Breeze" in 1927, and other hits included "All Alone Monday, "'Deed I Do," "Me and My Shadow" and "Blue Skies."

Frankie Marvin was working as a barber in Butler when Johnny returned and the two went off to New York. Frankie played slide guitar, later called steel guitar; in New York his first job was with music publisher Shapiro-Bernstein because "they were looking for a yodeler" and Marvin could yodel.[1]

Frankie Marvin's first recording session was in July 1927 when he did "The Bully of the Town" for Grey Gull. After this, Marvin recorded songs for Brunswick, Columbia and Edison (sometimes under the name "Frankie Wallace").[2] Frankie also did comedy with his brother; they played the Palace several times.

The duo traveled quite a bit performing but were in New York when Gene Autry arrived. Autry wanted to sing on the radio and reasoned the best way to do that was to sing on records. On his first trip to New York, he rode free on his railroad pass with $150 hidden in a sock. He stopped in Chicago on the way and watched the Jack Dempsey–Gene Tunney fight at Soldier Field on September 22; he also looked up Jack Kapp, then head of Brunswick Records. Kapp gave him the name of Tommy Rockwell, a friend and record executive in New York, to look up.

At the end of September 1927 — close to Autry's twentieth birthday — the Baltimore and Ohio train pulled into Newark, New Jersey; Autry then caught a ferry across the Hudson River and then a bus to the 42nd street station. He arrived in New York City on a Sunday morning about six o'clock.

Autry checked his guitar and suitcase into a locker and asked a policeman for directions to Times Square; when Autry arrived it was virtually empty. He checked into the Riley Hotel on Forty-fifth Street and knew he could stay for three weeks — his leave time from the railroad. It is clear from this first trip to New York that Gene Autry had a burning ambition and belief in his own talent. In a short while he looked up the Marvin brothers; they hit it off and Autry then moved into the Manger Hotel, where Frankie Marvin stayed.

Because the Marvins had an "in" at the record labels, they took Autry around. Frankie Marvin took him to the Edison Company first, where Autry sang the Al Jolson song "Sonny Boy." The next stop was Victor, where, according to one story, Autry sat in the lobby for several days, waiting for an appointment with Victor executive Leonard Joy. While waiting in the lobby area, Autry took out his guitar and sang "Jeannine, I Dream of Lilac Time," a song that had been a hit for Gene Austin. Joy heard Autry singing, came out front and asked if he would like to meet the person who had written the song. Joy then took him back to meet Nat Shilkret. So goes the story. However, Johnny Marvin was a successful band vocalist who had recorded with Shilkret's orchestra, and he probably arranged an audition for Autry with Shilkret and Leonard Joy.

Nate Shilkret was an important figure with Victor. He was a top band leader in New York who became a musical director and multi-purpose accompanist at recording sessions. Shilkret played clarinet with the New York Philharmonic, the New York Symphony, in the orchestra of the Metropolitan Opera House, and in the concert bands of John Philip Sousa and Arthur Pryor. In the early 1920s he began working for Victor and from the mid–1920s was conductor of the firm's house orchestra and accompanist for singers who recorded current popular songs. As a singer, Johnny Marvin had recorded several hit songs with Shilkret and the Victor Orchestra.

Joy invited Autry back for either a test recording or an audition but afterward told the young singer he needed more experience, which would give him more confidence when he performed. Shilkret reportedly told Frankie Marvin, "He doesn't sing too bad, but another Jolson he's not."[3] The ever-resourceful Autry managed to cajole either Joy or Shilkret into writing a letter for Autry to carry back to Oklahoma saying the young singer had potential.

According to Frankie Marvin, "he couldn't sing 'Sonny Boy' yet!" Later, back at the hotel, Marvin told him, "Better forget that Jolson stuff as well as the pop songs. Sing some yodel songs like we're doing. Carson Robison ... that's what they want." Then Marvin asked Autry if he could yodel, and Autry replied, "I don't know; I never did try." Marvin remember that "he tried to yodel, and he had just a very little falsetto voice, and I said, 'Well, go home and practice on your singing and yodeling and come back and I'll get you another test record.'"[4]

****

Gene Autry arrived in New York about two months after a seminal event which would change country music in general and his life in particular. In August 1927, Ralph Peer, working for Victor Records, went to Bristol, Tennessee, and set up his recording equipment. There, he recorded the Carter Family and Jimmie Rodgers. The Carters provided country music with a body of songs that became standards in American music. Jimmie Rodgers, "America's Blue Yodeler," became the biggest star in country music in the late 1920s and early 1930s and a major musical influence on Gene Autry.

Rodgers had spent the first thirty years of his life as "more or less a failure at everything he tried." He "wasn't much of a musician — couldn't read a note, keep time, play the 'right' chords, or write lyrics that fit"[5] and yet became the most influential country music artist in the first half of the twentieth century. Rodgers was not attracted to the country music of that time — primarily old fiddle numbers by people such as Fiddlin' John Carson. He was attracted to "pop" music but was from the rural South — born in Meridian, Mississippi. Rodgers was primarily interested in an audience and, like most entertainers, preferred to perform songs that went over well.

In a two and a half hour session for Ralph Peer in Bristol, Rodgers recorded "The Soldier's Sweetheart" and "Sleep, Baby, Sleep," the two sides of his first single, which was released in October 1927. Rodgers moved to Washington, D.C., where he obtained a radio show, then traveled to New York and contacted Peer for another recording session; he preferred not to wait until Peer called him. Rodgers was ambitious and anxious to put more songs on record, so a session was arranged on November 30 in Camden, New Jersey, where Rodgers recorded "T For Texas," his first "Blue Yodel" and the song that established him as a distinctive recording artist. This "yodel" — or a sort of slipping into falsetto during the song — gave Rodgers a distinctive sound on his recordings and influenced country singers for years. Rodgers's blue yodel songs were in standard blues format, with the first line repeated before a tag line (AAB) sums up the verse. According to Nolan Porterfield in his biography of Rodgers, it is "impossible to exaggerate the popularity of Jimmie Rodgers during the late '20s and early '30s when he was alive and recording ... it spread across all age brackets."[6]

"Blue Yodel #1 (T for Texas)" was released in February 1928, when Gene Autry was back in Oklahoma. There is no doubt that Autry heard this recording; it sold over a million copies and was the second major hit in country music, after Vernon Dalhart's "The Prisoner's Song." Jimmie Rodgers was an original; there was nobody like him before he came, so there was no one to copy. During the 1930–1933 period he recorded "Pistol Packin' Papa," "Jimmie's Mean Mama Blues," "T.B. Blues," "Jimmie the Kid," "My Good Gal's Gone Blues," "Hobo's Meditation," "My Time Ain't Long," "Mother, the Queen of My Heart," "Peach Pickin' Time in Georgia," "No Hard Times" "Miss the Mississippi and You," and six more blue yodels (for a total of 12).[7] The rural audience loved him, bought his records and wore them out on their phonographs.

Although Rodgers became the first country music "star" after "T For Texas (Blue Yodel #1)" was released in 1928, during the time when Autry was first in New York, the biggest seller in the hillbilly business was Vernon Dalhart's "The Prisoner's Song."

Vernon Dalhart was born Marion Try Slaughter in Jefferson, Texas. He studied voice at the Dallas Conservatory of Music and moved to New York in 1910 in hopes of becoming an opera singer. Dalhart originally recorded "Wreck of the Old '97" for Edison, then recorded it for Victor in 1924 with "The Prisoner's Song" on the back side. This recording eventually sold over a million copies and ignited an interest in country music from the New York–based labels. A secret to Dalhart's success is that he took the "whine" out of country music. According to a letter Ralph Peer wrote to *Variety* in 1955, "Vernon Dalhart was never a hillbilly and never a hillbilly artist. Dalhart had the peculiar ability to adapt hillbilly music to suit the taste of the non-hillbilly population. Perhaps we could characterize him as pseudo-hillbilly. Dalhart was extremely successful as a recording artist because he was a professional substitute for a real hillbilly."[8]

Dalhart was backed by Carson Robison, a studio guitarist for Dalhart and a prolific songwriter. Carson Robison, whose first job in radio was in 1920 at WDAF in Kansas City, moved to New York City in 1924. Robison met singer Vernon Dalhart in late 1924 and became his guitar accompanist. Dalhart reportedly recorded over 60 of the more than 300 songs Robison wrote. Included in these were "The John T. Scopes Trial," "Wreck of the 1256," "My Blue Ridge Mountain Home," "Maggie Andrews," "The Engineer's Child," and "My Little Home in Tennessee."

Vernon Dalhart was an important influence on Autry, who learned a number of the songs that Robison wrote and Dalhart recorded and sought the kind of popular appeal that Dalhart had.

****

Back in Oklahoma, Autry continued to work for the Frisco railroad as a telegrapher; he also approached radio station KVOO in Tulsa about singing. One of the big attractions on KVOO was Jimmy Wilson's Catfish String Band. The group had recorded a session in Dallas for Okeh Records in October 1925, doing four numbers, including a "Medley of Old Time Popular Songs" in addition to "Over the Waves" and "Let Me Call You Sweetheart."

Jimmy Wilson was a popular figure in Tulsa, an active citizen and humorist "of the same general type as Will Rogers" whose first band performed on KFRU in Bristow, Oklahoma, when that station went on the air in 1926. The station then moved to Tulsa and became KVOO and Wilson's group went with it. At one time they had a weekly one-hour show sponsored by Casco, a cold remedy and at another time were sponsored by SkellGas on a one-hour show.

The Potter brothers, Orin and Charlie, had a music store where the band gathered to practice. Band member Bob Dennis remembered that Gene Autry "often came by the store ... and sat in on some of the rehearsals. He was just there learning to play the guitar then and once learned he would go down to the Harvey House and play for the waitresses."[9]

However, Autry had a vivid, remarkable memory and during the 1980s related to Johnny Western a story about playing with Jimmy Wilson and the Catfish Band in 1927 on KVOO. Autry said they broadcast from a subsidiary station in Sapulpa and "walked around the conference room and showed how the chairs were set up, with one microphone in the room where the singer was and how the Catfish Band was set up so they got the best balance for sound in that little room," said Western. "He was talking about 1927 and named every one of those guys who were in those seats, which guy played what instrument and where they stood, for those who were standing."[10]

Gene Autry performed wherever and whenever he could around the Tulsa area, on KVOO whenever the opportunity arose and on personal appearances, building his repertoire and gaining experience as a performer. During 1928 he fell under the influence of Jimmie Rodgers, singing songs he learned from Rodgers's records and imitated him to the point that sometimes it was hard to tell it wasn't actually Jimmie Rodgers singing. Autry was joined in his enthusiasm for singing by his supervisor, Jimmy Long, a railroad dispatcher who was 18 years older than Autry and had been transferred from his home in Springfield, Missouri, to Tulsa.

James W. Long was born in Blevins, Arkansas, in 1889. He worked for the Frisco Railroad and lived in Springfield most of his life, but had been transferred to the Tulsa area, where he was living in 1928 when he met Gene Autry and invited him to his home for some singing and playing. Jimmy Long was a talented singer who had composed a number of songs and obviously connected with Autry because of their shared love of music. Long had a high tenor voice and sang harmony.

Around the first of October 1929, Gene Autry and Jimmy Long used their railroad passes to catch a train from Tulsa to New York City; when he arrived, Autry found his friends Johnny and Frankie Marvin and moved in with Frankie at the Manger Hotel (later known as the Taft), where they had adjoining rooms with one bath. Johnny Marvin was appearing at the Palace Theater, and Autry was invited on stage to sing a song, "Sonny Boy," a hit by Al Jolson.

By the fall of 1929, Frankie Marvin had established himself as a recording artist under his own name and under the name "Frankie Wallace." During 1928 Marvin did 25 recording sessions for a variety of labels, including Banner, Conqueror, Challenge, Edison, Okeh, Harmony, Diva, Velvet Tone, Columbia and Victor. By the time Gene Autry arrived in New York in October 1929, Marvin had already done 28 sessions that year.

Autry had a sixty-day pass from the railroad. On October 9, Autry, Jimmy Long, Frankie and Johnny Marvin went to Liederkranz Hall and recorded two songs for the Victor company, "My Alabama Home," written by Jimmy Long, and "My Dreaming of You," written by Johnny Marvin. "My Alabama Home" featured Frankie Marvin yodeling (Autry had not yet learned to yodel well) and playing the slide guitar, while Johnny Marvin and Jimmy Long added harmony vocals. That recording was not released immediately.

Autry remembered he had "been given the name of Arthur Satherley, the new head man at American Record Corporation." So Autry went to 1776 Broadway, where the American Record Company's offices were located and walked into Satherley's office.[11] Although he was unaware of it at the time, this meeting connected Gene Autry to one of the most important people in his professional career.

Arthur "Uncle Art" Satherley was born in 1889 in Bristol, England and emigrated to the United States in 1913. He found a job with the Wisconsin Chair Company at a plant in Grafton, Wisconsin, that made chairs and phonograph cabinets for Thomas A.

Edison. Satherley graded the lumber, then became a traveling salesman. The Wisconsin Chair Company sold their New London plant to Thomas Edison and Satherley went to work for the inventor as an assistant secretary for about nine months, then went back to the Wisconsin Chair Company, which had decided to start a record company. The company had several subsidiary labels: Paramount, Famous, Puritan and Broadway. In this job, Satherley traveled to Chicago to record artists, then brought the discs back to Wisconsin where the records were pressed.

In 1921 Satherley moved to New York, where the company had a recording studio at 28th and Broadway (1140 Broadway), and stayed until 1928, when he joined the Plaza Music Company, which owned a number of labels, including Crown, Regal, Domino, Jewel and Oriole Records. The company also had a publishing division and made most of its money selling sheet music. The company hired Satherley in order to get into the hillbilly business. Satherley noted, "If we sold 5,000 of a popular record, we'd go out and have a little banquet ... yet we'd sell 20,000 of a country number!"[12] By this point, Jimmie Rodgers and the Carter Family were doing well for Victor while Columbia went to Atlanta to record the Skillet Lickers, Charlie Poole and the North Carolina Ramblers, and others—mostly string bands.

In July 1929, the American Record Company was formed by consolidating several small companies, including the Plaza group of labels; Art Satherley had the job of recording acts for this new firm. Satherley had his job with the new American Record Company about three months when, according to Satherley, "All of a sudden a fellow walked into my office—his name was Gene Autry ... we were at a very low ebb, and weren't making any money ... and he said, 'My Name is Gene Autry.' He had nothing but an ordinary suit on, and he looked like the devil in an ordinary suit, and a guitar in a case. I said, 'Yes, what do you know?' He said, 'I sing, I'm from Oklahoma; Tioga, Texas.' He gave two addresses.... So I said, 'What have you got?'"

Autry sang several songs for Satherley, including "The Preacher and the Bear." According to Satherley, "I said, 'We can use you,' but he said, 'I've got another deal—what can you give me?' I said, 'Well, I'll give you a deal. We're going into this thing with a lot of money and a lot of chain stores back of us, and if you care to come with us that's up to you, Mr. Autry, and if you don't I have someone that I'm sure will come.' Well, he said, 'I've got a deal with Victor. I'll go over and see the Victor company.' I said, 'All right, go and see the Victor company ... and if you don't care for over there or want to come back here, just come back and tell me so I can go to work.' So he came back in about two days and said, 'Well, I'll need quite a draw. I think I'll throw in my luck with you.'"

Satherley recalled: "He didn't tell me he'd made a couple of records for Victor. So I challenged him, I said, 'If you do go with Victor, please yourself. But if you do go with us we expect you to stay if we want you—bear in mind it's our money!' So he didn't say a word about those two records, but he said, 'Well I don't think I want Victor.' I said, 'You're trying to yodel and you're trying to imitate Jimmie Rodgers.' I said, 'Mr. Autry, if you imitate Jimmie Rodgers, you're sunk!' I said, 'You're done before you get started with—that's their star, and they're not looking for a young fellow that's not known. Jimmie Rodgers is known!'"[13]

Autry remembered Satherley saying, "'Victor is big, but they have lots of stars. You can get lost over there. With us, you can be Number One.' That sold me." So, according to Autry, "Next day I called and gave my regrets to Loren Watson, the boss at Victor. Then I walked over to the American offices at 1776 Broadway ... and signed a contract with Art Satherley. I was to be paid an advance of fifty dollars a side for each record I cut, against royalties."[14]

The first session that Art Satherley supervised for Gene Autry probably occurred in mid–October 1929, shortly after the Victor session. This session was recorded on Long Island for the Cova Record company. Autry, backed by Frankie Marvin on guitar did "Stay Away from My Chicken House," "My Oklahoma Home" and "Living in the Mountains," all written by Frankie Marvin, and four songs credited to him: "I'll Be Thinking of You Little Girl," "Why Don't You Come Back to Me," "No One to Call Me Darling" and "Cowboy Yodel." Three records — six songs — were released on the QRS label, the first recordings by Gene Autry to be released publicly. Later, Grey Gull, a Boston-based label, purchased these masters and released several songs on their labels, which were sold through the Montgomery Ward catalog. Autry's name is not on these releases; instead the names Sam Hill, John Hardy and Tom Long are used.

On October 24, Gene Autry recorded "Left My Gal in the Mountains," a song written by Carson Robison, and a Jimmie Rodgers song, "Blue Yodel #5 ("It's raining here, storming on the deep blue sea") under the supervision of Satherley. These songs were immediately released on chain store labels Velvet Tone, Diva and Harmony, selling for 35 cents each. Many chain stores sold recordings under their own label; Diva was sold in W. T. Grant's five and dime stores. These budget items were hits for the label and led to invitations for Gene Autry to make more recordings.

Five days after this session it was "Black Tuesday" on Wall Street, October 29, 1929. It was the beginning of the Great Depression.

3

NEW YORK

On December 3, less than two months after his first recording sessions, Autry went into a New York studio and recorded six songs: "Why Don't You Come Back to Me," "Hobo Yodel," "No One to Call Me Darling," all credited to Autry as a songwriter; "Dust Pan Blues" and "Yodeling Them Blues Away" by Frankie Marvin; and the old song "Frankie and Johnny," which had been recorded by Jimmie Rodgers. Two days later, on December 5, Autry recorded two Jimmie Rodgers songs, "Waiting for a Train" and "Lullaby Yodel"; three songs written by Frankie Marvin, "My Dreaming of You," "Slue Foot Lou," "Stay Away from My Chicken House"; and one song by Jimmy Long, "My Alabama Home." The next day Autry recorded three Jimmie Rodgers songs, "Blue Yodel #4 ("I'm going to California where they sleep out every night")" "I'm Sorry We Met" and "Daddy and Home."

In spite of Art Satherley's admonition for Autry to steer clear of a Jimmie Rodgers sound on his recordings (recounted by Satherley many years later and probably a combination of two conversations with Autry that occurred several years apart) Jimmie Rodgers was the best-selling country act by 1929, so labels sought to cash in on Rodgers appeal by recording singers who sounded like Rodgers (including Frankie Marvin, who recorded Rodgers's numbers under the name Frankie Wallace).

Autry recorded Rodgers's songs soon after they had been released. At this point, Gene Autry was a Jimmie Rodgers imitator. Even the songs Autry is credited with writing — "Hobo Yodel," "No One to Call Me Darling" and "Why Don't You Come Back to Me" — sound like Jimmie Rodgers songs with the same themes (hobos, trains, low-down women and rambling men) and similar guitar runs on the accompaniment. Autry usually accompanied himself on guitar with Frankie Marvin sometimes adding a slide guitar. Satherley noted the first releases by Autry "didn't mean too much," meaning they didn't sell particularly well and that other hillbilly acts he recorded, like Welling and McGhee, outsold Autry. He encouraged Autry to find some original songs — either write them himself or find a songwriter with some songs — so there'd be some fresh material.[1]

If you think of a songwriter as someone who sits alone in his room, plumbing the depths of his soul in self-reflection, agonizing over a melody and words, sweating out a song until he or she gives birth to a new creation, then Gene Autry was no songwriter. Never was.

16

Autry often bought songs in his early years. There is little doubt that he bought a number of songs from Frankie Marvin. While this might be considered dishonest today, at that time, it was a fairly normal business practice. There was no great income from writing country songs, and no prestige attached to being a country songwriter. Writing a song was like building or crafting something and then selling the product. Frankly, songs weren't worth a whole lot of money. There was no money for airplay or public performances for country songs because ASCAP, the only performance licensing firm until 1940, simply would not allow country (or blues) songwriters to become members and collect those fees. The primary way a country songwriter made money was through the sale of songbooks. Sales of recordings allowed a publisher to collect two cents for each record sold, but they often did not split that income with songwriters 50/50 as they do today.

Country songwriters were, in general, happy to give a recording artist co-writing credit who recorded the song. Or even sell a song outright for cold hard cash. Better to have half of something than a hundred percent of nothing and better to have dollars in your pocket rather than the chance that pennies might come in the future. Gene Autry often came up with ideas or titles for songs, and other writers wrote the bulk of the song; this was a lifelong practice of his, and he felt justified in taking partial writer credit because of his initial input. Autry probably had a hand in writing some of his earliest songs, was active in the creative process of bringing a song to life through a recording and may, in fact, have written a few of his earliest songs, but he was never a "songwriter" in the strictest sense of composing words and music all by himself.

Gene Autry commuted between New York and Oklahoma during his early recording career. He used the railroad for regular employment and the benefit of railroad passes. His personnel file at the railroad notes he took leaves of absence "to see folks" when he actually went to New York to record. Apparently his superiors knew the truth but did not object, although the files note that Autry was reprimanded for being lazy, lax on the job and sleeping when he should have been working. Packy Smith observed, in the liner notes to the nine–CD boxed set released by Bear Family Records, that "Gene must have been well liked, and all his co-workers were pulling for his success." As a relief telegraph operator, Autry generally worked the midnight to 8 A.M. shift.

On March 3, Autry was in New York and recorded (with Frankie Marvin on steel guitar) "That's Why I Left the Mountains" (written by Frankie Marvin) and "Cowboy Yodel" (credited to Autry). Two days later Autry did two more recordings, the Jimmie Rodgers song "My Rough and Rowdy Ways" and the Autry-credited "I'll Be Thinking of You Little Girl." Autry was not signed to an exclusive contract with the American Record Company, so he took the opportunity to record for other companies when the opportunity arose, although he probably did not reveal these to Art Satherley.

Gennett was the label of the Starr Piano Company, founded by Harry Gennett in Richmond, Indiana, located almost due east of Indianapolis near the Indiana-Ohio line; it was a five hour train ride from Chicago. The studio was in a single-story gray, wooden building beside the Whitewater River with a rail spur for the Chesapeake & Ohio Railroad about three feet from the main entrance and a pump house that adjoined the building. The noise from the train, the river and the pump house interrupted a number of recording sessions. The studio itself was about 125 feet by 30 feet. The engineer sat in a tiny chamber, separated from the main room by a glass window. There was sawdust in the walls and draperies, making it a very "dead" room. The chief engineer was Ezra Wickemeyer, who recorded a number of jazz musicians during the 1920s and hated the fact that Gennett was the Ku Klux Klan's unofficial recording company.[2] In addition to the Gennett label, the firm also released recordings on Champion, which sold at a cheaper price originally through the Kresge store chain. Later, Gennett created another low-price imprint, Superior.

On June 5, 1930, Autry went to Richmond, Indiana, and recorded four songs credited to him as a songwriter, "Why Don't You Come Back to Me," "Hobo Yodel," "I'll Be Thinking of You Little Gal," and "Cowboy Yodel," one written by Frankie Marvin ("Dust Pan Blues"), one by Johnny Marvin ("The Girl I Left Behind"), a Jimmie Rodgers song, "Whisper Your Mother's Name," and a song written by Hattie Lummis and G. O. Lang, "In the Shadow of the Pine." On August 4, Autry returned to the Gennett Studio and recorded seven Jimmie Rodgers songs in addition to "Dust Pan Blues." On November 16, Autry recorded five Jimmie Rodgers songs for Gennett; obviously, the firm tried to capitalize on the popularity of Jimmie Rodgers with a Rodgers sound-alike. On most of the Gennett recordings, Autry appeared under a pseudonym, such as Tom Long or Johnny Dodd. Many of the Gennett recordings were leased to the Sears, Roebuck Company for release on the store's record labels.

Two days after the Gennett sessions, Autry was in New York to record three sessions for the American Record Company. On November 18, he did three songs he is credited with writing ("Yodeling Hobo," "Pictures of My Mother," and "Blue Days"); on November 20, he recorded two songs where he is listed as songwriter ("Cowboy Yodel" and "Dad in the Hills") and a Jimmie Rodgers song ("In the Jailhouse Now #2"). Four days later he recorded two songs on which he is credited as composer ("I'll Be Thinking of You Little Gal" and "Yodeling Hobo") and two Jimmie Rodgers songs ("High Powered Mama" and "Whisper Your Mother's Name"). In the meantime, another key figure entered Gene Autry's life.

****

In October 1930—a year after Autry made his first recordings for the American Record Company—that company was purchased by Consolidated Film Laboratories, owned by Herbert Yates. This was Yates's entry into the recording business and brought into Autry's life a person who would be a key factor in his opportunity to become a movie star.

Herbert Yates was born in 1880 in Brooklyn, New York, to immigrant parents who came from Great Britain seven years earlier. Yates's father was an accountant, and Yates himself graduated from Columbia University. When he was 19 Yates became a sales executive with the American Tobacco Company; he was so successful that in 1910, at the age of 30 he retired and became a gentleman farmer. That same year, he lent Roscoe "Fatty" Arbuckle, an early silent movie star, $100,000 at six percent interest and 25 percent of the profits from the movies Arbuckle was committed to make. Within three years Yates's investment had reportedly multiplied by 200 percent.

In 1912, Yates joined Hedwig Film Laboratories in New York. Then, along with his brother George, he purchased the firm. Hedwig was in the business of processing film for movies, a lucrative enterprise because the film industry was growing. The film industry was centered in New York, although this was the year *The Squaw Man* was filmed in Hollywood, which marked the beginning of a shift to southern California.

In 1915 Herbert Yates set up Republic Film Laboratories, then organized the Allied Film Laboratories Association, a consortium of film developers. In 1922 Yates combined several film processing companies into Consolidated Film Industries, again a lucrative and profitable business venture that developed film for the movies. This gave Yates the cash to purchase the American Record Company in 1930 when a number of companies went out of business and could be purchased at a bargain price for anyone with ready cash.[3]

4

THAT SILVER HAIRED
DADDY OF MINE

Autry's recordings sold well enough for him to do a number of sessions during 1931, mostly Jimmie Rodgers songs or songs that *sounded* like they were Jimmie Rodgers songs. On January 29, Autry recorded for Gennett, doing four Jimmie Rodgers songs and two songs credited as self-penned; on February 9 he went back to Indiana and recorded another Jimmie Rodgers song and three others. In February, Autry went to New York and recorded a session for the American Record Company. On February 17 he did three songs credited as self-penned ("A Gangster's Warning," "Pictures of My Mother," and "That's How I Got My Start") and one by Frankie Marvin ("True Blue Bill"). The next day Autry recorded four songs for Victor: two credited as self-penned and two by Frankie Marvin. On February 25, he did another session for ARC, recording a song honoring a labor organizer, "The Death of Mother Jones," re-recorded "A Gangster's Warning" and "True Blue Bill," and three more by Frankie Marvin.

The first record released on Conqueror, Sears's label, was "The Death of Mother Jones" and the next was "A Gangster's Warning." Both sold well, but "A Gangster's Warning" proved to be a genuine hit on the cut rate label in the Sears catalog. Victor released "Bear Cat Papa Blues" backed with "Money Ain't No Use Anyway" first, then "Do Right Daddy Blues" backed with "That's How I Got My Start." These Victor releases sound a lot like fellow Victor artist Jimmie Rodgers but, at 75 cents a copy, did not sell as well as Rodgers's since the Great Depression deepened considerably in 1931.

On the last day in March, Autry recorded for Victor, doing three Jimmie Rodgers songs ("T.B. Blues," "Jimmie the Kid," and "Travellin' Blues"), and four by Frankie Marvin. It is interesting to note that while Autry had previously recorded Jimmie Rodgers songs that had been released, on this session Autry did Rodgers's songs *before* the Rodgers records had been released: "T.B. Blues" by Rodgers, was released on April 24 — over three weeks after Autry's session — while "Jimmy the Kid" and "Travellin' Blues" were released in the summer of 1931.

This *may have* come about through Ralph Peer, Rodgers's record producer; however, it is more likely this occurred because Eli Oberstein had replaced Ralph Peer as head of Victor's hillbilly and race recordings and sought to undermine Peer by getting test copies of Rodgers's recordings to Autry. Since Autry learned songs by ear — he did not read or write music — he needed a test pressing to learn the song. While it is possible that Peer provided these pressings, it is not likely; Oberstein had an incentive to do so. It is also possible this arrangement of Gene Autry recording Jimmie Rodgers songs developed because Autry had met Rodgers. The connection came through Gene Austin, the pop singer whose "My Blue Heaven" was one of the biggest pop records of the 1920s. Austin was one of the first crooners and an artist on Victor Records, and Autry may have met him through Frankie and/or Johnny Marvin. Autry told Austin he wanted to meet Rodgers; while in New York, Autry received a message from Austin to come over to Austin's office at a certain time. When Autry walked into the office, there sat Jimmie Rodgers.[1]

Because the Depression cut sharply into sales of recordings, Victor made an attempt to capture sales with a budget line. They named their label "Timely Tunes," which sold for 25 cents each and was marketed through Woolworth's; the first release for the label was Autry's "T.B. Blues."

It is apparent that Autry was hedging his bets; if he couldn't get a hit from the American Recording Company, then he might get one from Gennett or Victor. Also, recording for Victor, the home of Jimmie Rodgers and the biggest, most prestigious label, still appealed to him. Since Autry usually received $50 for each song he recorded, it was good business to record as much and as often as he could. The Victor recordings sold for 75 cents each, which was a lot of money during the Great Depression and, consequently, Autry's Victor recordings did not sell well. What sold well were the cheaper, low price recordings issued through the chain stores. "A Gangster's Warning" was probably Autry's first hit, and "The Death of Mother Jones" also sold well during 1931.

Autry continued to split his time between Victor and the ARC companies in April. On the first day of that month he and Frankie Marvin went into Victor's studio and recorded two songs credited to Jimmie Davis as a songwriter ("Bearcat Mama from Horner's Corner" and "She's a Hum Dum Dinger"). Although Jimmie Davis would later develop a crooning style — similar to Autry — at this point he was a Jimmie Rodgers imitator and singer of risqué blues numbers such as "Tom Cat and Pussy Blues." Davis, who later became governor of Louisiana, recorded for Victor from 1929 to 1933. In addition to these two songs, Autry recorded seven other songs and played guitar while Frankie Marvin sang "Old Man Duff" and "I'm a Truthful Fellow."

On April 10, 13 and 14 Autry did sessions for the American Record Company; he was accompanied by Frankie Marvin on the ten songs he recorded. Autry then returned to Sapulpa, Oklahoma, where he continued his work as a relief telegrapher for the railroad. In October, he went to New York for some more recording sessions, carrying the song that would make him a major recording star.

Gene Autry was really part of a team, and although he would eclipse all the other members in the coming years, each provided Autry with key elements to the singer's ultimate success. The recordings of Jimmie Rodgers were a major influence, as was Rodgers's success as a recording artist. Johnny and Frankie Marvin were key players in New York, and Autry needed their friendship and musical talents — especially Frankie's — to launch his own recording career. Frankie Marvin continued to record prodigiously during the

1930–1931 period as a solo artist, although the names "Frankie Wallace, "George White," "Jack West," "Martin Craver" and possibly other pseudonyms were listed on the records released.

Art Satherley was a key business connection while Jimmy Long, Autry's boss on the railroad, was a mentor to the young artist, providing song material and harmony vocals. Ironically, after Autry's first recording session with Long in October 1929, they did not record together again for about two years. During this period Long recorded for Victor, Gennett, Champion, Superior and the Montgomery Ward labels. He recorded six sessions in 1930, including a session on December 2 of that year as a duet with Cliff Keiser. Among the songs they recorded was a song Long wrote, "That Silver Haired Daddy of Mine," which was released on the Champion and Superior labels.[2]

"That Silver Haired Daddy of Mine" was not a hit for Jimmy Long, but the song appealed to Gene Autry, who went to New York with Long in October 1931 for a historic recording session. The opening line, "In a vine covered shack in the mountains," was reminiscent of the hits by Carson Robison and Vernon Dalhart. And Autry was no doubt aware that Jimmie Rodgers had recorded some "Daddy" songs. The melody had a traditional sound that listeners could imagine was straight from the mountains. And the emotional appeal of loving your dear ole Dad was timeless.

In terms of musical influences, Autry was influenced by Jimmie Rodgers, Vernon Dalhart and Gene Austin. The fact that these artists were all extremely popular and successful was as influential as their musical styles. Rodgers provided the sound of the "blue yodels," which Autry essentially copied on his early recordings while Dalhart and Austin, with their smooth crooning-type vocals pointed the way that Autry would head in the future as he sought a wider audience, expanding beyond the rural, country music audience.

****

Gene Autry was at the Hotel Taft on Seventh Avenue and 15th Street on October 20, 1931, when he wrote a letter to his cousin, Callie Jane, back in Oklahoma. The letter states, "Sorry I didn't get a chance to see you before I left but the way it rained I just couldn't make it. I've had a good time so far since I came up here. We are doing a lot of recording and have a lot of fun. Wish you were here with us — we would stage a good one ... I like it up here but its cold as H — and my blood is plenty thin and, no fooling, but I almost freeze everytime I get outside."[3]

On October 29, 1931, Autry, Jimmy Long, Frankie Marvin, and Roy Smeck went into the studio of the American Record Company and recorded two songs credited to Autry, "Rheumatism Blues" and "I'm Atlanta Bound," and a Frankie Marvin song, "High Steppin' Mama," before they turned their attention to "That Silver Haired Daddy of Mine," the song Jimmy Long wrote and recorded with Cliff Keiser ten months before. On this song, as well as the next two ("Missouri is Calling" and "My Alabama Home") Long sang harmony with Autry.

The next day, Friday, October 30, Autry recorded "Mississippi Valley Blues," "My Old Pal of Yesterday" (both of which had been previously recorded by Long) and "My Cross-Eyed Girl" for ARC. That same day, after the ARC sessions, Autry went over to the Victor studio and recorded two sessions. The first consisted of duets with Long on songs Long had written but were credited as compositions to Long and Autry: "Mississippi Valley Blues," "My Old Pal of Yesterday," "Missouri Is Calling," "Cross Eyed Gal That Lived Upon the Hill," "I'm Always Dreaming of You" and "Why Don't You Come Back to Me." On these recordings they are credited as "The Long Brothers." After a break, Autry recorded four songs with just his guitar: "Jailhouse Blues," "Rheumatism Blues," "I'm Atlanta Bound," and "Wild Cat Mama."

Autry recorded 19 sides over a two day period for two different companies, but he recorded some songs for both companies, such as "Rheumatism Blues," "I'm Atlanta Bound," "Missouri is Calling," "My Old Pal of Yesterday," and "My Cross-Eyed Gal."

This was not unusual during this period of the recording industry; an artist was not signed to a label exclusively unless he was a major seller. And it was not unusual for an artist to record the same song for several different labels. Autry probably did it for money. He received $50 for each song recorded, so the ten he recorded for Victor gave him $500 — a nice sum in Depression America. Also, he may have tried a shotgun approach to recording — doing a number of songs and seeing which sold.

What is interesting is that he only recorded "That Silver Haired Daddy of Mine" for ARC. It seems most likely that Autry had performed the song back in Oklahoma and received a good response from audiences. Or perhaps he saw Long perform the song and the audience responded positively. It is also possible he promised Satherley he would not record it for Victor because Satherley felt the song was a hit. What is a fact is that ARC released "That Silver Haired Daddy of Mine," and it became a huge hit.

Jon Guyot Smith observed that after recording the first three songs, the musicians took a break, and when they returned "the next three songs ... were as different from the first three as a ripe nectarine differs from a hoecake." Smith notes Autry turned "aside from the Rodgers style which had gained for him a major foothold in the doorway to commercial acceptance" and adopted the style of Long, who "had grown up with the parlor ballads of the late 19th century." Indeed, "That Silver Haired Daddy of Mine" resembles a 19th century sentimental parlor ballad much more than a Jimmie Rodgers blue yodel. Stylistically and artistically, it was a complete turn for young Gene Autry.[4]

Actually, it may have been completing a circle more than making a turn. Autry's original audition songs were sentimental pop songs, and that's where his heart was, although his initial success came from Jimmie Rodgers–type and other blues-related songs. In his heart, Gene Autry always wanted to be known as a singer of sweet, romantic songs. Ironically, he had to achieve success in blues-related, then western-themed songs, before he was able to be a successful singer of "heart" songs.

In addition to a change in direction musically, these sessions may have marked a turning point in Gene Autry's professional life because it was probably during this time that Autry and Satherley discussed Autry moving to Chicago to be on radio station WLS.

On Wednesday, November 11, Autry was back in New York for another ARC session with Frankie Marvin playing slide guitar and Roy Smeck on banjo. On that day, they recorded three songs credited to Autry as songwriter: "Birmingham Daddy," "Why Don't You Come Back to Me," and "She's a Low Down Mama." On Monday, November 16 he recorded "I'm a Railroad Man (Without a Railroad Fare)," "Under the Old Apple

Tree," and "There's a Good Gal in the Mountains" (all of which have Autry listed as song-writer) and Frankie Marvin's "Wildcat Mama."

Art Satherley had been approached by Jeff Shea, music buyer for Sears, about Autry appearing on a show on WLS in Chicago sponsored by Conqueror Records, one of Sears's labels. Sears was a mail-order and retail giant by the beginning of the 1930s and had begun selling products under its own brands. Sears did not have a record label in the tra-ditional sense; instead of signing artists and recording them in studios, they leased record-ings from record companies and then released them under their own imprint. Silvertone was the oldest label formed by Sears; it began around 1916 and leased material primarily from Brunswick/Vocalion. Sears discontinued this label in 1930 (although it brought the imprint back briefly during the 1940s). Supertone began in March 1931 and was discon-tinued the following year.

Challenge was the cheapest line from Sears with prices between 19 and 24 cents a record, with further discounts if the records were bought in tens. The label generally assigned a pseudonym to the artists on this label. Conqueror leased almost exclusively from ARC and were sold for 29 cents each or three for 85 cents. Sears began Conqueror in 1928, and this imprint lasted until World War II.

Jeff Shea told Satherley that Sears could not pay Autry, but "we have quite a pro-gram" and "if you can afford to keep him in here, I'm sure it will be big for us all." WLS, the station in Chicago that Sears had previously owned and on which they continued to sponsor programs, could not pay Autry either. So Art Satherley offered Autry $30 a week from the petty cash account at ARC, telling him he could get a room at the YMCA for $1 a night. Someone in the room, listening, told Autry, "The rest can go for wine, women and song." This brought some laughter and Autry agreed.[5]

It is possible that at this time Satherley told Autry he had to decide between ARC and Victor. The earlier conversation where Satherley told Autry he could not succeed as a Jimmie Rodgers imitator and that ARC and Sears were putting money into his career so he needed to make a firm commitment may have occurred at this time. Gene Autry only did two more recording sessions for Victor after this time, and he may have bar-gained with Satherley to honor a commitment to Victor.

Satherley insisted that Autry capitalize on his Texas and Oklahoma background and present a western persona, although at this point Autry dreamed of mainstream, popu-lar success. "That sort of stuff didn't sound very glamorous to me," remembered Autry. "My recollections of ranch life included aching muscles and endless days in the sun and dust. I wanted to be a dreamy eyed singer of love songs like Rudy Vallee."[6]

Gene Autry went back to Oklahoma after his New York sessions, tied up his per-sonal affairs and caught a train to Chicago. On his way from Oklahoma to Chicago, Gene Autry stopped off in Springfield, Missouri, to visit his singing partner, Jimmy Long. The train pulled into the station early in the morning, and Autry went to Long's home for breakfast. This was probably the weekend of November 28–29.

Staying with Jimmy and Jessie Long and their children Jack and Barbara was Jessie's niece, Ina Mae Spivey. Ina Mae was born April 19, 1911, in Francis, Oklahoma, daughter of a telegrapher who worked for the Rock Island Railway. Ina Mae and her sister, Anita, attended school in Duncan, Oklahoma, where the family had moved when she was young.

After high school and a stint working in the Duncan Western Union office, she moved to Springfield, Missouri, to attend the Missouri State Teachers College.

Gene and Ina Mae had a lot in common. Gene and Ina's father were both telegraphers; Ina Mae was athletic (she played basketball for her high school team in Duncan) and musical (she appeared in school plays, was a member of the Glee Club and was proficient on the piano). When she left Duncan, Ina Mae's ambition was to become a music teacher. Years later, Ina Mae reminisced that she was "very excited" when she heard that Gene Autry was coming because "he was somewhat of a celebrity in our part of the country." When they met she was struck by "his round face and bright blue eyes," remembering that "before the weekend was over, I knew I had never met any fellow I liked as well."[7]

The feeling was mutual. Gene Autry left the Longs' home that day, but his mind stayed on Ina Mae Spivey.

5

CHICAGO

On December 1, 1931, Gene Autry debuted on WLS in Chicago on an early morning radio show, "Tower Topics," hosted by Anne Williams and Sue Roberts and sponsored by Sears. The show appeared Monday through Friday at 9:30 A.M. "Conqueror Records Time" was a segment of that show, which featured news from the Sears company. On the "Conqueror Records" segment Autry was billed as the "Oklahoma Yodeler."

Each morning, Anne Williams introduced Autry with a big build-up, saying something like, "Here he comes—he's fence riding—I see he's got a break, he's repairing a fence right now. Now he's got that done, and he's very fast on his horse and just as fresh as a daisy early in the morning. It's our own Gene Autry!" By doing this, Williams created a western persona for him, providing him with an image for his fledgling career.

Sears gave Gene Autry a big push towards stardom the winter of 1931–1932. The store's mail-order catalog offered the "Gene Autry Roundup Guitar" for $9.75 and a song folio, *Gene Autry's Cowboy Songs and Mountain Ballads*, for 39 cents. In the spring and summer catalogs from Sears, Autry's records sold for 19 cents each—a bargain basement price aimed at the Depression-era country music fan.

The musicians union was strong in Chicago, and a performer could not appear on either network, NBC or CBS, without being a member of the union. On December 9, 1931, Autry went to the union's office and paid $100 to join. On December 17, he was officially elected to membership and given card number 9269; his quarterly dues were four dollars.

On Christmas Eve that year, Gene Autry met someone who played a major role in his life, particularly during the Chicago years. Joseph Lee Frank, better known as J. L. or Joe Frank was born in Limestone County, Alabama, in 1900 and grew up in nearby Giles County, Tennessee. As a young man he worked in the steel mills in Birmingham, then moved to Illinois where he worked in the coal mines before opening a dry cleaning business, Champagne Cleaners, in Evanston, a suburb north of downtown Chicago.

Joe Frank, who later became known as "The Flo Ziegfeld of the Country Music Business," was bitten by the show biz bug. While he had his dry cleaning business, he spent evenings helping a local theater company haul their sets around. Gradually, through connections at WLS, Joe Frank became a booking agent, booking the country acts on that station. Joe Frank "loved country music, loved what it was and what it stood for," remembered his wife, Marie.[1]

That love of country music and connection to WLS led to someone from WLS calling Joe Frank and telling him, "Joe, we've got a cowboy who needs a booker." That's how Gene Autry met Joe Frank.

Joe and his wife first met Autry on Christmas Eve, shortly after Autry arrived in Chicago. Joe had picked up Autry as well as some puppies before he went home. Marie Frank worked for a detective agency, and the attorney who served as her connection to this agency told her the police department needed someone to take care of three police dog puppies. That's the reason Joe Frank held a box with three puppies under one arm while Gene Autry stood slightly behind him when Marie Frank opened her apartment door on Thursday, December 24, 1931.

"He was such a humble young man — shy in a word," remembered Marie Frank about her first meeting with Gene Autry. "Gene didn't drink or smoke. He was one of the cleanest young men you'd ever want to meet." Mrs. Frank remembered that Gene was wearing a black overcoat. "I don't think he was wearing cowboy boots," she observed. It would be tough start. "It was the hardest thing in the world to book him at first," remembered Marie Frank. "But Joe Frank could take anyone and build them. He loved to get someone, an unknown, and build them up. His happiest moments came when they struck it big."[2]

A common bond between Frank and Autry was membership in the Masons. J. L. Frank was dedicated to freemasonry and encouraged all the young men he worked with to also become Masons. Autry had joined the fraternal organization in 1929. On June 6 of that year, he received his Apprentice Degree from the Lodge in Catoosa, Oklahoma, a stop on the Frisco main line about 14 miles from Tulsa. On July 4 he was promoted to Fellowcraft and on August 2 to Master Mason.[3]

During that Christmas season, the young lady that Gene Autry met back in Springfield, Missouri, paid him a visit. By this time, Jimmy Long had joined Autry and was rooming with Gene in an apartment in Aurora, just west of Chicago. Autry told Ina Mae Spivey that her uncle hoped his family could visit during the Christmas holidays, adding, "I'd sure like you to come along." Jessie, Jimmy Long's wife, could not make the trip, but Ina Mae and a cousin did go for a weekend visit over the Christmas holidays in 1931, and after she left the two corresponded.[4]

****

Autry arrived at WLS in Chicago at the right time. Earlier that year the station became a 50,000-watt clear-channel station, which allowed Autry to reach a large audience throughout the Midwest, home to about ten percent of the population of the United States during the 1930s.

Chicago was a wide open city in the 1920s and early 1930s. The administration of Chicago's mayor, William Hale Thompson, was "a carnival of corruption."[5] Thompson was legendary; during Prohibition "Big Bill" announced that he was as wet as the middle of the ocean, and so was Chicago. The racketeers "owned" Thompson — they delivered the votes to get him in office and then bribed him to do their bidding. By 1931, Al

Capone had become the unofficial ruler of Chicago, his name synonymous with organized crime and corruption in the Windy City. But the end of Capone's rule over Chicago began on June 5, 1931, when the United States government indicted Capone on 22 counts of income tax evasion. Capone's trial began on October 6 and ended on Saturday, October 24 when Capone, wearing a dark purple suit, stood before the judge and heard his sentence: a total of 17 years in prison. After the sentencing he was taken to the Cook County Jail.

That's why Al Capone was in the Cook County Jail when Gene Autry arrived in Chicago at the end of 1931.[6]

In 1923, Sears received a license for a 500-watt radio station. The station, WSL, was actually started by the Agricultural Foundation of Sears, and "farm service" would be the core of programming. On Saturday night, April 12, 1924, WLS ("World's Largest Store") debuted from the Sherman Hotel at Randolph and Clark Streets. The following Saturday, April 19, saw the debut of "The National Barn Dance."

"The Barn Dance" was really a variety show for a rural audience; it sought to present "old familiar tunes" or "folk songs," as they were called at the time. On those early programs a listener might hear "Down By the Old Mill Stream," "When You Wore a Tulip," "Till We Meet Again," "Whispering," "Memories," "Love's Old Sweet Song," or "When You and I Were Young, Maggie."

On October 1, 1928, Sears sold the station to the *Prairie Farmer* magazine, owned by Burridge D. Butler. The headquarters for WLS became the *Prairie Farmer*'s new office building at 1230 Washington Blvd. Sears agreed to remain a major advertiser on the station, but did not want to deal with any issues of "conflict of interest" with the station. Butler was 65 at the time of the sale and did not manage the day-to-day affairs of the station. However, "Butler conceived of the National Barn Dance as a big, wholesome country party.... [This] fit Butler's view of life in the country."[7] Butler insisted on a moral, uplifting program, and would not allow songs about drinking or marital infidelity.

By the end of 1931, when Gene Autry arrived in Chicago, WLS and its "Barn Dance" was the biggest, most important stage for country music. The station, broadcasting at 890 on the AM dial, covered the Midwest and, during the Depression, had the most impressive lineup of country talent, the most programming with country artists and the best country music show on the air.

When Gene Autry moved to Chicago, he found a room at the YMCA, then stayed at the Union Park Hotel, on West Washington in a rooming arrangement with Red Foley, a member of the Cumberland Ridge Runners. The two shared a common living room but separate bedrooms; Autry remembered the bed folded up into the wall. Autry observed later that Red Foley was the most talented singer he ever met but was "lazy."[8] If Foley didn't feel well in the morning, he didn't show up for his radio show. Not so with Gene Autry; nobody ever accused him of being lazy and he *always* did his early morning show.

"Tower Topics Time," sponsored by Sears and hosted by Anne Williams and Sue Roberts, came on at 9:30 each morning except Sunday. There was no special mention of Gene Autry in the *Prairie Farmer*, the magazine that owned WLS, when he arrived. The first mention of Autry came on February 1, 1932, when "Gene Autry — Oklahoma Yodeler" was listed in the published lineup with a daily ten-minute show at 9:20 in the morning followed by "Tower Topics" at 9:30. This is the first indication of his popularity in Chicago, which, by the end of 1932, made him one of the most popular acts broadcasting on WLS.

"That Silver Haired Daddy of Mine" had been released. It was advertised in the Sears catalog and sold a reported 30,000 copies during its first month. Autry performed the song regularly, and it soon became a favorite with listeners. Since Autry was billed as a cowboy he began to dress like one — getting his first western outfits from Sears, reportedly after a suggestion made by Harry New, a salesman for the American Record Company. Previously, Autry wore street clothes when he sang.

On March 19, 1932, about three and a half months after Gene Autry joined the station, the WLS "Barn Dance" moved to Chicago's Eighth Street Theater, located at Eighth Street and Wabash Avenue on the south edge of Chicago's Loop. The theater seated 1,200, and there were two shows every Saturday night: 7 to 9:30 and 9:45 to 12 midnight. Admission was 50 cents for adults and 25 cents for children during the first few months, then rose to 75 and 35 cents. Every seat was filled, and there was a waiting list to buy tickets to the performances. The "Barn Dance" remained at the Eighth Street Theater for twenty-six years.

The popularity of the "Barn Dance" generated coverage from national publications. An article in *Radio Guide*, written in show biz slang by a cosmopolitan writer from New York, noted: "While the intellectuals of wireless entertainment were racking their brains to build a Packard, WLS came along with a Ford among the amusements.... Theirs is the Alpha and the Omega of all the bucolic revues. Potentially theirs is the last roundup for hillbilly talent, and artists of this type who have not faced its microphones are still on the fringe of the best yokel society."[9]

In addition to the "Barn Dance" on Saturday nights, WLS created several traveling units which featured "Barn Dance" acts. As *Radio Digest* reported, "The traveling units were the answer to countless pleas by out-of-towners who cannot come to Chicago. They were also an outcropping of the WLS practice of sending their popular performers to state and county fairs, and the myriad other outdoor and indoor advertisements that make up the rural entertainment program. They have become standard appurtenances of corn-husking contests, agricultural shows, stock shows and all the other public meetings which engage the agriculturist."[10]

The traveling acts became an integral part of WLS and the "Barn Dance" reaching beyond Chicago. "Most of the people made their money doing personal appearances in those days," said Autry years later. "I know when I was there I played most of the theaters and some auditoriums and fairs. I played all through Wisconsin, all the way up in the upper peninsula of Michigan. And I played all down through Indiana, Illinois, all the way down to Cairo, as we used to call it, and over into Iowa. You could play about five or six states right out of Chicago because WLS had that 50,000 watt channel...."[11]

"I was on WLS about five days a week. On Monday, Tuesday, Wednesday, Thursday and Friday I would play around Chicago where I could get back in time to do my show in the morning. Then on Friday, a lot of times we'd take a longer trip because we'd have Friday night, then Saturday and Sunday."[12]

Although Gene Autry appeared on WLS during the week, and often appeared on the "Barn Dance," he was not considered a member of WLS because he was aligned with Sears, which sponsored him on shows. Because Sears was interested in selling merchandise — specifically records — Autry invested a lot of time and interest in his recording sessions, recording more than any WLS act. Sears also sold the aforementioned "Round-Up Guitar" endorsed by Autry; Sears paid Autry 10 cents for each guitar sold.

Soon after the WLS "National Barn Dance" moved to the Eighth Street Theater, Gene Autry married the young lady he met in Springfield, Missouri.

The first time Gene and Ina saw each other was at the end of November, while Autry was on his way to Chicago. Several weeks later, Autry went back to Oklahoma to either purchase a car or pick up one he owned, and on his return he stopped in Springfield and visited Ina — the second time they met face to face. This is when Autry invited her to Chicago for the Christmas holidays.

In late 1931 or early 1932 Autry wrote to Ina Mae, "I made my first personal appearance today at Rockford, Illinois. I made thirty dollars. I think that's pretty good, don't you?" By this time they corresponded regularly and Autry sometimes wrote to her, saying something along the lines of "be sure to listen to my show next Thursday morning. I'm dedicating a song to you." He even sent her an autographed picture of himself.[13]

On Wednesday, March 16, 1932, Ina Mae went to Richmond, Indiana, with her uncle Jimmy and cousin Beverly to record a session as "The Long Family Trio." They recorded for two days, and two songs from the first session ("I'm So Glad Trouble Don't Last Always" and "Beautiful Isle of Sorrow") were released on labels (Superior and Chapel), whereas all five songs on the second day were released. The second session consisted of gospel songs ("Abide with Me," "Nearer My God to Thee," "Jesus Savior Pilot Me," "Rock of Ages" and "God Will Take Care of You").[14]

The following week, Ina Mae received a letter from Gene that caused her to run into Aunt Jessie's kitchen. Jimmy Long and Gene were scheduled to do a show in St. Louis on Thursday, March 31, and Gene wanted her to meet him. At the end of the letter, Gene wrote, "Plan to stay because I'm not going to let you go back home." Ina Mae told Jessie about the letter and her aunt asked, "Do you want to marry him?" Ina confessed she hadn't considered marrying anyone at that time because, she said, "I always thought I'd finish college first." Ina said to Aunt Jessie, "I guess I'll meet him in St. Louis, but you better come with me."[15]

On Friday, April 1, 1932, Gene and Jimmy Long met Jessie and Ina Mae at the train station. Gene asked the Longs if he could take Ina for a drive alone. During that drive, Gene convinced Ina Mae to marry him, although she had only brought along enough clothes for the weekend. Apparently, it took Gene and Ina about four hours to find a minister to marry them that day after they obtained a marriage license. There is a bit of a discrepancy in later interviews about what time they were married — it was either six or ten in the evening — but it was by Richard Jesse, a Lutheran minister, of the Mt. Calvary East Lutheran Church in St. Louis.

Gene listed his name on the marriage license as "Orvon Autry" and his address as "Springfield, Missouri." Ina Mae also listed Springfield, Missouri, as her address and stated that she was over 21 (she was 19 days short).[16] He did not have a wedding ring for her that day but bought one later in Chicago.

The young married couple's first home was the apartment in Aurora that Gene shared with Jimmy Long.

About a month after Gene and Ina Mae were married, Elnora Ozment Autry died in Tioga, Texas. She was buried in the Indian Creek Cemetery next to the Indian Creek Baptist Church where Gene's grandfather had preached. Nora was buried in the northeast quadrant of the graveyard, where a number of Autrys would be buried in the red clay Texas ground.

The two girls at home — Wilma, who was 20 and Vida, who had just turned 18 — and ten-year-old Dudley were sent to southeastern Oklahoma, where they stayed with Mr. and Mrs. Robert Ozment. Their father, Delbert Autry, did not stay around long; he soon drifted off. Gene felt an obligation to his siblings and brought them to Chicago, where they moved in with him and Ina Mae. The newlyweds became a family of five shortly after their marriage.

****

During the first four months Autry was on the radio in Chicago he regularly returned to Oklahoma to work for the Frisco Railroad as a relief telegrapher. Since he was relief, he did not work every day and often took a LOA (leave of absence). No doubt he wanted to keep a connection with the railroad because that connection allowed him to obtain railroad passes. But his personnel file with the railroad states, "He left work at Henryetta in April, 1932, and never returned." By this time things were going well in Chicago, and he had gotten married, so he felt he could leave the railroad.

In the middle of April, "Tower Topics" moved to 8:20 in the morning and became a 25-minute show. Hal O'Holloran and his Smile-A-While Crew now began at five A.M. instead of six, although WLS signed off one hour earlier both in the afternoon and evening, because of daylight saving time.[17]

In mid–May, the WLS "National Barn Dance" had "gone NBC." The National Broadcasting Company broadcast the last half hour of the show from the Eighth Street Theatre stage to broadcasters in various parts of the country.[18] In June the *Prairie Farmer* announced, "Two full houses each Saturday night continue to be the rule at the two National Barn Dance shows at the Eighth Street Theatre each Saturday night. There's just as much fun at either performance — 6:30 or 9:30 P.M. The antics of Bessie and Prof Dunck, Slim Miller, Spareribs, Wilbur and Ezra, Maple City Four, Old Timers and others never fail to amuse the audience highly. And the house is 'as still as a mouse' when Linda Parker, Gene Autry, Hugh Cross or 'Aunt Sally' sings and Bill Vickland reads his closing poem. Our own entertainers enjoy each show thoroughly because no one is sure just what is coming next so far as 'clowning' is concerned."[19]

On Monday, June 27, 1932, Autry recorded for Art Satherley and ARC in New York. On the first day he did "Back Home in the Blue Ridge Mountains." The next day, accompanied by Jimmy Long (with Roy Smeck on steel guitar), he did three songs then, the following day, did four songs. On Thursday, June 30, he recorded three songs for ARC, then went over to Victor where he recorded "Gangster's Warning" and four other songs with just his own guitar accompaniment.[20] After these sessions "The Crime I Didn't Do" b/w "I'm Always Dreaming of You" and "Have You Found Someone Else" b/w "Alone with My Sorrows" were released on the discount labels Oriole, Banner and Conqueror. The sessions done for Victor were released on Victor with "Gangster's Warning" b/w "That Ramshackle Shack" released on Montgomery Ward. These would be the only recordings Gene Autry made in 1932 when he was busy with radio work in Chicago.

At the end of June, Autry was listed on "Sears Tower Topics Time" at 8 A.M. as "Anne & Sue — Gene Autry."[21] This schedule remained throughout the summer and into the fall. Autry and Anne Williams also appeared, beginning November 1, on a daily show on WJJD in Chicago at 7:30 A.M.[22]

At the end of 1932, the daily "Sears Tower Topics" time featuring "Anne & Sue, Gene Autry, Oklahoma Yodeler" was on each morning from 8:50 to 9:10.[23] His morning show was followed by the Cumberland Ridge Runners on Monday, Wednesday and Friday with Mac and Bob appearing Tuesday, Thursday and Saturday. Autry also appeared on most Saturday nights on the "National Barn Dance."

In addition to his time on the radio, Autry toured with Jimmy Long and Frankie Marvin and played local venues in the area; they often toured with members of the Prairie Ramblers as a backing group. He toured within broadcast range of the station, playing county fairs, high school auditoriums, and theaters.

Gene Autry established a pattern in Chicago. He was a self-starter who knew the value of promoting his records. He did not wait for the record company to do things for him; instead he (with the help of Joe Frank's booking talent) took the initiative to appear everywhere he could — everything from Rotary lunches to intermissions in movie theaters — and performed his latest records. As demand for him grew, so did his income. He brought songbooks and other merchandise to sell, adding to the money he earned from the performances. Gene Autry loved to travel and perform, and he did this enthusiastically in Chicago in 1932. He also made sure he had an amicable parting with the Frisco Railroad. In a letter dated October 14, 1932, written with "Gene Autry/Radio & Recording Artist/Yodeling Blues & Oldtime Songs" on the letterhead, Autry apologized for not giving proper notice when he left and thanked the company for eight years of employment.

6

THE COWBOY

Country music in the 1920s was the era of early recordings, beginning with fiddle tunes, then country songs sung by New York singers, and then field recordings, most significantly the 1927 sessions in Bristol, Tennessee. But country music during the 1930s was defined by radio.

Radio had developed programs that appeared regularly at scheduled times. The most popular time for country music programs was early in the morning because the rural audience listened to radio before going off to work. On weekdays, noon was important because farmers came in from the fields for their noon meal and listened to the radio before going back to work. Saturday night had once been radio's dead night, but country music found a home here, playing to rural listeners after they'd finished their week's work; most of the early barn dances were on Saturday nights.

These barn dances were actually variety shows aimed at the rural audience. The shows attempted to offer a smattering of entertainment and songs that would later be called "country." There were old folk songs, songs from the minstrel and vaudeville stages, and newer songs written by performers. There were harmony groups, comedians, instrumentalists and square dancers. Although the original roots of country music were southern, these shows soon came to embrace western too. But the shows primarily embraced the ideas of "family," "wholesomeness" and "fun." There was a lot of comedy, a lot of gaiety, and a lot of laughter at these shows with the expressed intent that audience members left a show with big smiles on their faces.

Radio exposure created a demand for live performances, and artists often played on a radio program for free in order to obtain bookings within a listening area. The most popular performers found sponsors who wanted to advertise a product. Sometimes a sponsor paid the performer but usually paid the radio station so the performer could have time on the air. Sponsors also worked on the "PI" (per inquiry) plan whereby a performer advertised a product on the air, then received a commission on those sold via mail order from their shows.

For performers, radio had a profound impact. No longer were amateurs who played music on the side part of the game. Professional entertainers emerged and, as country music became more commercial, country performers had careers instead of an avocation.

Also, because radio demanded a huge repertoire, no longer could a musician or group get by with a few tunes. Audiences no longer accepted the songs they had heard for years. Performers had to either compose new songs or find songs from professional songwriters.

The new carbon microphones demanded a new type of singing. Gone was the belt-'em-out style and in was the crooning sound where singers sang softly with emotion. The most popular singers, like Jimmie Rodgers and, later, Gene Autry, developed an easygoing, conversational vocal style that appealed to listeners who felt the singer was accessible and sincere.

Tape technology was not available during the 1930s. But performers did record transcriptions. These large discs held fifteen minutes worth of material and were recorded direct to disc by performers and then shipped to radio stations. Popular shows and performers could be broadcast without the performer in the studio; at this point, records by country artists were almost never played on the air.

****

On May 27, 1933, the Chicago World's Fair opened. Officially titled "A Century of Progress International Exposition," the event commemorated the 100th anniversary of the incorporation of the city of Chicago. The Fair covered 427 acres on Lake Michigan, just south of the downtown area from 12th to 39th Street. (Today Meigs Field and McCormick Place occupy this site).

The Prairie Farmer and WLS held live broadcasts all during the World's Fair and attracted over 30,000 to the "Barn Dance" shows, broadcast from the Fair each weekend in September. Gene Autry, along with other WLS singers and musicians, performed before large enthusiastic crowds during the Fair's run.

The "Century of Progress" closed on November 12; however, because the Fair was popular but ended in debt, it was staged again the next year.

****

NBC broadcast the last half hour of the "National Barn Dance" as early as May 1932. Meanwhile, Miles Laboratories had advertised on WLS and received good results. Through the Wade Advertising Agency, Miles Laboratories decided to advertise their product, Alka-Seltzer, nationally. With this sponsor, the "National Barn Dance" was broadcast over 18 stations on the NBC Blue network beginning September 30, 1933. These 18 stations were all east of Omaha. However, a year later, there were 30 stations carrying the program coast to coast at 8:30 Central time on Saturday evening.

****

Gene Autry did not record his first cowboy songs until January 27, 1933, even though he cultivated the cowboy look in his stage appearances. Further, he recorded those first western songs for Victor on a cold windy day in Chicago. He had collected some cowboy material for recording. "Cowboy's Heaven" was written by Frankie Marvin and previously recorded by him, and "Little Ranch House on the Old Circle B" was written by V. Blanchard. "The Yellow Rose of Texas" was an old song in the public domain that Autry probably knew as a youngster growing up in Texas. "Your Voice Is Ringing," written by Percy Wenrich was a song that Autry sang as a youngster in Tioga, although the original title was "Silver Bell." The final song on the session, "Louisiana Moon," showed Autry receiving songwriting credit.[1]

These were the last recordings Autry made for Victor. From this point forward he recorded solely for ARC and its related companies, having signed an exclusive contract with Art Satherley to record only for the American Record Corporation. Autry had apparently decided that his future lay with Satherley and ARC and not Victor. Five of the songs were released on Victor's line that sold for 75 cents. "Little Ranch House on the Old Circle B" b/w "Cowboy's Heaven" was released first, followed by "Louisiana Moon" b/w "Yellow Rose of Texas" second and then "Your Voice is Ringing" was released with a song by Dwight Butcher on the flip side. In terms of content, this session pointed the way Autry was headed as a recording artist while, in terms of style, Jon Guyot Smith noted that "Louisiana Moon" "was essentially the Gene Autry sound of the future."[2]

Autry was on a daily show on WLS from January through May. However, on March 1, 1933, he was in New York recording for ARC, supervised by Art Satherley. He did "Louisiana Moon," "Cowboy's Heaven," "Little Ranch House on the Old Circle B" and "The Yellow Rose of Texas" again; he also recorded a Jimmy Long song, "If I Could Bring Back My Buddy" and the old standard "Old Folks at Home." The next day he recorded four more songs for ARC: "Gosh I Miss You All the Time" by Long; "The Answer to 21 Years" by Bob Miller; "Lamplighting Time in the Valley" by Joe Lyons and Sam C. Hart; "Watching the Clouds Roll By" by Jimmy Long; and the self-credited "Don't Take Me Back to the Chain Gang."

In mid–April 1933, Gene Autry had his own 15-minute radio show on WLS at eight every morning, then appeared with the "Sears Sunshine Express" at 9 A.M. The *Prairie Farmer* magazine promoted that show to its listeners, stating, "It's a new program with a new announcer, Jack Kay, presenting Ralph Waldo Emerson and Bill O'Connor, with your daily Sears friends, Gene Autry, Log Cabin Boys and Sue Roberts. There will be lots of cheer and melody on this half hour."[3] Two weeks later, Autry's morning show was moved to 7:15 A.M.,[4] and in May the "Sears Sunshine Express" was moved up to 8 A.M.[5] On Saturdays, from May 20 through mid–June, Gene Autry appeared at 7:30 P.M. on WLS, then was replaced by Arkie the Arkansas Woodchopper.[6] Although Autry was on WLS from January through May, he continued to appear on WJJD with Anne Williams for a 7:30 A.M. show.[7]

At the end of April, Gene Autry suffered a minor set-back in his career; according to a news release, he entered Chicago's American Hospital where he had his tonsils removed.[8]

With the help of Anne Williams, Autry compiled a songbook, *Cowboy Songs and Mountain Ballads*, published by M. M. Cole, that was sold through the Sears catalog as well as on personal appearances and over the air. An article in *Variety* in June 1933 commented on the songbook: "Another big seller among the hillbilly gentry... Sales on this publication in a few months are reported over 40,000, but in Autrey's [sic] case there's a commercial to be reckoned with on the split." The article also mentioned that Autry's "air contract" had him on the Sears-Roebuck payroll and that M. M. Cole published and distributed the song book.[9]

Autry also sold two self-published books, *Rhymes of the Range* and *The Art of Writing Songs/and How to Play the Guitar*, both of which gave Gene credit as author. Anne Williams helped with these books, and Joe Frank probably assisted on the business end of getting them printed. The "business" that marketed these books was "Frontier Publishers," at 2424 Lawndale Avenue, Evanston, Illinois. This may have been Gene Autry's home address.[10]

On May 26, 1933, Jimmie Rodgers died in New York at the Hotel Taft, two days after he finished his last recording sessions for Victor. Biographer Nolan Porterfield notes that Rodgers's "impact on country music can scarcely be exaggerated. At a time when emerging 'hillbilly music' consisted largely of old-time instrumentals and lugubrious vocalists who sounded much alike, Rodgers brought to the scene a distinctive, colorful personality and a rousing vocal style that in effect created and defined the role of the singing star in country music."[11]

On his next recording session, less than a month after Rodgers's death, Gene Autry recorded two tribute songs to the great Victor artist. On June 20 and 22 in New York with Roy Smeck on steel guitar, Autry recorded "The Death of Jimmie Rodgers" and "The Life of Jimmie Rodgers" in addition to nine other songs, including "Way Out West in Texas," "The Dying Cowgirl," and "There's an Empty Cot in the Bunkhouse Tonight."[12]

In the fall, Autry had three recording sessions in Chicago, all for Conqueror. Art Satherley lived in New York but often brought equipment to the WLS studios in Chicago, where he recorded Autry and other acts for ARC. On Autry's second session, on October 9, 1933 he recorded "The Last Round-Up" and on November 1 he recorded two more tribute songs: "When Jimmie Rodgers Said Goodbye" and "Good Luck Old Pal (In Memory of Jimmie Rodgers)." This session symbolically marks the end of an era for Autry as a recording artist and the beginning of another. The songs about Jimmie Rodgers demonstrate the significant influence Rodgers had on Autry's past career, but his recording of "The Last Round-Up" represents an arrow pointed toward the future.

"The Last Round-Up" was written by Billy Hill in New York and published in 1933. It became one of the most popular cowboy songs of all time, emerging during the Great Depression. It first achieved fame in the *Ziegfeld Follies of 1934* when performed by Don Ross. Radio broadcasts of the song soon followed, as well as recordings.

Songwriter Billy Hill was born in Boston in 1899 and studied violin. As a teenager he visited the West and worked briefly as a cowboy and miner. During a visit to a Texas ranch in the mid–1920s he and a friend watched a cowboy trampled to death after a fall from his horse; this incident became the inspiration for this song. A professional songwriter who wrote songs for the movies in the 1920s, Hill married DeDette Walker, the model for "The Columbia Lady" logo of Columbia Pictures, and the two moved to New York where Hill struggled to make a living. In 1930 he wrote "The West, a Nest, and You." Hill wrote "The Last Round-Up" in 1931 when he was penniless. When his wife gave birth to their daughter in an elevator because a hospital refused to admit them without payment in advance, Hill almost sold "The Last Round-Up" for $25, but was advanced $200 by Gene Buck, head of ASCAP, the performing rights organization, just in time. In 1933, Shapiro, Bernstein, and Co., a top New York firm, published the song, and it was first sung by Joe Morrison at the Paramount Theatre in New York.

In his book, *Singing in the Saddle: The History of the Singing Cowboy*, author Douglas Green notes that prior to Billy Hill and "The Last Round-Up" "the focus of the folk poetry that became cowboy music, and of the music of the early cowboy recording artists, was the cowboy himself" and that "in the public mind the cowboy was a rough-hewn adventurer who lived in a country where cattle drives and Indian uprisings unfolded in a raw and untamed land." The Sons of the Pioneers and Billy Hill "changed all that." According to Green, they "gave us a romantic, visionary West that turned the way the public thought of cowboy music upside down; at last the haunting beauty of the music matched the haunting beauty of the West."[13]

Certainly the Sons of the Pioneers and Billy Hill came along at a fortuitous time for Gene Autry, whose image would be linked to a "romantic, visionary West" instead of the old image of the "rough-hewn adventurer" and working cowboy.

****

The WLS booking office organized traveling road shows for their performers. A "unit" would have a number of performers and would be booked throughout Chicagoland, promoting the station and allowing the performers to earn more money. In December 1933, Gene Autry headed a road show, The WLS Roundup.[14] However, Autry generally put together his own show because he was signed with Sears, Roebuck and not WLS, although he appeared on a number of WLS programs, including their "Barn Dance."

On Christmas Eve, 1933, Gene Autry and Smiley Burnette performed together for the first time. On the show, a Sunday night performance at the Eighth Street Theater, these two began a partnership that proved fateful in 26-year-old Gene Autry's life.

Lester Alvin Burnette was born in Summum, Illinois, in 1911, the only son of ministers Almira Hezlep and George Washington Burnette. When he was ten, young Lester Burnette lived next door to part-time orchestra leaders Bill and Maude Baird in Concord, Illinois, who lent him musical instruments to learn to play. Burnette was a fast learner and extremely talented. Jon Guyot Smith notes: "By the time he entered high school, Burnette had mastered several dozen instruments."[15] He achieved some popularity when he sang at local functions, which led a furniture store in Champaign-Urbana to hire 19-year-old "Buzz" Burnette (as he was then nicknamed) to sing on WDZ in Tuscola.

James and Edith Bush, who owned station WDZ, hired him as a staff announcer and entertainer in the spring of 1930. The name "Smiley" came from a children's show he hosted. In 1931 Burnette needed a character's name, so he took "Mr. Smiley" from Mark Twain's story "The Celebrated Jumping Frog of Calaveras County." "Mr. Smiley" soon became "Smiley," and "Buzz" was dropped.

There are several stories about how Gene Autry came to hire Smiley. In one story, Autry's manager, J. L. Frank, heard Smiley and recommended him to Autry. In another story, Autry needed an accordion player, and a theater owner recommended Burnette to him. At any rate, on December 19, 1933, Smiley received a telephone call from Gene Autry, who offered him a job sight unseen. The 22-year-old Burnette quickly accepted, and on December 22 both met for the first time. Autry and J. L. Frank had to assure Burnette's parents that their son would not be booked into any place that served liquor or any other disreputable joint.[16]

"We met him somewhere and then drove over to his house," remembered Autry. "He had on a typical farmer outfit — some Levis, only they were brown or tan, and he had on a pair of those country shoes and had some kind of hickory shirt on. After we hired him, we went over to the Sears in Champaign and got him a suit."[17]

****

In the *WLS Family Album of 1933* (an annual keepsake book released at the end of 1932) there was a picture of Gene Autry dressed in a suit and tie wearing a hat that looked like a combination cowboy hat and fedora. The blurb accompanying the photo stated that "no program with Gene Autry is quite complete until he sings 'Silver Haired Daddy.'"[18]

In 1933, in the depths of the Great Depression when over a fourth of the country was out of work and the average income in the South was less than $1,000 a year, Gene Autry made $15,000.

7

GOODBYE, CHICAGO

During the spring of 1934, Pee Wee King was in Racine, Wisconsin, performing on the "Polish-American Hour" over WJRN, while Autry toured the area with his band, the Range Riders, accompanied by his manager, J. L. Frank.

According to King, in Milwaukee a car sideswiped the vehicle Autry was traveling in, bending the fender into one of their tires. The tire blew out near Racine, which caused the car to veer into a ditch injuring three members of the band. Autry and J. L. Frank took the car to a service station to repair the tire and bent fender. The radio at the service station was broadcasting the show with King's band. J. L. Frank called the station and inquired if the band members were available for Autry's next engagement. Frank and King agreed the four-member group would meet Autry at a theater in Port Washington, about twenty miles north of Milwaukee, for a three o'clock matinee. The group arrived just in time to do the show.

Pee Wee King was born Frank Julius Anthony Kuczynski in Milwaukee, Wisconsin, in February 1914. He grew up in a Polish-German family and played polkas on the accordion in his father's band. He adopted the name "King" after popular big band performer Wayne King and formed Frankie King & the King's Jesters in high school. In 1933 he had his own radio show on WJRN in Racine and was a member of the "Badger State Barn Dance."

King's band only played that one engagement with Autry, but King himself was asked to finish the tour with the Range Riders. According to King, in addition to the accordion, Autry also had a fiddle, bass, guitar and steel guitar in his band. The group stayed on the road for about two weeks. Since it was during Lent in a heavily Catholic area, King's band was not booked for dances. The tour went from southern Illinois to Iowa, then back through Illinois to Chicago.

Meeting Autry and J. L. Frank was a lucky break for King; Joe Frank eventually became King's manager, and Pee Wee later married Frank's daughter. Joe Frank also changed King's name to "Pee Wee" because there were too many "Franks" in their group.

****

At the end of March 1934, Gene Autry had three recording sessions in Chicago. On March 26 he recorded, for the first time, a song written by Smiley Burnette, "The Round-

Up in Cheyenne." In the coming years, Burnette would be a major songwriter for Autry, replacing Frankie Marvin and Jimmy Long. In addition to "The Round-Up in Cheyenne," Autry also recorded "Memories of That Silver Haired Daddy of Mine," "After Twenty-One Years," and "Eleven Months in Leavenworth" during the March 26 session. The next day he recorded duets with Jimmy Long on "Little Farm Home," "There's a Little Old Lady Waiting," (written by Long and Smiley Burnette) and "Dear Old Western Skies" (which may have been written by Smiley). On March 31 he recorded a duet with Jimmy Long on "Beautiful Texas," a song written by W. Lee O'Daniel, leader of the Lightcrust Doughboys and a future governor of Texas. On April 28, Autry re-recorded the duet with Jimmy Long on "There's a Little Old Lady Waiting." These recordings were released on the Perfect, Melotone, Banner, Oriole and Romeo labels.

In April *Billboard* reported that "Gene Autrey [sic] was made an honorary deputy sheriff of Champaign County, Illinois in April."[1] Even at this early stage of his career, Autry collected awards from city and town officials and made sure the press was aware.

At the end of May, Autry was in New York with Jimmy Long and Smiley Burnette. On May 28 and 29 he recorded duets with Long on five songs. During the session on the second day, Smiley Burnette made his first recordings for ARC, doing "Mama Don't 'Low No Music," "He Was a Traveling Man" and "The Lone Cowboy." On Thursday, May 31, Autry recorded "My Shy Little Bluebonnet Girl" while Smiley recorded "Peg Leg Jack" and "Matilda Higgins." On June 11 and 25, Autry was back in New York to re-record five of the songs he had done previously. They were the last recordings Gene Autry made in 1934.

From the end of June through July 21, Autry performed on WLS at 5:30 on Tuesday, Thursday and Saturday mornings.

****

The Chicago World's Fair extended its run for a second year in 1934, opening on May 26 and closing on October 31. Autry met a future sidekick, Pat Buttram, at WLS during the World's Fair in 1934. Maxwell Emmett "Pat" Buttram was born in 1915 in Addison, Alabama, the son of a Methodist preacher. He moved with his family to Nauvoo and then finished high school in Mortimer Jordan. Although he usually portrayed an unlettered hick cowboy when he performed with Autry, in real life Buttram was a graduate of Birmingham Southern College.

"I was in the first year of college in Birmingham, and I did a play and a guy named Steve Scissler saw me," said Buttram. "He'd been at WLS, and he owned a station in Birmingham. He put me on the air there and in two months brought me up to Chicago during the World's Fair in 1934.... So they put me on WLS doing the same type of humor and country boy stuff."[2] Autry claimed that he and Buttram "took to each other right away. I was all business then, in a hurry to get my career and my life organized. Buttram was just starting, not yet sure of what he wanted to do or how to find out."[3]

Years later, Pat Buttram recalled their early friendship: "Gene and I hit it off right away. We both liked to drink and admire the women.... His word was impeccable. You could put it in the bank. But Gene was always a horse trader. When he signed an autograph for a little girl, he saw dollar signs instead of curls. I remember he used to say on the radio, 'Send me 50 cents for the Gene Autry songbook.' Then he'd come in on Saturday and pick up his mail. He'd sit in front of a wastebasket, shake each envelope so the coins would slide down to one corner, and then hit it on the rim of the wastebasket. The envelope would break open, the money would fall out and he'd hand the envelope to his secretary. I'll always remember that wastebasket half filled with silver."[4]

During the 1934 Chicago World's Fair, Gene Autry performed at a rodeo for the first time. "That was my first appearance in Soldier Field," remembered Autry. "A fellow by the name of Tex Austin put on the rodeo and then took that same rodeo to London.... A good friend of mine, Hardy Murphy, performed in that show, too. He had a trained horse and did the 'End of the Trail' pose and those kinds of things. I was with Hardy a lot during those years."[5]

Autry's performance in Chicago — he performed some songs about halfway through the schedule of rodeo events — gave him the idea of performing during rodeos when he became a major movie star. And Murphy's "End of the Trail" pose gave Autry the idea to feature his own "End of the Trail" pose during his later rodeo performances.

****

In 1934 the American Record Corporation (ARC) purchased the Columbia Phonograph Company from Grigsby-Grunow, which had rights to the Vocalion, Melotone, and Brunswick labels. The Columbia and Okeh names were put on the shelf at the time, and the labels used for ARC's recordings were Perfect, Banner (sold by W. T. Grant stores), Oriole (McCrory's stores) and Romeo (S. H. Kress stores). Sears Roebuck leased product for its Conqueror label until the late 1930s. Artist and repertoire (A&R) responsibilities at ARC were handled by Art Satherley and his protégé Don Law. In addition to Gene Autry, other acts who were either on ARC's labels or would soon join included Roy Acuff, Big Bill Broonzy, Bill and Cliff Carlisle, the Chuck Wagon Gang, Al Dexter, Red Foley, Blind Boy Fuller, Robert Johnson, the Light Crust Doughboys, Patsy Montana and the Prairie Ramblers, and Bob Wills.

8

HELLO, HOLLYWOOD

Ken Maynard was a major western star who had sung in a number of his movies. He first sang in *Wagon Master* (1929), then played fiddle and sang "The Drunken Hiccough" in *Voice of Hollywood*, a short Tiffany film released in April 1930. In 1930 Maynard starred in *Song of the Caballero* and *Sons of the Saddle*, in which he sang and accompanied himself on the fiddle and banjo. He sang "Down the Home Trail with You" in *Sons of the Saddle* and recorded eight songs for Columbia Records.

In March 1933, Universal released its last Tom Mix movie and needed another cowboy actor. The studio hired Ken Maynard for $10,000 a week, with another $10,000 added if he wrote the story. He also received a percentage of the profits and had his own movie unit, Ken Maynard Productions.

On Ken Maynard's first two Universal pictures, *King of the Arena* and *Fiddlin' Buckaroo*, he performed a few songs on the fiddle. That same year, he composed and performed the theme song to *The Trail Drive*. Maynard sang twice and played the fiddle in the movie *The Strawberry Roan*, which was based on the cowboy song by Curley Fletcher. Maynard was not a great singer; although he could carry a tune, his voice was thin and did not have the resonance nor range of a professional singer.

Watching Maynard's career was Nat Levine. Born in New York City in 1899, Levine worked for theater owner Marcus Loew as an office boy when he was 13 and then became Loew's personal secretary. In 1919 Levine went to work for Margaret Winkler in Kansas City as sales manager for the organization that distributed *Felix the Cat* cartoons. Levine learned about film distribution with the Winkler organization but wanted to be a producer, so he moved to Hollywood in 1921. Levine purchased a movie, *Every Woman's Problem*, and made a lot of money through its distribution, which led to him buying a number of other films and distributing them through an independent exchange, which held rights to a film for a certain number of years (usually five) for a flat amount paid to the producer.

In 1926, Levine, Samuel Bischoff and some other investors produced a ten-chapter film series titled *The Sky Skidder* and starring Silver Streak, a German shepherd. Levine sold the serial to Universal, who re-titled it *The Silent Flyer*. Since Levine knew distribution and production and felt he could make more money with his own company, he decided to form Mascot Pictures in 1926, a firm that would specialize in chapter plays. Mascot's first serial was *The Golden Stallion*, directed by Harry S. Webb. It was released in 1927 and two more followed that year, *Isle of Sunken Gold* and *Heroes of the Wild*. In *Heroes of the Wild*, a western, Levine featured a male star with a horse and a dog to create a western with a trio of heroes. This idea may have originated in the western novel *The Untamed* by Max Brand, published in 1918, which featured hero Dan Barry with his horse Satan and dog Black Bart. Zane Grey also used this device in *The Heritage of the Desert*, his debut western novel. Levine later used a dog and horse as heroes in *The Adventures of Rex and Rinty*, a Rin Tin Tin serial released in 1935.

Because Mascot's serials depended upon lots of fast action, stunt work was essential, so Levine hired Yakima Canutt to coordinate stunts for Mascot. Born Enos Edward Canutt in 1896, Canutt picked up the moniker "Yakima" after competing at the Pendleton Roundup in Oregon in 1914. Since Canutt was from the Yakima Valley in Washington state, a reporter named him "Yakima Canutt." Canutt was a rodeo champion, and he was "World's Champion All-Around Cowboy" in 1917 at Pendleton. He was awarded the *Police Gazette* Cowboy Championship Belt 1917–1919, 1921 and 1923. Canutt first appeared in movies in 1924 and, when no feature roles were available, became a freelancer, doing stunts or bit parts.

Levine developed a successful formula for serials: he kept the budget at $30,000 per serial and did two or three a year. He hired talented actors, directors, writers, stunt men and technicians for little money and long hours. Levine had an eye for talent — he signed Boris Karloff, Harry Carey and John Wayne — and gave them artistic freedom.

In 1931 Levine produced three serials: *The Galloping Ghost*, starring football star Red Grange; *The Vanishing Legion*, starring Harry Carey; and *The Lightning Warrior*, starring Rin Tin Tin. The serials had constant action, and each chapter ended with a cliff-hanger. The film crews worked 12 to 20 hour days. To maximize use of time, Levine hired two directors — one for interiors and the other for exteriors. Armand "Mandy" Schaefer was hired for interiors; on days when exterior shots were done, Schaefer would set up interior shots as well as any other job the production required.[1]

Levine capitalized on current trends in his serials. He signed John Wayne in 1931 to star as a stunt pilot in the series *Shadow of the Eagle*, which capitalized on the appeal of Charles Lindbergh's flight across the Atlantic in 1927 and the growing buzz about aviation. After *Shadow of the Eagle*, Wayne starred in two more serials for Mascot — *Hurricane Express* and *The Three Musketeers*. In 1933 Wayne finished at Mascot and signed with Warner Brothers to remake six silent westerns originally done by Ken Maynard.

When Nat Levine saw Maynard's *The Strawberry Roan*, it gave him the idea of doing a series of musical westerns — possibly as a serial. Levine called Maynard — who was in London — and asked if he was interested. Levine offered him $10,000 a week to come to Mascot but, at that time, Maynard elected to remain with Universal.

Levine had ambitious plans in 1933. Mack Sennett's lot on Ventura Boulevard in the San Fernando Valley had gone into receivership, and Levine negotiated a lease with an option to purchase. Someone else with ambitious plans in 1933 was W. Ray Johnston with Monogram Pictures. Johnston formed Rayart Productions in 1924, then changed the company's name to Syndicate Film Exchange in 1928; in 1931 he renamed the company Monogram. A small, independent company, Monogram was known for producing serials on the Bowery Boys, Charlie Chan, the Shadow and the Cisco Kid. Monogram signed John Wayne to star in a series of westerns in 1933; the first, *Riders of Destiny*, was produced by Paul Malvern and directed by Robert North Bradbury. Wayne starred as "Singin' Sandy Saunders." The movie opened with Wayne on horseback, strumming a guitar and singing; unfortunately, Wayne could neither play nor sing, and his voice had to be dubbed in by Bradbury's son, Bill.

Johnston planned to create a series of singing cowboy movies based on Singin' Sandy, but Wayne nixed the idea; he hated the idea of appearing to sing in the movies when, in fact, he couldn't sing at all.[2]

Herbert Yates, owner of both American Record Corporation and Consolidated Film Industries, took notice of the young singer in Chicago who was sold so many records during the Great Depression. There was too much money being made from the sales of Gene Autry's records *not* to notice. So one day Yates asked Art Satherley about Autry. Satherley took some of the singer's records to Yates, who listened and thought they were horrible.[3] Herbert Yates was not a musical connoisseur, nor was he a fan of country music, so Gene Autry's voice and sound had no appeal to him. Still, Autry made money, and Herbert Yates respected anyone who made money for him.

There are several different versions of how Gene Autry received a movie contract, but there is one undeniable fact: The man who made the decision to give him one was Nat Levine, who owned Mascot Pictures. Levine met regularly with Herbert Yates because Yates owned Consolidated Films, a processing facility, in New York. Banks were loath to lend money to the entertainment industry, especially independent movie producers, so these producers had to find other sources of money, or credit, within the industry. For Levine, and other independents, this meant credit for film processing from Yates. Levine needed to inform Yates of his plans about making pictures for the coming year, so the processing could be anticipated.

According to Autry, interviewed on radio in 1974, Nat Levine and Herbert Yates met at Yates's office in New York, and Levine informed Yates that he wanted to do a picture with Ken Maynard. Yates reportedly told Levine, "We have an artist out in Chicago working on WLS, and we sell a lot of records with him. You should take a look at him because if he can sell pictures like he does records, why you may have something." Levine called Autry and arranged to meet in Chicago, where Levine told Autry, "I'm going to make a picture with Ken Maynard. We will write a barn dance sequence in it if you want to come out and do the picture rather than just make a test. That can be a test for you. If it works out well, we'll try to use you."[4]

In an interview with *Daily Variety* in 1980, Autry told the reporter that "Levine ... was going to make a western, but he wanted something different.... Herb Yates told him, 'Look, we've got a kid out there in Chicago who's on WLS. He's selling a hell of a lot of records." Autry then related that "they called me in Chicago to tell me that Nat Levine was coming through. I'll never forget, I met him at the Sherman Hotel. It was in September. 'I'll have the writer write in a singing barn-dance sequence,' he told me, 'if you want to come out to the Coast and do it. We could sort of get a test out of this sequence you're going to do.'"[5]

In another version, Art Satherley claimed that he lobbied Yates on Autry's behalf and demanded he listen to Autry's records. Yates, according to Satherley, at first was indifferent to the idea of his record star going into the movies, primarily because he (Yates) did not care for Autry's type of music. And Yates only processed the film — he didn't do the actual filming or casting. Satherley said he knew that Nat Levine had received letters from Autry and would be in Chicago to meet with his motion picture distributors. Satherley claimed he called Autry, told him to dress neatly in his best western garb, and meet Levine at the Blackstone Hotel. According to Satherley, Levine was "not overly impressed with the singer."[6]

In Autry's autobiography, he does not mention Satherley, his closest working relationship at the record label, but says he received a call from Herb Yates and Moe Siegel, who was president of the American Record Corporation. Autry stated, "It seemed clear to Herb Yates that the Western movie needed a shot in the arm. He discussed it with Moe Siegel, then the president of American Records, and they agreed that the straight action Western was a thing of the past. So they met again with Levine and Yates said, 'Nat, I'll give you the money, but on one condition. We have a fellow who sells a helluva lot of records for us. He's on radio in Chicago, on a national hookup, does the 'Barn Dance.' Nat, it would be worth your while to take a look at Gene Autry.'"[7]

There is a good reason that Yates suggested Levine put Autry in the movies: Yates owned the label that sold Autry's records. An appearance in the movies meant greater exposure for Autry and more record sales, thus more profits for Yates. And there is good reason that Levine would take this suggestion seriously — he could gain favor with Yates. Also, Autry sold a lot of records through the Sears catalog, had a major national hit with "That Silver Haired Daddy of Mine," a number of other recordings that sold well and was a regional star in the Midwest with national exposure on the NBC network through his work at WLS. Gene Autry was a proven singing talent, and Levine needed as much star power as possible to entice audiences to attend his movies, especially in the South and Midwest, which were prime markets for the type of pictures that he produced.

According to Autry's autobiography, Levine was in Yates's office discussing a Ken Maynard movie, and "a day later" Autry received the phone call from Yates and Siegel and met with Levine, who told him "we've written in a barn dance scene. You can call the square dance, do a few songs. That can be your screen test. We'll see what kind of reaction we get when the movie plays." Then, according to Autry, Levine asked him to call before he came out.[8]

However, according to Nat Levine, he had "received a half dozen letters from Autry during 1933 asking for an opportunity to work for me in anything I would suggest in pictures. Autry's name value at the time was limited to an independent radio station in Chicago, practically an unknown with questionable ability. On one of my trips East, I stopped off in Chicago, not to meet Autry, but for business I had with my distributor. But I did get to meet Autry and he virtually begged me for an opportunity to come to Hollywood and work in pictures. While he was nice looking, it seemed to me he lacked the commodity necessary to become a Western star: virility! I was not impressed and tried to give him a nice brush-off, telling him I would think about it. For a period of six months he wrote to me continually, conveying that he would do anything for the opportunity."[9]

Tracing these stories, it is apparent there wasn't one meeting that led to Gene Autry's entry into the movies. If the initial meeting between Levine and Autry occurred in September 1933, then the meeting inviting Autry to be in the Maynard movie must have occurred in the spring of 1934. This would explain the letters from Autry to Levine between September 1933 and spring 1934 (although none have surfaced).

Although Levine initially met Autry in September 1933, he was not impressed and did not feel that Gene Autry was the person who could fulfill the singing cowboy role. Autry was persistent (hence the letters that Autry reportedly wrote to Levine), and Levine did not find anyone else to fill that role. Plans for a musical western were put on the back burner, and Levine announced plans in the trade magazines to produce 12 features and four serials, at a cost of over $1 million during the coming year. The first production was *Burn 'em Up Barnes*, a 12-episode serial on auto racing.

Those plans were suddenly changed when Ken Maynard, who was at Universal working on *Doomed to Die*, had a confrontation with Carl Laemmle, the head of the studio, because Maynard had gone over budget on seven movies. Laemmle was angry at his son, Junior, who was supposed to be overseeing these budgets. The final straw came when the elder Laemmle saw Maynard's film *Smoking Guns* and disliked it. He confronted Maynard, who walked off the Universal set. Since Nat Levine had previously offered him $10,000 a week to make movies, Maynard went over to Mascot and accepted the contract from Levine.[10]

At this point, Levine was confronted with a dilemma: he had finally signed Maynard and was prepared to try a musical western; but, although Ken Maynard wanted to sing in movies, he did not have a strong voice and Levine, believing that songs could have a place in westerns, needed a strong singer for the movie. An added problem was that Ken Maynard was a difficult man to work with — he drank heavily and often lost his temper. Having a sequence that could be shot without Maynard might have given Levine some added insurance that he would not lose valuable shooting time if Maynard walked off the set for a day or two.

That would explain Levine making a trip to New York to talk with Herbert Yates about financial help for a Maynard movie. In addition to solving the problem of getting his film processing done on credit, Levine could also placate Yates by casting Gene Autry in the Maynard movie. The fact that Gene Autry was a proven, successful singer with a following in the Midwest was an added bonus. Also, Nat Levine did not have anyone else to fill the role of a western singer!

This led Levine to stop in Chicago and invite Autry to Hollywood (as well as meet with his distributor). Levine then told Autry that a part would be written for him in Maynard's movie — a role similar to Autry's real life experience on WLS and the "National Barn Dance" — and this would, in essence, be a "screen test" for Autry. There was not much for Nat Levine to lose — the scene would only last ten minutes in the movie — and Ken Maynard's films generally did well. This device of bringing on a guest star to sing recurred later in Autry's movies when top name country acts appeared as guests in his singing cowboy movies, which added to the appeal of the picture.

The July 14, 1934 issue of *Billboard* announced that "Gene Autry, WLS Oklahoma yodeling cowboy, will depart for Hollywood in about three weeks. Gene has not signed any contracts, but has been offered a part in Ken Maynard's forthcoming picture, being produced by Mascot Pictures, Inc. Tentatively he is scheduled for the master of ceremonies job in a great barn dance sequence. Mascot officials indicate they expect to rely to a large extent on Gene's experience with the WLS National Barn Dance for information on technique and routine for a live barn dance sequence."

The article also stated that "Autry was offered a part in Mascot's Wampas star production, *Young and Beautiful*, but a contract for Chicago theater appearances prevented him from going to Hollywood in time for the filming in June."[11]

Autry, his wife Ina Mae and Smiley Burnette drove to California, probably arriving in early to mid–August. On the way out, Smiley Burnette wrote several songs while sitting in the back seat of Autry's Buick. For "Ridin' Down the Canyon," which became a western classic, Autry gave Smiley $5 for the copyright, so they are listed as co-writers. Burnette also wrote "The Old Covered Wagon," "Wagon Train," "Hold On, Little Dogies, Hold On" and "Someday in Wyoming," which Autry performed in the Maynard film.

In Hollywood, Autry had to meet with Ken Maynard and get the star's approval before it was certain he was in the film. Apparently things worked well, and he received the nod.

The filming was set to begin in September; meanwhile Autry had to find work, and performed around the Los Angeles area. One evening, he and Smiley Burnette walked into the radio station where Stuart Hamblen did his "Lucky Stars" radio show. Autry introduced himself and asked if he could sing a song; Hamblen let him do one. According to Wesley Tuttle, who was in Hamblen's group at the time, "That was the first time I'd ever heard of Gene Autry, but Stuart probably knew about him out in Chicago because he kept up with other singers."[12] Also, Autry later recorded one of Stuart Hamblen's songs, "Texas Plains," in September 1935, and the two may have corresponded about songs.

On September 4, 1934, Autry signed a "term" contract with Mascot, giving him $100 a week for his debut appearance in a movie.

The movie was originally entitled *Down in Old Santa Fe.* Autry's part was to perform during a hoedown dance written into the script, accompanied by Smiley Burnette. The filming had some tense moments. Director David Howard started the film but did not complete it; his contract with Levine was up before the film was finished, and Levine did not want to renew it, so he hired Joe Kane to finish directing. Maynard's sidekick was George Hayes, later known as "Gabby." After this movie, Harry Sherman signed Hayes to play in the Hopalong Cassidy/Bar 20 films.

Kane caused Maynard to lose his temper when, trying to kid around with the star, he handed him a revised script and said, "I understand you need a few minutes to memorize that much." Maynard responded by drawing his gun and aiming it straight at Kane, inviting the director to take up a gun as well. (The guns fired blanks, but these could hurt at short range.) Autry intervened in the flare-up and walked Maynard off to a side and calmly talked him down.[13]

Another time, director David Howard was photographing the heroine, Evalyn Knapp, back lit by the fireplace. Since Miss Knapp wore no undergarments, it took no imagination to see all there was to see. Maynard walked on the set during this session and erupted "in a state of moral indignation."[14]

In Old Santa Fe had contemporary elements in an Old West setting. During the film, Evalyn Knapp drove a sports car, some of the characters wore clothing that was a mixture of East and West, and Maynard battled big city gangsters. This mixture of the Old West infused with modern devices — cars, airplanes, radios, etc.— would be a hallmark of Gene Autry's westerns. The idea probably originated with Nat Levine, who needed fresh ideas for the western and wanted a more contemporary setting.

In the movie, Autry called a square dance and sang "Someday in Wyoming." Smiley Burnette did "Mama Don't 'Low No Music in Here," the song he recorded earlier that year, playing all the instruments in the band. Autry then sang "Down in Old Santa Fe." In terms of sheer talent, Smiley Burnette showed he had it in abundance, but the rotund musician did not look like a movie star — Gene Autry did. Also, Autry's voice sounded good, and he had a large following in the South and Midwest through the WLS "National Barn Dance" and Sears. Indeed, the unsung hero of this story might be the Sears catalog, which carried Autry's records and the "Gene Autry Round-Up Guitar" for several years before this appearance.

After *In Old Santa Fe* was completed in September 1934, Autry and Burnette had a small role in Maynard's next project, a serial titled *Mystery Mountain*. In this serial, Autry and Burnette drove a wagon — there were no songs. Autry and Burnette were just a step above extras and benefited from being in the right place at the right time. Upon completion of their roles in *Mystery Mountain*, the two musicians went back to Chicago for personal appearances and radio shows.

During the filming of *Mystery Mountain*, Levine decided to fire Maynard. The actor had proven to be increasingly difficult; he wanted to change the story and film it on the Universal lot. Budgeted for $65,000, the serial cost $80,000. Maynard was drinking heavily, was always in a sour mood, and beat the horses mercilessly. Levine confronted Maynard and fired him. That solved one problem, but now Mascot needed a cowboy actor.[15]

In Old Santa Fe was released on November 15, 1934, and the first chapter in *Mystery Mountain* was released on December 1.

The Hollywood movie business had made a dramatic change in July 1934, around the same time Autry was shifting his career from Chicago to Hollywood. Four years earlier, in March 1930, the Motion Picture Producers and Distributors of America pledged to abide by the Production Code, which imposed a moral standard on the movie industry after criticism was directed at Hollywood because of off-screen scandals and onscreen antics and innuendoes. There was also the problem of gangster movies, which, according to community leaders, led young people astray.

Heading up the Motion Picture Producers and Distributors of America was Will H. Hays, the former postmaster general during the Warren Harding administration. The Production Code was written by Catholic priest Daniel Lord and Martin Quigley, a prominent Roman Catholic and editor of the *Motion Picture Herald*. The problem was that the Code had no effective enforcement; whenever Code administrators made an unfavorable decision against MPPDA members, these members appealed to the next level of executive authority. In other words, the movie producers and directors could appeal to themselves; a "transit visa" was then granted for theatrical release. As a result, gangster movies and movies with sexual themes were on movie screens in Middle America.

Beginning in late 1933 and continuing through early 1934 — just before Autry went to Hollywood for his first movie appearance — the Catholic church launched a campaign against Hollywood immorality. A group called the Motion Picture Research Council published reports that linked bad behavior with movies. After Franklin D. Roosevelt was sworn in as president in March 1933, he brought a number of businesses and industries under the scrutiny of the federal government. One of the laws passed in 1934 was the Federal Communications Act, which mandated that the radio airwaves should be used for the public interest, as determined by the federal government. At the end of 1933, the *Hollywood Reporter* published an article stating the movie industry had to clean up its act or else face the possibility of federal censorship. During this period, a number of bills were proposed or introduced in Congress to regulate the movie industry with strong, bipartisan support.

Also in 1933 the Legion of Decency was formed by Catholics to force Hollywood to present moral and wholesome stories on the screen. Catholic priests and bishops warned parishioners against Hollywood films, and priests stood outside movie box offices to confront parishioners buying a ticket.

All of these events — the Legion of Decency, FDR's New Deal legislation, the decline in movie attendance because of the Depression — combined to force Hollywood executives to put some teeth into the Production Code by hiring Joseph Breen to enforce it. The MPPDA's board of directors also changed the Code's enforcement policy by abolishing the power of studio heads to reverse decisions by the Studio Relations Committee, allowing Production Code Administration decisions to be reversed only by a court of appeals in New York, dominated by the bankers and financiers of the movie industry. A. P. Giannini, president of the Bank of America, sealed the deal when he announced there would be no financing of a film without prior clearance from the Production Code Administration.[16]

Nearly overnight, the Hollywood movie business became wholesome. One of the first beneficiaries was Shirley Temple, the six year old child star, who rocketed to fame in 1934. Temple sang in her films; in 1934's *Bright Eyes*, for example, she sang "On the Good Ship Lollipop." Another beneficiary was Gene Autry, who began singing in western movies in 1934 and the following year starred in a string of singing cowboy movies. Both children and cowboys were considered quintessentially American and presented a wholesome, moral message.

Beginning in 1934, the Hollywood musical was back. In 1935 it was in full swing as movies like *Top Hat*, starring Fred Astaire and Ginger Rogers; *Born to Dance*; a series of *Gold Diggers* movies; *Showboat*; and numerous others were filmed. It was the right time for a musical western star to emerge, and Gene Autry was in the right place at the right time with the right talent in the right vehicle.

9

THE PHANTOM EMPIRE

In the fall of 1934, Nat Levine told his script writers to alter a serial to allow Gene Autry to sing in most chapters. The script was originally written for Maynard, and the promotion material had been created to feature Maynard. The plot was rather far-fetched — it was a science fiction/western — and starred a western radio entertainer who uncovers an underground kingdom. In most episodes, Autry managed to get back to the fictional radio station to sing a song.

Autry and Burnette came back to Hollywood to film *The Phantom Empire* in early December. They finished filming in late December 1934, and headed back to Chicago. An item in *Variety* on Christmas day noted, "Mascot's new serial star, Gene Autrey [sic], after completing his first thriller, flew to Chicago Friday (21) to resume broadcasting for Sears Roebuck. He returns here for another serial which will be produced after Tom Mix's Texas Ranger."

On January 14–17, 1935, Gene Autry was in New York, accompanied by the Prairie Ramblers and Smiley Burnette for four consecutive days of recording sessions. After duets with Jimmy Long on "Angel Boy" and "Red River Lullaby," Autry sang solo on the song he performed in his movie debut, "Someday in Wyoming." The following day he recorded "Dear Old Western Skies" and "The Old Covered Wagon," both written by Smiley Burnette. On the third day, again accompanied by the Prairie Ramblers, he did "Hold On Little Dogies Hold On," "Answer to Red River Valley," "That Silver Haired Mother of Mine," and "Ridin' Down the Canyon." On the final day, along with the Prairie Ramblers and Smiley Burnette, he recorded "Wagon Train," "Old Missouri Moon," and "Ole Faithful."

On February 23, 1935, the first chapter of *The Phantom Empire* was released. When film critics speak of *The Phantom Empire*, they generally focus on its mixture of science fiction and westerns. In fact, in terms of science fiction, it was a pioneer serial, arriving at theaters a year ahead of Buck Rogers and other sci-fi serials. Obviously, the success of *The Phantom Empire* inspired Mascot and studios to pursue these futuristic serials for Saturday morning fare. What has been overlooked is the importance of this serial to the singing cowboy genre. It was the introduction of the singing cowboy to movie audiences. Although Gene Autry had appeared in Ken Maynard's *In Old Santa Fe* in a ten-minute

50

segment, the plot was built around Maynard, not Autry. In *The Phantom Empire*, the plot was built around Gene Autry, who blended singing with his acting in the plot. Interestingly, it presented Gene Autry as a star in his first starring vehicle.

The serial took advantage of Autry's success on radio. His dude ranch is known as Radio Ranch, and there are two basic settings: the Radio Ranch of Autry and the underground city of Murania, ruled by Queen Tika. A young person in the 21st century undoubtedly considers *The Phantom Empire* much too hokey with all the implausible cliffhangers as well as the gizmos and gadgets on the obvious stage set of Murania. But for a ten-year-old rural youth in 1935, this was exciting stuff. There are lots of action scenes, a suspension of disbelief, and the constant wondering of "how in the world is Gene Autry going to get out of this mess?"

On the same day *The Phantom Empire* was released, Autry appeared at WLS in Chicago with Sue Roberts on "Sears Junior Roundup." He continued on that show each Saturday at 10 A.M. during February.

A full-page ad in *Billboard* on March 9, 1935 announced that Autry was "now making a personal appearance tour of the country with his own show."[1] At the end of March, Autry began a fifteen-minute weekly show on WHAS in Louisville at 12:45 P.M. Soon, he was on twice daily and performed theater dates in the Louisville area.

WHAS was the largest radio station in Louisville, an NBC affiliate with 25,000 watts. In 1934 J. L. Frank moved from Chicago to Louisville after he decided not to accompany Gene Autry to Hollywood. He brought along Pee Wee King and the Log Cabin Boys. Autry went to Louisville, where he remained based for a couple of months because J. L. Frank was there. Frank obtained bookings for personal appearances as well as exposure on the radio for Autry. During the period from March through April, Autry said he received a call from Levine while "on the road" to return to Hollywood. This would probably have occurred in late spring of 1935. Autry wanted Joe Frank to go to Hollywood with him, but Frank refused. Joe Frank's dream was to return to Tennessee, so he set his sights on the Grand Ole Opry in Nashville, although first he had to go to Knoxville before he landed at the Opry with the Golden West Cowboys, headed by Pee Wee King.[2]

****

Levine was pleased and surprised at the positive reaction Autry had received. At that time, people wrote letters when they liked an actor or singer, and Gene Autry received a lot of letters addressed to him at Mascot in Hollywood for *The Phantom Empire*. And so Nat Levine got his script writers to meet Autry and develop a feature.

In *In Old Santa Fe*, Autry appeared as "Gene Autry," which was logical, considering they wanted to capitalize on his popularity with the record buying public in the South and Midwest and attract more ticket-buyers to the movie. In *Mystery Mountain*, Autry and Smiley Burnette used the names "Thomas" and "Hench." If Levine had seen movie star potential in Autry, he would have given him the name of a character in *Phantom Empire* so he could play other roles in future movies. Instead, Autry played "Gene Autry." Levine probably figured that Autry's name brought in ticket sales in the small, rural theaters, so it would be an asset. Also, for Levine, the initial idea of a singing cowboy seemed to reside in serials or chapter plays, like *The Phantom Empire*, where the singer had a fairly short amount of time to work in a plot and a song. Further, it was fairly easy to write a story about a radio star; the fact that Autry was a radio star in real life was a nice coincidence.

Finally, Levine, an astute judge of talent, probably realized that Gene Autry could play Gene Autry quite well, but he was not an actor in the traditional sense, able to convincingly play different characters in a wide variety of roles.

Hollywood musicals were big, lavish affairs, so the idea of a "western musical" just didn't seem to fit the cowboy movie genre. At that point, it was difficult to imagine how a cowboy movie could have songs sprinkled through it and still be effective. And so *Phantom Empire* became an important bridge in the development of the singing cowboy movies from the traditional westerns, which had sometimes incorporated a song or two.

On May 17, 1935, Gene Autry signed a contract in Los Angeles with Mascot for eight pictures. According to Levine, "Autry was completely raw material, knew nothing about acting, lacked poise, and was awkward. A couple of days after his arrival I had him at my home and invited my production staff to meet him. The next day all my associates questioned my judgment in putting him under contract. They thought I was slipping. But I persisted, and for the first four months he went through a learning period. We had at that time in our employ a professional dramatic and voice teacher, and Autry became one of her pupils. He wasn't much of a horseman either, so I had Tracey Layne and Yakima Canutt teach him how to ride."[3]

According to Levine, Autry received $100 a week, and Smiley Burnette and Frankie Marvin received $75 a week each. However, according to Burnette, he and Marvin received $35 a week.

Nat Levine had an uncanny eye for unusual talent. Obviously, he saw something in Autry, but he may have seen a "package" and not just Autry alone. Smiley Burnette, who was probably with Autry when he met Levine, was an incredibly talented musician and comic. In fact, Burnette was cast in other Mascot movies without Autry. Frankie Marvin was also with Autry and played a key role writing songs, playing on his recordings, and performing with him. While it was obvious that Autry was the star and leader, these two were important to Autry's success. And when Levine signed Gene Autry, he also signed Burnette and Marvin. It was a good move from the beginning. *The Phantom Empire*, budgeted at $70,000, became the third highest grossing serial in the history of Mascot.

****

In mid–1935, Gene Autry moved to California for good. He had to send his sisters and brother to Oklahoma at first, where they stayed with the Ozments until Gene and Ina Mae could find a place to live. As soon as they did, Gene and Ina sent for his siblings, who lived with them in California until they were married.

Autry added several key people to his team who would remain with him for the rest of his musical career. George Goodale, a newspaper reporter who interviewed Autry when the singer was on KVOO in Tulsa, had gone to work for the *Los Angeles Examiner* but was fired. According to Goodale, he walked into the Brass Rail one day while Gene Autry was singing. After a re-introduction, Autry hired him on the spot as his publicity agent.[4]

(According to Autry, he ran into Goodale at the Brown Derby restaurant while at lunch.)[5]

Autry later claimed to have spoken with Will Rogers, one of Autry's heroes, shortly before the humorist died on August 15, 1935. This is possible because Rogers was at Gilmore Stadium in Hollywood for a rodeo on August 3. Rogers sat in the stands and chatted with a number of people during the evening, so it is possible that he may have chatted with Autry as well.[6]

The biggest change for Gene Autry during 1935 concerned the business arrangements of Nat Levine and Herb Yates. Levine leased, with an option to purchase, the old Mack Sennett Studio on Ventura Boulevard, but never exercised the option because he needed all the money he could find in order to expand his film production. Mascot and Monogram both owed money to Consolidated Film Industries, owned by Herbert Yates. Yates proposed to Levine that Mascot and Monogram merge their production and distribution operations with Consolidated's processing laboratories and invest capital to create a single firm: Republic Productions. They would then buy Liberty Pictures, Majestic Pictures, and Chesterfield Pictures, which included all contracts and any corporately-owned distribution outlets.

Yates, who planned to stay in New York with the film processing plant in Fort Lee, New Jersey, offered Levine the job of production head, which is what Levine always wanted to do. Trem Carr, head of Monogram, would work in production supervision while W. Ray Johnston would serve as president and take care of distribution, while Herbert J. Yates would hold the title Chairman of the Board. This meant the new entity would have to increase production to increase cash flow, control distribution, and make more effective use of the studio. Levine was always short of cash and knew that without a large pipeline of product, he could not match the distribution networks of the major studios. The central argument from Yates was that production could increase in both quality and quantity by merging resources. Levine would be a stockholder in Republic and have authority over production — so he agreed. Also, the financial problems of Levine and Johnston would be solved.

Levine did not realize at that time that he was moving from a relatively small operation where he had complete control to a situation where he would have to answer to partners, some of whom knew little about production. This would lead to increased frustration on Levine's part as time progressed. Mascot brought to the table a cast of technicians, stunt men, directors and actors — including Ann Rutherford and Gene Autry. Monogram had a network of distribution exchanges, producer Paul Malvern, director Robert North Bradbury and actor John Wayne. For Gene Autry and John Wayne, who had contracts with Mascot and Monogram, respectively, this meant they would now be contractually tied to Republic.[7]

The first movie released under the new Republic arrangement was *Westward Ho!*, starring John Wayne, and it was a singing western. Again, this proves how influential *The Phantom Empire* serial — and Gene Autry — was to movie-making even before his first starring feature was released. John Wayne filmed *Westward Ho!* at the same time Gene Autry filmed *Tumbling Tumbleweeds*. Also, Warner Brothers had a singing western, starring Dick Foran, scheduled for release around the same time Autry's first feature was released.

Westward Ho! featured a group, the Singing Rangers, who sang "Covered Wagons Rolling West." The Singing Rangers comprised a group of singing actors, not a "name" singing group. In the movie, John Wayne sang "The Girl That I Love in My Dreams" to a young lady — but the voice was dubbed in (probably by Jack Kirk) because, in real life, Wayne could not sing.[8] Although there was music and singing in the film, there was no singing star to build a plot around. John Wayne could never fill that role.[9]

Clearly, Nat Levine as well as other Hollywood executives felt the singing western was an idea worth trying, and Gene Autry benefited from being in the right place at the right time.

10

THE SINGING COWBOY

On July 12, Autry finished filming *Tumbling Tumbleweeds*, which was done on location in Bakersfield and Barstow, California, at the Placerita Canyon Ranch. The film was released September 9, 1935, and created a standard for Autry's pictures. Following the pattern of *In Old Santa Fe*, Autry's movies would combine cowboys with current times. There were cars and airplanes as well as cowboys and horses; sometimes cowboys on horses chased city slickers in cars. Cowboys wearing guns stood in saloons where a radio played; sometimes a hay wagon pulled by horses shared a road with a truck. There was also a lot of songs, capitalizing on Autry's success as a recording artist.

Tumbling Tumbleweeds featured Gene Autry as a singer in a medicine show (perhaps inspired by his real life experience with the Field Brothers). At the time this was released the only country music heard on the radio was on the barn dances or early morning shows, so those who loved this music were not overexposed to it. The singing cowboy movies gave audiences who wanted to hear this music another chance to do so. Autry's first full-length starring movie featured the songs "Tumbling Tumbleweeds," "That Silver Haired Daddy of Mine," and "Ridin' Down the Canyon."

On September 23, 1935, Autry was in New York to record with the Prairie Ramblers. He did the Bob Nolan song "Tumbling Tumbleweeds," "Texas Plains" (written by Stuart Hamblen) and Smiley Burnette's "Uncle Noah's Ark." These songs were first released on Conqueror, the Sears label; Sears and Republic were in a joint marketing campaign to promote Gene Autry.[1]

About two weeks after the release of *Tumbling Tumbleweeds*, on September 24, *Melody Trail*, co-starring Smiley Burnette and Ann Rutherford was released. In *Melody Trail*, Autry's horse, Champion, received his first billing. Champion had been owned by Tom Mix and appeared in *The Phantom Empire* series. The horse was ridden by Autry, who rode several different horses in that series. The horse was brought to Autry's attention by Tracey Layne, a stunt man and movie horse wrangler. Autry probably purchased Champion after he moved to Hollywood in the summer of 1935.

Ann Rutherford, Autry's co-star in *Melody Trail*, remembered that on the last day's shoot for that movie, Ina Autry "came on the set and their car was piled high with boxes." Ina told her the boxes "contained Gene's fan mail, from people who liked *The Phantom*

Empire." Ina told Rutherford that after Autry finished filming they were "going to get Champion in a trailer and ... play all the towns in California.... Gene's been answering his fan mail and signing pictures, but I set up a filing system where, for instance, if we go to a town I have the cards from all the kids there who wrote to him. We'll get a local phone book when we get there and Gene will call them." Rutherford observed that Gene Autry "had the greatest good fortune in choosing wives who can really help him."[2]

That fall Autry went on a cross-country tour promoting his movies. In Oklahoma City, where Johnny Marvin was broadcasting on WKY, a station owned by *The Daily Oklahoman*, Autry had an outdoor appearance near City Hall with free admission on November 11. On this bitterly cold day Autry wore a ten-gallon hat, dungarees, cowboy boots, but no coat. Johnny Bond, who was in the audience, remembered that he sang "Old Faithful" and "strummed restlessly on his guitar in between songs, leading me to wonder if he was quite certain as to what he was going to do next."[3] Autry was the special guest of the Theater Owners of Oklahoma, who were holding their annual convention at the Biltmore Hotel. He rode into Civic Center park on a horse loaned to him. After the performance, the movie was shown at the Majestic Theater.[4]

****

On October 27 the last Mascot serial, *Fighting Marines*, was released. By this point there were two more Autry features completed, which were initially listed as *Sage Brush Troubadour* and *Tex Comes a Singin'*. Armand Schaefer, who joined the studio that year, handled production duties on Autry's pictures. Schaefer would be an important member of Autry's team for the next twenty-five years.

The Sagebrush Troubadour was released on November 25, 1935; Autry's co-stars were Smiley Burnette and Barbara Pepper. On December 5, Autry was in Chicago recording "My Old Saddle Pal," "Riding the Range," "End of the Trail," "Don't Waste Your Tears on Me," and "You're the Only Star in My Blue Heaven." On Christmas Eve, he recorded "Mexicali Rose." These were first released through Sears. In *Singing Vagabond* (originally titled *Tex Comes A-Singin'*) which was released December 11, the star appeared as "Tex" Autry; co-stars included Smiley Burnette, Ann Rutherford, Barbara Pepper, and Ray "Crash" Corrigan. The plot involved television, a new technology which would not be known to the public until 1939.

Red River Valley was released March 2, 1936, and co-starred Smiley Burnette and Frances Grant. The movie opens with an orchestra performing an instrumental version of "Red River Valley." The plot involves a drought problem in the West — this was the era of the Dust Bowl storms in Oklahoma and Texas, which led a number of migrants to venture West — which could be solved by a dam. However, someone was sabotaging the dam, blowing up gates so the dam could not irrigate the region. Autry becomes a "ditch rider," working to protect the dam as he tries to uncover who is behind the dynamiting. The villain turns out to be a respectable banker.

Early in the movie there are three songs in a row: an instrumental coming from a saloon piano, a song for an African-American tap dancer, and another instrumental by a novelty band. These gimmick bands were popular in Autry's movies. Reminiscent of the Hoosier Hot Shots on WLS, these bands played kazoos, washboards, and other assorted instruments. Autry sang "Red River Valley" in the saloon, then Smiley Burnette (as Frog Millhouse, his standard character name in most Autry pictures) sang "Hand Me Down My Trusty .45." The next song, "We're Digging a Ditch" or "Construction Song," was sung by a group of farmers working on irrigation ditches. One of the villains, the construction foreman, is forced to sing "Red River Valley" before Autry and the group of workers join in. The plot thickens when the payroll is stolen and Autry is blamed; this is a recurring device in Autry's films — the hero is falsely accused of a crime and has to prove himself innocent. Autry escapes and finds the villains in their hideout; they spill the beans on the mastermind behind the dirty tricks, and the movie ends with Autry again singing "Red River Valley."

Autry's movies generally had a respectable businessman as the villain, a theme that resonated with Depression–era audiences who tended to blame business and businessmen for the Depression. Musically, Autry's early pictures featured a variety of performances; Autry himself only performed a few songs while Smiley Burnette did one or two; there might be a large group or chorale singing off-camera, while on-camera a known group would do a guest appearance and perform some songs. There were some instrumentals and even big band numbers that came from a radio on the set. Although these early Autry movies had six to eight songs in the roughly one hour movie, Gene Autry did not sing all of them; instead the music was parceled out, and fans heard a smorgasbord of musical selections, but the title or "hit" song in the movie was always sung by Autry.

In *Comin' Round the Mountain*, released at the end of March 1936 and co-starring Ann Rutherford and Smiley Burnette, the setting is the Old West, making this one of only two films he did for Republic that did not have a contemporary setting. As Autry's movies became successful, and his star rose, he had more input into his films and clearly preferred his westerns be set in the modern world. Also, the ideas that originated with Nat Levine had proven popular and successful.

Autry was a modern man himself; he liked living in the current world. He had grown up in the Old West and wanted to escape it; the reality of working cowboys had no appeal for him. He wanted to be a modern day star. The audiences agreed with him and as the twentieth century progressed, with inventions like radio and automobiles becoming more commonplace, audiences related to those movies. The problem is that Autry's westerns are dated when watched by audiences who didn't grow up in the 1930s and 1940s; old cars and primitive radios in the wild west don't seem to mix. The historical westerns are more timeless and more likely to become classic westerns. But Autry knew his audience, and he knew the vehicles that worked to make him a major star in his time.

****

The Singing Cowboy was released in May 1936 and co-starred Smiley Burnette, Lois Wilde, and Lon Chaney, Jr. *Guns and Guitars* was released June 22 and co-starred Smiley Burnette, Dorothy Dix, and Denver Dixon. In September *Oh, Susannah!*, co-starring Smiley Burnette, Frances Grant, Frankie Marvin, and the Light Crust Doughboys was released. This movie began a trend of using established country acts in Autry's movies. The idea was to make it more appealing to audiences in various regions. The Light Crust Doughboys came from Fort Worth, Texas, and were popular on radio. *Variety*'s review of the movie stated, "The banjo-plinking horseman and his guitar laze through this fancy sagebrush opera in which there is more singing than action. Song stuff is cowboy yodeling and hillbilly whining. Too much of it."[5]

It is interesting to note the *Variety* reviewer did not know a banjo from a guitar; Autry never played a banjo in his movies (although a band member in this movie did play the banjo). Since *Variety* was (and still is) the major trade magazine for the movie industry, the publication's reviews give an insight into what the mainstream movie industry thought of Autry's pictures. In general, it was dismissive of Autry and his movies.

The B westerns were not filmed in the same manner as the A films from major studios. The majors spent a lot of time and money on a movie, while the B western filmmakers generally filmed six to eight features in a row. Each feature took two to four weeks to film, then the next would start. There was stock footage — perhaps a cattle stampede or a horse chase — from previous films which could be dropped into a movie — or perhaps several movies. The movies were leased by theater owners, who generally showed the movies once or twice. So these B studios cranked out numerous movies with the result that audiences were not saturated with a movie, the theory being that movie fans wanted to see something new each week.

Work on those early B movies was draining. Ann Rutherford remembered that the cast and crew "worked until midnight on Saturdays. We even worked on Sundays.... The cry we heard all day was 'Fighting light! Fighting light!' That put the fear of God in everybody. You see, the big klieg lights were just too expensive. They took a few on location, but they couldn't take many.... They'd start shooting at the first light. I remember getting up at 4:00 in the morning and trying to put a face on. You know, we'd stay in these rotten little motels. We'd go to a place like Lone Pine, where they have those wonderful Alabama Hills ... where all the villains or crooks could hide behind rocks and come out and kill people — and they had rattlesnakes there, too.... We did exterior shots there, and then we'd scuttle back — because it cost them money to house people ... maybe eight or ten dollars a day in a hotel there — and Nat Levine counted every penny. We started working at first light, and it behooved everybody to know their dialogue. You didn't get a second shot at it, unless you really stumbled badly — and then they'd say 'cut' and they'd pick it up from where you stumbled. We had scant rehearsals — and it wouldn't have helped much if we had rehearsed, because most of the directors had previously been electricians or second assistant directors or something else!"

Rutherford recalled that those movies were made "on a dead run. One of the films had Indians in it. In the morning, the cowboy riders were cowboy riders. In the afternoon, they'd put dark make-up on and they were Indians — and they spent the rest of the day chasing themselves." Rutherford observed that Autry wasn't bothered by the grind. "He was just as happy as he could be," she said. "He had been on the radio, but being in pictures was really paydirt. He would sing and play his guitar, and Smiley would accompany him on his 'Stomach Steinway,' as he called it, and it was the best of all possible worlds. He was getting acquainted with the fine points of riding, and he got real good at it."[6]

****

Ride, Ranger, Ride, released September 30, 1935, co-starred Smiley Burnette, Max Terhune, Chief Thundercloud, Frankie Marvin, Iron Eyes Cody, and the Tennessee Ramblers. The movie opens with Autry and a group on horseback, riding towards the camera, singing "Ride, Ranger, Ride." Autry and a group sang this song several times in the movie; Autry sang "On The Sunset Trail" twice and a large group off-camera sang "Song of the Pioneers."

On November 16 *The Big Show*, filmed at the Texas Centennial in Dallas, was released, co-starring Smiley Burnette, Kay Hughes, Max Terhune, Sally Payne, Frankie Marvin, and Sally Rand the fan dancer. This movie was an attempt by Republic to do an A movie from a B studio and was billed an "Autry Special." The movie featured five musical groups: Sons of the Pioneers, the Light Crust Doughboys (whose star, Bob Wills, had just quit to go out on his own), the Beverly Hill Billies, the Jones Boys, and the SMU school band. The film featured songs written by Hollywood songwriters Ted Koehler and Ned Washington. The movie opens with Autry singing "The Martins and the 'Coys" with a group. Tom Ford, also played by Autry, then enters as a prima donna movie star who demands his double appear for a stunt. After the movie making is finished, Tom Ford disappears into the mountains on a camping trip before it is discovered that he is supposed to appear at the Texas Centennial in Dallas. Since there was no way to reach Ford, Autry has to go to Dallas.

Tom Ford owes gangsters $10,000 from gambling; the gangsters believe Autry is Ford and intend to shake him down. But first, Autry rides in a parade as Tom Ford while a group sings "Ride, Ranger, Ride." The Sons of the Pioneers play for a dance, and then Gene and Smiley Burnette sing "Way Out in the Wild and Wooly West." In a studio, backed by the Sons of the Pioneers, Autry sings "Be Nobody's Darling But Mine." A twist in the plot occurs when Tom Ford, during his camping trip, hears on the radio that Gene Autry is impersonating him. Further, Tom Ford cannot sing while Autry is winning over crowds with his singing. Autry sings "Mad About You" while the gangsters, who discover the ruse, threaten to blow Autry's cover. The Sons of the Pioneers sing "Roll Wagon Roll," and Gene sings "Old Faithful" to his horse during a dramatic presentation to the Centennial crowd. In the meantime, the comedic PR agent for "Mammoth Studios" is having a fit. The gangsters manage to kidnap a girl and get $25,000 in ransom money. Autry recovers the money, saves the girl and, in the end, he was the star while Tom Ford was his double.

The *Variety* review called the film Republic's "humdinger" of the season and said, "it's by far his [Autry's] best in many starts, and it packs a lot of entertainment for the action and western fans.... Congress of cowboy tunesters is one of the features — the Beverly Hill Billies, the Lightcrust Doughboys, the Jones boys, and the Sons of Pioneers, all taking a crack at guitar strings and song at various times.... As bronc operas go, this is a different story and a better class production."[7]

In *The Old Corral*, a young actor using the name "Dick Weston" has a fistfight with Autry. Autry forces Weston to sing — which he does, although it humiliates him. Dick Weston was the stage name used by Leonard Slye, who eventually changed his name to Roy Rogers. In addition to Weston, other co-stars include Smiley Burnette, Hope Manning, Lon Chaney, Jr., Frankie Marvin, and the Sons of the Pioneers.

****

In December 1935 it was reported in the press that Autry had offered to build a resort hotel and develop a spa around the mineral water wells in his hometown of Tioga, Texas, if the town changed its name to "Autry Springs." Jason Hodges, editor of the *Tioga Herald*, wrote an editorial stating, "Tioga has been a good enough name for the town for 55 years, and it ought to be good enough for another 55."[8]

There was a vote held, but a prominent physician, Dr. E. Eugene Ledbetter, was against re-naming the town. According to legend, Ledbetter was bitter because Delbert Autry never paid him for delivering Gene. It was noted that Gene "had played at Sam Anderson's barbershop," but he "left Tioga High School before his senior year to pursue a career as a relief telegrapher for the Frisco Railroad."[9] After the vote the name of the town remained Tioga.

At the end of 1936 Gene Autry was voted the number three western star, behind Buck Jones and George O'Brien. He was becoming comfortable as a movie star and had licensed his name for a number of products. During this year he also began making appearances on major radio shows, such as those hosted by Rudy Vallee and Eddie Cantor.

11

PUBLIC COWBOY
NUMBER ONE

In 1937 Gene Autry emerged as the top western star in the United States. It was a pivotal year for him. Autry's first movie in 1937 was *Roundup Time in Texas*, released on February 28; co-starring Smiley Burnette, Maxine Doyle, and the Cabin Kids, the movie was set in South Africa after a brief opening in Texas. The title came from the song "When the Bloom Is on the Sage" whose opening line is "when it's roundup time in Texas." In the plot, Autry's brother is kidnapped, so the star has to go to South Africa to rescue him.

This is the last film where Nat Levine is listed in the production credits because in April Levine, who first signed Gene Autry to a movie contract, left Republic. At the time, Levine was 37 years old and had produced four Republic serials a year, in addition to Autry's movies and the *Three Mesquiteer* series. During the original merger, in the fall of 1935, Levine had folded everything — his staff, production unit and contracts with actors (including Gene Autry) — into Republic. Herbert Yates then bought out Nat Levine for $2 million and gained complete control of Republic. This led to a conflict with Autry during the fall of the year as Yates flexed his muscles and Autry looked towards greener pastures. As for Levine, he left for New York, then spent a couple of months in Europe after the buy-out. In August, Levine returned to Hollywood and signed a contract with M-G-M to be an associate producer.

The reviewers at *Variety* had begun to appreciate Gene Autry and the executives at Republic a little more by this time; a review stated, "In this simple little fable he gives evidence of why he's building in locales where they go for the oats operas. Possessing nice physique, passable acting, and an ingratiating voice, he has the prerequisites to take him places."[1]

On March 22 *Git Along Little Dogies*, co-starring Smiley Burnette, Judith Allen, the Maple City Four, and the Cabin Kids, was released. The movie opens with Autry and a four man group riding towards the camera singing the title song. In this film, Smiley Burnette used his "double" voice — a unique talent the sidekick had. Burnette would begin singing in a tenor, then drop down to a growly baritone bass that sounded completely different from his supposedly normal voice; he did this in every Autry movie where he sang.

In the film a novelty group — playing piano, funnels for horns and a washboard — performs the jazz song "China Town," with Autry singing a little; Autry then sings "Cowboy ABCs." Several songs are performed by the Maple City Four, a group from Chicago well known to the WLS audience while Autry was there: "The Boys from Circle A" and a medley of "Wait for the Wagons," "Red River Valley," "She'll Be Comin' Round the Mountain," "Long, Long Ago," "Oh Susannah," "Goodnight Ladies," and "For He's a Jolly Good Fellow" with lyrics to the songs appearing on the screen so the audience could sing along. There is an instrumental background number, and a female duo sings "Calamity Jane." The Cabin Kids sing "After You've Gone," Autry sings "To the Valley Where the Sun Goes Down," but the song is interrupted when someone shoots out the radio broadcasting Autry's voice. At the end of the picture, Autry and the group sing "All's Well That Ends Well" before the entire group performs "Happy Days Are Here Again."

On May 12 *Rootin' Tootin' Rhythm*, which co-starred Smiley Burnette, Armida, Ann Pendleton, Hal Taliaferro, and Al Clauser and His Oklahoma Outlaws, was released. This movie begins with Autry and Smiley Burnette singing "The Old Home Place" backed by a big production. Smiley then sings "Kick Him Until He Is Dead" with Clausen's group before Autry sings "I Hate to Say Goodbye to the Prairie." The Clausen group — who appeared as Texas Rangers — perform "Trail of Trails" and "Down the Trail of the Mountain Road." The movie ends with Autry singing "Mexicali Rose" to the young actress Armida.

On May 29 and June 2, Autry was in Chicago and recorded two duets with Jimmy Long, "Down a Mountain Trail," and "When the Golden Leaves are Falling" in addition to eight other songs. These songs would first be released on Conqueror and sold through Sears catalogs.

On June 14 *Yodelin' Kid from Pine Ridge* was released. Co-starring Smiley Burnette, Betty Bronson (Hollywood's original Peter Pan), Charles Middleton, Russell Simpson, Frankie Marvin, and the Tennessee Ramblers (Dick Hartman, W. J. Blair, Elmer Warren, Happy Morris, and Pappy Wolf), the movie opens with Autry yodeling, then he sings "Sing Me a Song of the Saddle" while riding alone. At the end of the song, he discovers a young lady stealing a calf; after stopping her he reprises "Sing Me a Song of the Saddle." In the film, Autry sings "Travelin' Slow," a vocal group sings "Land on the Rio," Autry and the vocal group accompanied by some young ladies sing "At the Jailhouse Rodeo." Smiley Burnette with the Tennessee Ramblers sings "Ma Put the Kettle On" followed by The Tennessee Ramblers singing three songs in a row: "Red River Valley," "She'll Be Comin' Round the Mountain" (with the young ladies singing)" and "Blue Danube Waltz." A record of Autry plays "Down in Santa Fe" (with Jimmie Rodgers–style yodeling), an African-American group sings "Swing Low, Sweet Chariot" and the movie ends with Autry singing "Sing Me a Song of the Saddle."

On August 23 *Public Cowboy No. 1*, co-starring Smiley Burnette, Ann Rutherford, William Farnum, and Frankie Marvin, was released. The plot involved using a short wave radio set to thwart cattle rustlers, who used an airplane! The title came from a phrase first coined back in Chicago by Crime Commission head Frank Loesch when the police were pursuing Al Capone. The term was popularized by J. Edgar Hoover and the FBI, who named criminals they were hunting "Public Enemy No. 1" and "Most Wanted."

Boots and Saddles was released on October 4 and featured a cast that included Judith Allen and Gordon Elliott as well as Smiley Burnette and Champion. The movie opens with an instrumental overture of "Boots and Saddle." The plot involves a man and a boy arriving from England at a ranch where Autry is foreman; the boy, who owns the ranch, is "royalty" and wants to sell the ranch. The first song is a Spanish-language number, sung by a group before Autry performs "Take Me Back to My Boots and Saddle." Autry sings "Ridin' the Range All Day," Smiley performs "Dusty Roads," a young lady sings "Celito Lindo," Autry sings "You're the One Rose That's Left in My Heart" and "Oh, Why Did He Get Married." The film ends with Autry singing the title song, "Boots and Saddle."

By this time, *Variety* and the rest of the movie industry acknowledged that Autry's pictures were profitable and popular with rural audiences. But the Hollywood crowd never quite understood Autry. This may have been because the United States was undergoing a metamorphosis during the 1930s as it moved from a rural to an urban nation. On the radio were the big bands, dressed in suits (or tuxes) with complex arrangements, presenting an image of sophistication and culture. Tin Pan Alley songwriters wrote in suits and ties and, although many had grown up as poor immigrants, they sought to distance themselves from their past. The movies in general were filled with escapist fare. In some A pictures the men wore tuxes and didn't work, while the women were elegant. Filmmakers in general distanced themselves from the everyday working world.

The cowboy pictures, on the other hand, were aimed at the rural audiences who lived in the working class world. In Autry's singing cowboy pictures the bad guys are the guys in suits — bankers and other businessmen — who are foiled in their attempts to fool the rural cowboys. This theme played well during the Depression because businessmen and bankers were often seen as untrustworthy and guilty of— or at least complicit in — creating the Great Depression. But this theme also played well on another level.

The rural audience was unsophisticated and uncultured as defined by the hip city-dwellers in New York and Hollywood who were more worldly wise. But the rural audience had a dignity of their own. They may have lacked worldliness, but they had common sense and basic, decent values. The values of the worldly urbanites seemed phony and pretentious to the rural dweller. In Gene Autry's pictures, rural audiences saw their values triumph and their down home approach to life rewarded and valued.

The westerns of the Great Depression and even the 1940s associated big cities and the East with corruption, immorality, economic exploitation and the distasteful, greedy, manipulative side of human nature. The heroes in westerns embraced traditional values, a clear right and wrong, and the idea that true justice will ultimately prevail. Later, when the United States became an urban and suburban nation, when most Americans considered themselves cool, hip, and worldly, these westerns were scorned. They were certainly scorned by the media in New York and Hollywood who believed themselves to be superior to the rural audience and tended to look down their noses at what they viewed as hicks, hayseeds and hillbillies who populated the rural heartland.

The Hollywood types failed to see that not everyone wanted to see themselves as Hollywood saw itself— cool, sophisticated and on the cutting edge, discarding outdated morals and fashions of the past and generally superior to those who make up the heartland.

Later movies would have the "hip" people living in cities and wearing suits (or fashion-able contemporary clothes) while those from the country would be dupes, living in a world that disdained them and their values. In other words, according to Hollywood, the coun-try folk didn't "get it" — with "it" being defined as the values promulgated by Hollywood and the pseudo-sophistication found among the self-absorbed "in" crowd. To the elite of Hollywood and New York, the people in between the two coasts were "flyover" people.

This was reflected in the *Variety* reviews, which referred to westerns as "oaters" (because horses eat oats) and whose casual use of the term "hillbillies" and other slang phrases drove home the point that Hollywood tastemakers were way ahead of the rural audience, who plodded behind. That's a major reason Gene Autry and his movies did not fare well with the media critics during his time or even today, while the rural audi-ence made him a hero and major star.

12

GENE AUTRY
AND BING CROSBY

The singing cowboy movies of Gene Autry changed western moviemaking as well as country music. During the 1935–1937 period, Gene Autry emerged as a major superstar in the United States, although the types of movies he did — and the types of songs he sang — did not appeal to the major critics at the time, and have certainly not appealed to most film historians since that time. Regardless, Autry by the end of 1937 was a major star in Hollywood.

The period 1927–1932 had marked a transition period for the western. First, westerns had suffered a decline in 1926, a result of the production of too many cheap westerns. Second, the coming of sound in 1927 with *The Jazz Singer* starring Al Jolson marked a new era for the movies. Most of the major studios stopped making westerns while a new group of small, independent studios, called "Poverty Row" studios or "Gower Gulch," became the dominant makers of westerns.

The period 1933–1937 has been called the "boom years" for the western. During these "boom years" about 530 western features were released and almost 500 of them were B movies. Also, 17 serials were released, accounting for 220 chapters. For fans of the traditional western the big star was Buck Jones, who rode his horse, Silver, in ten releases for Columbia, 22 features for Universal and four Universal serials. Tom Mix and Ken Maynard made the transition from silents to sound westerns, and Johnny Mack Brown got his start in Western features.

During this time the United States was in the depths of the Great Depression, and westerns provided a welcome relief with their escapism from daily life. On Saturday afternoons and evenings, people would spend a quarter for the movies, their major source of entertainment outside the radio. Americans seem to face adversity in two ways: by directly confronting it, on one hand, and by the use of escapism on the other. B westerns were escapist entertainment, creating a West that never was. Here, westerns moved from an attempt at realism with the William Hart silents — cowboy work clothes, lots of dust, rough-hewn actors — to the pure escapist entertainment of Gene Autry and other singing cowboys.

In addition to Buck Jones, B Western serial stars included Tim McCoy, Randolph Scott, George O'Brien, Charles Starrett, William Boyd, Ken Maynard, and Gene Autry. Other major cowboy stars of this era include Harry Carey, Hoot Gibson, Tom Mix and John Wayne.

The most interesting phenomenon of this period was the development of the singing western, with Gene Autry leading the charge and becoming the most popular movie cowboy of his era. With his sidekick Frog Millhouse (played by Smiley Burnette), Autry's films pioneered several areas: the extensive use of music in westerns (a new development in the genre which had basically repeated the old formulas of the silent westerns); the increasing emphasis on escapism as the role of westerns; gaudy costumes no real cowboy would ever wear on the range; use of the contemporary West in traditional plots; and the use of the "fool" sidekick, who caused as many problems as the outlaws.

During the mid-to-late 1930s there were several trends in the movie industry reflected in Autry's movies. There were screwball comedies that were popular with audiences; these comedies juxtaposed rich and poor, smart and stupid and, especially, male and female for comedy that was illogical, unconventional, impossible and hilarious. In 1931 there was *Platinum Blonde*, starring Jean Harlow, and then *Bombshell* in 1935; in 1934 there was *The Thin Man*, starring William Powell and Myrna Loy, and *It Happened One Night*, starring Clark Gable and Claudette Colbert, and *Twentieth Century*, starring Carole Lombard (often regarded as the first true screwball comedy); in 1936 there was *My Man Godfrey*, starring Carole Lombard, and *Mr. Deeds Goes to Town* starring Gary Cooper.

Other screwball comedies include *The Awful Truth*, starring Irene Dunn and Cary Grant; *Stand-In*, starring Leslie Howard, Joan Blondell, and Humphrey Bogart; *True Confession*, starring Carole Lombarde and Fred MacMurray; *Nothing Sacred*, starring Lombard, Fredric March, and Walter Connolly; *Topper*, starring Cary Grant and Constance Bennett; and *Stage Door*, starring Katharine Hepburn, Ginger Rogers, Lucille Ball, and Eve Arden.

Autry's movies, with Smiley Burnette as his sidekick, certainly had elements of the screwball comedies, especially in the "smart vs. dumb" routines as well as the male vs. female situations where the two sexes battle each other before falling for each other.

Gene Autry's movies were not musicals in the strict definition of the term, but they were certainly musical, and this would be an important genre for Hollywood during the 1930s. In 1933 movie musicals included *42nd Street, Gold Diggers of 1933* and *Footlight Parade*; in 1934 there was *Dames* starring Dick Powell and Ruby Keeler. In the 1930s Fred Astaire and Ginger Rogers starred in a series of pictures: *Flying Down to Rio* (1933), *The Gay Divorcee* (1934), *Roberta* and *Top Hat* (both in 1935). In 1937 Jeanette MacDonald and Nelson Eddy began a series of musical movies and, like Autry's, they featured actors bursting into song throughout the movie. There were child stars, led by Shirley Temple, and Autry often included children in his movies, especially Mary Lee, beginning in 1939.

Gene Autry's major influences in entertainment when he made his first recordings were Will Rogers, Al Jolson, Vernon Dalhart, Gene Austin and Jimmie Rodgers. Musically, Rodgers had the greatest influence, but Autry was also attracted to success. There is a difference between popularity and influence — many influential musical artists, musicians and songwriters are not popular, and many popular acts are not particularly influential. But popularity itself is usually influential, especially with struggling up and comers who dream of escaping the working-class world. Certainly Gene Autry's ambition led him to dream far beyond the Texas and Oklahoma roots that anchored his early years.

In the early 1930s, Bing Crosby became the most popular performer in America, and this fact did not escape Gene Autry. Crosby's voice was especially suited to the microphone, which had been introduced to the recording process in 1925. Crosby's voice was relaxed and informal, a pleasant baritone, and he projected the image of a friendly, accessible, unassuming American. Like Autry, Crosby was influenced by Al Jolson.

Bing Crosby came to Hollywood from his hometown of Tacoma, Washington, in November 1925 with his buddy and bandmate, Al Rinker, and stayed with Rinker's sister, singer Mildred Bailey. Crosby and Rinker soon joined Paul Whiteman's big band—the most popular big band of its time—and Whiteman teamed them with a third member, Harry Barris, to form the Rhythm Boys. Barris was a songwriter; he wrote the trio's first hit, "Mississippi Mud," as well as later hits such as "Pack Your Troubles in Dreams (And Dream Your Troubles Away)."

Crosby performed with the Rhythm Boys for several years before striking out on his own. In 1931 he landed a radio show on the CBS network, and this established him as a national star. Crosby made his first recordings in 1926 and recorded extensively during 1927–1929 with the Rhythm Boys and Whiteman's orchestra. His first hit was "If I Had You," recorded with Sam Lanin's orchestra in 1929. During that year, he increasingly recorded as a solo singer instead of as a member of a group.

Bing Crosby's most prominent years were 1935–54 when he starred on recordings, radio and in the movies. This parallels the career of Gene Autry, whose best years were also 1935–54.

Crosby's first appearance in the movies was in the 1930 film *King of Jazz*, which starred Paul Whiteman and his band. Crosby was in three other movies that year—generally appearing as a singer with a group doing a song. His appearance in *The Big Broadcast* in 1932 launched him as a major movie star. During the 1931–1935 period he appeared in a number of films and increasingly starred as a character with a talent for singing, so that songs were woven into the plot, performed by Crosby at opportune moments as a natural extension of his character. This is the same formula which worked in Autry's movies, although Autry's movies were westerns, while Crosby's were aimed at the contemporary audience. Still, though Autry's films were westerns, most were set in the contemporary West of the 1930s. This was believable because the West in the 1930s was in reality a mixture of the Old West of ranches, horses and cowboys and the new America of telephones, automobiles and airplanes. Autry's movies have been criticized as being out of touch by critics who expected (demanded!) that westerns be set in the late 1800s or perhaps very early 1900s. But for rural westerners, the settings for the Autry movies were as contemporary as anything that starred Bing Crosby or Fred Astaire.

To those who deride Autry's movies as escapist entertainment, the question must be asked: were Autry's movies more escapist than movies like *Anything Goes*, which starred Bing Crosby in 1936 and which took place on a luxury liner, or *Waikiki Wedding*, which starred Crosby in 1937? Or any of the Fred Astaire movies where people didn't work, wore tuxedoes and lived a life of luxury in the midst of the Great Depression?

Bing Crosby was only four years older than Autry — the pop singer was born May 3, 1903, while Autry was born September 29, 1907 — so the two were contemporaries. But in terms of success in show business, Bing Crosby was miles ahead of Gene Autry when the latter arrived in Hollywood in 1934. Crosby continued to be well ahead of Autry in popular appeal throughout the 1930s because Crosby appealed to the broad, pop audience while Autry's audience was seen as juveniles. Also, country music did not have respect and prestige attached to it as popular big band songs and jazz music did.

Crosby was shaped musically by jazz, while Autry was shaped by Jimmie Rodgers and other country singers. Autry first found his recording voice by imitating Jimmie Rodgers in the 1920s and early 1930s. However, by the time Autry recorded "The Last Round-Up" on October 9, 1933 (ten days after Crosby recorded the song) it is obvious that Gene Autry had reached a turning point in his singing career. On "The Last Round-Up," Autry begins the song with a yodel reminiscent of Jimmie Rodgers, but the verses are sung in a crooning style, similar to Bing Crosby's singing style.

Crosby began recording western songs on September 27, 1933, when he recorded "The Last Round-Up" and "Home on the Range" with the Lennie Hayton band. In 1935 he recorded "Take Me Back to My Boots and Saddle" and in 1936 recorded "We'll Rest at the End of the Trail," "Empty Saddles," "A Roundup Lullaby," and "I'm a Old Cowhand." That same year, influenced by the success of the singing cowboy movies, Crosby starred in *Rhythm on the Range*. In *Rhythm on the Range*, the Sons of the Pioneers appeared with Crosby, and he sang two of their biggest hits, "Tumbling Tumbleweeds" and "Cool Water." In the movie, Crosby played rodeo performer Jeff Larabee, who captured the heart of a wealthy and beautiful heiress. The role — which Crosby claimed was one of his favorites — led him to purchase a working ranch in Elko, Nevada, several years later.

Crosby made country and western songs respectable — he didn't ham it up or look down his nose at them; he sang those songs straight, as he would any other pop song and, in doing so, gave those songs a dignity and respect they had not received when done by country entertainers. In 1937 Crosby recorded "My Little Buckaroo" and "There's a Gold Mine in the Sky"; in 1938 he recorded "Home on the Range" again, "Silver on the Sage," "Mexicali Rose," and "When the Bloom Is on the Sage." In 1939 he recorded "El Rancho Grande" and in 1940 recorded "Tumbling Tumbleweeds," "The Singing Hills," and "Sierra Sue." By this point Crosby listened to Autry's repertoire for material; after Autry recorded "Mexicali Rose," Crosby sang it on his radio show a number of times, then recorded it. Later, it became the title of one of Autry's movies.

Crosby was signed to Decca Records, a label that began in 1934, and label head Jack Kapp was Crosby's producer. Crosby allowed Kapp to select the material he recorded, and Kapp selected a wide variety, covering western and Hawaiian music as well as jazz and pop songs. Crosby wanted to reach as large and wide an audience as possible. Autry did too, but was hemmed in by his image as a singing cowboy. Autry reconciled this by aligning himself closely with his cowboy image in dress and in his movies, while singing an increasingly wide variety of pop songs in addition to his western numbers.

Bing Crosby and Gene Autry had something else in common. Each became defined by his image in the media — in Crosby's case an easy-going, friendly older brother type who was always relaxed and approachable, while Autry's image was as a clean-cut cowboy hero. Both represented the image of a quintessential American — regular guys — with a demeanor that was comforting during the Great Depression. Crosby and Autry were both ambitious men who worked hard for their success, but always gave the impression of never striving for wealth or prestige. Crosby and Autry both chased fame and fortune while convincing others that they were not ambitious men and that fame and fortune just happened to them. Neither Crosby nor Autry were models of piety in their private lives, but both guarded and nurtured their images and grew into their public personas. Those personas became a role they played on and off screen.

Bing Crosby and Gene Autry were both lucky when it came to meeting people early in their careers who helped them. For Crosby it was his musical partner, Al Rinker, and his sister, Mildred Bailey, then Paul Whiteman, who teamed him with Harry Barris. For Autry it was Frankie and Johnny Marvin, Joe Frank, Jimmy Long and Smiley Burnette. In the recording studio, Crosby was fortunate to be teamed with Jack Kapp, while Autry had the fortune to work with Art Satherley. Kapp and Satherley helped their young artists find their voices and guided their early recordings. In later recordings, their producers became less important. Still, without the guidance of Kapp and Satherley, both Crosby and Autry might never have gotten to the position — or certainly gotten there as quickly — of being major record sellers.

Neither Crosby nor Autry claimed to be great actors, yet both were extremely effective on the screen. Studio executives and casting directors quickly saw their faults: Autry supposedly wasn't masculine enough to be a cowboy (prior western stars had been former rodeo riders and working cowboys), while Crosby had thinning hair, ears that stuck out and a not very masculine build. Both fought weight problems, although Autry had better luck during the 1930s, while Crosby had to wear a girdle in some of his movies.

The biggest difference between Autry and Crosby was in their off-hours. Crosby loved golf, fishing and horse racing and cherished his relaxation as much as his work, while Autry never really stopped working. Autry did not hunt, fish or play golf until much later in his career; he didn't take vacations, and when he wasn't filming movies, he was on the road performing. Crosby made much more money from his movies and recordings than Autry did; also, Crosby did not enjoy performing for a live audience. Autry needed to play on the road in order to promote his movies and recordings, while Crosby had a network radio show. In 1936, Crosby began hosting the "Kraft Music Hall" where he performed each week for a national audience estimated at 50 million. Autry's radio show did not begin until 1940 and, although it was certainly a popular show, never had an audience the size of Crosby's. Then again, no entertainer did; Bing Crosby dominated musical entertainment in the 1930s, which is why Gene Autry was influenced so much by Bing Crosby.[1]

Autry's success inspired a number of other studios to try singing cowboys. This move came because Autry's pictures were financially successful, but also because they breathed new life into the old westerns. The genre had been popular for a long time but needed some new, fresh ideas. The singing cowboy provided this. Another major reason for singing cowboys is because they were considered safe from the Legion of Decency and Hayes Office in Hollywood, which sought to control moral content in films and restricted gangster violence and romantic passion on the big screen.

After Autry, the next successful singing cowboy was Tex Ritter, who starred for Grand National studio, although Dick Foran also starred as a singing cowboy in several pictures beginning in 1935. In fact, Foran's singing cowboy debut came less than a month after Autry's first starring role, which indicates that the idea of singing cowboy movies was circulating in Hollywood. Others who played singing cowboys include Fred Scott, Smith Ballew, Jack Randall, Tex Fletcher, and John "Dusty" King. Later there followed Roy Rogers, George Houston, James Newill and Bob Baker.

During the 1935–1940 period, Gene Autry wasn't the only singing cowboy, but he was certainly leading the pack.

13

THE WALK-OUT

An article in *Variety* on October 12, 1937, reported that Gene Autry had committed to two movies for Paramount, the first in December, the second in January. Reports of the deal were quickly denied by Republic chairman Herbert J. Yates and by Autry himself. Even Paramount production chief William LeBaron said that Autry wouldn't make films for Paramount "if there is any hitch in his Republic tieup." Yates told his exchange managers that Autry would make pictures for Republic only for the life of his contract, which would be in effect for five more years.[1]

The next day a *Variety* article noted the popularity of Gene Autry and the singing cowboy pictures. The article stated that movie distributors "have noted a decided trend in popularity of cowboy singing stars in the last few years, based on actual sales and fan mail." The article continued: "The 1937-type westerns are those having a cowboy who can wield a guitar and warble in the off-moments when he is not punching the villain or shooting it out with his rival. Yodeling cowboy stars on personals in the middle west, southern areas and as far east as Chicago, have helped build strength with exhibitors. Thus far these p.a.'s [personal appearances] don't mean much in the east but they are rated stalwart draws elsewhere."[2]

That same day, October 13, 1937, Leonard Slye, later to become known as Roy Rogers, signed a contract with Republic Pictures.

Herbert Yates was a man who wanted to be in control and he did not like the idea that somebody working for him was bigger than he was. Such was the case with Gene Autry. Yates paid him a salary for appearing in movies that Yates financed, and by 1937 Autry wielded a lot of power. So Yates decided to take Autry down a peg or two. He believed stars were interchangeable and that money was the constant, unchanging factor. He'd made Gene Autry a star, so now he'd make somebody else a star and dilute Autry's power. After this it would be easier to keep him in line.

The first choice of Yates and the other executives at Republic was Tex Ritter, who was starring in singing cowboy movies with a rival studio. They approached Ritter, but Tex wanted to bring along his producer, Edward Finney, and Republic nixed that. They reportedly offered Stuart Hamblen, the most popular cowboy singer on Los Angeles radio, a $200 a week contract, but he turned it down.[3] They also reportedly approached Red

Foley, back in Chicago at WLS, but Foley wasn't available. Republic also conducted some open auditions at their studio, just to see if they could turn up anyone — an unknown — who had potential.

Leonard Slye wasn't an unknown. He was a member of the Sons of the Pioneers, the most successful western singing group in America, and had appeared with them in several movies — including several by Autry (*The Big Show* and *The Old Corral*). But Republic executives just hadn't thought about him as a solo singing cowboy star at the time.

Slye learned about the Republic auditions when he went to get his cowboy hat cleaned and another actor there mentioned the auditions. So Slye hurried over to Republic but could not get inside the gate. Finally, at lunch time, with people coming and going, he tried to slip in. He was caught by the security guard but, at the same time, saw Sol Siegel, president of Republic, walking by. Slye called out to Siegel, and Siegel was glad to see him — here was a good prospect they had forgotten about.

Slye auditioned for Republic singing "Haddie Brown" and "Tumbling Tumbleweeds" and got the job. He signed his contract on October 13, 1937, but Republic wanted him to change his name. They first decided he would remain "Dick Weston," the name Slye had used when he appeared in Autry's picture *The Big Corral*. "Weston" would also appear in Autry's *The Old Barn Dance*. But Republic executives decided that "Dick Weston" didn't quite sound like a star so they renamed him.

The name "Rogers" sounded good; the memories of Will Rogers, who died two years before, were still warm and current. "Roy" seemed to go with the last name, and so Leonard Slye became Roy Rogers.[4]

When Leonard Slye signed his contract with Republic Pictures, he was still under contract with his group, the Sons of the Pioneers, at Columbia. Columbia released him from his contract, and Slye contacted Pat Brady, who was appearing as a singer, comedian and bass player at Sam's Place on Sunset Beach, to replace him with the Sons of the Pioneers.

The Sons of the Pioneers continued to appear in Columbia movies, but the last movie Slye appeared in with the Sons was *The Old Wyoming Trail* starring Charles Starrett, which was released on November 8, 1937. Meanwhile, the Sons of the Pioneers had been recording for Decca but, under Slye's new agreement with Republic, began recording for the American Record Corporation, which was owned by Herbert Yates. On October 21 the group — consisting of Slye, Bob Nolan, Lloyd Perryman, guitarist Karl Farr, violinist Hugh Farr, and steel guitar player Sam Coki — went into ARC's Los Angeles Studio and recorded seven songs; on October 26 they returned and did 11 more. On two dates in December, the Sons of the Pioneers recorded 14 more songs, primarily gospel.

Although Gene Autry emerged as the biggest star of the singing cowboy era, the Sons of the Pioneers created a distinctive, influential sound. While many groups on radio dressed in cowboy outfits — influenced by Autry — they often formed trios and sang in harmony like the Sons of the Pioneers.

The original members of the Pioneers — Leonard Slye, Bob Nolan and Tim Spencer — were joined in 1935 by fiddler Hugh Farr and his brother, guitarist Karl. In 1935 they made their first movie appearance in *Old Homestead*, followed by an MGM short, *Slightly Static*, and a Joan Davis film, *Way Up Thar*. They also appeared in the first Charles

Starrett westerns, *Gallant Defender* and *The Mysterious Avenger*. In early 1936 the Pioneers filmed an appearance in the Bing Crosby movie, *Rhythm on the Range*. After this movie they went to Dallas where they appeared at the Texas Centennial and served as musical back-up for Gene Autry in his movie *The Big Show*. In 1937 the Sons of the Pioneers signed with Columbia to appear in a western series starring Charles Starrett. Ray Whitley, who later achieved fame as the songwriter of "Back in the Saddle," represented the group as their manager during this time.[5]

Clearly, Herbert Yates thought he had Gene Autry over a barrel — not only had he signed a singing cowboy who could replace him, but he also signed a top group whose records could sell like Autry's. But Autry stuck to his guns.

Gene Autry had three recording sessions in Los Angeles in mid–October. On October 11 he recorded "Blue Hawaii," "Dust," "Rhythm of the Range," and two others; on October 15 he recorded five songs, and on October 18 he recorded "When It's Springtime in the Rockies," "Take Me Back to My Boots and Saddle" and three others. It is interesting that Autry recorded a number of western tunes on this session but also did a Hawaiian number ("Blue Hawaii"), obviously influenced by the success Bing Crosby had with Hawaiian songs. He also did several non-western songs, branching out into pop in order to have his recordings appeal to a larger audience.

On November 13 *Manhattan Merry-Go-Round* was released. Directed by Charles Riesner, the movie featured performances by Phil Regan, Leo Carrillo, Ann Dvorak, Cab Calloway, Joe DiMaggio, Louis Prima, Max Terhune, Smiley Burnette and "Guest Star" Gene Autry. The *Variety* review noted, "Republic bids for big time booking consideration with this filmusical which is enlivened by four — count 'em — name bands, five featured players, a corps of dialect comedians and a world's series home-run by Joe DiMaggio. Not least in interest among the interpolated talent is the hard-riding guitar crooner, Gene Autrey [sic]...." The reviewer also noted that "Joe DiMaggio speaks excellent center-field English."[6]

A few days later *Springtime in the Rockies* was released. Co-starring Smiley Burnette, Polly Rowles, Frankie Marvin, George Montgomery, and Jimmy Wakely's Saddle Pals, the title song was sung in the movie twice by Autry, who also did "You're the Only Star in My Blue Heaven," which is credited to Autry but which Don Weston probably wrote. In the movie, which has a sheep vs. cattle ranching theme, Autry stops a hanging, then gets a bad guy to sing "Springtime in the Rockies." A group of cowboys then join in as Gene leads the chorus, saying, "A song solves the problem" and "It's hard to sing and be mean at the same time." This would be a recurring theme in Autry's pictures.

During the filming of this movie, which was done in the mountains near Palm Springs, the cast and crew stayed in a motel in Palm Springs and one night found an old stuffed Indian. Autry and some others brought the wooden Indian to Polly Rowles's room, sat it on the toilet, then waited outside after she had gone in her room to go to bed. Soon, a blood-curdling scream was heard. It was the kind of practical joke that Autry and the boys loved to play, then re-tell a thousand times.[7]

On November 24 Autry went into a Los Angeles recording studio and recorded "There's a Gold Mine in the Sky," written by Charles and Nick Kenny; "Sail Along Silv'ry Moon," written by Charles Tobias and Percy Wenrich; and "The Old Barn Dance," written by Peter Tinturin and Jack Lawrence. By the end of 1937 Gene Autry was successful but restless in his stardom, wanting to reach beyond his status as a cowboy singer and actor confined to Republic Pictures.

Musically, Autry took a big step forward in 1937 when he hired Carl Cotner during a Midwestern tour. Cotner, a versatile musician, filled the role of fiddle player in Autry's band but also did arrangements and conducted an orchestra. During the coming years, he would play an increasingly important role in the musical career of Autry.

Summing up the movie industry for 1937, *Variety* noted that Autry was the "one outstanding shining light" for the western. He "proved a big draw in the provinces and is a leading factor in piling up profit and grosses for Republic."[8]

At the end of 1937, Gene Autry finished *The Old Barn Dance* for Republic and vowed not to make any more movies for the studio until they increased his pay. He had interest and offers from two others studios — Twentieth Century Fox and Paramount — and wanted to be with a major studio.

On January 12, 1938, *The Old Barn Dance* was released. The cast featured Smiley Burnette, Helen Valkis, Frankie Marvin, Denver Dixon, the Stafford Sisters, the Maple City Four, Walt Shrum and his Colorado Hillbillies, and "Dick Weston." Exactly one week later a headline in *Variety* announced, "Autry Demands More Money from Republic." The article stated that Autry had threatened to stay on the road until a new agreement with Republic had been reached. Attorneys for Republic and Autry were trying to work out a deal agreeable to both sides, but other companies were eager to sign Autry — it was reported that Paramount and 20th Century–Fox were prepared to top Republic's top offer. *Washington Cowboy* was delayed due to the negotiations.[9]

This article summed up the situation with Gene Autry and Republic at the beginning of 1938. He had, in fact, signed a two-picture agreement with Paramount.

In 1937, Republic earned $4,076,102 in distribution fees for its movies. Consolidated Films, also owned by Yates, had earnings of $4,478,180 after $200,000 was paid out on preferred stock. The net earnings for Consolidated Films was $605,755, down from $919,515 the previous year. On January 12 *Variety* announced that Republic planned to produce 30 features, 16 westerns and four serials by September 1, the end of their production year. The studio planned to begin the year with *Washington Cowboy* starring Gene Autry. But that wasn't in Autry's plans.[10]

A January 26 article in *Variety* headlined "Republic Counting on Autry's Peaceful Return Despite Walk." Republic was still hopeful it would win Autry back, and even proceeded with plans for more movies with him. Autry's agent, however, had let Republic know that their star wouldn't be returning unless a money agreement could be reached. The agreement would have to compensate Autry for giving up a two-film deal with Paramount.[11]

The article noted that Autry was to have started a new production on December 27 but found the movie wasn't ready to be filmed. He waited until January 5, then hit the road for personal appearances. Autry, according to this article, had been promised by Republic that they would counter the offer made by Paramount, but had failed to do so. The article concluded that Autry was on his way to New York to discuss a deal with Charles Sparks of the Downey Brothers circus, who offered him $4,000 a week for 32 weeks of personal appearances.

Autry was in Nashville on Saturday, January 15, and appeared on WSM. A newspaper reporter interviewed him in the restaurant at the Hermitage Hotel, where Autry had a breakfast of chicken livers and scrambled eggs. Dressed in a sharp-looking western outfit, Autry was joined at the table by J. L. Frank; Grand Ole Opry performers Sarie and Sallie; Asher, Little Jimmie and Buddy Sizemore; and WSM announcer David Stone. He told the reporter that he was on his way to Kentucky for some personal appearances and would appear in Nashville at the Paramount Theater on January 27.

Autry told the reporter he was on strike against Republic because "my contract calls for eight pictures a year at $5,000 per picture and, if the studio desires, I have to make one or two more. In the first place, I think that's too many pictures per year. That kind of work has killed many players in Hollywood. In the second place, some of the other Western stars out there, like George O'Brien and Buck Jones, get from $15,000 to $20,000 per picture."

Autry continued, "If they get that much, and my pictures are ranked above theirs in drawing power, I think I am entitled to more money. I know this much — when I begin to slip, Republic isn't going to show any sympathy for me. They're going to kick me right out."[12]

Gene Autry returned to Nashville for the January 27 date, which featured J. L. Frank's Golden West Cowboys with Texas Daisy and the comedy duo of Sarie and Sallie in addition to Autry, who was scheduled to perform with Frankie Marvin. The show was scheduled to take place at the Paramount Theater before the movie, *Blonde Trouble*, starring Eleanor Whitney and Johnny Downs was shown; the price for admission would be 25 cents for children and 40 cents for adults. Across town, *Heidi*, starring Shirley Temple, was playing at another movie theater.

Autry would not perform at the Paramount because just before he was to go on stage, two representatives from Republic, New York attorney Meyer Lavenstein and William Saal, assistant secretary for Republic, presented him with an ultimatum: either sign the contract from Republic they carried or face an injunction against any personal appearances. Autry refused to sign.

Variety reported the show "had standees with hundreds streaming in by the time the first stage show went on." Autry was in his costume while the opening performers tried to keep the audience satisfied. Emcee Milton Estes told the audience that Autry wouldn't appear at the first show due to "circumstances beyond his control" but would appear for the second show. The audience remained seated for four hours, through a second feature, waiting for Gene to appear. Autry was talking frantically with his Nashville attorney and agent George Goodale, trying to resolve the conflict. Finally, they decided to put his horse, Champion, on stage at three o'clock, but three police offices stopped him. However, Champion did appear later "with nothing on his back but his master's $2,000 silver-trimmed saddle" and went through his paces.[13]

Tony Sudekum, president of Crescent Amusement Company (which owned the Paramount theatre), "was boiling at Republic about the whole thing but wouldn't say whether or not he intends to boycott its pictures at the 150 theaters" he booked.[14]

Autry insisted that December and January were his "exclusive period" when he could do personal and radio appearances. The Republic production year ran from July 1 to June

30, and Autry made only four pictures during that period. Autry's Nashville attorney argued that it was not Autry but Republic that breached his contract. "Autry could have saved the date by 'signing his life away' but didn't," argued the attorney, "nor did the theatre management want him to." The article concluded, "To rub the sore spot, Autry realizes that while he is definitely big time, his salary is still comparatively minor league. He ranks first among western stars in the annual box office audit, but he still is tied down by his contract to $5,000 a picture while Bill Boyd, No. 2 mustanger, gets $12,500 a picture; Buck Jones, No. 3 draws $16,000; and George O'Brien, who placed fifth, tops them all with $21,000."[15]

Variety reported that Autry sent a telegram to film columnists in Los Angeles in which he stated that exhibitors he had met during personal appearances had convinced him that he was not getting what he deserved. Autry's statement read: "[Exhibitors] have told me that they are more than willing to pay top money for my westerns if they aren't forced to buy dozens of pictures at fancy prices that they don't even take the trouble to play. Republic, if it wants to make adjustments with exhibitors, can get more money for my releases and still sell its other product at reasonable prices."[16]

The discovery about "block booking" added fuel to the flame and, in Autry's mind, further justified his walk-out. Ironically, in later years as he recounted the story of his walk-out from Republic, the block booking issue was the major reason he cited.

The article continued, "Republic studio will not compromise its position with Autry. Herbert Yates ... declared Autry will be allowed to buy his release from remaining three years of the contract if he so desires. Action will be predicated on apology from Autry for statements he has given out in the course of his several weeks' tour, particularly the one he wired Hollywood from Nashville last week."[17]

In Nashville, Autry announced that he intended "to fight, sue for damages, and ask cancellation of contract" with Republic; he also filed a suit in Chancery Court to get the injunction against his personal appearances lifted.[18]

Another part of his contract with Republic bothered Autry: a clause that entitled the studio to half of any money he received from endorsements, radio or public appearances. There had been no attempt to collect that money, and Republic had assured Autry — verbally — there would be none. But "I didn't want some lawyer rediscovering those rights later and deciding they should be enforced," said Autry.[19]

Back in California in December, Autry had instructed George Goodale to book a tour headed East. Goodale had been barred from the Republic lot when he went there after Autry and Yates had a confrontation. According to Autry, "Yates said he would make a film without me and create a new cowboy star." Further, "Yates threatened to break me — 'if you won't work here, you won't work anywhere,'" he reportedly told Autry.[20]

Republic hired a new executive, James Grainger, formerly with Universal, as president in charge of distribution and sales. The company planned "the biggest and most expensive production schedule in its history," according to *Variety*. There was one big problem: no Gene Autry.[21]

The showdown was covered thoroughly by *Variety* and showed Autry losing his fight in Nashville. On Monday, February 3, 1938 at 9 A.M. a hearing was scheduled for Autry and Republic. Chancellor R.B.C. Howell ruled in favor of Republic, and Autry appealed.

Howell set Autry's bond at $25,000 while Autry remained in Nashville. The next day, Autry told a reporter that he was going to Chicago to visit friends "then go on a hunting and fishing trip." On Friday, he left Nashville.[22]

During the hearing, the Chancery Court Room was packed. Autry stayed in a suite at the Hermitage Hotel and "created a little riot among the small boys, many of whom had been disappointed at not seeing him on the stage at the Paramount theatre." It was noted that on Sunday, February 2, Autry planned to visit Mammoth Cave in Kentucky, about a hundred miles away but his car, with Champion in a trailer on the back, slid down the street and crashed into a plate glass when the brakes slipped. The newspaper noted "Autry is protected by insurance."[23]

Autry planned to go to St. Louis on February 13 to participate in the "1938 Radio Stars' Jamboree," where a national fiddling contest would take place. Instead, on February 16, Autry was back in Hollywood where a *Variety* article noted that Republic was "giving serious consideration to scheduling a series of westerns featuring a new star, with Dick Weston already set for the spot."[24] Meanwhile, according to *Variety*, Republic had given up on trying to settle with Autry and was waiting for him to decide what he would do. Smiley Burnette, whose Republic contract had five months left, had asked Republic for release from that contract. He didn't want to work with Dick Weston — Republic called him Roy Rogers and was grooming him to take Autry's place.[25]

On March 16 *Variety* reported that "if 20th Century–Fox can get Gene Autry, Republic's western star, the company may schedule horse operas for the 1938-39 season." It had proposed buying out Autry's contract to Herb Yates, but no deal had been reached. 20th would not make any westerns during the coming year if they could not obtain Autry.[26]

On March 23 *Variety* reported that Autry was planning a tour of South America unless Republic agreed to pay him $25,000 per picture. The tour would begin April 9, unless Republic agreed to his demands before then. It noted that Smiley Burnette would "accompany Autry should the latter decide to go through with the deal, for which the promoters have already posted $25,000 as a partial guarantee." Autry would receive $4,000 a week, while Burnette would receive $1,000. Autry agreed to go forward with the negotiations for the tour after his attorney informed him the injunction against him did not apply outside the United States.[27]

On April 6 an article in *Variety* discussing Hollywood studios plans for the coming year noted that 456 pictures were scheduled for production by movie studios in 1938–39 "not counting 74 Westerns." That compared with 504 features and 111 westerns scheduled the past production year by 12 companies. The article provided numbers for each studio: 20th-Fox and Universal would not produce any westerns, Republic would do 24, Columbia 22, Paramount 6, Monogram 16 and RKO 6.[28]

Republic scheduled its sales meeting in Los Angeles for four days starting May 2 and planned to produce "three groups of regular features totaling 30, in addition to three series of westerns with Gene Autry, Three Mesquiteers, and Roy Rogers, plus four serials."[29]

Variety reported on April 13 that "Roy Rogers, being groomed as Gene Autry's successor at Republic, and Smiley Burnette, Autry's former supporting comic, are en route to Dallas, where they will open a series of personal appearances arranged for them by the studio. Kansas City and Oklahoma City are also on the schedule. Tour is planned to cover those territories where Autry stood out as a box office favorite." The article noted that Autry, scheduled to leave for South America on April 11 for 30 weeks of personal appearances, had set back his departure date for two weeks to continue to negotiate his contract with Republic.[30]

On April 15 *Under Western Stars*, starring Roy Rogers, was released. The *Variety* review stated, "Apparently it cost some coin, but Republic got away from the norm and produced a western that is different. In addition to being entertaining, it's plausible sage stuff that will hold the adult mind as well as the credulous kiddies." Roy Rogers was praised not only for his looks — a boon to the females in the audience — but for his acting and singing talent. Smiley Burnette, Carol Hughes and other supporters were praised, too.[31]

Variety continued its coverage of the Autry walk-out and, in its April 20 issue reported that Autry and Republic had made up and that Autry was going back "to the fold." The article noted that Autry's lawyers had objected to the use of "Dust" in the Roy Rogers film, *Under Western Stars* because Autry owned the copyright to the song and that Republic "had no right to dispose of the song's publication rights." Republic countered that Johnny Marvin had written "Dust," and that the producer had purchased it from him. But Autry did hold the copyright, and songwriting credit is given to Autry and Martin.[32]

Finally, Gene Autry and Republic came to terms. The agreement was announced in the May 14 issue of *Variety* under the headline, "Autry Yippees Again for Republic; Peace Terms in His Favor." The article noted that Autry would work under a revised contract, getting $7,500 instead of $5,000 for the three movies he still owed Republic and $10,000 instead of $6,000 each for the eight scheduled during the 1938-1939 season. The agreement also allowed Autry to make "outside pictures" and let him have control over his radio engagements and personal appearances. In addition, Autry was in the clear to produce movies for his own company, Autry Pictures, Inc.[33]

Four days later, an article in *Variety* noted that "contracts-within-contracts will be a problem for Republic execs when all the talent, corralled by Gene Autry on his recent stampede, arrives at the studio gates." Autry had signed two bands, a songwriter and a comedienne — all would "hit the trail" for Republic.[34] Another article noted that "what to do about Smiley Burnette is the latest problem at Rep, caused by Autry's return." Now that Roy Rogers and Gene Autry were working again, Burnette's future was uncertain.[35]

Actually, that problem had been solved when Gene Autry negotiated a clause in his new Republic contract guaranteeing that Burnette would only appear in Autry's pictures.

14

BACK TO REPUBLIC PICTURES

The final agreement between Autry and Republic was not signed until September 22, but they agreed that, beginning July 1, 1938, Autry would do ten movies a year for Republic with $6,000 paid to the star for the first two, then $10,000 each for the remaining eight. Like most five-year contracts in the movies, it was actually a one-year contract with four one-year options. In the following options, there would be an annual increase of $1,000 per picture for Autry so that in the final year of his contract he received $14,000 per film.

Before Republic signed Autry they signed John Wayne on May 7, giving the actor a five-year contract guaranteeing $24,000 a year for eight westerns; after the contract was signed, Republic cast him in the "Three Mesquiteers" series as Stony Brooke, replacing Robert Livingston and co-starring with Crash Corrigan and Max Terhune.[1]

The first movie Gene Autry made under the new agreement with Republic was *Gold Mine in the Sky*. In addition to some amendments in the contract — more money and no claim on his income from merchandising — Autry got more of a say-so for this movie. He wanted top notch songs, so he hired Fred Rose, then living in Nashville, to come west to write songs for his films.

Fred Rose is a key link between western and country music, or the music that came from the singing cowboys and the music that would later come from Nashville. Born in Evansville, Indiana, in 1897 Rose spent most of his early life in St. Louis and Chicago. In the late 1920s he was a radio performer and recording artist and wrote pop hits such as "Deed I Do," "Red Hot Mama" and "Honest and Truly."

Rose moved to Chicago and played piano for silent movies and at Chicago night spots; he also made piano rolls and wrote songs for publishing companies such as Leo Feist, Ted Browne Music and Irving Berlin, Inc. that were recorded by big bands such as those led by Paul Whiteman and Isham Jones. Beginning in 1928 he appeared on WLS, KYW and WBBM with Elmo Tanner as the Tune Peddlers, playing pop favorites as well as his own compositions. Also in 1928 he joined ASCAP. Around 1930 he joined Ted Weems's band and continued to record for Brunswick. But Rose had a drinking problem, causing him to lose his job at WBBM in 1932. He first went to New York for work, then returned to Chicago before hearing of an opening in Nashville with WSM. In May

1933 he moved to Nashville where he had a late-afternoon 15-minute show, "Freddie Rose's Song Shop," on week days. While in Nashville, he divorced his second wife and married his third, Lorene Harmon, in March 1935.

In Nashville, Rose met Ray Whitley, in August 1935 — just after the plane crash that killed popular humorist Will Rogers and his pilot, Wiley Post — and wrote two songs, "Will Rogers, Your Friend and My Friend" and "Last Flight of Wiley Post" that Whitley recorded for Decca. In late 1935 or early 1936, Rose made a commitment to Christian Science, probably led by songwriter Ed G. Nelson in New York. This conversion "transformed his outlook, instilled a new optimism and drive within him, and fostered ethical attitudes that would prove highly influential.... All observers who witnessed the change considered him a new man."[2]

In 1936 Rose went to Hollywood and played a song he wrote, "We'll Rest at the End of the Trail," for Decca executive Jack Kapp, who sent the song to Bing Crosby and Tex Ritter, who both recorded it. Rose had known J. L. Frank in Chicago, and Frank helped Rose with some Hollywood connections, including a connection with Gene Autry. Frank sent some songs to Autry in Hollywood written by Rose.[3]

****

By May 24, 1938, the cast and crew for *Gold Mine in the Sky* were at Keene Camp, California, doing location shooting. They had already been in the studio and recorded eight songs for the movie: "Tumbleweed Tenor" by Eddie Cherkose; "That's How Donkeys Were Born" by Smiley Burnette and Cherkose; "Hummin' When We're Comin' Round the Bend" by Al Columbo and Cherkose; "Dude Ranch Cowhands" by Autry, Johnny Marvin and Fred Rose; "As Long as I Have My Horse" by Autry and Marvin; "I'd Love to Call You My Sweetheart" by Joe Goodwin, Larry Shay and Paul Ash; "There's Gold Mine in the Sky" by Charles and Nick Kenny, and "Hike Yaa" by Burnette.

Autry wanted to hire a top country band for the movie; he called J. L. Frank and hired the Golden West Cowboys for $7,500. Gene Autry always remembered his friends.

The call from Gene Autry came to a high school auditorium in New Hope, Alabama, on May 13, 1938, a few minutes before showtime at 8 P.M. Autry wanted the group in California in a few days so after the show the group drove out in two cars. The day they arrived they went to Smiley Burnette's home where the sidekick hosted a cookout. Burnette was an excellent cook and produced a caesar salad, cutting up and mixing the ingredients himself, including a special dressing. The group went over the songs for the movie that evening.

The group checked into the Padre Hotel and stayed for four weeks, although the actual shooting took 15 days. The group was taken by studio buses to Big Bear Lake for exterior shots where they were housed in cabins. There was plenty of food for the cast and crew, usually sandwiches for lunch but a full meal — steaks, pork chops or chicken with homemade bread — for dinner. Back at Republic Studios, where they filmed shots on the soundstages, they ate at the commissary.

The cast had to be ready for make-up at five A.M., then waited until their scenes were shot. Sometimes the cast sat around all morning without doing a scene, playing cards or talking in the shade. Pee Wee King remembered that when they shot the first scene inside the dance hall, Autry walked on the set and saw him standing there in a white cowboy suit. Autry looked at King and asked, "Kid, who told you to wear a white suit?"

King replied, "Nobody. This is all I brought. We came here directly from the Opry, and it's what I wear down there."

Autry said, "I know you wear it on the stage at the Opry, but I'm the only one who wears a white suit in my movies. Now you get on up to the costume wagon and get another suit."

King pleaded, "But Gene, that's way up the hill, and I'll never make it back in time to shoot this scene. Anyway, I'll bet they don't have a suit in my size."

Autry relented "Okay, we'll figure out something. You go over there to the piano and make believe you're playing."[4]

King remembered: "The accordion I took to Hollywood ... was a new thousand-dollar instrument with rhinestones all over it that spelled out my name. In one scene where I'm supposed to be riding on the stagecoach, Smiley said, 'Kid, you want to be seen, so we'll put you up there on top next to the driver.' The driver was Joe Yourogoin, who was one of Gene's doubles. As I was climbing up, the director saw me and said, 'No, we can't let you get up there. It's too dangerous. You might fall off.' I pleaded with him and finally Smiley said, 'Oh, once we get him up there, he won't fall off. We can boost him up there, then haul up his accordion and put it in his lap, then strap him to the seat. He'll bounce around, but he won't fall off.'"[5]

The scene suffered no mishaps, and Pee Wee King sat on top of the stagecoach playing "She'll Be Coming 'Round the Mountain" as the horses ran. Pee Wee King was surprised he was allowed to use his rhinestone-studded accordion because "the girls weren't allowed to wear wristwatches, rings, or any kind of jewelry."

King remembered that "Gene wanted to do his own stunts.... He was an excellent horseman. He did his own riding and took his own falls and did his own fighting. He loved the fight scenes and got a big kick out of all the action."[6] However, there was one accident with Autry where the star was supposed to jump off his horse onto another actor and tumble down a hill. Autry got tied up coming out of the stirrups and had to be transported to a hospital in Hollywood for two days.

"All the guys that worked for Gene just loved him," said King. "They worshipped him. Smiley told me that once he was working with Gene on a movie right before Christmas, and the producer decided to stop production for a couple of weeks. It bothered Gene that the actors and crew wouldn't have paychecks just before Christmas, so he turned a piece of his bad luck into their good fortune. Gene got his knees injured in a fight scene and had to spend a week recovering, but he made sure everyone got paid for the time he was laid up. That's the kind of guy he was."[7]

Off camera, the cast and crew killed time by playing practical jokes. One day the cook at the chow wagon yelled, "Come and get it," and Frankie Marvin came running with a long rubber hose yelling, "Snake," causing the cook to flee. After a good laugh, the cook admonished Marvin, "Don't you ever do that trick again. If I had stumbled into that hot tub of water over there, I'd be boiled by now."[8]

Pee Wee King concluded that "movie making was not all glamour. I learned it was a lot of hurry up and wait. It was long hours. It was regimentation."[9]

While in Hollywood, the Golden West Cowboys appeared with Autry on "The Eddie Cantor" radio show.

Gold Mine in the Sky was released on July 4, 1938. Co-starring Smiley Burnette, Carol Hughes, Frankie Marvin, George Montgomery, the Stafford Sisters, and J. L. Frank's Golden West Cowboys of WSM Nashville. Autry made a personal appearance in Nashville, with the Golden West Cowboys, to promote the movie.

Pee Wee King noted that Autry "taught me a lot about stage conduct. He showed me how to bow with my hat and make an introduction.... He said, 'First take the hat off, then crush it with your hand because it's not going to break. Then go down and sweep the floor with it. If it gets dirty, you can have it cleaned. Then you put it back on and say, 'Ladies and gentlemen, the singing star of Republic Pictures, Gene Autry!' Then you look and point toward the side I'm coming from."[10] King also stated that Autry gave him good advice, saying, "Memorize people's names, especially the names of booking agents and show managers. They are the ones who can give you an audience, and without an audience you can never be a star." King added that "Gene loved to make money, but he loved the work he did to make it."[11]

By the time that cameras were finished with *Gold Mine in the Sky*, Gene Autry had a new member on his team. Mitchell Hamilburg may have become Autry's agent when Republic decided to sign Autry to a long-term deal in 1936 and thus may have been an important instigator in the walk-out staged by Autry. One of the factors in Autry's disagreement with Republic was the clause permitting Republic to have his income from merchandising. Autry certainly realized the value of merchandise; he had collected ten cents for each "Gene Autry Round-Up Guitar" sold by Sears, and his songbooks had proven to be a lucrative venture back in Chicago. As a singing cowboy movie star, Autry was in the position to endorse a number of items, which could — and did — prove to be quite profitable in the future.

There was certainly precedent for merchandise endorsements by celebrities. Souvenirs had been sold at Buffalo Bill's *Wild West Shows*, and cowboy actors Tom Mix, Hoot Gibson, Ken Maynard and Buck Jones had endorsed products such as lariats, air rifles and western costumes. In the early 1930s, Kay Kamen directed a licensing program for Walt Disney's Mickey Mouse, putting Mickey's image on hundreds of products.

The contract with Republic in 1938 let Autry keep sole rights to his merchandising. It is possible that if Autry had not signed with Mitch Hamilburg prior to the walk-out, he signed with him soon after the contract re-negotiation with Republic in order to acquire endorsements for merchandise.

Hamilburg was born in Boston in 1900 and came to Hollywood during the early years of the Great Depression. Originally with the Plymouth Rubber Company, Hamilburg came to work with movie tie-ins and endorsements with that firm. He began representing Deanna Durbin, who was the toast of Hollywood in 1936. Following in the footsteps of Shirley Temple, the 15-year-old Deanna starred in *Three Smart Girls* in 1936. Hamilburg's agency continued to grow, representing a number of actors and actresses in the coming years. Hamilburg played an enormous role in the career of Gene Autry.[12]

Hamilburg arranged a wide variety of merchandise endorsements for Autry, from cap pistols, cowboy boots and dolls to puzzles, pennants, lunch boxes, watches and bicycles.

It provided Autry with a lucrative income in the coming years and showed musical acts throughout the twentieth century how to mine the gold in merchandising. During his career, Autry became a wealthy man. He made a lot of money from his record sales, movies, and personal appearances but, in the long run, his greatest source of show business wealth was in merchandising. Getting "a piece of the action," usually a royalty, for each item sold with his name and/or image on it, Autry parlayed his fame in the movies and on radio to amass a small fortune.

****

As soon as *Gold Mine in the Sky* was finished, Autry did three more films in a row — *The Man from Music Mountain*, *Prairie Moon* and *Rhythm of the Saddle*, to be released throughout the year.

Man from Music Mountain was released on August 15 and co-starred Smiley Burnette, Carol Hughes, Sally Payne, Frankie Marvin, and Polly Jenkins and Her Plowboys. Autry sang "Built Upon the Sands of Yesterday, "The Man from Music Mountain," "I'm Beginning to Care" and "Burning Love"; a group of four young ladies joined Smiley in "All Nice People," and Burnette performed "She Works Third Tub at the Laundry" as a solo. The movie featured a child in a starring role, and Polly Jenkins performed a song on bells and then did "The William Tell Overture" on a marimba.

On September 25 *Prairie Moon*, co-starring Smiley Burnette, Shirley Deane, and Peter Potter, was released. In *Rhythm of the Saddle*, originally titled *Rodeo Buster*, Autry's co-stars were Smiley Burnette and Peggy Moran. The *Variety* review was not kind; the writer opined, "Fumbling badly, it's one horse opera that doesn't jell.... Credibility is stretched to the straining point in episode after episode. Autry is his usual self, placid, unruffled, with a heart full of sentimental songs. He sings four numbers and well ... but Autry's following may dwindle if they turn out many more like this."[13] On December 2 *Western Jamboree*, formerly titled "Bloom on the Sage," was released, co-starring Smiley Burnette, Jean Rouveral, Kermit Maynard, Jack Perrin, and future singing cowboy star Eddie Dean. That month Autry, accompanied by Frankie Marvin, Carl Cotner, Ben Roscoe, George Goodale and Champion, returned to Los Angeles after a six-week tour of the South and Midwest.

In the December 24 issue of *Motion Picture Herald*, Gene Autry was named the number one film cowboy, with William Boyd (Hopalong Cassidy) a close number two. Tex Ritter, Roy Rogers and John Wayne finished ninth, thirteenth and eighteenth, respectively.

In November 1938, it was announced that Autry's record label, the American Record Company, had been sold by Yates to the Columbia Broadcasting System (CBS), headed by William Paley. CBS resurrected the "Columbia" logo and made it the flagship label. Art Satherley remained with the new company, handling the duties of country and blues music A&R. This sale linked Gene Autry with CBS.

15

BACK IN THE SADDLE AGAIN

In early February 1939, *Home on the Prairie*, co-starring Smiley Burnette, June Storey, Jack Mulhall, and the Sherven Brothers Rodeoliers was released. *Mexicali Rose*, co-starring Smiley Burnette, Noah Beery, Sr., and Luana Walters was released at the end of March.

This is the first Autry picture in which June Storey starred as the heroine; in total, she starred in ten films with Gene Autry. The blonde actress was a perfect female leading lady for the cowboy with her winsome looks, spunky personality and competent acting. Storey was born in Toronto, Canada, in 1918; she obtained a screen test with Fox in 1934 and appeared in nine movies before her appearance in *In Old Chicago* caught the attention of Republic executives. She was signed to Republic from April 1939 until October 1940 and starred in 15 films for that firm before she left after working on her final Autry film, *Rancho Grande*.

On April 13, 14 and 18 Autry recorded a number of songs in a Los Angeles studio, including his first cut of "Back in the Saddle Again." The song was written by Ray Whitley who, in 1938, received an early morning call from a movie executive telling him they needed another song for a movie Whitley was to sing in that starred George O'Brien. Whitley had to come up with a song in two hours and told his wife, "I'm back in the saddle again." When she commented that was a good title, he sat down and composed one verse and the tune quickly. He told his wife as he was leaving that "I'll put in a whoopie-ti-yi-yay or something when I get to the studio." A member of Whitley's band, Willie Phelps, helped Whitley with the song, but did not claim any songwriting credit.[1] The song was first performed in the movie *Border G-Man* and later recorded by Whitley with his group, the Six Bar Cowboys, for Decca in 1938. Gene Autry first sang the song on the screen in *Rovin' Tumbleweeds*.

Although Ray Whitley was a talented singer and songwriter who appeared in several singing cowboy movies, he never attained star status. "I never made any great effort to promote myself too much," he said. "I never hired a publicity man. Gene Autry always told me that I was silly not to put something back in. He says, 'You know, Ray Whitley is just like an automobile or a farm or any other enterprise. You've got to grease it and you've got to put something back into it in order to make it function." Autry, according to Whitley, "definitely had the right idea on promotion and how to make more of your-self."[2]

In May, *Blue Montana Skies*, co-starring Smiley Burnette, June Storey, Walt Shrum and His Colorado Hillbillies, was released, and *Mountain Rhythm* was released in June. On June 6, 1939, a long article on Gene Autry appeared in the *Boston Globe*. Headlined "Encouraged Him to Go Into Movies" and written by Mayme Ober Peak, the article began with the story of Autry meeting Will Rogers one night in a telegraph office in Oklahoma. Peak noted that Autry had been the leading western film star for four consecutive years and received 10,000 to 20,000 fan letters a week. She also noted that he received royal-ties from records, books, toys, games, pistols, sweatshirts, chaps, and leather gloves.

Discussing his acting, Autry said, "I just try to act natural. I'm no actor. I don't expect to win any Academy Awards." However, he also observed, "The reason Tom Mix held on for so long is because he lived in character. That is the reason I live in character. You walk down the street and people see you in ordinary shoes and clothes, they are disillu-sioned. They like to see you as they do on the screen — fancy cut shirts, high-heeled boots, a big white sombrero." Autry wore a cadet blue suit with moon-shaped pockets and cuffs, a paler blue shirt piped in navy, a cream white sombrero, and boots decorated with intri-cate stitching during the interview. Peak observed that the "reigning idol of cowboyland doesn't look the part." She added, "Gentleness is outstanding quality of the screen's hard-riding, straight-shooting, sweet-singing star. There is no dash to his makeup."

The article noted there were eight people on Autry's staff and quoted Autry saying, "After you get to making money — good money, you have to have people working for you. I like that. Money doesn't mean anything to me. You get at the top and you have to work harder, for the fans are more critical."

Autry's wife, Ina Mae, was described as "a charming, brown-haired young woman in a dusty rose linen sports dress, as simple of manner as her famous husband." She "has not permitted an interior decorator to touch" her home, which was described as "a ram-bling yellow stone ranch house with windows placed so as to bring much of the outdoors inside and to get full benefit of the panoramic view of the mountains. Rooms hung sim-ply in flowered chintz and furnished in comfortable things.... Outside were rustic fences, winding brick walks, and an old well."[3]

****

ASCAP was the only performing rights organization until 1940, which meant a song-writer had to be a member of ASCAP in order to collect money from radio airplay and live performances. However, ASCAP was a membership organization, dominated by the major publishers in New York who refused to allow country or blues songwriters to join. This meant there was no way for songwriters or publishers of country music to earn income from their songs other than the sale of songbooks. ASCAP was a closed society and limited its membership to Broadway, movie and Tin Pan Alley writers or "respectable" music. Gene Autry had sought membership in ASCAP since 1930, when he was still in Oklahoma, but "I could not get an audience, or could not even get in," said Autry, because it was a "closed door."[4]

In Chicago, Autry had a number of songs published by M. M. Cole, a major Chicago-based publisher. Cole began his company in 1925, publishing primarily music instruction books at first, but by 1930 the company was publishing folios and songbooks, including a number of songbooks and folios in country music. Cole wanted to join ASCAP but "it became obvious that ASCAP was not interested in my companies or my catalog."[5] Cole was told that it might be possible for his company to become a member of ASCAP "on probation" for a year, but that would not entitle him to any royalties collected by ASCAP and, after that probationary year, his companies might receive "about $50 per quarter, or a total of $200 a year." Cole turned down that offer.

"During the years 1930 to 1934 I was told repeatedly that ASCAP was not particularly interested in country and western music, or as a matter of fact in any music which did not receive 'plugs' in New York City," said Cole. "Country and western music at that time was less popular in large urban areas than it has become and most of the performances of my works were not on New York stations or network broadcasts but were rather on local stations throughout the country, particularly in rural and semi-urban areas."[6]

Autry's songs had been in songbooks, folios, on records, carried in the Sears, Roebuck catalog and in movies, "but I still never could get into ASCAP. You had to have a couple of ASCAP publishers to sponsor you for membership and you had to have quite a few songs — in fact, I think it was five — published by publishers recognized by ASCAP before you got in," said Autry. Eight years after he had first applied for ASCAP membership, Autry noted, "I finally was admitted as a nonparticipating member on October 27, 1938. This meant I was a member, but I received no payment for my rights. Finally, almost nine years after I began my search for membership, I was admitted as an active member on March 29, 1939.

"I think what actually got me into ASCAP was, after being in Hollywood for about three years, out of all the people that were here I was voted the fourth biggest box office attraction in motion pictures. I think that probably had more to do with getting me into ASCAP actually than the songs that I turned out." Autry noted the music he performed appealed to "that very large group of Americans who do not live in New York or in Beverly Hills" and said that "writers and publishers of this kind of music were not admitted to ASCAP in any substantial number." However, he became an exception to that policy and finally obtained ASCAP membership. Later, Autry noted that "while country music could not get me into ASCAP, it did get me into the White House."[7]

****

In July 1939 Autry traveled to New York and performed at ten theaters. He also performed at the Boys Brotherhood Republic for Lower East Side kids. After these performances, he made his first tour of the British Isles. On July 26 Gene and Ina Mae Autry, Herbert Yates and his wife, and Bill Saal, an executive with Republic who conceived and organized the tour, boarded the U.S.S. *Manhattan* at Pier 58 in New York and joined a group that included James Farley, Mrs. and Mrs. John Roosevelt and a number of government and military folks to sail for Britain. Autry performed in a number of cities during the next several months, including London, Liverpool, Dublin, Glasgow, and Danzig, in theaters filled with people who had seen his movies.

Autry was mobbed like later rock stars. After he appeared at the Paramount Theater in London, a crowd of 5,000 had to be restrained by mounted police. This gave Bill Saal the idea of getting a picture of Autry in the midst of that enthusiastic crowd. Saal instructed Autry to come out the front door when he finished his act, where a group of photographers waited. Autry did so, but the crowd literally lifted him off his feet as he moved towards the door. The three photographers snapped their pictures, but a problem was soon evident — how to safely get out of this situation! Once outside the building, Autry and Saal went to a small convertible and climbed on the roof, smiling and waving as they sank through the canvas. Finally, someone backed the horse van and lowered the ramp, allowing Autry and Saal to join Champion in his traveling stall.

Champion did not spend all his time in the van; at a luncheon for Autry at the Savoy Hotel, Autry led the horse through the elegant lobby.

Gene Autry was in Liverpool on September 1, 1939, when Hitler sent his blitzkrieg across the German border into Poland, causing Great Britain and France to declare war on Germany. "The signs of war were everywhere, unmistakable," said Autry. "And the people talked about it. They talked of little else. In their hearts they knew it was only a question of time. But no one seemed to be preparing for it." Autry remembered a newspaper headline that said, "Hitler Says He Is Losing Patience" and underneath, "Cowboy Takes Liverpool."[8] "Some thought Hitler would start bombing England right away," remembered Autry. In Dublin, the theater manager was a captain in the British Army reserve. "He received his orders one night before I went on stage," said Autry. "By the time I got off, he was gone."

"The war talk, the guns going off in our imagination, had something to do with the size of the crowds and the emotion they showered on us," reminisced Autry. "It was a kind of last hurrah, I guess. People had a sense of their lives changing, of time running out on make-believe things."[9]

Gene Autry rode a wave of adulation in Dublin, and a memory was created he would never forget. He rode through the city on Champion while 300,000 lined the streets, watching. At the end of the tour, which concluded at the Theater Royale in Dublin, Autry was in his second floor dressing room and heard people outside chant, "We want Gene." Finally, a microphone with loudspeakers was assembled on the fire escape, and Autry performed a few songs for those who could not get tickets for the shows.

On his last night in Dublin, Autry recalled, "I went outside and sat down on the fire escape and told them how much I loved Dublin, and all of Ireland, and how great it had been, and how grateful I was. Then the crowd sang to me. First a few voices, then more, until it seemed all of them had joined in and you could hear it for blocks, the words of 'Come Back to Erin.'"[10] Autry cherished this treasured memory the rest of his life, "one of the most touching, one of the purest moments of my life."[11]

Another treasured moment came backstage in Dublin, when Autry heard the song "South of the Border" for the first time. The song was written by Michael Carr and Jimmy Kennedy, two Brits who had never been to Mexico; however, they had seen a number of Gene Autry movies and hoped he would record the song. This wasn't the first western song from these writers. Carr had written "Ole Faithful" with Hamilton Kennedy, Jimmy's brother, about five years previously. Jimmy Kennedy was a well-known British songwriter, having written "Red Sails in the Sunset," "Harbor Lights," "Roll Along Covered

Wagon," "My Prayer" and "Serenade in the Night." Gene Autry was not dealing with two unknown writers when he listened to their song in Dublin. He wasn't dealing with a totally unknown song either; Captain Jimmy Kennedy had performed the song for British armed forces at the front, and the tune had proven to be popular with the troops.[12]

Those treasured moments in Dublin led to a treasured career opportunity when Autry returned to the United States. P. K. Wrigley, owner of the Wrigley Chewing Gum Company as well as the Chicago Cubs and the minor league Los Angeles Angels, wanted to sponsor a radio program to advertise Doublemint gum. He was in Dublin during Autry's tour and noted how much the crowds loved the cowboy. When he returned to Chicago, Wrigley called his advertising agency, J. Walter Thompson, and told them he wanted to explore the development of a radio program starring Autry that advertised Doublemint.

During the time Autry was in Britain, several of his films were released. *Colorado Sunset*, a movie filmed in June 1939 co-starring June Storey, Barbara Pepper, Buster Crabbe, Patsy Montana, William Farnum, Kermit Maynard, Frankie Marvin, and the CBS-KMBC Texas Rangers was released at the end of July. *In Old Monterey* was released in mid–August and featured a bigger production and more money than previous releases. It co-starred Smiley Burnette, June Storey, George "Gabby" Hayes, Stuart Hamblen, Ken Carson, Sarie and Sallie, and the Ranch Boys.

On September 11 and 12, after Autry returned to the United States, he recorded "South of the Border" and five other songs in Chicago. Republic purchased the rights to use "South of the Border" in a movie for $1,000 and began pre-production.

South of the Border was released on December 15 and co-starred Smiley Burnette, June Storey, Lupita Tovar, Duncan Renaldo, and the Checkerboard Band. The movie was filmed after his return from England, and in it Autry introduced a new co-star, Mary Lee.

Born in Centralia, Illinois, in 1924, Mary Lee Wooters came from a musical family; her father — who owned a barbershop — and older sister, Vera, sang on a small radio station in LaSalle. In May 1938 she auditioned for the Ted Weems Band and landed the job of singer. During that summer, the Weems Band played at the Avalon Ballroom on Catalina Island in California, which led to Mary Lee's first movie role in *Nancy Drew, Reporter* in early 1939. Autry heard Mary Lee sing on a Weems broadcast and arranged for her to audition for Republic, which signed her to a series of movies with Autry and Roy Rogers.

The 1930s were an era of child stars; Shirley Temple, Judy Garland and Deanna Durbin were all young film stars during this period. The addition of Mary Lee in Autry's films was an attempt to capitalize on this trend. In his movies, she generally played a spoiled brat and added another female element to his movies.

South of the Border began with an overture of the song. Gene, Frog and the group sang "Come to the Fiesta," and Autry sang "South of the Border" during a dream-like sequence. Autry sang "Moon of Manana," and "Girl of My Dreams," did a duet with Mary Lee on "Goodbye, Little Darling, Goodbye," and Mary Lee sang a solo on "Merry-Go-Roundup." Gene sang "When the Cactus Blooms Again," a radio is heard playing "South of the Border," Autry performed a duet with June Storey on "Swing," Smiley

Burnette did "Fat Caballaro," and the movie ended with Gene again singing "South of the Border" as he rode away. The plot is about a planned revolutionary overthrow of the Mexican government that Autry and his gang thwart.

South of the Border was Autry's top grossing movie. The film had hit songs and a good, well-written plot that flowed well and never stumbled over itself. The song and the movie were so successful with audiences that Republic made plans for a second movie, *Down Mexico Way*, the title coming from the second line in the song. However, *South of the Border* was not shown in Mexico because censors there, nervous about a plot involving oil and revolution, forbade the showing of the movie anywhere. In Mexico City, the only American-operated cinema, the Cine Olimpia, booked the film and spent a good deal of money promoting it. Apparently foreign oil companies and fears of a revolution caused a last minute program change.[13]

****

During the 1935–1940 period, the big three singing cowboy stars were Autry, Roy Rogers and Tex Ritter, although the Sons of the Pioneers were also featured prominently in a number of movies and their sound was influential. In 1935, Autry starred in five movies, while the Sons of the Pioneers (with Roy Rogers as a member) were featured in seven. In 1936 Autry starred in eight movies, with the Sons of the Pioneers featured in two of them, *The Big Show* and *The Old Corral*. The Sons of the Pioneers were featured in four other movies, including *Rhythm on the Range*, starring Bing Crosby. Tex Ritter made his debut that year, starring in two singing cowboy movies.

In 1937 Autry starred in eight movies, while Tex Ritter starred in six; the Sons of the Pioneers were featured in two movies, starring Charles Starrett. In 1938 Roy Rogers began starring in singing cowboy movies and headlined in four that year; Autry starred in six, while Ritter starred in eight and the Sons of the Pioneers were featured in eight Charles Starrett movies.

16

MELODY RANCH

While filming the movie *Shooting High* in late 1939, Autry received a call on the set from Danny Danker, an account executive with the J. Walter Thompson Agency in Chicago, which handled the Wrigley's chewing gum account. "When I put down the phone I told Carl Cotner and Frankie Marvin, 'Hey, stick your fiddles in the car tomorrow. We're going to do an audition for CBS for a radio show for the Wrigley people," remembered Autry.[1] The next day the three went to the CBS Studios on Sunset Boulevard and auditioned for the ad agency. Out of that audition came the "Melody Ranch" radio program.

On January 7, 1940, the "Melody Ranch" radio show debuted on CBS. The first show was 15 minutes and began with announcer Ken Ellington introducing Autry, who sang one of his recent recordings, "I'm Gonna Round Up My Blues." After a short talk extolling Doublemint Gum, Autry was in a brief sketch that dramatized Autry's version of his encounter with Will Rogers. During that sketch, Autry sang "Back in the Saddle Again," then reprised that song at the end of the show. The first regular announcer for the show was Wendell Niles, and a singing group billed as the Texas Rangers performed on the earliest shows.

A *Variety* review of that first show stated, "Autry talks easily about the purple hills of the west like a New Yorker talks about the traffic jams on Madison Avenue and sings pleasantly about pinto ponies. To an accompaniment of good wheezy fiddlin' he gets nostalgic with a lot of showmanship. There's the inevitable horse opry comedy relief called (also inevitable) 'Shorty,' but a nice cuss under the unschooled exterior.... The story blends in and fades out with ballads fore and aft or, if the mood or the running time suggest, ballads in the center, too."[2]

The previous summer Johnny Mack Brown and the Texas Rangers had a radio program on CBS structured almost exactly like Autry's, but it was not renewed after the summer. But Wrigley's was a powerful advertiser, and Autry had enormous box office appeal.

Autry used "Back in the Saddle Again," the song composed by Ray Whitley, as a sort-of theme song for that first broadcast but then switched to "Sing Me a Song of the Saddle" for the next several months until he obtained the copyright and publishing to "Back in the Saddle." Chappell had originally published the song, and it took Autry a pretty good while to negotiate a release from that publishing company. Autry paid Whitley a sum of money (it may have been from $500 to $750) for the copyright and co-writing credit. It was a good move for Whitley; the song would never have become as popular as it did without Autry singing it so often, and Gene Autry would not have made it his theme song if he did not own the copyright and publishing.

President Franklin Roosevelt's birthday was January 30; at the president's birthday party, Gene Autry performed and presented him with a ten gallon Stetson hat. As he presented the hat to FDR, with Eleanor Roosevelt nearby, he told of all the ways to use a hat, then concluded by saying, "They're good throwing hats too, Mr. President, in case you choose to throw one into the ring." There was speculation during this election year about whether FDR would try for a third term, and the President took the hat, laughed and said, "I shall check the hat's qualifications this summer at Hyde Park."[3]

On March 22, 1940 *Rancho Grande* was released, co-starring Smiley Burnette, June Storey, the Brewer Kids, and Pals of the Golden West. As usual, Autry hit the road to promote the picture. On April 22 he was in Okemah, Oklahoma, to help celebrate Pioneer Days, and rode down main street with Governor Red Phillips, while thousands lined the streets, standing and cheering. The Light Crust Doughboys came from WBAP in Fort Worth, and the Jimmy Wakely Trio came with WKY; Autry appeared on both shows. The Wakely Trio and Autry then went to the Crystal Theater to watch *Rancho Grande*.

The meeting with Wakely's group came from a flash of lighting. Wakely's group was driving one night when lightning allowed them to see a poster of Gene Autry announcing his appearance in Okemah. The trio — Wakely, Johnny Whitfield and Scotty Harrell — drove to Okemah, and convinced Bill Slepka, manager of the local theater, to allow the trio sing on a radio broadcast from the theater. They also promised Slepka they'd get Autry to sing on the program.

During the parade, Wakely's trio climbed on an old store building as Gene passed. According to Wakely, "As he approached on his horse, Champion, we waved our cowboy hats. He spotted us and waved his white Stetson. 'Come on over to the hotel!' he shouted. I told Gene of my promise to my sponsor and he and Champion walked to the theater with us — with hundreds of fans following behind. Champion followed Gene into the elevator, then onto the stage, where he stood quietly at his side and listened to Gene sing 'South of the Border.'"[4]

In 1937 Wakely had joined "Little Doc Roberts Traveling Medicine Show," then formed the Bell Boys, who appeared on WKY on three 15-minute shows a week. This trio consisted of Scotty Harrell, Jack Cheney and Wakely, with staff guitarist Mel Osborne performing with the group. The group wore bell boy uniforms and pill box caps and were sponsored by the Bell Clothing Stores. Wakely's biggest influence was Gene Autry. "He is the reason I chose to be a singing cowboy," Wakely said. Because of Autry's influence, Wakely "wanted to wear western clothes and sing cowboy songs."[5] He dropped Jack Cheney and Mel Osborne from his group and brought in Johnny Whitfield, who had a 15-minute show on KTOK, "Johnny Whitfield, the Lonesome Cowboy."

The Bell Boys made their first trip to Hollywood in 1939; they also changed their name to Jimmy Wakely and the Rough Riders. In Hollywood, they made some transcriptions for Standard Radio and signed a contract to appear and sing in a Republic film,

Saga of Death Valley, starring Roy Rogers. Failing to find more movie work, the group returned to Oklahoma.

Wakely had dreams of being a singing cowboy in Hollywood, so he took to heart what Autry told them as they parted in Okemah: "If you fellows should decide to come back out to California again, be sure and look me up!" That was good enough for the trio, who were, as Johnny Bond remembered, "Young, ambitious and fearless."[6] The group gave their notice to WKY that they were leaving, but group member Scotty Harrell chose to remain behind; he was replaced by Dick Reinhart.

On May 29, 1939, Wakely with his wife and two daughters, and Johnny Whitfield with his wife, Dorothy, climbed in a Buick and headed to Hollywood, pulling a trailer which carried their instruments, luggage and household furnishings; during the drive out, Whitfield decided to change his name to Johnny Bond. In June, the group reached California. Autry was out of town at the time, so the group scrambled to obtain some work before their money ran out. Wakely managed to acquire a spot in a western radio series, *The Range Busters* and his first movie was *Trailin' Trouble*.

When Autry arrived back into town, he "arranged an audition for Jimmy's trio with his sponsor, Mr. Wrigley," according to Linda Lou Wakely in her book, *See Ya Up There*. "He told them if they were accepted and could get into the musician's union, he would put them on his radio show." The group "auditioned on closed circuit radio to Chicago for Mr. Wrigley's representatives," who turned them down. But "Gene said, 'Hell with it! I'm gonna put you on my show for two weeks. If Wrigley likes you, you can stay.'"[7]

According to Johnny Bond, Autry commented when the trio first auditioned for him that he preferred the Oklahoma trio with Harrell instead of the new trio with Reinhart so, on their way to Duluth, Minnesota, for a rodeo date, the group stopped in Oklahoma City and sought out Scotty Harrell. Autry told the group he would put them on his "Melody Ranch" CBS Radio show if Harrell would re-join. Reinhart remained, and sometimes the trio was a quartet with two tenors; Harrell and Reinhart alternated in the trio for the next several years.

In April 1940, *Shooting High* was released, co-starring Jane Withers, Carl Cotner, and Frankie Marvin. In May, *Gaucho Serenade* was released, co-starring Smiley Burnette, June Storey, Duncan Renaldo (who later became famous playing "The Cisco Kid"), and Smith Ballew; the *Variety* review slammed the picture, stating, "Story is not only unbelievable and rehashed, but a slower-upper. It makes of the picture neither fish nor fowl, neither musical nor western, and as result it will please nobody. With Autry's personality, his pleasant singing voice and the splendid tunes he is handed, 'Gaucho' had the essence of a humdinger. But some attention should have been paid to the story."[8]

On July 31, a syndicated story on Gene Autry by Hedda Hopper appeared in newspapers across the country. The article proclaimed him "one of wealthiest stars," who "hates being judged on the basis of his material success." The article noted Autry "did not attend many Hollywood parties." Autry related that he "once attended a party thrown in a Hollywood mansion. It was practically a marble castle, and it was so cold the guests gathered in a little room in the basement and wouldn't leave it." Autry was more down to earth: "When people visit us we want them to feel at home."

The article noted that Autry's home was a ranch house with six rooms "decorated in western style. Every time you turn around you bump into a set of polished long-horns mounted on a wall. One pair is over 10 feet wide." The article also noted, "You step through the living room door directly into the training ring for the horses. A loud speaker and spot lights provide the show atmosphere when the animals are being put through their paces."[9]

In August, Autry spent four days in the studio recording. On August 20 he recorded "Be Honest with Me." Autry and Fred Rose wrote this song, which would be nominated for an Academy Award. Autry did a variety of songs during these sessions. "The Call of the Canyon," by Billy Hill was a western classic, while "Broomstick Buckaroo" was a children's song, and "The Last Letter" was a country hit. "When the Swallows Come Back to Capistrano" and "We Never Dream the Same Dream Twice" were both pop tunes. Again, Autry followed in Bing Crosby's footsteps, recording a wide variety of material to reach a broad market.

In September 1940, *Ride, Tenderfoot, Ride,* co-starring Smiley Burnette, June Storey, Cindy Walker, and Cactus Mack was released.

The Jimmy Wakely Trio joined Autry on the 30-minute "Melody Ranch" radio program in September, singing their hit "Cimarron." For the radio show, the group gathered each Friday night for a script rehearsal. When Autry came in, he generally stopped in the doorway and said "Gentlemen" or "Ladies and Gentlemen" to the entire cast, then everyone gathered in an informal circle and read the script, making changes along the way. Johnny Bond remembered that Autry's "first reading was usually a bit on the rough side, leading us to wonder if he was going to be able to handle it or not. After a couple of times through he fell into it pretty good, although he was never completely relaxed."

"He took direction well," said Bond, "hardly ever making changes or suggestions of his own. When he did he usually tried to drive home his point with gentle emphasis. He was a quiet, easy going sort. Director Tony Stanford drove everyone pretty hard. After rehearsals, Gene always stayed around for a short while and had conferences in the corner with the director or Johnny Marvin, the musician's contractor on the show. Mitch Hamilburg, his agent, was always around. Then he'd say, 'Goodnight, everybody. See you Sunday morning,' and leave."[10]

There was a musical rehearsal at ten on Sunday mornings. Autry would come in, speak to everyone, then go to the orchestra leader's podium and go over each song alone before singing it with the rest of the group. After the songs were rehearsed, there would be another script reading, then a full dress rehearsal that was clocked with a stop watch. That usually left about an hour between dress rehearsal and show time.

The radio show was performed before a live audience, who had free admission in one of CBS's small studios at Columbia Square, located on the corner of Sunset and Gower Street in Hollywood. About ten minutes before going on the air, the curtain opened and Autry walked out unannounced and talked to the audience, telling a few jokes and requesting that they applaud when the applause light was on.

By September, "Melody Ranch" had settled into a routine. The show began with his theme song, "Back in the Saddle Again," which replaced "Sing Me a Song of the Saddle." Autry opened each program with a few remarks, then sang an uptempo song with the orchestra and trio. A commercial for Doublemint typically followed—read by the announcer—and Autry did another song, usually a ballad. A comedy routine followed that involved Autry, Horace Murphy (as Shorty) and Frank Nelson (as Reno). Mary Lee, a regular on the show, usually sang a solo, then there was another comedy spot, followed by a song by the Jimmy Wakely Trio. About halfway through the show was a "Western Tale," a ten minute story with musical cues and sound effects. Good always triumphed over evil in these stories, and Gene Autry was always the hero. This drama was followed by another commercial, then Autry and the Trio would perform a classic cowboy song. After this, the cast said, "Good night," and Autry sang "Back in the Saddle Again" to close the show.

Each show was recorded on a transcription disk that Autry kept, often reviewing and critiquing the show afterwards. "Melody Ranch" was broadcast over KNX in Los Angeles in the afternoon, so it was heard at 6:30 on the East Coast. Since it was on the CBS network, it was heard in most cities throughout the United States and Canada. When Autry toured, he broadcast his show live from wherever he was. Sometimes these broadcasts came from a high school or city auditorium and sometimes from a CBS outlet in that city.

The pre–World War II show of "Melody Ranch" had a stronger cowboy flavor than those during and after World War II did. After the trio of Wakely, Bond and Reinhart, known as "The Rough Riders," replaced the Texas Rangers as Autry's vocal group, a few other changes occurred. During that first year, Tom Hanlon became the announcer, and Lou Bring's orchestra provided the backing with production assistance from Johnny Marvin.

When Johnny Bond and his group joined Autry, they fell into Autry's social circle. Bond noted that this social set held a lot of parties in their homes. Gene and Ina Mae seldom arrived late, and when they did, Autry shook hands all around. Although Autry was usually in one of his cowboy outfits, it was "just plain old visiting like ordinary folks." A jam session usually followed, which might last until midnight. "We learned that Autry loved to sing whether on stage or off," remembered Bond. "He would begin with some of the older, more familiar favorites, followed by some new songs that he and others were working on. In this manner we all learned the new songs, sometimes even helping him revise certain parts of them."

Bond remembered "our new boss would always suggest that each of us come forward with new compositions so, naturally, we began writing." Smiley Burnette generally wasn't there—he might be out on the road with his own show—or he just might not come. The Burnettes were teetotalers, and there was usually some drinking at these parties. However, the Burnettes sometimes hosted huge outdoor backyard parties at their home in Studio City, not far from Autry's home.[11]

The Autrys' circle of friends during this period included Johnny and Gloria Marvin, Frankie and Mary Marvin, Kitty and Carl Cotner, Ray and Kay Whitley, Fred and Lorene Rose, Jimmy and Inez Wakely, Dick and Juanita Reinhart, Johnny and Dorothy Bond, and the Wooters family, which included daughter Mary Lee.

On September 29, 1940, Gene Autry turned thirty-three years old. He had been a movie star for six years and a recording star for ten. "Observing him in person," noted Johnny Bond, "one got the impression that he had just stepped out of a steam bath.

Standing there, five feet eleven, blue-green eyes, sandy hair, both his person and his form fitting costumes were always spotless. His ten-gallon Stetson was always solid white with the traditional 3½ inch brim. He had many of those white hats at his fingertips in case the one he was wearing became even slightly smudged or soiled. It was immediately replaced without anyone noticing. He wore the hat always, seldom taking it off in public except during those occasions and in places where it would have been indiscreet to do otherwise. Whenever he was introduced to a lady, you could bet your boots that it would be tipped or removed promptly.

"Almost everything that he wore was tailor made for him. Even his boots. He didn't go for the 'loud' cowboy clothes except for those occasions when the script called for it. For street wear, he would have a conservative Western suit made with just enough trimming to show that it was Western only after close inspection. The suits, too, were always immaculately cleaned and pressed. The boots and belt buckle might be considered about the most colorful thing that he wore, the buckle being studded with precious gems while the better part of the boots were hidden underneath the bottoms of his trousers." Bond also observed that "Mrs. Autry had much influence upon Gene's dress and mannerism, but it was always done in private. There was never any direct word of that nature to him in public."[12]

In Philadelphia, Autry had discovered cowboy tailor Rodeo Ben's, who made many of his early custom-made costumes.

In October 1940, Gene Autry made his first appearance at the big Madison Square Garden Rodeo in New York. The cast and crew drove across the country, while Autry flew in. The group stayed at the Belvedere Hotel, which took up its carpets when the cowboys arrived. On a big billboard overlooking Broadway was Gene Autry's picture.

There were several aspects to this booking that played a role in Autry's career. First, Republic wanted to promote him in big cities; next, Autry saw the rodeo as good exposure that fit with his cowboy image; and finally, the rodeos needed a boost in terms of entertainment. Previously, rodeos had featured clowns and events like donkey basketball games or trick ropers for their entertainment between events. Having a movie cowboy star appear at a rodeo would give a definite entertainment boost to the event.

The problem with this initial New York booking was that Autry was working on a movie with Champion until two days before the rodeo began. It was impossible for someone to drive Champion across country during that time, so Champion became the first horse to fly in an airplane. The price tag was $3,400 because TWA had to rip out seats, install a stall for the horse, and obtain a special license to carry the animal. Autry, ever mindful of publicity, had pictures taken and used the event to promote his show.

On October 9, 1940, Wakely's group opened for Autry, who wore a solid white cowboy outfit, at Madison Square Garden, and "Gene fell off his horse and got some bad publicity," according to Wakely.[13] (Rumors circulated about Autry's riding ability as well as sobriety.) During that same tour, Franklin Roosevelt was re-elected to his third term as president, and the group listened to election returns on Dick Reinhart's radio in Autry's dressing room.

On November 5, according to Wakely, "A wild bull broke out of the pen and took right out through the arena when Gene was introducing 'South of the Border.' It passed us then came right back after us. Gene was standing in the spotlight and could not see. It could see us though and ran full speed right at Gene. The crowd almost fell out of their seats. We all stood there behind Gene and when he finally saw the bull after him, he couldn't run as it was too late. He just let out a 'Yippi!' and waved his hat. The bull turned a little and just missed him. Gene was quite a hero after that."[14]

The group played before 25,000 in Madison Square Garden each night for six weeks — seven nights a week with four matinees. On the show, announcer Abe Lefton first introduced Jimmy Wakely and the Melody Ranch Gang, who ran to the center of the arena and performed four or five up tempo songs. Then came the Grand Entry, with every cowboy and cowgirl connected to the event riding on horses, dressed in colorful costumes and carrying flags as they circled the arena. The band played louder and faster as the horses went from a walk to a trot then to a gallop, with the cowboys shooting blanks. Autry and his cast were not part of this.

Rodeo contests followed this spectacle — bareback bronc riding, calf roping, women's saddle bronc riding, and Abe Lefton provided a running commentary of the events. After about 45 minutes of rodeo contests, Autry made his entrance on Champion, who jumped through a large hoop covered with paper with Autry's picture on it. This was an extremely difficult trick for a horse, which naturally would want to stop when it saw a "wall" in front of it; however, trainer Johnny Agee had coached Champion to do this trick.

Another trick was even more difficult. A baby grand piano, with the top down, was covered with a rubber mat. Champion came in on a gallop, jumped up on the piano and stopped as Autry waved to the crowd from his back. Agee generally sat at the piano, pretending to play, during this trick. After jumping down from the piano, Autry put Champion through his series of steps, tricks and dances, taught by Agee. This section ended with Autry and Champion in an "End of the Trail" pose.

After this, it was back to the rodeo contests — bulldogging, trick riding and specialty acts. Then Gene Autry and Champion rode into the center of the ring, and the band joined them. Autry performed for about 15 minutes; he usually sang "Back in the Saddle Again," "Mexicali Rose," "Be Honest with Me," "South of the Border," "Tumbling Tumbleweeds," "Cool Water," "Empty Saddles," and "The Last Roundup." Following these musical performances, Autry circled the arena on Champion, then rode out and the rodeo contests continued. The last contest was the Brahma bull riding, and Autry usually stayed around to watch this event — the most dangerous and exciting event in rodeo. At the end of the rodeo, Autry was mobbed with thousands of screaming youngsters, wanting an autograph or souvenir. To those kids, he was a hero, larger than life.

After Madison Square Garden, Autry and his troupe went to Boston, where they performed at the rodeo in the Boston Garden.

****

In November the movie *Melody Ranch* was released, co-starring Jimmy Durante, George "Gabby" Hayes, and western swing star Bob Wills and His Texas Playboys. The *Variety* review stated, "The most pleasant surprise of the whole vehicle is how funny Jimmy Durante proves as announcer to the cowboy radio star in the story. The schnoz has never been funnier on the screen, the new surroundings meaning nothing to his typical line of wisecracks and mangling of the English language."[15]

In December a headline in *Variety* announced, "Autry Leads the Herd in Rep's Western Pix." The article stated, that 1940 had been Republic's best year: "Gene Autry, the topper, has hit into the 'A' house field in key centers and aided by his radio strength may be in the position that Tom Mix occupied years ago at Fox of playing the select houses." The article added that "John Wayne, a Republic star who worked off [the] lot more than on, is the prestige asset of the studio and helpful to product."[16] This statement referred to Wayne's value as a "loan-out" at Republic; the studio found it profitable to allow other studios to use him, receiving a payment for this. The article also named Republic's other top western stars as Roy Rogers, Don "Red" Barry, and the Three Mesquiteers (Robert Livingston, Bob Steele, and Rufe Davis). The article noted George "Gabby" Hayes' move from feature roles to co-star roles for Rogers films for 1941.[17]

Overall, the top stars at Republic in 1940 were Gene Autry, John Wayne, Judy Canova, Roy Rogers, Bob Livingston, Claire Trevor, Don "Red" Barry, Chester Morris, the Gleason Family, Lloyd Nolan, Edmund Lowe, Richard Cromwell, and the Weaver Brothers and Elviry.

On Saturday evening, December 4, Autry appeared in a benefit for Britain's child victims of German bombing raids. The event was broadcast live and then sent to radio stations on transcriptions. The event was organized by the Cowboy Association for British War Children's Relief, headed by Ben Roscoe. In addition to Autry, Roy Rogers, Tex Ritter, Jack and Tim Holt, Buck Jones, Bill Boyd and other cowboy stars appeared in the show, which featured mock "hold-ups" at various places around the Los Angeles area to raise money.

17

GENE AUTRY, OKLAHOMA

In January 1941, *Ridin' on a Rainbow*, co-starring Smiley Burnette, Mary Lee, and Carol Adams was released. Songs in the movie included "Be Honest with Me," which was nominated for an Academy Award that year. In February, Autry appeared at the rodeo in Houston, then went to rodeos in Hershey and Pittsburgh, Pennsylvania, New Haven, Connecticut, and Washington, D.C. At these events, Autry usually began the day with an early morning breakfast with a group of prominent ladies, then toured a children's hospital, followed by a luncheon and a radio interview before the matinee performance. The purpose of all this activity was to gain publicity and promote his appearance, which increased the paying crowd.

While in Washington, Autry and Bond drove past the Washington and Lincoln monuments and went to the Smithsonian. They attended a luncheon sponsored by Oklahoma's senators and congressmen, and Bond noted, "It was during these times that we all came to realize that Gene was very much interested in politics and on each subsequent visit thereafter he always placed the Capitol or White House on his itinerary. Years later he would say to us, 'I guess I shoulda run for Governor or Senator.'"

During the drive around Washington, Autry surprised Bond by asking, "So what do you think of all that's happening." Bond was stumped and asked what he meant. "I believe we're headed towards a war," replied Autry. Bond was surprised that Autry followed the news so closely.[1]

Autry took Bond with him to play the guitar. That way, Autry wouldn't have to carry a guitar in case someone called for a song and would be free for shaking hands and signing autographs. After the Washington appearance, Autry played a rodeo in Cleveland. Autry had signed a contract with the Arena Managers Association guaranteeing him a minimum of $100,000 for appearances in at least eight rodeos. The organization acted as Autry's agent and booked him for nine rodeos between April 1 and the end of May.[2]

In March *Back in the Saddle* was released. Co-starring Smiley Burnette and Mary Lee, songs in the movie included "Back in the Saddle Again" (the third time Autry sang it in a movie) and "You Are My Sunshine." Autry sang the Jimmie Rodgers song "In the Jailhouse Now," Mary Lee sang a jazzy "Swingin' Sam, the Cowboy Man," a female vocal group sang "Where the River Meets the Range," Autry sang "When the Cactus Is in

Bloom," Gene and Mary Lee sang the Johnny Mercer song "I'm an Old Cowhand" and actress Jacqueline Wells reprised "Where the River Meets the Range."

On June 18, 1941, Gene Autry did a session for the first time with the Wakely trio backing him. He recorded two songs by Jimmie Davis — "You Are My Sunshine," which soon became a standard, and "It Makes No Difference Now" — as well as two others. On July 28 they were back into the studio and recorded "Under Fiesta Stars" and three other numbers then. Two days later they recorded four songs, including "Don't Bite the Hand That's Feeding You." On August 1 they recorded four numbers; ten days later they recorded another four songs and on August 27 they recorded three songs, including "Blue Eyed Elaine," the first hit from Ernest Tubb, a young singer in Texas and future star in country music. In August *Under Fiesta Stars* was released, co-starring Smiley Burnette and Hal Taliaferro. On September 26 Autry was back in a Hollywood studio recording "I Wish All My Children Were Babies Again," "Amapola," "Maria Elena," and "I Don't Want to Set the World on Fire."

In October, Autry again performed at the Madison Square Garden rodeo and managed to attend some of the World Series games, an added bonus of playing New York in October when one of the New York teams was almost certain to be in the World Series. In 1941 it was a subway series, with the Yankees playing the Brooklyn Dodgers, and the Yankees winning in five games. That same month *Down Mexico Way*, co-starring Smiley Burnette, Duncan Renaldo, Eddie Dean, and the Herrera Sisters, was released, featuring the songs "Maria Elena," and "South of the Border." On November 12 *Sierra Sue*, Autry's 50th movie, co-starring Smiley Burnette, Fay McKenzie, Eddie Dean, Kermit Maynard, and Frankie Marvin, was released. Songs in the picture included "Sierra Sue," "Be Honest With Me," "Ridin' the Range," "Heebie Jeebie Blues," and "I'll Be True While You're Gone."

During the first week in November, Autry began a two week series of performances at the Boston Garden for the rodeo there. Just before his last performance on Saturday night, November 15, as he was ready to ride into the ring for the start of his show, his pilot Herb Green informed him his house on Bluffside Drive in North Hollywood was on fire. "Anybody hurt?" asked Autry. Green, taken aback by Autry's seeming nonchalance, stressed again, "Your house is on fire." Autry replied, "Well, I can't put it out from here," then rode into the ring and did his show.[3]

The destruction was nearly total to Autry's home, and he lost a number of valuable mementoes. Still, he continued with his professional obligations.

The next day, Sunday, November 16, Autry performed in Berwyn, Oklahoma, population 227, which changed its name to "Gene Autry, Oklahoma" that day. There were about 35,000 people in attendance for the hour of festivities, including Governor Red Phillips, all sweltering in 83 degree heat. At two in the afternoon, the "Berwyn" sign was replaced by a sign that said "Gene Autry." Autry then performed his "Melody Ranch" radio show live before the crowd.

The re-naming of the town came after Autry bought a ranch in Berwyn, near Ardmore, for his Flying A Rodeo Show. Lonnie Rooney, a three time World Champion All-Around Cowboy worked for Joe Greer, managing stock for rodeos, when he received a call "from a guy who said he knew me." The man said he worked for Autry, adding, "Gene wants to go into the rodeo business and a lot of people recommend you." Rooney was in Chicago, where Greer's company was supplying stock for a rodeo when Autry flew in from New York to meet him. Autry asked, "Lonnie, if I could buy Joe out, would you come over with us?" Rooney replied he would never leave Greer unless the contractor decided to completely sell out, which he did.

Hardy Murphy was one of Rooney's best friends; Murphy was also an old friend of Autry. Since the Flying A needed a permanent home, Rooney and Murphy decided to talk to Autry about locating it near Ardmore, where both lived. Leon Daube had a ranch just west of Berwyn that was available; Autry looked it over, decided to buy it and then he sent someone from California to construct the barns and buildings under Rooney's supervision.[4]

****

On Sunday morning, December 7, 1941, the Autry troupe rehearsed for the "Melody Ranch" radio show at the CBS studio. The band consisted of Jimmy Wakely on guitar, Dick Reinhart on bass, Johnny Bond on guitar, Carl Cotner on fiddle, Frankie Marvin on steel and Paul Sells on accordion — the same line-up that accompanied him on his rodeo tours during 1940 and 1941. The group was working on a movie with Autry tentatively titled *Deep in the Heart of Texas*. This would be the only movie the Jimmy Wakely Trio performed in with Autry, although the group traveled with him and were regulars on his radio show.

Both Autry and Bond remembered there was a buzz around the studio that something big had happened, although most found it hard to believe. About twenty minutes before air time, the troupe took their places on stage, then about ten minutes before the show was scheduled to go over the airwaves Autry came out, told a few jokes, then was interrupted by a voice over the speakers saying that a special announcement would be coming from the CBS newsroom in New York.

Instead of Gene Autry singing "Back in the Saddle," the cast, crew and audience stood on the stage and heard the Japanese had bombed Pearl Harbor. Bond remembered: "It goes without saying that each of us, Gene included, was stunned. We looked at our room full of people while they sat motionless looking up at us on stage. Autry made no comment but began his theme song upon cue from our director.

"It was an awkward and difficult show for us, the performers as well as the listeners. We sang, played and spoke in one mood, always a carefree, lighthearted air, while millions of terrifying thoughts raced through our minds."

"I can only suppose that there were plenty of things that Gene would liked to have said to his fans, but like a true showman, he stuck to the script and let it go at that."[5]

Autry remembered: "We had to put on a show as though nothing had happened. No one told us the control room had received word that 'Melody Ranch' was to be delayed for a special report from the CBS newsroom in New York. At the moment our theme usually began, the report was piped into the studio. Those of us on the stage — and the hundred or so seated in the audience and the millions riveted to their radios across the land — listened numbly to the details of the attack on Pearl Harbor. For the next vacant seconds the people in the studio were like figures in a wax museum. No one stirred. Or spoke. Then the director gave a cue, my theme came up, and almost by reflex, we started the show.... One of the most awkward of my life. We sang. Joked. Went through our lines. And when it was over the audience got up and walked out in a silence that was like leaving a tomb....

"We stuck to the script. It didn't strike me as a time for making a speech. Or a pep talk.... People got through that day on reflex and instinct, mostly. And by following a script.... We knew nothing would ever be the same again.... You were too full of the flag to feel sorry for yourself."[6]

Autry and the Jimmy Wakely Trio finished their movie, which was re-titled *Heart of the Rio Grande* because Universal purchased the rights to the provisional title song "Deep in the Heart of Texas." Ironically, the Jimmy Wakely Trio also appeared in that picture, backing Tex Ritter and Johnny Mack Brown.

Working with Autry on a movie, Johnny Bond noted that "he worked before the camera with the same ease that he did before the radio microphone or in the center of the rodeo arena. He never 'blew his stack,' but took it all in stride, reading his lines in a semi-amateurish way, donning a boyish-bashful approach to the leading lady, Fay McKenzie, while working the horses and fight scenes with much authority."

During the filming of the picture, Bond observed Autry "had several strangers visiting, talking with him between takes. He would do one of his scenes, then, while the crew was changing camera angles, he would rush over into a distant corner and a few of them would get their heads together in conversation that didn't reach our ears." These visitors were helping him organize a Wild West type show he planned to mount.

Bond also noted there were several teenaged girls on the set "who began to needle Gene with some kind of verbal heckling," trying to get the star to notice them. "After a while," said Bond, "he rode Champion over to the group of gigglers, giving them a firm, but polite dressing down. 'Listen, you kids,' he said to the group of girls. 'Don't bug me when I'm talking business with somebody.'" Bond noted "that was about as close to losing his temper that he had come to since we joined him."

However, on the movie set the next day, Bond recounted, "It was noted that the strangers of yesterday were absent. On this day Gene was now talking between takes with many of the actors, actresses and extras who were working on this particular picture. As it later turned out, he was approaching these people, inquiring as to their availability during the next month as to whether or not they would be interested in working the Houston Fat Stock Show and Rodeo which he had booked."[7]

On the Saturday following Pearl Harbor, Autry recorded four songs; among those he recorded was "I Hang My Head and Cry."

18

ARMY AIR CORPS

Gene Autry reportedly made over $600,000 in 1941, but he was quick to tell folks, "I never made more than a dollar a day until I was 20 and, fortunately, I've got a poor man's estimate of values. I mean, I don't need a lot of fine things to make me happy. I'm a lucky man and I hope I'll never forget it."[1]

Although Autry was always friendly and outgoing, he kept many plans to himself; also, he moved in several groups of people, and one group might not know about the other. Johnny Bond remembered: "Gene was not in the habit of revealing everything about his personal plans and movements, but we did get rumors from sources close to him that he was preparing to enter the service in some manner. We knew that he was taking flying lessons when various strangers in uniform began to appear upon the scene either at rehearsals or some other gathering."[2]

Gene Autry did four movies in the first six months of 1942 before he entered the service. In January, *Cowboy Serenade*, a movie he finished in 1941 co-starring Smiley Burnette, Fay McKenzie, and Frankie Marvin, was released. In February Autry transported a huge cast and crew to Houston for a two week appearance at the rodeo. The show was a giant production that featured actors doing square dances in colorful costumes under newly installed strobe lights that gave a fluorescent glow. The show itself featured actors portraying historical figures Buffalo Bill (played by Tex Cooper), Teddy Roosevelt (played by Eddie Dean), Kit Carson, Davy Crockett, Sitting Bull, Annie Oakley, and General Custer. Each of the characters came out and stood in the arena. It was a colorful addition to the rodeo, but it was the only time Autry mounted that show. Production costs and the impending possibility of Autry entering the armed services stopped it after its first run. When he returned to Hollywood, Autry recorded "Tweedle-o-Twill," "Deep in the Heart of Texas," "I'm Thinkin' Tonight of My Blue Eyes," and "Rainbow on the Rio Colorado" on February 24, 1942.

In March *Heart of the Rio Grande* was released, co-starring Smiley Burnette, Fay McKenzie, Frankie Marvin, and the Jimmy Wakely Trio (with Jimmy Wakely, Johnny Bond, and Dick Rinehart). The *Variety* reviewer threw a barb at the singer, saying, "Autry, who's not getting any slimmer these days, is still a stiff actor, and his numerous vocals only impede the action. Smiley Burnette's clowning is on the oafish side."[3] In April *Home in Wyoming* was released; the next month *Stardust on the Sage* came out, then *The Singing Hill*.

Gene Autry was ordered to report for an army physical on April 20, 1942, and was immediately classified "1-A." He was 34 years old, married, but had no children. He knew he needed to make a decision about the armed services.

On July 4 Autry and his troupe performed in a rodeo at Soldier Field in Chicago, and the next day, with media in tow, he went to the recruiting station and enlisted in the Army Air Corps, although he was sworn in during a broadcast of "Melody Ranch" later that month. If Autry had to serve in the army, he wanted some publicity mileage out of it — and so did the army, which used Autry's enlistment as a recruiting tool. Autry preferred to enlist so he would have some say in his job with the army. "I wanted to get into something that I knew a little bit about, and I had a pilot's license at that time," he told an interviewer some years later.[4]

Autry had gone to Washington before his Chicago appearance and arranged with military chiefs of the Army Air Corps to enter the army with the rank of sergeant. He was initially offered an officer's commission, but a committee headed by Senator Harry Truman, investigating favoritism by the military toward Hollywood celebrities, caused that offer to be withdrawn. However, he did negotiate with the army to be allowed to finish one more movie, *Bells of Capistrano*, which began production on July 6.

The *Hollywood Reporter* noted, "Enlistment of Gene Autry in the Army Air Force automatically halts all preparations for his 1942–43 film program, which had been set up as the most important of his career."[5] Autry was scheduled to star in eight pictures, four of which would be top budget musicals. The article also noted that Autry was "long the mainstay of the company" and "was to be given his biggest buildup during the coming season," adding that Republic "will have three unreleased Autry pictures on its hands when *Bells of Capistrano* is finished." The others were *Call of the Canyon*, a big budget picture, and *Stardust on the Sage*, which had a lower budget. The article continued, "Due to the importance of Autry pictures to Republic, and the advisability of avoiding a sudden complete blank in his releases, it is considered probable that a quick consultation will be held between the home office and all Republic exchanges with a view to holding up immediate release of the trio of Autry's and spreading them over the next several months or even the entire release year."[6]

Autry's movies were scheduled to be released every six weeks but, because of the war, that schedule had to be altered. Republic's schedule was also threatened because other actors might enter the service. Don Barry, who starred in a series, was scheduled to enter the military, while the status of Roy Rogers was uncertain, although he held a deferred classification because he had two children. The Three Mesquiteers series was a little safer because Tom Tyler and Bob Steele were both too old for the draft; however, the newest member of the trio, Jimmy Dodd, was waiting to hear from his draft board.

In an interview at that time Autry stated, "I think the He-men in the movies belong in the Army, Marine, Navy or Air Corps. All of these He-men in the movies realize that right now is the time to get into the service. Every movie cowboy ought to devote time to the Army winning, or to helping win, until the war is over — the same as any other American Citizen. The Army needs all the young men it can get, and if I can set a good example for the young men, I'll be mighty proud."[7] Not all the movie cowboys took his advice; John Wayne received deferments engineered by Republic.

Herbert Yates wanted to keep Autry out of the armed services and on the Republic lot making movies. He pleaded with Autry to let Republic obtain draft deferments for him and was angry that Autry turned him down. This made Yates all that more determined to keep John Wayne at Republic. When Wayne raised the issue of joining the service with Yates, the studio head "became apoplectic. 'You should have thought about all that before you signed a new contract,' Yates bellowed. 'If you don't live up to it, I'll sue you for every penny you've got. Hell, I'll sue you for every penny you hope to make in the future. God damn it! Nobody walks out on me.'"[8]

In their book, *John Wayne: American*, authors Randy Roberts and James S. Olson note, "But Gene Autry did, and Duke could have. He just did not. Yates told Wayne that he would sue him for breach of contract if he enlisted ... [and] would make certain that he would never work for Republic or any other studio. Although his threat went against government policy — every person in uniform was guaranteed his or her civilian job once the war ended — Duke did not press the issue. He feared poverty and unemployment, and perhaps he feared even more losing the status he had achieved and sinking into obscurity."[9]

Although he did not serve in World War II, John Wayne won the war on the screen. Republic cast him in *Flying Tigers* in 1942, a year in which Wayne made five films. Throughout the war, Republic appealed Wayne's status, so he received a 2-A deferment, "deferred in support of national health, safety or interest." In other words, John Wayne served his country by starring in movies about World War II. By the end of the war, he was Republic's top film star.

****

There had to be a lot of changes in short order when Autry decided to enlist. Out in Gene Autry, Oklahoma, at the Flying A Ranch, Lonnie Rooney "was cutting stock at the ranch to do ten shows back East when my wife came and told me they'd bombed Pearl Harbor.

"He got everything built just like I wanted," said Rooney. "Then the war came along. If it hadn't, he would have been the world's greatest rodeo promoter."

During the year and a half that Rooney worked with Autry, the Flying A Rodeo Show went to 11 cities — ten of them on the East Coast after the war had started. The show's stock and cowboys made their way from city to city in baggage cars. "We had two train loads," said Rooney. "Autry would buy enough tickets for a whole baggage car and the cowboys could all go along." The last stop on that tour was Chicago, where Autry appeared with his rodeo, then joined the armed services.

The ranch in Oklahoma was bought by "a guy from Texas," said Rooney. "We didn't even have the ranch complete when Gene sold it. Everything just happened at the wrong time." Rooney remembered that during the construction of the buildings on the ranch, Autry came and visited, staying with Rooney and his wife, Thelma. "He'd spend the night with us," said Rooney. "He could eat more biscuits than any man I ever seen.

"The only way we could bring Gene here was to slip him in," remembered Rooney.

"Autry was a great man to work for. He never interfered with my business. Whatever I decided to do was alright with him."[10]

On July 24 Autry finished production of *Bells of Capistrano* and on July 26 was sworn into the Army Air Corps on his "Melody Ranch" broadcast. On August 1 he reported for duty at Fort Bolling, Washington; on August 17 Autry was transferred to the air base at Santa Ana, California, for basic military training. By this point, he had logged over 200 hours as a civilian pilot and wanted to fly. However, the army preferred he perform shows for the troops.

"They put me in Public Relations and Special Services," remembered Autry later. "And I said, 'Look, I've been doing that kind of stuff for so long and I want to do something else. I want to get in the flying end of it. So I was transferred to the Air Transport Command."[11]

After Autry started basic training, *Call of the Canyon*, his 55th movie, was released, co-starring Smiley Burnette, Ruth Terry, Bob Nolan, Pat Brady, and the Sons of the Pioneers.

Carl Cotner entered the service around the same time Autry did, but Smiley Burnette stayed in Hollywood and co-starred in movies with Roy Rogers, Bob Livingston and Sunset Carson. The Jimmy Wakely Trio split; Dick Reinhart moved back to Texas, Wakely pursued a solo career in the movies and Johnny Bond stuck with Autry. Fred Rose moved back to Nashville where, in October 1942, he formed Acuff-Rose Publishing Company with Roy Acuff. Although Autry's enlistment gave Rose a convenient reason to move back to Nashville, in truth Rose's wife was tired of Hollywood and wanted to move back to where her family lived.[12]

Autry and Cotner were transferred to Luke Field in Phoenix where they continued the "Melody Ranch" broadcasts. Gene and Ina Mae stayed together in Phoenix, but during weekends they caught the Southern Pacific train back to Hollywood for the "Melody Ranch" radio show. After the Sunday show, Autry usually had a quick dinner, then caught a Pullman for an eight-hour sleeper back to Phoenix.

In the fall of 1942, Autry boarded the train in Phoenix at the last minute for the trip to Hollywood, but there was no private compartment for him. Instead, he roomed with Johnny Bond, who remembered Autry saying, "They let me live off base. Outside of that I'm just another one of their blasted soldiers." Discussing the war, Autry said, "It'll last as long as Hitler is alive. He's not going to give up until he buries every one of us."[13]

Autry talked to Bond about his career, saying, "You spend half your life getting it all together like you want it, and wham! Something like this comes along and puts the skids on it overnight. One day you're making good money and the next day you're on Army pay." Autry continued, "Our overhead is pretty steep. Now with the Republic money cut off there's nothing coming in but some royalties and you damn sure can't depend on them alone. I'll tell you one thing, though. I'll never again let myself get into a position where I'm depending on a salary alone which might be cut off by something like this. I'm going to get some investments which will pay me whether I work or not." Autry elaborated that he was going to invest in "lots of things. Real estate, hotels, radio stations. I've got my eye on a couple of stations. One here [in Phoenix] and one down in Tucson. They tell me they're little gold mines."

Autry kept up with Hollywood news by having *Daily Variety* and *Hollywood Reporter* forwarded to him. He talked about the movie *Deep in the Heart of Texas* from Universal and asked Bond — who was in the picture with the Wakely Trio — some questions about the film.

"Do they have Ritter sing the title song?" he asked.

Bond replied, "No. Fuzzy Knight sang it."

"What time setting did they use?" asked Autry.

"About 1840," replied Bond.

"That's about what I figured," said Autry. "You see, that just goes to show you how short-sighted and stupid some of these Hollywood executives can be. We offered the publisher a good deal for the title rights to that song. But no, they run right over and sell it to Universal for a few bucks more. I recorded the song. That makes the publisher more money, but do you think that makes any impression upon them? Now, you take Universal. Here's a modern song and they take it all the way back to the middle ages. They have Tex Ritter and Jimmy Wakely, both recording artists. Do they give them the song? Hell no, they give it to Fuzzy Knight who hasn't made a record yet. You should give your hit songs to your star, especially when they are recording stars. We had a modern, up-to-date story built around the song ["Heart of the Rio Grande"]. As I see it, both the publisher and Universal missed the boat.

"I think they'd better get somebody in there that knows something about making singing westerns. Ever since I started making the musicals, every studio in town has tried to jump on the bandwagon. They think all you have to do is get some guy, any guy who can carry a tune, stuff a few Public Domain songs down his throat, hire some two-bit writer and turn out a money-making Western. We don't do it that way. We spend money on songs, stories, and we turn out a good, modern picture. The rest of them want to stay back in the Stone Age. Do you ever see an automobile in one of their pictures? Hell, no. We even use motorcycles, radio — we go modern. Why? So, they finally go out and buy a hit song and look what they do to it. Louse it up. You just can't get through to them that it's important to use hit songs. Not just one hit, lots of them. They just won't put out the money on songs. They spend it all on everything else. If it wasn't for the Screen Actor's Guild they'd be having you work the picture for practically nothing."

By this point, Autry was getting heated. "I learned one thing about these Hollywood executives," he told Bond. "The only way you can get them to respect you is to make them pay. Remember that — make 'em pay! Republic didn't pay me in the beginning. Much, that is. I had to go on strike to get another dime out of them. That and a few other things. There wasn't that much to it. I was going along fine. I didn't pry into the studio's business. I knew the pictures were selling — that was good enough for me, but when I learned that they were using my pictures to move a lot of that other crap they'd been turning out, it kinda got my goat, really teed me off. Anyway, that's when I decided to make 'em pay. They did. And now they respect me more for it. But, you have to demand it. They don't force it on you...."

"Frog [Smiley Burnette] didn't strike. He wasn't even with me at the time. Frog was out on tours of his own. I'm not going to use him in my future pictures anyway. Not only him, but Republic as well. They're too slow for me. I've given them every good idea that they ever had. Then they turn right around and fire up another series with this one and that one — some unknown who never made a picture, never made a record, never rode a horse. Now they think they can make stars out of just anybody. I'll show 'em. I plan on making my own pictures. They'll be bigger and better Westerns. What's more, they'll be in color, every one of them."

In reference to Smiley Burnette, Autry said, "William S. Hart never used a comic side-kick. Neither did Tom Mix, Buck Jones or any of the rest of them. I don't know if you need one or not. If I do though, I have a guy in mind, Sterling Holloway. He hasn't been in westerns but we can dress him for the part. Besides, I like him. He has that 'Stepin Fetchit' look about him and he enlisted in the service. I'm going to stay with the patriots because when this thing is over I think the public is going to remember who served and who didn't."[14]

As they got ready to go to bed, Bond learned that Gene Autry always slept in the nude.

By October 1942 about 12 percent — or over 2,700 — of the men and women in the movie business had entered the armed services. In addition to Gene Autry, these included actors Jimmy Stewart, Henry Fonda, Ronald Reagan, Clark Gable, Tyrone Power, Robert Montgomery, William Holden, Laurence Olivier, David Niven, Sterling Hayden, and Burgess Meredith; directors Frank Capra, William Wyler, John Huston; and producers Hal Roach, Jack Warner, and Darryl F. Zanuck.

After Autry and Carl Cotner completed basic training, they were notified by the J. Walter Thompson Agency of arrangements between the military and Phil Wrigley to send them on a tour of bases, where they performed daily shows for servicemen. Performing with Autry were Johnny Bond, Eddie and Jimmy Dean, and Carl Cotner on fiddle as well as the orchestra director for the radio programs. CBS arranged for staff musicians and radio engineers to travel from Chicago to wherever Autry performed for the radio broadcasts. During this period Autry broadcast from Denver; Casper, Wyoming; Indianapolis; Louisville; and Birmingham. On the regular shows, a local officer at the base would introduced Autry, who sang several of his hits.

"I had mixed feelings about doing camp shows," wrote Autry in his autobiography. "It was soft duty. For the cut in pay I had taken, I felt I was entitled at least to get shot at. I didn't want to play show-and-tell, or beat the drums for war bonds or the Red Cross or WAC enlistment drives. I knew how to fly.... But I had a problem. My age was against me. I had flown only small aircraft, so just to get into flight school I needed a higher rating — so many hours flying [with] so much horsepower. I found a private field in Phoenix and, on my own time, at my own expense, I started checking out bigger aircraft, the Stearman and Fairchild 84 and the AT-6.

"I flew two or three times a week for six months and, finally, I was accepted for flight school at Love Field, in Dallas. Believe me, when you are competing with nineteen-and-twenty-year-old boys, trying to match their reflexes and their stamina, it is mighty tough. But I had no intention of washing out. And I guess I should make it clear. Being Gene Autry had nothing to do with that. Didn't help, didn't hurt. I didn't take any hazing, either. Anyone who cared to look could see I was earning my way. That's why I considered it a break, not coming in on a cushion, as an officer. Gene Autry's name and reputation meant little. But love of flying did. And I was hooked on those clouds."[15]

Gene Autry did not give up his entertainment career completely or the comforts of home during the time he was in the Army Air Corps. He continued to do his radio show until 1944, when he stopped because of his active work as a cargo co-pilot. He was also helped by the fact the Musicians Union had called a strike for recording musicians that lasted from August 1, 1942 until the end of 1944, so he could not have made any recordings even if he had been in Hollywood at the time.

In October 1943, Autry performed at the Madison Square Garden rodeo, and Herbert Yates came backstage and spoke angrily with him after Yates insisted Roy Rogers should have Autry's dressing room. Yates told Autry, "Well, you wouldn't cooperate and I'll break you if it's the last thing I ever do. And I'll make Roy Rogers the biggest thing that ever happened in this business."[16]

Yates had tried to cajole Autry out of enlisting, now he threatened to ruin his career, but Autry always stood up to him.

The advantage Autry had over John Wayne was that Autry did not have to depend solely on movie work for an income; he could sing on records and perform at live shows. Also, the merchandising deals Autry engineered continued to bring in money.

The last movie Gene Autry made before entering the service was *Bells of Capistrano*, released on September 15, 1942, after he entered the army. Co-starring Smiley Burnette and Virginia Grey, the movie featured the song "Don't Bite the Hand That's Feeding You." The *Variety* reviewer was not a fan of Autry's acting; he gave him a backhanded compliment, noting, "Crooner Autry, of course, is still the better b.o. bet than Actor Autry. The star must depend on the cast's lessers for the better performances, for he's still the same expressionless, stodgy performer. But he's still the best of the cowboy songsters."[17]

In September Republic rereleased *Man from Music Mountain*, a picture originally released in 1938. Although Republic reissued some of Autry's movies during the war, the studio reacted to Autry's departure by building a major promotion behind Roy Rogers, naming him "King of the Cowboys." The war gave Roy Rogers a big career boost.

19

WORLD WAR II

The build-up of Roy Rogers as King of the Cowboys began with a film of that title released in April 1943. In the movie was Autry's old sidekick, Smiley Burnette, and the Sons of the Pioneers. Rogers starred as a rodeo performer who worked as an undercover agent. Songs in the movie were "A Gay Ranchero," "Ride Ranger Ride," "Ride 'Em Cowboy," "Red River Valley," "Roll Along Prairie Moon," "I'm an Old Cowhand," "They Cut Down the Old Pine Tree" and "Biscuit Blues."

During the war years, Rogers began to play a character named "Roy Rogers," and more songs were included in his films, making them more like Autry's. Rogers began wearing more colorful clothing — more a star than an authentic cowboy — and developed a supporting cast of horse Trigger, dog Bullet, and female lead Dale Evans. Lavish production numbers were incorporated into the films, a direct result of the influence of the musical *Oklahoma*, which studio head Herbert J. Yates saw in New York. After Yates saw *Oklahoma*, he directed his writers to use the idea of a musical in Rogers's movies; the result was that the movies of Roy Rogers became, in effect, western musicals with big production numbers instead of cowboy movies with some singing.

The budgets for the Roy Rogers films increased during the war years, and the movies were marketed to A theaters in major cities, rather than B movie houses, primarily in small towns and rural areas, particularly in the South and Midwest, which were the previous markets for westerns in general and singing cowboys in particular. After *King of the Cowboys*, Rogers starred in fifteen more movies during World War II. Republic reissued Autry's pictures during World War II, which kept that singing cowboy in the public spotlight.

Looking at Gene Autry and Roy Rogers one may conclude that Roy Rogers may have been a better actor, but Gene Autry had a more complete career in entertainment. Autry consistently took care with his recordings, and they sold extremely well. Rogers, who was never comfortable as a solo performer, never achieved the record sales of Autry and, in fact, did not pay as much attention to his recording career as Autry did. In terms of personal appearances, Autry spent time and money to present a great, crowd-pleasing show.

The major contribution Roy Rogers made to music was through his formation of

the Sons of the Pioneers and the early recordings he made with them. The group's har-
monies — especially with their yodels — influenced several generations of country singers.
But it was Gene Autry who was consistently more successful as a recording artist, seeking out new songs to record and putting together a traveling show. Autry worked as hard
on his singing career as he did on his movie career, while Rogers concentrated his efforts
on his movie career.

Roy Rogers was certainly a major influence on kids growing up in the 1940s and
1950s, becoming a hero in an age of heroes, and although Autry was also a hero, Rogers's
influence probably lasted longer simply because his television career during the 1950s and
early 1960s lasted longer than Autry's, who moved into the world of business after 1960.

****

During World War II, a group of dedicated fans helped keep Gene Autry's name in
the news. The Gene Autry Friendship Club was started by Dorothy Pinnick of Gary, Indiana, in February 1938, during the period of Autry's walk-out from Republic Pictures.

Dot Pinnick became Dot Crouse when she married Ted Crouse in 1941. Described
as "amiable, charismatic and possessing strong organization and leadership skills," Dot
was a beautician who owned and operated her own beauty parlor. The fan club started
with about 30 members but, by writing to magazines such as *Radio Mirror*, *WLS Stand-
By*, *Screen Book*, *Modern Movies* and others with fan club listings, the club grew to about
400 members in two years. Members were kept informed of Autry's activities through
mimeographed monthly journals edited by Dot. Autry approved of the formation of the
club, and his secretary, Dorothy Phillips, was a steady source for material.

The first Gene Autry Friendship Club convention was held in Chicago; Autry was
not present, but Arkie the Arkansas Woodchopper treated club members to breakfast. At
an earlier appearance in Chicago, on November 4, 1938, when Autry performed at the
WLS "National Barn Dance," he had a severe cold, and the only ones permitted to visit
him backstage were members of his fan club. In 1939 Bev Barnett began work for Gene
as a press agent and became a steady, reliable source of information for the club. Johnny
Marvin was a regular contributor to the published journal, which became known as *Autry's
Aces*.

The first individual GAFC chapter was organized in New York City in 1941; the following year a chapter was started in Chicago by Virginia Siegers. Jon Guyot Smith, who
wrote a history of the club for their newsletter, states that during the club's convention
in Chicago in 1942, members of the club "were waiting with others to be admitted to the
studio for Gene's show. Gene came into the foyer and a lady in the group called to him.
She had with her a small child, a little blind girl. Gene stooped down and let the child
run her hands over his face to 'see' him.... Another incident at the same broadcast: a small
crippled boy was in the audience. At the close of Gene's broadcast, the crowd surged forward to get Gene's autograph, endangering the child ... but Gene noticed it first and asked
the crowd if they would please move out and he would come down from the stage and
sign their books."

Blanche Linton (of Allentown, Pennsylvania) and Bonnie Baker (of Toronto, Canada)
formed the Post Card Patrol. According to Jon Guyot Smith, "Members joining the Patrol

were expected to send a bunch of postcards to Blanche and Bonnie each month, which the ladies would then imprint with instructions as to which magazine editors should be bombarded with requests for Gene Autry articles." Smith noted that "hundreds of members joined the Post Card Patrol, and magazines did indeed cover Gene constantly throughout the war years." In addition to the Post Card Patrol, the journal, edited by Bessie Faye Fairbanks, published current news on Autry. Fairbanks, who lived in California, received most of this news from Autry's staff.[1]

****

In January 1944, *Billboard*, the music trade magazine, began a chart of country songs, called "Folk" at that time, which listed the top-selling country records based primarily on sales to jukeboxes. Since jukeboxes had bought the majority of country music singles during the Great Depression — and would continue to buy the majority until the 1960s — this seems like a fair way to determine the top artists and recordings from the inception of that chart. On January 29, 1944, Autry's recording of the old Carter Family standard "I'm Thinking Tonight of My Blue Eyes" was on that chart; on April 29 his recording of "I Hang My Head and Cry" was listed.[2]

However, that chart started 16 years after Gene Autry began recording, so the period when Autry sold a huge number of records is mostly unaccounted for by any chart, although there were weekly lists of the "ten most popular songs," based primarily on sheet music sales. A few of Autry's songs, including "The Last Round-Up" and "Tumbling Tumbleweeds" were on those charts. Also, Gene Autry was the rare country artist whose records were bought by consumers in large numbers. Although jukeboxes certainly bought Autry's recordings, the sales to jukeboxes alone cannot accurately gauge the success of Autry as a recording artist during his career.

Jon Guyot Smith has confronted this problem and determined that "the best-selling Gene Autry records are the ones which most often surface on the collectors market" because "more copies were pressed and thus the supply is far greater than for lesser hits." Smith notes that "a Gene Autry fan seeking to build a library of 78s today will have little difficulty in finding copies of 'Rudolph, The Red-Nosed Reindeer' 'Peter Cottontail' or 'Mexicali Rose.' These huge hits were pressed and sold in enormous quantity and may be very easily located." Smith notes that Autry's first release, "Left My Gal in the Mountains" b/w "Blue Yodel Number 5" on Velvet Tone "is comparatively easy to find." In fact, according to Smith, "all the Velvet Tone records are fairly easy to locate." On the other hand, "My Oklahoma Home" on Radiex and "Oh, for the Wild and Wooley West" on QRS "are all but impossible to locate," primarily because those records, made at the beginning of the Depression were released by companies that went out of business.

Smith contends that a "more reliable method of judging the success of Gene's early recordings may be to study the marketing patterns of the record companies." The bulk of Autry's hits during the 1930s were done for the American Record Corporation, which had contracts with various chain stores which sold their records for 25 or 35 cents (instead of the 75 cents that Victor charged for their top line of product). It stands to reason, then, that examining which records remained in print the longest indicates those with a continuing demand and, hence, greatest sales.

Autry's earliest records were released on labels such as Melotone, Perfect, Oriole, Banner, Romeo and Conqueror. According to Smith, "the biggest sellers were retained in the catalogue, and pressed several times, while the less spectacular selections were pretty quickly deleted." Examining the Conqueror label, which was sold exclusively by Sears, Autry's records began appearing in the 1931 catalogue. By 1941—a decade later—Sears still offered twelve of Autry's early recordings:[3]

"A Gangster's Warning"
"That Silver Haired Daddy of Mine"/"Mississippi Valley Blues"
"When It's Lamp Lighting Time in the Valley"/"The Old Folks Back Home"
"The Yellow Rose of Texas"/"Gosh, I Miss You All the Time"
"The Last Round-Up"/"There's an Empty Cot in the Bunkhouse Tonight"
"Tumbling Tumbleweeds"/"Old Missouri Moon"
"Nobody's Darlin' But Mine"/"Mexicali Rose"
"I'll Go Ridin' Down That Texas Trail"/"The Old Gray Mare"
"That's Why I'm Nobody's Darlin'"/"The Convict's Dream"
"The One Rose"/"I Hate to Say Goodbye to the Prairie"
"Take Me Back to My Boots and Saddle"/"I Want a Pardon for Daddy"
"There's a Gold Mine in the Sky"/"Sail Along, Silv'ry Moon"

****

In December 1938, when CBS purchased the American Record Corporation, Columbia became the flagship label. Earlier that year ARC discontinued the labels Melotone, Perfect, Banner, Oriole and Romeo. The discount label for CBS then became Vocalion, which reissued a number of Autry's recordings. In 1940, the CBS-owned firm discontinued the Vocalion label and put its 35-cent line of recordings on the Okeh label. Autry's records were then released on Okeh until World War II, when shortages in shellac caused labels to cut back on their releases.

Jon Guyot Smith notes the Autry records recorded during 1931–1936 that were on Okeh during World War II were[4]

"That Silver Haired Daddy of Mine"/"Mississippi Valley Blues"
"Tumbling Tumbleweeds"/"Old Missouri Moon"
"Nobody's Darlin' But Mine"/"Don't Waste Your Tears on Me"
"Mexicali Rose"/"You're the Only Star in My Blue Heaven"
"Answer to Nobody's Darlin' But Mine"/"Answer to Red River Valley"
"I'll Go Ridin' Down That Texas Trail"/"My Old Saddle Pal"
"That's Why I'm Nobody's Darlin'"/"The Convict's Dream"
"Beautiful Texas"/"There's a Little Old Lady Waiting"
"My Old Pal of Yesterday"/"Why Don't You Come Back to Me"
"There's an Empty Cot in the Bunkhouse Tonight"/"Louisiana Moon"
"Old Faithful"/"Someday in Wyoming"
"The Last Round-Up"/"Way Out West in Texas"
"The Yellow Rose of Texas"/"Little Ranch House on the Old Circle B"

****

In 1944, Republic released *The Phantom Empire* as a two-part feature titled *Men with Steel Faces* and *Radio Ranch*. Autry was concerned about his career as a movie star during the war. In March 1944, he confided to Johnny Bond that he felt if the war lasted much longer he would be too old to be a cowboy star. Gene Autry turned 37 that year.

On November 29 and December 6 Autry was in Hollywood recording—the musicians' strike had just ended—"Don't Fence Me In," a song written by Cole Porter and introduced by Roy Rogers, and "At Mail Call Today," a song written by Autry and Fred Rose that became popular during World War II. Autry received the idea for "At Mail Call Today" when he was stationed at Love Field in Dallas and read a letter in *Yank* magazine from a G.I. whose girl jilted him; he found out "at mail call today." Autry called Rose in Nashville, who flew to Dallas, where they wrote the song in Autry's apartment at the Stoneleigh Hotel.[5]

Gene Autry earned his pilot wings in the Army Air Corps on June 21, 1944, and was sworn in as a flight officer at Love Field in Dallas, Texas. Assigned to the 91st Ferrying Squadron of the 555th Army Air Base Unit, Air Transport Command, Autry was certified to fly the AT-6, AT-7, AT-11, C-104 and C-109.

In the Asian theater during World War II, the "Burma Road," 715 winding miles of paved cobblestone, ran between the railhead city of Lashio in Burma and the Chinese city of Kumming. Created by 200,000 Chinese laborers in 1937 and 1938, it was the key route for American, British and Allied forces to supply food and equipment in China as the Japanese army advanced steadily south and west thorough Asia. By February 1942, General Joe Stilwell commanded the China-Burma-India theater (CBI); in March, Rangoon, the commercial capital and major port for Burma, was taken by the Japanese and on April 29 the Japanese took Lashio, severing the Burma Road.

CBI had been promised C-46 cargo plans to create the Air Transport Command, which would ferry goods over the Himalayan "Hump" to China from air fields in Assam, India. However, the planes were not delivered as promised, and the Army Air Corps had to make do with C-47s and the B-24 Liberator, rechristened C-87s for cargo, and C-109s, which carried fuel.

From the airfields at Assam it was 500 miles over the Hump, first crossing the 10,000-foot Naga Hills of India and Myanmar, then the 20,000-foot peaks of the Himalayan Santsung Range of southwest China, before landing on Chinese airfields. For pilots, this was one of the most dangerous missions of World War II. Allied maps were unreliable, and the most powerful navigational radios reached only 30 to 50 miles. Japanese fighter aircraft and anti-aircraft fire from the ground, which launched flak explosives (called "black roses"), were constant threats. There were monsoons from May to October, and freak winds could blow as hard as 248 miles per hour over the highest Himalayan peaks; air turbulence could cause an aircraft to flip over when it skirted the Himalayas, and random gusts could bounce an aircraft up or down a thousand feet in a minute.

In his book, *The Burma Road: The Epic Story of the China-Burma-India Theater in World War II*, author Donovan Webster quotes pilot Charles F. Linamen, who flew C-109s over the Hump, on what it was like:

"The first thing you'd do when you climbed into the cockpit for a Hump run was to cinch down the leg and chest traps of your seat harness until they were so tight you could hardly breathe. Because when that aircraft would hit turbulence, you'd get bounced all over the place. The plane would meet an updraft, and you'd be pushed down into the seat until the belts were so loose you wouldn't even know you had them on; you could easily pass your hand between your leg and the belt. Then, a minute later, you might get slammed by a downdraft and you'd be thrown against the harness belts — they were the only things keeping you in that seat. Sometimes, in an up-or downdraft, I'd look at the altimeter and it would be spinning so fast my eyes couldn't follow. You'd rise one thousand feet or fall one thousand feet in no time, the aircraft sometimes tilting over on one side or the other to ninety degrees or more: you'd look out the side windows and see the ground directly below your shoulder. After especially rough flights, my shoulders and legs would be bruised from the pressure of the harness against them. And we did that every day, the way people these days get in and out of cars.[6]

Sometimes known as "Operation Vomit," these flights saw an average of eight planes go down each month; by the end of the war, almost 600 planes had crashed along the route. The C-109s were particularly dangerous because they were loaded with fuel, and the plane could quickly turn into a ball of fire.

Gene Autry was co-pilot on one C-109 flight over the Hump. For the rest of his life, Gene Autry carried a lot of pride for completing that mission. Although he was awarded the American Campaign Medal, the Asiatic-Pacific Campaign Medal and the World War II Victory Medal, Gene Autry was most proud of carrying card number 939 of the Hump Pilots organization.

There was tragedy for Autry during the war years as well; his close friend and music director Johnny Marvin died on December 20, 1944, in South America after he contacted a fever.

On June 13, 1945 Autry was in Hollywood recording four songs; on June 15, he returned to the studio and recorded three more. He was getting ready for his discharge and wanted a good stock of recordings for release.

On July 17, Gene Autry transferred to Special Services and arranged to do a tour of the Pacific, performing for the troops. Beginning in August 1945, when he flew into Saipan, he spent ten weeks traveling from island to island with Rufe Davis, Will and Gladys Ahern, Marjorie Alden and Sandra Shaw, playing approximately 85 shows for G.I.s on a USO Camp Shows trip arranged by the Hollywood Victory Committee.

"Everywhere we went the first thing the boys said was: 'where's your horse,'" Autry told a reporter after he returned. "And I sure could have used Champ on those islands. I walked up hills and down hills and into Jap caves, until I had walked off 22 pounds. The only time I got to ride was on Guam, where they gave me a water buffalo."

The troupe covered 35,000 miles, performing at Guam, Saipan, Tipnian, Kwajalein, Angar, Palau, and Iwo Jima.

"We were on Iwo Jima when the news came that the Japs were going to give up, and I never saw a bunch of men go quite so crazy," said Autry shortly after he returned. "Most of them were Marines who were getting ready for the next invasion, and that news meant that a lot of them would not have to die....

"We never had less than 3,500 in the audience and a lot of times we played to an entire division of 15,000 men in a day. The boys are a wonderful audience and next to wanting to go home, they want entertainment, and they will continue to want it as long as they are overseas."[7]

In his autobiography, Autry told of having a drink with General Ramey on August 4, 1945, two days before the *Enola Gay* took off to drop the atomic bomb on Hiroshima. Autry and the troupe were in Tinian on August 6 when the bomb went off.

"All over the islands, the news touched off a wild celebration," wrote Autry. "The kind that ends at four in the morning with people trying to hold each other up and sing barbershop harmony. There was no question of what we felt then. Pride. Relief. In all the moral agonizing that has taken place in the years since, we sometimes seem to forget how few doubts anyone had at the time that decision — Harry Truman's awesome decision to use atomic power — was the right one."[8]

Autry's days in the armed service were numbered; during his time in the Army Air Corps he had one perk while in uniform — he was allowed to wear cowboy boots — and one idiosyncrasy: he refused to salute female officers.

Within hours of the Japanese surrender about a week later, Autry and the troupe were on a plane headed back to the United States. "I had gotten up close to a very wide screen, had felt a lot of emotions I probably would never feel again," remembered Autry. "But it was behind me now. Somewhere over the blue Pacific, a few hours outside of Honolulu, it occurred to me that I was a civilian again. More than that, I was a free agent. The way I had it figured, my contract with Republic had run out while I was in the service. From my seat I could see the metallic blur of the plane's propellers. They were turning no faster than the thoughts turning in my mind."[9]

However, once again, Herbert Yates, head of Republic, did not see things the same way Gene Autry did.

20

HERBERT YATES
AND REPUBLIC, REVISITED

In September 1945, the "Melody Ranch" radio program, known as "Sgt. Gene Autry" during the war, went back on CBS but, due to a crowded schedule, was only a 15-minute program until the spring of 1946, when it resumed as a 30-minute program. There were some changes in the line-up for the new show. The Cass County Boys were the featured trio; Fred Martin played accordion, Jerry Scoggins played guitar, and Bert Dodson played bass. Carl Cotner remained, playing fiddle and directing the band, and Johnny Bond also remained, playing guitar for Autry. The Pinafores — Beulah, Eunice and Ione Kettle — were also now part of the show.

The fight to be released from his Republic contract occupied most of Gene Autry's time and attention during the fall of 1945. Autry had signed a seven-year contract with Republic in September 1938, then joined the service in July 1942. Autry, who long wanted to own his own movie production company, reasoned the contract expired in September 1945, allowing him the freedom to pursue an independent movie production deal. Herbert Yates and Republic argued that Autry, by joining the service, had not fulfilled his contract, that it was "suspended" during the time he was in the service and so, when he returned, he was obligated to three more years, or 21 more movies for that studio. Autry appealed to patriotism, arguing that he owed a duty to his country greater than his duty to Republic during the war, and also pointed out that Republic had not paid him anything during his service years.

At the time Autry enlisted in the armed services there were five movies left to be filmed under the third option in the five-year contract. This meant if the contract ran the full five years the termination date would be March 6, 1945. However, on May 11, 1942, before Autry enlisted, he and Republic agreed that one more year would be added to the 1938 agreement, obligating him to appear in eight more movies for $15,000 each. Republic picked up his fourth option, notifying Autry on March 3, 1944, even though Autry was in the service. But on June 17 of that year, Autry served Republic "a notice of termination of the agreements and employment thereunder by reason of military service." On June 27 he filed his case against Republic.

There is a California law (the "Shirley Temple law") that states no contract can run more than seven years, and Autry based his case on that. He hired attorney Martin Gang, who won a case for Olivia de Havilland against Warner Brothers based on this law. The case was decided in Republic's favor in February 1945 (although not entered on the court records until March 20), and Autry appealed. On November 7 the case went before Judge Louis Palmer of the Los Angeles District Court. Autry spent a week on the stand testifying. The Court ruled in Autry's favor, but Republic appealed the decision.[1]

On September 24, 1945, John Wayne signed a new seven-picture contract nonexclusive with Republic. In this contract he received ten percent of gross profits on his films, with a guaranteed minimum. If any of Wayne's films were profitable, he could make $200,000 or more.

On October 27 Autry's song "Don't Hang Around Me Anymore," was on the *Billboard* chart. On November 11 he recorded four songs. On December 29 Autry's recording of "Don't Live a Lie," backed with "I Want to Be Sure," was on the *Billboard* chart.[2]

Gene Autry was still a singing cowboy; he certainly dressed the part. But he increasingly recorded pop songs and sought a more pop-sounding backing on his recordings after World War II. This was the direction that country music increasingly took in the coming years, although that was not so obvious when World War II ended.

On January 11, 1946, Autry recorded "I Wish I Had Never Met Sunshine" (Dale Evans was a co-writer on this song), "Ages and Ages Ago" and two others.

At the end of January, District Court of Appeals Judge Charles E. Haas ruled that Autry owed Republic 21 more pictures. At this time, Autry had not made a movie since 1942, although some of his older films were reissued, and he realized the legal proceedings would keep him off the screen even longer. He had a successful career on the radio — although "Melody Ranch" was only a 15-minute program at this point — as well as a recording career and did well on personal appearances, but the movies provided him with a broad, national exposure that was vital to selling merchandise and created a demand for his recordings and personal appearances. And so Autry arranged to play golf with Herbert Yates.

During their golf game, Autry and Yates apparently came to an agreement, finalized shortly afterward, that Autry would do five more movies for Republic, receiving a percentage of the profits, during this legal battle. Further, if the courts decided in Republic's favor, he would oblige their terms — although there was little choice except quit the movies totally at this point. On the other hand, if the courts decided in his favor, Yates and Republic agreed not to fight further, tying him up in endless court battles.

Autry and Yates agreed to a minimum 18-day shooting schedule for his movies, and Autry received song and producer approval. On every other movie, Autry would receive $22,500 for starring; for the rest, he would receive a percentage of the gross revenue. Autry could also name Sterling Holloway as his co-star and sidekick. Smiley Burnette had left Republic for Columbia.

Gene Autry felt he was at a severe disadvantage if he remained at Republic because the studio had built up Roy Rogers during his absence. The two would compete for the best scripts, actors, songs, budgets, advertising and publicity at Republic — and a studio could maneuver things in such a way that Autry's movies always received the short end of the stick. This concerned Autry, who always wanted the best productions for his own movies and detested a situation where he did not come out first class.

In the summer of 1946, Autry worked on two movies, *Sioux City Sue* and *Robin Hood of Texas*, for Republic.

****

During the 1943–1944 movie season there were nine low-budget films under the "Smiley Burnette Productions" imprimatur. There wasn't much notable about them except Burnette introduced his best-known song, "It's My Lazy Day," in *Bordertown Trails*, released in 1944. After this series, Mitch Hamilburg negotiated a lucrative deal for Smiley at Columbia to co-star with Charles Starrett in the "Durango Kid" series. This meant he was unavailable for Gene Autry when Autry resumed making movies for Republic after the War.

****

Autry purchased a radio station in Tucson through his Pueblo Broadcasting Company. Autry owned 46 percent of the company, and already had a 15 percent interest in KPHO in Phoenix. Autry owned 25 percent of the World's Champion Rodeo Company and had Golden West Publishing company, which held copyrights to the songs he wrote and a number he recorded. All those trips to Washington and time spent with Congressmen paid off when Gene Autry needed help building his budding broadcast empire.

Autry signed an agreement to do a two-month tour as headliner for the Arena Managers Association (AMA) rodeo, which included appearances in Washington, D.C., beginning April 23, 1946, then on to Cleveland, Toronto, Pittsburgh, Providence, Rhode Island, and New Haven, Connecticut. The year before, Roy Rogers was the headliner. The rodeo tour was scheduled to end in June.

The rodeo tour was a smashing success and proved Autry's star had not dimmed during the years he was in the army. An article about the Washington appearance in *Variety* stated, "Autry could do nothing wrong for the several thousand youngsters who piled out to see him.... Autry makes two appearances, one in which he puts the oat burner through a series of fancy circus tricks, and the other in which he sings to string accompaniment by the Melody Ranch boys." He performed "Back in the Saddle Again" and a medley of "Marine Hymn," "Wild Blue Yonder," "Caissons Go Rolling Along" and "Anchors Aweigh." The article also noted that Autry had gained weight since going into service, and that his songs seemed a little corny for his city audience. That didn't matter much, since the kids were as entertained as ever: "Autry sings from the back of Champion, which, in turn, stands atop a large white grand piano in the middle of the arena."[3]

During the Washington appearance, a congressman from Mississippi stated he "couldn't stand Autry" because he "looks too much like Harry Truman." Autry related that story to the president when he visited the White House.[4]

May of 1946 was a busy month with appearances at rodeos. Then on June 5 and 6 he recorded eight songs in Hollywood. In June he had three songs on the *Billboard* Folk chart: "I Wish I Had Never Met Sunshine," "You Only Want Me When You're Lonely," and "Wave to Me, My Lady."[5] On July 2, Autry recorded "Cowboy Blues," "Gallivantin'

Galveston Gal," and "Someday." He received offers from Hill & Range and Peer International to purchase his music publishing companies for $60,000 but refused. Autry's publishing companies had no foreign distribution, which hampered his business, but he decided to work on that problem rather than sell to someone who did have overseas distribution. Besides, he owned 100 percent of the companies and saw the assets as a good business investment that would grow.

Gene Autry was building a business empire. In addition to the Tucson radio station, Autry and Tom Chauncey, who owned a jewelry store in Phoenix's Adams Hotel and whom Autry met while stationed in Arizona, purchased the newly licensed television station in Phoenix, which became KOOL. Television did not begin broadcasting until 1947, and 1948 would be the first full year of TV programming. Those early years were rough; Autry and Chauncey lost a reported $35,000 a month on the Phoenix station those first few years. They enjoyed profits from the radio market, but continued to depend on lines of credit and loans from banks to stay afloat. Although these assets would grow into great wealth in the future, at the time they were a financial drain that hampered his cash flow.

In the fall of 1946, Gene Autry performed at the Madison Square Garden rodeo for 21 days. On the way, Autry stopped in Cincinnati for some business, then boarded the train in that city, headed for New York. Eddy Arnold was on his way to New York for a recording session, having gotten on that same train in Nashville. Arnold went to the dining car and saw Autry talking with "someone from Columbia Records." Arnold remembered: "I waited until he'd finished talking, then went over and introduced myself. As soon as I said my name he said, 'I've heard your record.' I had 'That's How Much I Love You' out, and that was my first big hit. Gene Autry was a big, big star then — and I was just beginning. But he didn't slough me off — he treated me like a gentleman, and we talked quite a bit and became friends."[6]

The Madison Square Garden rodeo was followed by the rodeo in Boston; from Boston, Autry and his troupe traveled to Baton Rouge, Louisiana, where he performed at a rodeo. The rodeo tour of 1946 featured another important change for Gene Autry — his original Champion was retired, and a new Champ was the featured performer in the spotlight.

In November, it was announced that Autry had completed an agreement under which he would star in his own rodeo for two years in Madison Square Garden, performing for 26 days at the show each year.

A new bio was written for his record company, which stated, "The Autry miracle, if such it is, rests on the fact that Gene Autry has a good singing voice, but not a great one, rides adequately but not brilliantly, and is personable, but by no means has the look of a matinee idol. Shrewd and aggressive, he lives his career and confines his activities to what he knows. There is no record of Gene Autry having taken a flyer in exotic ventures or going overboard to develop talents he is frank to admit he lacks."[7] The bio also contained some digs at Republic and put an Autry spin on his walk-out and other disagreements with the studio.

By the end of 1946, Gene Autry had a new team in place for his organization. His personal secretary before the war, Dorothy Phillips, married a navy man and moved away. While at Luke Field in Phoenix, Autry met Louise Heising, who replaced Phillips. Heising was an accomplished musician — she played violin — and often played in the string section during the "Melody Ranch" broadcasts. Autry's publicist was Bev Barnett, who had served with him since 1938, while David Whalen headed the rodeos. Mitch Hamilburg remained Autry's agent, Armand "Mandy" Schaeffer was the producer of Autry's film unit, Bill Burch produced the radio show, Art Satherley supervised Autry's recording sessions, Carl Cotner was the musical director for Autry's shows, Oakley Haldeman headed the publishing companies, Johnny Brosseau was the ranch foreman and person in charge of construction at Autry's properties, and legal advice came from John O'Malvaney and Martin Gang.

An article on Autry in 1946 stated, "Despite his enormous wardrobe, the cleaning and pressing bill for which is fabulous, Gene Autry does not employ a valet. He is extremely fastidious about his appearance. His wife cares for his clothes at home. A handy man named Johnny Brosseau lays them out when on the set, and his horse trainer, John Agee, doubles in this respect while on the road with the rodeos. Otherwise, Gene takes care of himself."

The article added that Autry "has an extremely well ordered and happy home life, due in large measure to his competent wife's management." It was noted the Autrys lived in a "low-slung white ranch house," which Autry had built "in a remote section of the San Fernando hills" during the 1940s that was "originally intended as a place where Autry might corral his horses and get away once in awhile for a breathing spell.[8]

"For other purposes, he and Ina live in a conventional semi–Colonial house in a well populated part of North Hollywood, a few hundred yards off busy Ventura Boulevard."

Surrounded by eucalyptus trees, the house was described as "comfortable and delightful" and "filled with Ina's antique treasures and souvenirs and trophies Autry had picked up." The backyard was an acre or so. The house was "furnished in thoughtful, unostentatious taste," while Autry "maintained a small semi-circular building in which was located his own business office, the swimming pool bath houses, a rumpus room, and another small office for members of his staff."

Their previous home was the one that had been destroyed by fire in 1941, and "from necessity, and because Autry was about to don uniform, the Autrys moved into the ranch house." Upstairs, a huge playroom was furnished like an old frontier saloon with swinging ruby glass chandeliers. A festooned bar had pictures and caricatures of days of Billy the Kid and Annie Oakley. After the fire, Autry had a business office in downtown Hollywood but, the article said, "He hopes to build a larger, more conveniently located house, possibly in one of the Hollywood canyons, as soon as building restrictions permit."[9]

21

RUDOLPH,
THE RED-NOSED REINDEER

Trail to San Antone, released in January 1947, co-starred Peggy Stewart, Sterling Holloway, and the Cass County Boys. The *Variety* review noted that in the movie "Autry conducts his search for the horses via airplane and, in a climax that won't be believed even though seen, lassos the stray horse from the air."[1] *Twilight on the Rio Grande* was released in April and featured Sterling Holloway, Adele Mara, Bob Steele, Frankie Marvin, and the Cass County Boys; this movie took a bit longer to produce than his earlier ones — 18 days.

In *Saddle Pals*, released in June, Autry's co-stars were Lynne Roberts, Sterling Holloway, and the Cass County Boys. In this movie, Autry wore jeans and a western shirt, not his usual flashy outfit. *Robin Hood of Texas*, released in July, co-starred Lynne Roberts, Sterling Holloway, Frankie Marvin, and the Cass County Boys. This was Autry's last film for Republic, and a press release from the studio, attempting to undermine the star, stated the studio was not picking up its option for another picture. A spokesman for Republic stated, "We concluded that the income we would receive would not justify present-day higher costs of production."[2]

Around the time *Robin Hood of Texas* was released, the courts decided in Autry's favor, letting him form his own production company. This helped with income taxes by allowing him to keep more money. He signed with Columbia, headed by Harry Cohn. "It was as good a deal as anyone in Hollywood had at that time," remembered Autry.[3]

The deal with Columbia was a 50–50 affair; Autry had to pay half the production costs and received half the profits. The original contract, signed in 1947, was for two years and required four pictures a year. President of Gene Autry Productions was Armand Schaefer; vice-president and treasurer was his agent, Mitch Hamilburg, while his wife, Ina Mae, was secretary, and Autry was chairman of the board.

Autry wanted his future movies produced in color and wanted new, original hit songs for the films. However, the Technicolor Corporation, which owned the color process, was inundated with demands for color films and could not start work on Autry's movies for a year. For that reason, Autry's first film for Columbia, *The Last Roundup*, was not shot in color. Also, to hold down costs, Autry could use footage of a number of stock chase scenes that Columbia had in its vaults — but these were all in black and white. And so Autry's plan to star in color movies was put on hold.

When Autry signed his production deal with Columbia, a publicist conducted a long interview and wrote a rough draft report that served as the basis for a studio biography. The report gave his birth date as September 29, 1908, shaving a year off his age. The draft bio stated, "Next to horses, baseball is tops with Gene," and proclaims, "At one time he entertained a hope of becoming a professional player, and even made a semi-pro team in the South West.... Recently, he was called upon to say a few words at a sports writer's dinner, and launched into such an astute analysis of the current baseball season, replete with baseball vernacular, that the scribes, who thought they had come to hear a Hollywood cowboy drawl a few pat remarks, were properly jolted."[4]

The draft bio noted the actor "likes ketchup with worcestershire sauce [on his] steak. For breakfast, likes orange juice and ham and eggs, 'once over lightly.'" For clothing, Autry "doesn't have conventional business suit other than an Air Force uniform and one Bond Street dinner jacket his wife wanted him to buy when in London in 1939. His entire wardrobe is more or less as it is seen on the screen and personal appearances. Away from the limelight, he does not change into 'street clothes.' His suits, tailor-made to his own specifications by a capable Hollywood tailor, run to fine gabardine and whip-cords in light colors. Gene's favorite color is powder blue, and he has several shirts and suits in this shade. Also wears beige, light tan and for evening, cream white. All his off-screen suits are tailored with tight trousers and well fitting jacket, cut rather long, with lapels and pockets piped in contrasting colors. Always wears high-heeled, hand-made Texas boots in bright color combinations, the pointed toes intricately tooled, and the tops appliquéd with bright colored leather designs in the shape of butterflies, steer-heads, branding irons and other cowboy symbols.... Usually prefers white hats in traditional Oklahoma or 'foreman's Crush' ... has a huge hand tooled leather and Indian silver holster with carved ivory handled revolver" for his movies and personal appearances.

An article on Autry noted he flew his own Beechcraft plane and was "an indefatigable question asker. Although his education included high school, he has always felt that it was deficient.... He wants to broaden his understanding of world affairs, and although he reads sporadically, and usually limits his reading to the daily newspapers, which he devours from editorial page to want ads, he has a terrific memory for facts."[5]

Autry handled his own monetary and financial affairs and had investments in publishing, merchandising and "anything that looks like a paying proposition." He liked to play golf at the Lakeside Country Club, where he was a member with Bing Crosby and Bob Hope. His wife collected antiques, and it was reported Autry owned a flying school and a small chain of theaters in north Texas. He had a twin-engine Beechcraft and twin-engine Lockeed Load Star airplane, which he piloted with Herb Green.

****

In 1947 Johnny Bond witnessed a rare display of anger from Autry. At one of the Sunday morning rehearsals for "Melody Ranch" Autry stormed into the studio and confronted Bond and the other musicians, complaining the songs they performed on the

"Hollywood Barn Dance" on Saturday night were the same ones he had programmed for the next day's "Melody Ranch." Bond admitted that was true, but said it was "purely coincidental." Autry accepted the explanation and apology and the show went on.[6]

In June 1947, Art Satherley was in New York and heard a Christmas song he loved, "An Old-Fashioned Tree." Satherley obtained a copy of the sheet music and took it to Autry, telling him, "You have never made a Christmas record, and I have a new song that has never been recorded. I'd like to see what we could do with it."[7]

They needed a song for the B side of the single, but "there wasn't a number we considered good enough, so we decided to write one," said Satherley. Autry had an idea for a song, "Here Comes Santa Claus," based on his experience as grand marshal of the annual Christmas parade in Hollywood. As he rode in the parade, down "Santa Claus Lane" (the street was renamed for the parade) he heard children yelling, "Here comes Santa Claus! Here comes Santa Claus!" Autry outlined his idea for the song and gave it to Oakley Haldeman, who ran Autry's publishing company.

According to Satherley, a group "went up to a lovely home in the hills near Hollywood and sat out near the swimming pool on a very hot night to write this Christmas song. They had a colored couple make us dinner, and at 11 o'clock they served dinner. At four in the morning, the dinner was still on the table and had never been touched. We had been busy writing."

In the group was Harriet Melka, a lady friend of Satherley's who received songwriting credit on the original version of the song; Satherley himself also contributed, although the songwriting credit was finally given to Autry and Haldeman, who was responsible for the melody. Autry was not present at the songwriting session, although his basic idea was used, so in order for him to learn the song there had to be a demonstration recording of it because Autry could not sight-read sheet music.

The following evening, Satherley and Haldeman went to Johnny Bond's home where Bond had a small home studio with a disc-cutting machine. Bond learned the melody from Haldeman and recorded the demo after he prepared some drinks for his guests. As Bond recorded the song, the ice cubes from Satherley's drink were heard jingling in the background, giving them the idea of adding "jingle bells" to the recording.

"Here Comes Santa Claus," "An Old Fashioned Tree" and "Pretty Mary" were all recorded on August 28, 1947.[8] Before the record was released, Satherley noted, "We have tested it on about 400 people — children and grownups — and they all agree that it is a great record." A sales representative from the chain of Kresge stores had agreed "to put on a special drive for the Gene Autry Christmas record."[9] During the Christmas season of 1947, "Here Comes Santa Claus" became a huge hit for Gene Autry, selling over two million copies. It was quickly covered by a number of other artists, including Bing Crosby, the Andrews Sisters, Doris Day and Red Foley.

In September, Gene Autry performed at the rodeo in New York's Madison Square Garden, then at a rodeo in St. Paul, Minnesota. He made national news by kissing Elena Verdugo in a movie he made for Columbia, *A Little Spanish Town;* Autry's movies had previously avoided on-screen kisses with his leading lady. In November, he performed at the Boston Gardens for the rodeo.

Autry's first picture with Columbia, and his 62nd overall, was *The Last Round-Up,* which co-starred Jean Heather, Ralph Morgan, Carol Thurston, Shug Fisher, Frankie Marvin, Iron Eyes Cody, and the Texas Rangers. *Variety's* review stated, "Gene Autry has teed off his new Columbia production slate with a top western entry. *The Last Round-Up* has everything a good, actionful western should have to make it click in the outdoor market. There's knowledgeable production, direction and writing to give the action plenty of substance. It's certain to please the many Autry fans and should attract some new ones. Film bears evidence of higher than average oater budget.... The story holds water, a point not too common in westerns."[10]

At the end of 1947, Gene Autry's fan mail came primarily from girls 16 to 19 years old who obviously saw him as a heartthrob. He received $1,500 per personal appearance and owned a crop dusting company, radio stations, newspapers, a string of theaters, two music publishing companies, a 100,000 acre ranch, and 3,500 head of cattle. In December he recorded twelve songs, including President Harry Truman's favorite song, "Missouri Waltz," and "Buttons and Bows." There was a musicians strike called for 1948, and Autry — as well as other recording artists — needed to get as much "in the can" as possible.

****

At the end of World War II, *Autry's Aces* was edited by Virginia Siegers, who moved from Chicago to Los Angeles. She was assisted by Bonnie Baker and Myrla McDougall, both Canadian natives who had moved to LA.

Meanwhile, one of Gene Autry's most dedicated fans — and later a dedicated employee — moved from England to New York after the War. Alex Gordon became a die-hard Gene Autry fan in 1936, when he saw *Guns and Guitars* in his native England. He organized and ran the Gene Autry Fan Club in Great Britain until he served in the military. Gordon was a regular contributor to *Autry's Aces* and first met Autry in 1947 at the World Championship Rodeo in New York at Madison Square Garden. Autry, well aware of Gordon's work, invited him backstage for that initial meeting, which began a lifelong friendship and working relationship.

The 1948 Gene Autry Friendship Club (GAFC) convention was held when Autry and his troupe were appearing with the rodeo. At the convention Autry, Johnny Bond, the Cass County Boys and Frankie Marvin all sang to convention attendees while Uncle Art Satherley and Bill Burch, producer of the "Melody Ranch" radio show, conducted a question-and-answer session.

By 1948, the Gene Autry Friendship Club had 52,000 members in 64 chapters. Autry encouraged and supported the club; members of the club could get backstage to meet Autry just by showing their GAFC membership cards. "It was not unusual in the least for Gene to invite long-time club members to have lunch or dinner with him while he was appearing in their home area. He would visit with them at the hotel where he was staying, and club members were able to attend both the rehearsals and the actual broadcasts of Melody Ranch radio programs. Dot Crouse and some staff members made pilgrimages to California, where the hospitable Gene and Ina would entertain them in their lovely home."[11]

In 1948, Gene Autry began a tradition of hitting the road twice a year for a series of one-night stands; this continued for the next ten years. These shows lasted about two hours and were performed twice a day. The first tour usually began in January and lasted about six weeks, then Autry returned to Hollywood to make movies and recordings. He generally did not tour in the summer, but toured again in the fall, finishing in New York and Boston, where the big rodeos were held.

The cast and crew were transported by bus while Autry usually flew with Herb Green, who was in charge of booking the tour. In the cast were Pat Buttram, who performed comedy; Carl Cotner, who played fiddle and was the orchestra leader; Frankie Marvin, who played steel guitar and did comedy; the Cass County Boys (Jerry Scoggins, Bert Dodson, and Fred Martin), who performed trio numbers; the Pinafores, Johnny Bond, and Autry's horses, Champion and Little Champ. The horses traveled in a van specially constructed for them.

During the next few years, the personnel changed with others joining the tour. Smiley Burnette did a few tours; Rufe Davis joined as a comedian; Jack and Bobbie Knapp did rope tricks, acrobatics and had a trained dog; the Strong Family had a dog and rope act; and Eddie Peabody played the banjo. In addition, the Hoosier Hot Shots, Ginny Jackson, Judy Clark, Gail Davis, Barbara Bardo (who had an act with ropes and acrobatics and later married Autry's brother, Doug), Merle Travis, Tony White Cloud and three Indians who did authentic dances, the Candy Mountain Girls, and various other dancers and acrobats were on the tour at one time or another.

The 1948 tour began in Dallas and covered cities in Texas, Arkansas and Louisiana. On February 15 Autry finished the first part of his tour with an appearance at the Houston Rodeo. By this time, Autry and his partner, Everett Colburn owned the Gene Autry Flying A World Championship Rodeo, which kept their livestock at the Lightning C Ranch in Dublin, Texas. On March 23 he began a second series of one-nighters. On April 25 Autry was in Chicago, where he recorded "A Boy from Texas, a Girl from Tennessee" and "Blue Shadows on the Trail." The next night he finished this second series of one-nighters with an appearance in Chicago.

By June it was reported that Gene Autry received about 80,000 letters a month — the most of any Hollywood star. The Whitman Publishing company published 100,000 Gene Autry comic books a month, and there were five million copies of dime novels about Autry scheduled to be published over the next four years. He had just signed with Dell Publishing Company to make monthly selections of his eight favorite western stories. Gene Autry Jeans were made by the J. M. Woods Manufacturing Company of Waco, Texas, and young cowpokes all over the country were wearing them.

He owned 120,000 acres in Winslow, Arizona; another ranch in Florence, Arizona; the Autry-Marsh Flying School in Phoenix; KOOL in Phoenix; controlling interest in KOPO in Tucson; four movie theaters in Dallas; was a shareholder in the *Arizona Republic* newspaper in Phoenix; and owned the *Phoenix Gazette* with Smith Davis.

On August 11 he began a one-week stand of appearances at the rodeo in Great Falls, Montana, then did one-week stands at theaters in Milwaukee, Chicago, and Baltimore. On October 29, he began his appearances at the Madison Square Garden Rodeo, where his shows had been scaled back from 54 appearances over 33 days to 43 performances. It was the 23rd annual World's Championship Rodeo, but performers had begun to see empty seats in the stands. *Variety* reported, "New this year is Autry's presentation of his famed horse Champion Jr. and Little Champion, a colt, in a circus routine that left much to be desired."[12] In November, he appeared at the Boston Gardens Rodeo.

In August 1948, *The Strawberry Roan*, co-starring Gloria Henry, Jack Holt, and Pat Buttram, was released. The movie featured two Autry horses, Champion and Little Champ, and was filmed in Cinecolor. The *Variety* review noted that Champion was the real star of *Roan*: "beautifully photographed in shades which set off animal's beauty. Horse's training is demonstrated at every turn."[13] This movie was the first in which Pat Buttram was his sidekick and the first that featured Little Champ, a Tennessee walking horse marked like the original Champion which Autry had bought at Maryland Farms in Nashville for $1,500, "the most I ever spent for a horse," Autry said.[14]

On October 9 Autry's recording of "Buttons and Bows," from the movie *Paleface* entered the country and pop charts, where it peaked at Number six and Number eight, respectively.[15]

In January 1949, *Loaded Pistols*, co-starring Barbara Britton, Chill Wills, and Jack Holt, was released; the *Variety* review noted, "Musical spotting is so expertly done that action movement is never slowed. That's a major credit in itself for an oatuner."[16] This was followed by *Riders of the Whistling Pines*, co-starring Patricia White, Jimmy Lloyd, Clayton Moore, Jason Robards, Sr., and the Cass County Boys, then *The Big Sombrero*, filmed in Cinecolor and released in March 1949 and co-starring Elena Verdugo and Vera Marshe. The movie was the longest Gene Autry ever did — 82 minutes — and his second, and last, movie filmed in color.

Autry noted his films at Columbia, after the first few, "had taken on a whole new look. Gone were the fancy shirts and pants and modern trappings and settings. What emerged for the most part was Gene Autry, frontiersman. The cycle had come nearly full circle. By then we were groping, guessing, trying to find a trend. The B Westerns were slipping."[17]

****

The original story of *Rudolph, the Red-Nosed Reindeer* was written by Robert L. May in 1939. Bob May worked as a writer in the advertising department for Montgomery Ward in Chicago, and his boss requested a Christmas story that could be given away over the Christmas season at Montgomery Ward's chain of department stores.

It took May about 50 hours to write the Rudolph story. First, he decided to do a take-off of "The Night Before Christmas" by Clement Moore and use a reindeer as his main character. Then he picked the "ugly duckling" story for his theme and set about writing his story. But first he needed a name for his reindeer. May first chose "Rollo," but decided it was "too jolly" and then tried "Reginald" before settling on "Rudolph."[18]

There were 2.4 million copies of the book given away in 1939, but then World War II brought a paper shortage, so the second edition of *Rudolph* was not published until 1946, when Montgomery Ward distributed 3.6 million copies. The following year, Montgomery Ward turned the copyright over to May, and a publisher released 100,000 copies of a new edition. There had been some changes along the way. In the first edition, Rudolph and the sleigh carrying Santa almost collide with a tri-engine plane; the second edition has a four-engine plane, and the third edition has a huge speeding plane (with a jet pictured).

Songwriter Johnny Marks wrote the song, based on May's book, and began pitching it to various artists—including Bing Crosby and Dinah Shore—who all turned it down. Gene Autry would have turned it down too, but his wife, Ina Mae, liked it, comparing it to the ugly duckling story and insisting that kids would pull for the underdog.

On June 27, 1949, Gene Autry recorded two songs: "Rudolph, the Red-Nosed Reindeer" and "He's a Chubby Little Fellow," written by Oakley Haldeman, the head of his publishing company. By this time, Columbia had decided to create a line of children's records and put Hecky Krasnow in charge. During the next few years, Autry worked with Krasnow more than he worked with Art Satherley as Columbia increasingly aimed Autry's recordings towards the kiddie market.

Two days after the recording of "Rudolph," Autry recorded a children's story, "Stampede." During this story, Autry sang "Night Herding Song" and "Cowboy's Dream."

Columbia decided to release "Rudolph" for the Christmas season of 1949, and Autry originally wanted "He's a Chubby Little Fellow" on the B side. But on August 4 he recorded three more songs: "Santa Santa Santa," written by Haldeman, "If It Doesn't Snow on Christmas," a song co-written by Johnny Marks, and "Story Book of Love." It was decided to release "Rudolph" with "If It Doesn't Snow on Christmas," probably because of a commitment by the publisher to promote the record heavily.

Johnny Bond remembered that Autry and his new producer were not getting along well during the recording of the Christmas songs. Bond recalled they spent a great deal of time recording the selections. "We thought they would never get the takes to his satisfaction, but they did."

Bond, who played on the sessions, remembered that "Rudolph" was recorded on the first take; Autry also remembered that. If that's true, then it's probably why Autry said "Donner" instead of "Donder," which was the actual name of the reindeer in the poem "T'was the Night Before Christmas." (Donder and Blitzen are "thunder" and "lightning" in German.) Plus, "Donner" was easier to say than "Donder."

Autry apparently said of the song before they recorded it, "Nobody is going to remember the names of all those damned reindeer!"[19]

****

In July 1949, Autry did a three-week tour of one-nighters in Canada and the western United States. That same month, *Rim of the Canyon*, co-starring Nan Leslie, Jock Mahoney, Alan Hale, Jr., Denver Pyle, and Frankie Marvin, was released. On July 31 an article by Hedda Hopper was syndicated to a number of newspapers around the country. Autry took Hopper to Melody Ranch for the article and told her, "When I close that gate, I'm cut off from the world. This is a fine place to rest." Hopper then observed, "Rest is one commodity that the cowboy star doesn't seem to be able to handle." She noted his wife hadn't seen him for two days because he'd been in Arizona. The next day he was scheduled to leave on a trip that would take him to Dallas, New York, Chicago, Minneapolis "and a few other points east."[20]

Autry explained, "I have to go to Minneapolis for a newspaper convention, so I figured that I might as well drop by Dallas and take care of a little business." Hopper noted, "That is how Gene Autry operates—on the road 7 months a year, makes 6 pix during 5 months in Hollywood, and does a radio show each week." Hopper added, "This summer, to give the other members of the show a vacation, he transcribed four of the programs. While they rest, Gene will do three rodeo shows and 21 one-night stands of personal appearances. That's his idea of a vacation."

She quoted Bill Burch, producer of Autry's radio show, who stated Autry "has marvelous powers of recuperation. Many times between acts at a rodeo, I've seen him lie down and sleep for ten minutes on the bare floor. Then he'll get up feeling as fresh as a child. With ten minutes sleep, he's good for another seven hours. He can sleep any time and anywhere."

Burch noted that Autry "knows people all over the country, so when we're on the road he usually sits up until 4 in the morning, chatting with cronies. But bright and early the next day, he's ready for work." Hopper reported that Autry flew his own plane but handed over the controls to his publicity man in order to take naps on long hops.

"Why does he work so hard?" asked Hopper. "He loves it," she answered. "It's not for money," said Autry. "After a certain amount the government gets practically everything anyhow." Another Autry pal was quoted saying, "At heart, Gene's a horse-trader. He gets a tremendous kick from outwitting sharpies in business deals. That's why he'll never quit working. It's like a tonic to him."

Autry stated, "I don't suppose a man in my spot can slow down. You get so involved that you can't afford to take even a month off. So many people depend upon me for work, I feel obligated to those who've been loyal to me."

Remarking on Autry's 15 years in Tinsel Town, Hopper noted, "He's been happily married to the same woman for 17 years, and not a breath of scandal ever has touched them." There were stories about animosity between Roy Rogers and Gene Autry, but Autry said of Rogers, "Roy got a break and he would have been crazy not to take advantage of it. I would have, and so would most any other fellow." Although Autry, like most performers, kept a wary eye on his competition—and Roy Rogers was his chief competition—his real conflict was with Herbert Yates.

Autry claimed he played for "the real America." "One of the saddest things about the average New Yorker is that he thinks Hollywood people are dumb," said Autry. "I don't go for sophistication. Neither does the average American." He also disapproved of blue humor in his shows. "A few so-called sophisticates may appreciate it, but most people won't even understand it," he said. "And I don't like that kind of humor." The humor in Autry's shows tended towards the corny but clean.

"My rodeo show has proved to be Madison Square Garden's biggest annual attraction," he told Hopper. "And I believe the reason for that is that I don't try to compete with the Roxy in slickness. If the people want good, old-fashioned thrills and corn, they'll get it. I try to give them a show just like they'd find in a place like Reno. And the biggest thrill of my year comes with the free show we put on at the Garden for underprivileged children. The kids come by the thousands, wearing their wooden guns, jeans, and sombreros. When I sing they join me. To me that's show business. And the blind kids. You should see their faces. They want to touch my horse, run their fingers over my guns, feel my clothes. They break your heart, Hedda. It's all a matter of sticking to the real spirit of humanity. That's why I try to keep both myself and my shows simple and down to earth. I think Bing Crosby's success for the last 20 years can be explained by the same formula."[21]

On September 3 he began appearances at the Madison Square Garden Rodeo. That same month *The Cowboy and the Indians* was released, co-starring Sheila Ryan, Frank Richards, Jay Silverheels, Iron Eyes Cody, and Shooting Star. Songs included "Here Comes Santa Claus," "Silent Night," "America," and "One Little Indian Boy."

During his 1949 appearances at the Madison Square Garden Rodeo, Gene Autry introduced "Rudolph," with Frankie Marvin dressed as Rudolph, complete with a flashing red nose. The single was promoted heavily by Columbia Records, whose executives felt strongly they had a hit. It was a fairly safe bet, considering the book with the original story was quite popular.

In November, Autry starred in the last rodeo held at the Boston Gardens. Times were changing, and the big rodeos in New York and Boston faced dwindling crowds and less public interest. From this point, the rodeos would hold less appeal for easterners, and would generally become a sport centered in the West.

In November, *Riders in the Sky*, co-starring Gloria Henry, Pat Buttram, Mary Beth Hughes, Robert Livingston, Kermit Maynard, Denver Dixon, and Stan Jones, came out. On December 10 two Christmas songs from Gene Autry entered the *Billboard* charts; "Here Comes Santa Claus" would again be popular in the nation, but "Rudolph, the Red Nosed Reindeer" would rise to the number one position on both the country and pop charts and eventually sell over eight million copies — the second biggest selling single, behind "White Christmas," in the United States before 1955.[22] It was Gene Autry's biggest hit of all time.

By the end of the 1940s, Autry's "Melody Ranch" program was heard on CBS at 6:30 P.M. on the East Coast. It featured musical selections as well as a "Western Tale" of the day, a ten-minute fictional story with sound effects that often featured Hollywood actors. The show was heard in Los Angeles over KNX.

The show had become a much bigger production than in its earliest years, and personnel had changed since Autry resumed the show after World War II. By the end of the '40s, regulars included Pat Buttram as Autry's comic sidekick; Jim Boles, Wally Maher and Tyler McVey played various supporting roles; musical performers included the Cass County Boys, the Pinafores, the Gene Autry Blue Genes, Alvino Ray, Carl Cotner's Melody Ranch 6, Johnny Bond, the King Sisters (Donna, Alice, Yvonne, and Louise) and Mary Ford. The announcers were Lou Crosby and Wendell Niles. Bill Burch produced and directed the series, which was written by Ed James and sponsored by Wrigley's Doublemint gum. The theme song was "Back in the Saddle Again."

The big news of 1949 concerned television, and the Hollywood community was abuzz about the effect it would have on movies. Most in the film community looked down their noses at the fledgling technology and tried to ignore the young upstart while, at the same time, felt threatened by it.

The movie industry, organized under the Producers Association, agreed not to sell old movies to TV. However, the *Hopalong Cassidy* series was owned by Harry Sherman, who was not part of this group, and he sold the series to TV, making "Hopalong Cassidy" the first cowboy show on TV. It was a huge success, revitalizing the career of actor William Boyd and the Hopalong Cassidy trademark; the merchandise for Hoppy outsold all the other cowboy heroes. At this point, Republic agreed not to sell its old movies — including those by Gene Autry — to television. Autry sensed the B western era was ending and wanted to get into the new medium, so he began plans to develop a television series. This caused much controversy in the Hollywood community, and much consternation among movie distributors.

22

TOURS AND TELEVISION

At the beginning of 1950, Gene Autry was probably worth around $4 million. He made about $1.5 million a year, but taxes took 90 percent of personal income at that level; however, Autry had structured his corporations to take the bulk of his income, saving him from the high personal tax rate in his income bracket.

Long-time friend and sideman Frankie Marvin noted, "What Gene's done doesn't mean beans to him. It's what he's doing and gonna do that counts." A magazine article stated, "Gene pretends to play golf," but during the celebrated golf match set-up between Autry and Roy Rogers, covered with a full spread in *Life* magazine, Gene shot 102 and Roy 105.[1]

"A quick game of bridge or canasta is really Autry's only frivolity," the article continued, and Autry "has just bought a half block on Sunset Boulevard where a big super market sat. He's remodeling it into 24 offices, and putting up a sound stage on the parking lot. He'll bring his TV operations there, his music publishing firm, his own offices, and several other Autry enterprises.[2]

In February it was announced that Autry, in business with former heavyweight boxing champion Jack Dempscy and S. D. Johnson of Wichita Falls, Texas, had struck oil in Oklahoma, with an estimated flow of 200 barrels a day. The partnership also operated in some north Texas oil fields.[3]

Autry's comment, when asked about his many activities, was usually "If it was easy, everybody'd be doin' it!"

Another article noted, "Probably the biggest disappointment of Gene's life is that he has no kids running round his house." It also noted, "Ina, Gene's wife, is a devout and practicing Christian Scientist. Gene's not."[4]

In 1950, Gene Autry's "Melody Ranch" radio show, heard on Saturday nights over CBS at 8 P.M. Eastern Time, celebrated its tenth anniversary, still sponsored by Wrigley's Doublemint. During this year, the production was increased, with more singers, writers and actors hired. Bev Barnett was hired to promote the show. During the year, the show began to be taped, which meant mistakes could be corrected.

In January, Autry's seventieth movie, *Sons of New Mexico*, was released, co-starring Gail Davis, Clayton Moore, and Frankie Marvin and produced by Armand Schaefer.

This was the first film that featured Gail Davis as Autry's leading lady; there would be thirteen more. Davis toured extensively with Autry during the coming years, appeared in 15 of his TV shows and starred in the Flying A Production of the "Annie Oakley" TV show.

Born Betty Jeanne Grayson in Little Rock, Arkansas, Davis studied drama at Harcum Junior College for girls in Bryn Mawr, Pennsylvania, and finished her studies at the University of Texas, where she was a beauty queen. She may have first caught Autry's eye in Texas, where he invited her to call if she came to Hollywood.

In her senior year in college, Gail joined a group that entertained soldiers at camp shows. During this time she met, fell in love and married Captain Robert Davis. In 1946, after Davis got out of the service, they moved to Hollywood.

Davis appeared in her first picture, *Room 303*, for RKO in 1947; her second picture, *The Romance of Rosy Ridge*, was also for RKO. That same year she was in *Merton of the Movies* (MGM) and the next year appeared in *If You Knew Susie* (RKO), which starred Eddie Cantor and Joan Davis, and *The Far Frontier* with Roy Rogers at Republic, while his co-star Dale Evans was pregnant. She did several more films with Republic — *Death Valley Gunfighter* and *Frontier Marshall*, both starring Allan Lane, and *Law of the Golden West* starring Monte Hale — then returned to RKO where she appeared in *The Judge Steps Out*. She appeared in a Durango Kid movie, *South of Death Valley*, starring Charles Starrett and Smiley Burnette in 1949 for Columbia, before her first movie with Autry.

Gene Autry kept up with other actors and actresses for possible roles in his movies; his partner, Armand Schaeffer, may have seen Davis in one of those movies and recommended her to Autry, which led to a role in *Sons of New Mexico*.

On January 7, 1950, Autry began a string of personal appearances in Pueblo, Colorado. During January, he performed in the states of Kansas, Nebraska, South Dakota, Minnesota, Wisconsin, Indiana, Michigan, New York, Pennsylvania, Massachusetts, Rhode Island, Connecticut, Maine, New Jersey, Pennsylvania, Virginia and North Carolina as well as three dates in Canada. Most of his performances were in towns or small cities, although he did perform in Chicago, Detroit, Toronto, New York City and Washington, D.C., on this tour.

On February 22 the movie *Mule Train* was released. Co-starring Sheila Ryan and Pat Buttram, this movie opens with Autry and Pat Buttram performing the title song; Autry then sings a current hit, "Room Full of Roses," followed by "Old Chisholm Trail" and "Mule Train" twice more. On March 2 Autry recorded "Peter Cottontail" in New York, then it was back on the road to South Carolina, North Carolina, Georgia, Tennessee, Alabama, and Mississippi. The tour concluded in Shreveport, Louisiana, at the end of March. In April, "Peter Cottontail" entered the *Billboard* charts; it reached Number Three. In May, the movie *Cow Town* was released, co-starring Gail Davis, Jock Mahoney and Harry Shannon. *Beyond the Purple Hills* — co-starring Pat Buttram, Jo Dennison, and Hugh O'Brian, with songs "Dear Hearts and Gentle People," "Beyond the Purple Hills," and "The Girl I Left Behind Me" — was released in May. This movie began with a group singing the title song as an overture; an instrumental of "Polly Woddle Doodle All Day" was performed, and Autry sang "Beyond the Purple Hills" and "Dear Hearts and Gentle People."

In April, Flying A Productions was formed to film "The Gene Autry Show," a half hour series for television. Mitchell Hamilburg and Armand Schaefer were Autry's partners in Flying A, and the offices were initially located at 6000 Sunset Boulevard.

Autry watched Bill Boyd as Hopalong Cassidy reap a huge income and renewed popularity from his TV series, which consisted originally of edited movies. Then he watched "The Lone Ranger," starring Clayton Moore and Jay Silverheels (who had both appeared in his movies), created with adaptations of radio scripts. Autry did not own the rights to his Republic features, so if Republic put those on TV, he had no say and reaped no rewards; therefore, he decided to (1) begin his own TV series and (2) block Republic's efforts to edit the 56 movies he had done and run them on television.

Television was in its formative stage so each new show was a bit of a gamble, particularly filming a half hour series when many of the early TV shows were either live or an adaptation of a successful radio show. But the biggest gamble was whether a movie star still starring in films could capture a television audience and, at the same time, have audiences pay to see him in theaters. Gene Autry was the first movie star to take this gamble.

Flying A Productions set up a permanent shooting location in Pioneertown, near Palm Springs, and Autry soon learned that filming a half hour TV series was quite different than filming a feature. First, the TV show had to be 26 minutes on the nose whereas his features had no set time limit, although most were roughly an hour in length. Next, the production crew had to adjust their shots for a small screen TV instead of the big screen in movie houses. To make this adjustment, the crew eliminated long shots and concentrated instead on close ups. The camera shot horseback riders at a closer range and riding across the screen rather than towards the camera. Whites and lighter shades were emphasized, while darker portions of the picture were kept deep gray instead of flat black.[5]

The production used 35 mm film and lots of music; in fact, Flying A licensed the first TV film music with the American Federation of Musicians. Carl Cotner composed and conducted the TV score, which had background music behind about 80 percent of each show's action, helping create the desired mood. Autry had to get special permission from James Petrillo, head of the American Federation of Musicians, for permission to use music; the union had turned down other requests, and some arrangers had scored TV shows in Mexico.[6]

Later, TV shows on the network would be shown coast-to-coast; however, "The Gene Autry Show" began on only six CBS-TV outlets. These six — in the biggest markets — were sponsored by the William Wrigley, Jr. Company, the same sponsor for Autry's "Melody Ranch" radio program. After the first couple of shows, the Autry show did appear coast-to-coast, but there were different sponsors in different markets, while Wrigley continued to sponsor the six original markets. The show was broadcast on Sunday evenings, and audiences grew as more and more people bought TV sets in the early '50s.

There were usually two shows filmed at the same time, using identical casts and crews; there would be 26 half hour shows filmed that first season. The first one completed was "Gold Dust Charlie," although the first show televised was "Head for Texas." The first six taught Autry and his production crew some valuable lessons. The first plots were too complicated for the half hour format, and Autry tried to fit in too many songs. Autry and his crew quickly learned that TV shows "needed to be simple and direct in order to entertain a home audience."[7]

"The Gene Autry Show" premiered on Sunday night, July 23, 1950. "Head for Texas," the first episode, featured Autry with Pat Buttram as his sidekick and Barbara Stanley as his love interest; he sang "Sing Me a Song of the Saddle" on that show. "Gold Dust Charlie," episode two, featured Autry, Buttram and Buttram's wife, Sheila Ryan. Autry had four songs in this show: "Mexicali Rose," "Cowboy Blues," "Home on the Range" and "Great Grandad." No other Autry TV show would ever have that many songs; most of the shows had Autry perform one song. On August 6 "The Silver Arrow" featured "Can't Shake the Sands of Texas from My Shoes" and "The Doodle Bug."

Since his recording career was increasingly geared towards children after the success of his Christmas songs, in late July and early August Autry recorded "Bucky the Bucking Bronco," "Rusty the Rocking Horse," "Little Johnny Pilgrim," and "Guffy the Goofy Gobbler," as well as the big pop hit by the Weavers, "Goodnight Irene."

The movie industry was scared that once TV arrived there would be no more demand for movies; further, a Supreme Court ruling led to movie studios getting rid of their chain of movie theaters. This left the movie industry wondering if they would make movies in the future and, if so, would anyone watch them. Some advocated a boycott of TV productions, while others tried to figure out how to capitalize on the new medium. Herbert Yates organized the Hollywood Television Service as a division of Republic to distribute the studio's films to TV networks and stations. Gene Autry and Roy Rogers would have no say in negotiations about their movies being used on television.

Autry caught heat from movie distributors for his television shows, which saw the move to TV as a betrayal of his movie career and a threat to movie distributors who saw TV in terms of loss of revenue. P. J. Wood, secretary of the Independent Theatre Owners of Ohio, criticized Autry for making films, and an Ohio exhibitor cancelled four Autry features, then wired Abe Montague, Columbia general sales manager, this message: "I cannot compete, charging admission for Gene Autry on my screen, with free home television showing Autry in new pictures. It's a sin to think Autry would betray theater owners who made possible his popularity and financial success in years past by switching his talents to television when theaters are in such critical times as at present."[8]

Autry responded, "I am not an enemy or traitor to the exhibitor. On the contrary, I have proved over a period of years that I am a friend of the industry, but let's look it square in the face — television is here, television is going to stay here and the sooner we all start figuring how to benefit from it rather than run from it, the better off we all will be."

He continued, "In all the years I have made pictures exhibitors in metropolitan situations have seldom given me a break. If they did run one in a downtown house it was always at the bottom of a twin bill, giving the major companies a better break. My pictures have always played the smaller towns. At present, TV does not reach these areas, so how could television hurt my pictures at the box office when they have not been given fair exhibition in the large cities in the first place?"

Autry concluded that exhibitors were buying his old pictures, reissued, instead of his newest films, "simply because they are a little cheaper," and observed, "I know that the exhibitor is complaining about bad business. But do you think that he always uses his best judgment in booking pictures?"[9]

On Monday, October 3, 1950, Gene Autry flew to Pittsburgh from New York, where he was appearing at the Madison Square Rodeo, to give a talk at a movie distributor's gathering. *Variety* reported he "twirled a mighty fetching lariat, but failed to corral any sizable number of exhibs." The article continued: "Everyone agreed that Autry's heart-to-heart was a sincere and warming statement of his case for making six pix for TV, but he still hadn't convinced them that they could sell what he was giving away."[10]

Autry came "to answer face-to-face exhib squawk that tele pix which he's making are unfair competition by a star who made his fortune in theaters — and furthermore are hurting b.o. of his own westerns." The article noted he encountered a "pea-shooter-size barrage of questions from the floor" and "most of the 200 exhibs Autry faced were deferential and many even friendly during his talk. He got a number of rounds of applause, with the boys who were blasting him so heatedly a couple weeks ago seemingly eating out of his hand as nicely as his own cow pony." However, after Autry left to fly back to New York, the *Variety* reporter observed, the talk "hadn't changed a single mind."

The article pointed out that Autry had "brought up a couple of old sores. He pointed out that exhibs had never paid high terms for his pix and have demonstrated they'd rather book old reissues (he owns no financial interest in 60 films made for Republic) than new and better product at higher prices. He likewise declared that in many large cities his pix still can't get dates, and 'many kids don't even know who Gene Autry is except through radio.' ... Autry slapped exhibs' wrist for failing to study radio and television to figure out ways it can help them." During the talk, Autry noted he'd paid $10,000 for the rights to the song "Mule Train," which sold five million records, but "theater men made no effort to capitalize on it and his pic of that title wasn't booked in L.A. until a year after the tune hit its peak."

Gene Autry attempted to placate the theater owners that fall by promoting the movie industry on his radio show. At the end of October, Autry asked the audience listening to his Sunday night "Melody Ranch" broadcast to 171 stations over CBS, "Have you been to a movie lately? Well, if you haven't you're missing some of the best entertainment there is, and I mean that. Of course, we'd prefer you saw one of our pictures, like 'Cowtown' or 'Indian Territory,' but the most important thing is that you see a moving picture. Make it soon, now, won't you?"[11]

Meanwhile, Autry's TV show appeared each week, with Autry usually singing one song per episode. On October 8 it was "Mellow Mountain Moon," on October 15 it was "Goodbye to My Old Mexico," on October 22 it was "Night Time in Nevada," on October 29 it was "Cool Water," and on November 5 it was "Painted Desert" and "Broomstick Buckaroo."

In late 1950, Autry was finishing the last of his initial group of 26 TV shows. In production were two episodes, tentatively titled "Scorched Earth" and "The Gray Dude." In "Scorched Earth," Pat Buttram played a rainmaker who set off a cannon that caused rain. Buttram stood about three feet away when the cannon exploded in the wrong direction, sending debris in Buttram's chest, jaw and through his left boot, where it severed an artery. Word of the accident was relayed to Herb Green, waiting with an airplane about four miles from Yucca Valley where the accident occurred. Green took off and picked up a doctor and some blood plasma in Los Angeles; meanwhile, Buttram was put in a pick-up truck and driven to a hospital in Twenty-Nine Palms, where Dr. Bill Ince, son of movie pioneer Thomas Ince, worked. Buttram was laid up for nine months but recovered.

Because of deadlines and production costs, filming had to continue. "Scorched Earth" was retitled "The Peacemaker," and popular character actor Chill Wills was hired to fill in for Buttram. Dressed in the Buttram costume, he appeared in that show and in the accompanying "The Gray Dude." In the next two shows, "Hot Lead" and "The Killer Horse," Alan Hale, Jr. was Autry's sidekick. In the final four shows shot that season, "The Sheriff of Santa Rosa," "T.N.T.," "The Raiders" and "Double-Barrelled Vengeance," Fuzzy Knight was Autry's sidekick. This accident with Buttram led to Smiley Burnette re-joining Autry in the last six movies Autry made.

Late in 1950 Flying A Productions began producing a second TV series, "The Range Rider," starring Jock Mahoney and Dick Jones. This show premiered during the 1951 season.

The movie *The Blazing Sun* was released in November, co-starring Pat Buttram, Lynne Roberts, Anne Gwynne, Alan Hale, Jr., and Frankie Marvin. On the *Billboard* country and pop charts were "Frosty the Snowman" (Number Four country and Number Seven on the pop chart) and "Rudolph, the Red-Nosed Reindeer (Number Five country, Number Three pop.) On Christmas Eve, his TV show aired, with guests Fuzzy Knight, Dick Jones and Stanley Andrews and Autry singing "Marquita" and "Tweedle-O-Twill." On New Year's Eve, those who stayed home could watch him sing "Tears on My Pillow" on his TV show. It was a fitting way to end the busy, productive year.

From January 13 through March 23, 1951, Autry played a string of one-nighters, beginning in Topeka, Kansas, and ending in Peoria, Illinois. On this tour he played in Kansas, Iowa, Nebraska, Illinois, Missouri, Indiana, Kentucky, Michigan, Ohio, Pennsylvania, New York, Connecticut, Maryland, West Virginia, Tennessee and Arkansas.

Gene Autry's tour in early 1951, with Smiley Burnette a special guest, drew record crowds and record profits. A *Billboard* article stated the 37-day tour played two standing room only shows in Bowling Green, Kentucky, turning away 1,500. Those shows grossed $19,785.45, while a stop in Peoria, Illinois, grossed $13,123.45 at the 6,000 seat Bradley Fieldhouse. On these shows, the top ticket price was $1.85 and the lowest was 60 cents.[12]

In Baltimore, Autry played to 11,000 people on Sunday, February 11; there were 7,000 at his matinee and 4,000 at the evening show at the Fifth Regiment Armory. The gross from ticket sales was around $19,800, with tickets priced at $1.20, $1.80, and $2.40. Earlier that day, Maryland governor Theodore R. McKeldin and Baltimore mayor Thomas D'Alesandro were at the airport, along with several thousand fans, to greet Autry when his private plane landed.[13]

By this time, Autry owned four planes: a light single-engine plane, two twin-engine cabin craft and a large twin-engine transport ship. The cabin planes were expensive to operate; it cost $60 to $75 an hour for either of the two in the air. Autry certainly needed the planes for travel. By 1951 he was doing six films each year, filming his TV program, doing about 120 personal appearances and touring with his rodeo 60 days annually.[14]

During his personal appearance tour two of his movies were released. *Gene Autry and the Mounties* co-starred Pat Buttram and Elena Verdugo, and *Texans Never Cry* co-starred Pat Buttram, Gail Davis, and Russell Hayden.

Autry always stayed in hotels during his tours, telling Johnny Bond, "You stay at someone's home, you're his prisoner for the day and night. You can't make a move without his knowledge or permission and his time is your time. That's why I always turn down such invitations regardless of who it is that might ask, even a close friend. Now, that's when you're working. If you're on vacation and have no deadlines, that's something else." Bond agreed, but noted that he "never knew Gene Autry to take a vacation!"[15]

Autry dressed well—he owned 50 to 75 cowboy suits that cost him an average of $250 each. Money was rolling in—in addition to his radio show, heard each Saturday evening, fans saw him on television each Sunday evening and purchased an array of items with Gene Autry's name and picture on it, including wrist watches, rubber and leather boots, toy pistols, hats, belts, dolls, and Gene Autry Jeans. Autry licensed his name and likeness, relying on one of his business dictums: "Operate on the other fellow's money."[16]

****

After the tour, Autry entered the recording studio in Hollywood and did "Mister and Mississippi" (a hit for Patti Page, Dennis Day and Tennessee Ernie Ford—all in 1951) and another song on March 21, three songs on March 26 and two Easter songs, "Bunny Round-Up Time" and "Sonny the Bunny," on March 31.

On April 20, Autry recorded his last song that would appear on the country charts in *Billboard*, "Old Soldiers Never Die," backed with "God Bless America." The song entered the chart in June, but only lasted one week. The recording was inspired by the firing of General Douglas MacArthur by President Harry Truman. This firing caught the American public by surprise and created a backlash against the unpopular president; MacArthur was considered a war hero.

Autry's recording of "Rudolph" was not the only record of his selling well. Jon Guyot Smith compiled a list of 43 two-sided 78-rpm records by Autry on Columbia in 1951 that were still in print, indicating continued sales. Smith also noted three records were released on 45-rpm records—a new format at the time—which indicated a market demand for "I Wish I Had Never Met Sunshine"/"You Only Want Me When You're Lonely"; "Have I Told You Lately That I Love You?"/"Someday You'll Want Me to Want You"; and "At Mail Call Today"/"I'll Be Back."[17]

In May, the movie *Whirlwind* was released, co-starring Smiley Burnette, Gail Davis, Frankie Marvin, and Stan Jones. In June, *Silver Canyon*—co-starring Pat Buttram, Gail Davis, Bob Steele, and Frankie Marvin, with the songs "Ridin' Down the Canyon" and "Fort Worth Jail"—was released. In November, Autry did a tour of Canada, playing nine cities as well as performances in North Dakota, South Dakota, Iowa, Illinois, and Michigan. On October 19 Autry and his troupe performed before 25,000 people at the Forum in Montreal; the next day they played in Burlington, Vermont.

During the tour, traveling from Edmonton to Saskatoon, the group faced a snow storm. Some members managed to fly ahead, including Johnny Bond. But Bond forgot to bring his guitar—his job was to go with Autry on visits during the day to hospitals, orphanages, and luncheons and if someone wanted a song, Bond played while Autry sang. The incident brought out a rare display of anger from Autry, who chastised Bond, saying, "Listen Bond. If it ever gets to the point where it looks like the show might be delayed — if YOU can get here, bring your damned guitar. At least you and I can start it and keep them entertained until the rest of the crew gets here. Have you got that straight?" Bond learned his lesson.[18]

Rodeos had a difficult time lining up top talent. The International Rodeo, held in Chicago in October, had Harpo Marx as their main talent, whereas the World's Champion Rodeo, which opened at the end of September, featured the Lone Ranger for the first 12 days and then Vaughn Monroe for the last two weeks. Gene Autry turned down appearances at rodeos he did not book himself, while Roy Rogers turned down all offers, and Bill Boyd (Hopalong Cassidy) refused to work any shows that charged admission.[19]

On October 30 Autry filed suit in federal court to stop Republic's sale of his films to television. Roy Rogers had just won a similar suit.

Autry put his brand on a variety of products in 1951. His Melody Ranch Food company endorsed food products, except candy and bread, through Martin Stone Associates.[20] Late in 1951, Autry signed a merchandising deal for Range Rider clothes for youngsters, the first time he merchandised a clothing line without his name on it. Autry knew the value and money in merchandising, so when his Flying A Productions began producing TV shows, he made sure he held the merchandising rights to those characters. An article at that time noted "Gene Autry cap pistols began sales in 1934," and since that time "over 10,000,000 have been sold."[21]

Everywhere he went, Gene Autry was seen and photographed wearing western clothing. "In my business, you always have to be the character that the kids imagine you are," he noted. "I don't mind wearing cowboy clothes because, if you don't, the kids lose the illusion."[22]

Valley of Fire, co-starring Pat Buttram, Gail Davis, Russell Hayden, Frankie Marvin, and William Fawcett, came out, but an important member of the Gene Autry team died in November. John Agee, the 80-year-old trainer who taught all the Champions their tricks for the past dozen years, passed away. Agee had worked as Tom Mix's trainer for 14 years before joining Autry, and prior to that time had worked with Buffalo Bill's *Wild West Show* and the Ringling Brothers Circus.

During the 1950–1952 period a number of stories on Ina Mae Autry appeared in fan magazines. Ina Mae had generally stayed in the background from her famous husband until this time. She was certainly active in his career, but in a behind-the-scenes capacity, helping with his fan club and businesses.

There were several articles with Ina Mae's byline. These types of articles "by" a celebrity tend to be written by a publicist or someone on the star's staff; however, the writer generally talks with the subject first to get an idea of what he or she wants to say. While everything in these articles cannot be accepted at face value, there are a number of interesting observations and insights in these pieces that ring true.

In *Radio Best*, Ina Mae stated Gene had "an easy-going, tolerant nature.... He absolutely refuses to allow anyone to get him really mad."[23] In an article titled "Marry

Your Man for Keeps," Ina Mae said Gene "has utterly no fears or inhibitions, never the slightest thought that he might fail."[24]

In "An Open Letter to Gene Autry," Ina Mae observed, "You sing around the house and in the corral, as much, if not more, than you sing in a picture or on the air. You are never angry with anyone, seldom lose your temper.... I believe I have your mother to thank for what you are."[25]

Mrs. Autry told her husband, "In the house, you are the most needing-to-be-waited-on-man a wife ever waited on! If left to fend for yourself at home, you'd surely starve. Not only can't you boil an egg, you would not boil an egg. Why, you won't even get yourself a glass of water! And you are not, emphatically, a picker-upper of your clothes. You keep your desk, the corral, the office, everything that concerns you in immaculate order but you don't always find your way back to the closet with your clothes. Yet you are the most fastidiously groomed of men! You never slop around the house in old clothes, never."

Discussing his eating habits, Ina Mae told Gene, "You are a funny man about food. You will not try new things to eat. You won't even give a new recipe an experimental taste. There are certain things you like and want to eat and do eat, every day in the year — steak for dinner, ham and eggs for breakfast and often the mustard greens, black-eyed peas and cornbread that you loved so when you were a boy in Oklahoma.... You won't eat candy. You eat very few desserts. You don't smoke ... but you are an inveterate gum-chewer."

Ina Mae revealed that around their home there was "never the conventional six o'clock dinner; more likely it's eight, or nine or even nine-thirty.... We never do the same thing two consecutive days or night.... You are not a reader, except of newspapers.... We watch television (you like the fights).... Once in bed, the instant your head touches the pillow, you are asleep.... You can sleep anywhere, at any time (except at a baseball game).... You have so many pairs of those pointy-toed, high-heeled, elaborately tooled Texas boots of yours, they bulge the very walls of the house."[26]

In another article, Mrs. Autry noted her husband had an "utter disregard for time. In his business life — on the radio show, for instance, and on his personal appearance tours — everything must be timed to the split second. Perhaps that is why, in his personal life, he refuses to notice a clock ... [although] one of his pet hobbies is collecting interesting and unusual timepieces." She said she "never expects him for dinner until he puts one boot inside the door. Sometimes when he's terribly late he finally remembers to call and say, 'Honey, I'll be home very soon now' ... [but] he's liable to show up an hour or even two hours later."[27] She noted, "Gene doesn't like to be pinned down to social engagements — or anything else for that matter — too far in advance and that's always been a great cross for me. All of our entertaining has to be pretty much a last-minute affair, except for the two big parties we give every year at Christmas and New Years." She concluded: "Gene likes to do most things on the spur of the moment — when the mood strikes him."[28]

Ina Mae noted, "We have quite a large home. It covers approximately 6,000 square feet, including 1,500 square feet of closet space. We have one full-time housekeeper (she's been with us ever since Gene returned from the service) and a man who comes once a week to do the heavy cleaning ... [then] along comes Gene and inside of ten minutes he can have any room looking as if a cyclone had just swooshed through it. He's immaculate about his person, but he's lived in hotel rooms so much of his life that he's forgotten how to pick up after himself, I guess."[29]

In a magazine feature titled "Gene Autry at Home," the writer stated, "Gene's study ... [has] a rope design carved in the ash paneling [which] outlines built-in book shelves; some old six shooters have been mounted on handsome walnut bases and fashioned into lamps. There's a western corral scene in a glass enclosed diorama occupying the length of one entire wall and on the other walls hang many handsome trophies." The article observed that their home in the San Fernando Valley had "a master suite ... [with a] fireplace (there are four fireplaces in all in the house) and a seven foot bed, private baths and separate dressing rooms for each.... Gene's long rows of closet space (1,000 square feet) which houses his enormous colorful wardrobe ... one closet built especially to hold 50 of his hats with shelves sized and spaced to accommodate the wide brims and high crowns of his identifying Stetsons. Another closet contains only boots."[30]

A special article on Gene and Ina Mae's home in Laurel Canyon noted the couple had twin white Cadillacs, and Gene had a telephone installed in his. The home was situated on four and a half acres. The article noted, "A long hall runs horizontally through the house linking the living room, playroom, and dining room on one side, with a stairway curving to the upstairs bedrooms, on the other. The three main rooms downstairs look out onto a flagstone terrace. All have outside windows, with a huge picture window in the playroom that is a solid wall of glass ... above the flagstone fireplace is Remington's "Bronc Buster." ... [On the] opposite wall is a life-size portrait of Gene by Howard Chandler Christy." The Autrys stated: "we can entertain anywhere from fifty to a hundred and fifty guests."[31]

The popularity of Gene Autry was so great that even his secretary warranted a feature story. "I've taken dictation from Gene Autry on planes, cars and trains, between hot action shots on a sound stage, in broadcasting studios, in his dressing room and the living room of his home, and over the long distance phone. Gene has enough business deals buzzing to keep me perpetually dizzy," said Louise Heising, in a by-lined article.

Heising worked as a violinist in the orchestra at the Arizona Biltmore in Phoenix in June 1943, when Autry trained at Luke Field. Since the "Melody Ranch" radio program was broadcast from Phoenix at this time, Heising worked as a violinist in the group backing Autry on his radio show. Autry's secretary decided to marry and left, so he needed a new secretary. According to Heising, "I knew neither stenography nor bookkeeping but he said I could learn both." About working with Gene, Heising stated, "I've never seen Gene unpleasant, but he sure knows how to get his way."[32]

In another article, Louise Moraweck, as she was known after her marriage, stated, "Gene is consistent and even-tempered. Perhaps I should say he has a complete lack of temperament. So many actors are 'stars.' He's not one of them. He's just Gene." Moraweck continued, "On the other hand, he's full of energy. On the road he doesn't mind a seven-day-a-week schedule, matinee and evening performances, Sunday rehearsal and radio show or visits to the governor, mayor, or city officials. Whenever there is a break in the day, his first stop is the children's hospital. He works best when he has most to do. Yet he never loses his temper — though I can tell you he's had plenty of occasions to do so."[33]

23

GOLDEN WEST

The tour of 1952 began on January 15 in Wichita with two days of rehearsals, then a show on the 17th. After the show, Autry and some of his cast members flew to an oil rig, in which he had invested. After Wichita, the show went to Missouri, Iowa, Illinois, Wisconsin, Indiana, Ohio, West Virginia, Pennsylvania, New York, Rhode Island, Massachusetts, Connecticut, Maryland, North Carolina, South Carolina and Florida, where it ended in Miami on February 23 after two days of shows.

The tour of one nighters attracted 243,844 fans.[1] A review of Autry's show in *Billboard* stated, "Autry is a polished showman. Obviously aware that his name will pull the moppets in droves to areas where his radio, TV and motion pictures are popular, he has infiltrated his routine with enough salable material to insure the attention of the adults as well as the kiddies."[2]

The reviewer noted the show began "with a darkened stage, shots are heard and the lights come up on a Western setting with three masked cowboys supposedly shooting it out with their victims. Into this scene comes Autry, his gun blazing, and the show is underway." There was a 12-piece house band, but "Autry, of course, is the focal point during the entire hour. He not only tells a few gags which fit in with his character, sings, and works his two horses, but emsees [sic] as well. There is also a strong supporting cast including the Marino Sisters, three top fem acro-dancers; Cass County Boys, Pat Buttram, Jemez Indians, Jack and Bobby Knapp, rope experts, and others." The show finished with "Autry bringing on Champion, who goes thru his paces with ease despite the confines of a theater stage."[3]

A fall tour, that began on November 17 in Wichita Falls, Texas, went to 18 different cities in 21 consecutive days (he played two days in Little Rock, Arkansas and three days in Columbus, Ohio) before it finished on December 7 in New Orleans.

On tour, Autry was usually awakened by an early morning phone call; he dressed in a costume cowboy suit with a white hat and colorful boots — always a different outfit from the day before. He had breakfast in his room and went over his schedule for the day. If the troupe was scheduled to be in a different town the next day, they traveled by bus with a truck and van carrying the horses. Trunks of costumes and stage props left the night before to set up in the next town.

Autry traveled either by car or plane to the next town. When he got to his plane, he put overalls over his outfit and co-piloted with Herb Green. In the plane or car he opened his mail and read *Daily Variety* and the *Hollywood Reporter*. When he landed he was met at the airport by VIPs, politicians, reporters and photographers, then went to a children's hospital where he sang a few songs, which was reported in the next day's newspaper, usually with a picture. There would usually be a luncheon with the mayor or the Rotary Club where Autry spoke briefly, often about national or local affairs. The motion picture distributors, radio stations and record stores all wanted Autry to stop by, and he obliged as many as possible.

Visiting children's hospitals was an important part of Autry's personal and professional life. He recalled his first visit to a children's hospital. "From then on I knew that I was a special being," he said. "I was a hero to the children of this country, whether I liked it or not. I didn't like it. It scared me. How could I — or anyone else — live up to the kind of hero worship you get from kids? I'm only human and I've got plenty of human failings."

Autry said his wife told him, "'Gene, you've been more blessed than most. Yours can be more than fame or money, if you'll have the courage to take hold of it.' More blessed than most.... Those words stayed with me."[4]

Autry actively promoted his appearances and believed strongly in a good publicity and public relations machine at work. He had an "advance man" who was in a city prior to his arrival and made sure everybody knew Gene Autry was coming to town by planting stories with local newspapers, purchasing ads in the papers, and arranging visits with key dignitaries, children's hospitals, and civic organizations.

At the hotel, he was met in the lobby by fans — generally kids and moms — wanting an autograph. The troupe usually did two shows each day, two hours each — a matinee generally scheduled for 4:30 P.M. so kids could come after school (except on Saturdays and Sundays when the matinees were at 2:30 P.M.) and an evening performance. Before the matinees Autry often hosted a cocktail party, a meet and greet for local VIPs, where he shook hands, had his picture taken, and spoke briefly.

The shows generally played before audiences of 3,000–4,000 people in auditoriums. The show began with Autry singing "Back in the Saddle Again" as the curtain opened on the troupe, followed by Autry greeting the crowd. The curtain backdrop had a western setting so the stage looked like the interior of a ranch house, with a fireplace and mountain and desert scenes outside the window.

Autry was active throughout the entire two hour show, introducing each act. He did comedy with Frankie Marvin (who sometimes sat in the audience as a jokester), then an act did trick roping or dancing. This was followed by a musical act, then comedy with Johnny Bond and musical numbers with the group — usually six or seven songs. After a ten minute intermission, when customers bought merchandise or snacks, Autry came back on stage in a new costume, then brought out the Cass County Boys, comedian Rufe Davis, did a comedy routine with Pat Buttram and Frankie Marvin, then a song.

In many ways, Autry's traveling road show used the same format as the WLS "Barn Dance" in which performers remained on stage during the performance and took their turn when the time came as a wide variety of entertainment performed for the audience.

During the time Autry was not on stage, he was usually in his dressing room, reading the movie and music trade papers or playing cards; gin rummy was a favorite.

For the closing, Autry rode Champion on stage, and they went through their routine of steps, dances and tricks. He finished with the "End of the Trail" pose. After "thank you's" and a farewell talk, Autry sang "Back in the Saddle Again."

After the matinee, there was a two hour dinner break, and the cast went back to the hotel for dinner. Then they came back to the auditorium and performed the show all over again. They did this every single day for about three months each year. It was a grueling pace, but Autry thrived on it. He was one of the hottest acts in show business, able to draw crowds wherever and whenever he played. He told friends and associates, "We gotta get 'em while we're hot," aware he would not always be a top draw. He admonished his cast, "We're young, we can take it." He was fond of saying, "I think we're gonna break even today" as he watched the crowd come into the venue.[5]

Some of the cast complained about the packed schedule. Autry confided to Johnny Bond, "I can't afford to let these tours tire me out. I know that a lot of guys are beginning to complain about them behind my back, but what would they be doing back home? I do these tours because I like them. A fellow has to get it while he can. When you cool off, you're a long time cold, remember that. Another thing, I need the cash to pay my income taxes. I make six to eight pictures a year — that's only sixteen weeks of work. Well, what the hell, I'm not about to sit around Hollywood and starve to death. You take Tom Mix and those guys. Buck Jones, Art Acord, and a lot of other Western actors. They made money but I doubt that they left a whole lot behind. That's not going to happen to me. I've been broke and I don't like it. I don't plan on going back to it if I can help it. I've got me a way of making money now and I aim to stick with it as long as possible. Money is the one thing that people respect. When you're hot you're hot and when you're cold nobody loves you."[6]

In the early 1950s, Autry told Bond, "I've got to make a lot of changes in my show. We're going to have to put a little more class into our show. I don't want us to get corny like that Grand Ole Opry bunch. Why they're still wearing those hick costumes, straw hats, smoking corn cob pipes, same sort of stuff they've been doing since the twenties. They never improve. Now, me I want more class. We've got to keep up with the times — switch to a regular western costume" because, as he was fond of saying, "For a little bit more you can go first class."[7]

In January 1952 it was announced that Flying A Productions, owned by Gene Autry, Armand Schaefer and Mitchell Hamilburg, had acquired the television, radio and merchandising rights to the Annie Oakley comic strip created by Eli H. Leslie. Autry announced plans for 52 episodes for the series, which was scheduled to film in the spring. Autry also announced he would hold contests around the country to find the right actress to play the role.

Gail Davis remembered: "I wanted to play the part, and I went in to talk to Mandy Schaefer, the executive producer. He said, 'Gail, you're too well-known as Gene Autry's leading lady in 14 feature films with him. We have to find an unknown for the part!' They tested over 200 girls throughout the United States, and when they came back I said, 'Mandy, please just let me test!' I went in one day and put on a pair of blue jeans and boots, a gingham shirt ... and no make-up. I put freckles on my nose with a pencil, and I put my hair in pig-tails. I told Mandy, 'Just give me a break!' And he replied, 'Well, I guess the least we can do is give you a test!' They did ... and I passed."[8]

On April 8 Gail Davis was signed to Flying A Productions to star in the Annie Oakley TV series. The first episode, "Bulls-Eye," was a pilot to pitch to agencies and clients. In addition to Davis, the show starred Brad Johnson as Deputy Sheriff Lofty Craig and Jimmy Hawkins as Tagg Oakley. But that pilot wasn't sold right away; in fact, it took quite a while before sponsors were found for the show. In a later interview, Gail Davis remembered: "The sponsors wouldn't buy it because they didn't think a girl could carry the show."[9]

On June 19 Autry went into Radio Recorders Studio where he recorded three songs; the next day, he went back and recorded two duets with Rosemary Clooney, "The Night Before Christmas Song" and "Look out the Window." After the session, some of the musicians went down to his office at the corner of Sunset and Orange, where he had a plush upstairs quarters with a bar. Reading *Daily Variety*, Autry said to his agent, Mitch Hamilburg, "Hey, Mitch! It says here that KMPC is for sale. Whatta you say we pawn one of our enterprises and buy it?"

The station belonged to the estate of George A. Richards, who died May 29, 1951. Just before his death, an examiner from the Federal Communications Commission recommended news slanting by KMPC should be dropped. Richards's widow did not want to deal with problems from the FCC or running a radio station, so she put the station on the market. Autry organized Golden West, a company that would own broadcasting stations, and on November 20, 1952, the *Los Angeles Times* announced the sale.

Autry's major partner was Bob Reynolds, a former All-American football player (he played tackle) at Stanford and pro player for the Detroit Lions. At Stanford, Reynolds became the only player to play the full 60 minutes in three Rose Bowl games. With the Lions, he played under owner George A. Richards, who hired him to work for KMPC in 1937. At the time of the sale, Reynolds was general manager of the station and a minority stockholder.

Golden West purchased KMPC for $800,000, paid in capital stock of $300,000, which served as the down payment. The loan was paid off from the station's cash flow. The firm soon added radio stations in San Francisco, Seattle, and Portland. The San Francisco and Portland stations reportedly cost about a million dollars each; a little less was paid for KVI in Seattle. The Seattle station, which carried mostly religious programming and gospel music, was losing money. When Golden West purchased it, they cancelled all existing contracts and made it a pop music station. During this period, Autry went to Washington frequently to meet with politicians and Federal Communications Commission members in regards to his broadcast licenses.

Gene Autry had turned 45 years old by the time of the announcement of his purchase of KMPC. He realized his days as a star performer were limited — few performers lasted into their 40s, and Autry wanted to be successful when his performing days were over. Besides, he liked business and being a businessman.

In 1952 Autry purchased his home on Brookdale Road in Studio City. On five and a half acres he built a Spanish style house with filigreed wrought iron posts in front. He added azaleas and crape myrtles, oaks and ferns. The home had a white brick patio, sloping lawn and large pool. Inside the home were red throw-rugs on hardwood floors with pictures of birds and animals on the wall. There was a piano, which Ina Mae played, and in the large study a collection of silver and gold rodeo buckles was arranged neatly on Autry's desk. There was also a trophy cabinet filled with signed baseballs.

In 1952 Monogram Studios folded, and Autry bought the 110-acre lot in Santa Clarita and renamed it Melody Ranch. The lot was a working movie set, with a western town built for location shots. Autry installed a miniature railroad and wanted to eventually turn the ranch into a museum and amusement park open to the public. During the years it operated as a movie set, actors such as John Wayne, Gary Cooper, William Boyd (Hopalong Cassidy), Clayton Moore (The Lone Ranger) and Autry filmed there. The opening scene of the TV series "Gunsmoke," starring James Arness, was filmed there. During the 1952–1953 season, "The Gene Autry Show" was to be filmed there.

Autry was fond of nicknames. He called Johnny Bond "Jonathan Q," Pat Buttram was "Big Butt," Roy Smeck was "Rick Smack," Red Foley was "Burr Head," Art Satherley was "The Chinese Hillbilly," and Carl Cotner was "Flutter Tongue."

Several new movies were released. In *The Old West* Autry co-starred with Pat Buttram, Gail Davis, Lyle Talbot, and Frankie Marvin. In *Night Stage to Galveston*, released in March, the co-stars were Pat Buttram, Robert Livingston, and Clayton Moore, who would gain fame as "The Lone Ranger." In *Apache Country*, released in May, Autry co-starred with Pat Buttram, Carolina Cotton, Iron Eyes Cody, and the Cass County Boys. *Barbed Wire* was released in July, and in September *Wagon Team* was released, co-starring Pat Buttram, Gail Davis, Dick Jones, Frankie Marvin, and the Cass County Boys (Fred Martin, Bert Dodson, and Jerry Scoggins).

In the fall of 1952 "The Range Rider" TV series began in syndication. It appeared originally on CBS sponsored by Table Talk pies. There would be 78 black and white shows filmed, and 23 issues of "The Range Rider" comic book appeared.

During 1952 it was announced "The Gene Autry Show," along with "The Range Rider," would be shown on Italian television for a three-year run beginning January 1953.[10] Autry also announced the formation of a booking firm, Melody Ranch Enterprises. Officers for the venture were Autry, his wife, Ina, and Herb Green, who had booked Autry's personals for five years. On November 18 Gene Autry headed out with his troupe for a series of 20 one-nighters.[11]

The last four months of 1952 were busy ones for Gene Autry; he filmed two movies for Columbia, filmed ten shows for his television series, did a ten-day rodeo booking and 23 one-nighters of personal appearances, hosted his weekly radio show and did a recording session.[12]

Things were changing for Autry in 1952. His long-time producer, Art Satherley, resigned from Columbia. In Hollywood news, CBS purchased Mascot's old property in Hollywood and renamed it Television City. Herbert Yates married Vera Ralston, a young actress he tried to promote as a star; unfortunately, she did not have the acting talent to match his promotional push.

Gene Autry made the news when the normally mild-mannered star was sued for $10,000 by Harrison Willard. Autry slugged Willard on the chin when the man called Autry a name; the suit was later dismissed.

24

THE END OF
THE SINGING COWBOYS

In 1953 Gene Autry filmed his last singing cowboy movie, *Last of the Pony Riders*. By this time, there were only 3,000 movie theaters that booked B pictures and small westerns, much less than the 8,000 in Autry's Republic heyday. Further, most of the 3,000 were in financial trouble. In May, an article in *Variety* noted that Paul Mertz, the composer who scored for Autry's movies, had left Columbia and Autry had completed his movie contract. It was noted "studio execs are awaiting returns on his latest pictures before considering a renewal."[1]

Autry was closing one chapter in his life at this point; this same year he went back to London for a three-week stand, continued production on his television and radio shows, did more recording sessions and kept up his hectic touring schedule.

In early January, it was announced the Federal Communications Commission had approved the transfer of ownership of KMPC in Los Angeles and KSWB in Yuma. KMPC would be owned by Melody Ranch Enterprises, with Autry holding 51 percent interest, while KSWB would be owned by Maricopa Broadcasters, Inc., with Autry holding 85 percent.[2]

On January 14 he began his annual tour in Wichita, Kansas, and performed two shows a day in Kansas, Nebraska, Iowa, Missouri, Iowa, Illinois, Indiana, Ohio, Michigan, New York and five Canadian cities. During the tour of one-nighters Autry grossed the incredible sum of $585,548, while amassing an attendance figure of 329,218. There were 27,672 more attending Autry's matinee performances than his evening shows. The matinees generally saw two children for every grownup, while the evening shows were split equally between children and adults. The top ticket price was $2.50 with children twelve and under admitted for half price. Some promoters wanted to eliminate the half price tickets in some of the smaller venues, but Autry insisted on that practice because he didn't want any kids turned away because of the cost of a ticket.

This was the most profitable tour since Autry began touring one-nighters in 1948. The tour finished at the Uline Arena in Washington, D.C., on March 1; that venue was sold out twice. In fact, over half the dates played were complete sell-outs.

There were some rough spots on the tour. In Omaha a fierce blizzard caused a number of cancellations, and in Kansas City, the flu epidemic resulted in less than half the house being filled. Still, half a house was considered good because the local newspapers had run stories warning parents against letting their children get in crowds. There were several other cities in the Midwest where the flu was the cause of less-than-capacity houses. In Vincennes, Indiana, a pouring rain held back fans.

In an interview with *Billboard*, Autry attributed the successful tour to three factors. The first was television, and Autry noted that in the cities where his TV show played, attendance was significantly up from the 1951 and 1952 crowds. This was especially true in Indianapolis, Providence, South Bend, Indiana, and the Illinois cities of Peoria, Joliet and Champaign. The second factor was the weather. Although Autry toured during the winter months of January and February when snow, sleet and rain are expected, there was a minimal amount of bad weather encountered during the tour. The final factor was "that unknown factor in show business that makes a performance hot or cold. Autry was hot this time around."[3]

In addition to Autry, there were about 25 performers on the show, including the Hoosier Hot Shots, Pat Buttram, Johnny Bond, Gail Davis, the Cass County Boys, Carl Cotner, Frankie Marvin, the Four Strongs, the Winter Sisters, Barbara Bardo and Gene's Melody Ranch Group.

Early that year several movies were released: *Winning of the West* co-starred Smiley Burnette, Gail Davis, Robert Livingston, William Fawcett, and Frankie Marvin, and *On Top of Old Smokey* co-starred Smiley Burnette, Gail Davis, Sheila Ryan, and the Cass County Boys. The title song for that movie was a current hit for the Weavers, whose earlier hits included "Goodnight, Irene." *Goldtown Ghost Riders* was Autry's 90th film; it co-starred Smiley Burnette, Gail Davis, and Denver Pyle. On three consecutive days in June (24–26), Autry recorded Christmas songs.

In April 1953, Gene and Ina Autry received a notice from Uncle Sam that they owed $142,400 in back taxes. The Autrys had claimed a net taxable income of $15,013 for 1952, but purchased $6 million in government bonds. In a petition filed with the government, it was revealed that Autry had borrowed the money from a finance company to buy the bonds and then claimed the interest paid was deductible from his taxes. The government disallowed his claim.

Autry wasn't the only one to get caught with this; Danny Thomas was also notified about back taxes. The tax shelter that Autry invested in involved purchasing bonds where the interest on the loan for the bonds was greater than the interest and appreciation on the treasury notes. Autry deducted the interest he paid from his regular income and reported the gain on the sale of the treasury notes as a capital gain. Autry claimed a capital gain of $37,500 on a $4 million dollar note and an $80,312 gain on a $2 million dollar note. His interest payments on the $4 million notes were more than $78,000 and $141,737 on the $2 million note.[4]

In June, Autry's long-time guitar player and right-hand band mate Johnny Bond resigned to go to Dallas. Autry said to him, "Hate to see you go. But, there comes a time in every man's life when he has to take that giant step. Tell you what. If things don't work out to your satisfaction, you can always come back. Your job'll still be here, waiting."

Before the end of the year, Bond came back and re-joined Autry. According to Bond, "Not once did he ask me to explain or go into any form of detail as to what had happened both here and in Dallas, or to otherwise explain my actions or what was going on inside my feeble brain. While some of the gang were digging me deeply, not Gene. This, to me, was the sign of a big, big man."[5]

Pack Train was released in July 1953 and co-starred Smiley Burnette, Gail Davis, Sheila Ryan, Frankie Marvin, and Kermit Maynard. The *Variety* review stung: "Autry's star duties are carried out satisfactorily in his customary style, but his kiddie fans will probably prefer that he slim down to hero size, if this oater series continues."[6]

On July 27, 1953, Gene Autry began an 11-week British tour at the Empress Hall in London with the Cass County Boys, Pat Buttram, Carl Cotner, Tony White Cloud and His Hoop Dancers, the MacQuaid Twins, and Gail Davis; Mrs. Autry and Mitch Hamilburg also went along. The tour concluded with a three-week stand at Earl's Court in London, where crowds filled the arena every night.

In July, "The Gene Autry Show" moved to Tuesday nights on CBS TV, while his next to last movie, *Saginaw Trail*, was released in September. On October 29 Autry went into the studio to record more Christmas songs.

On September 25, 1953, Jimmy Long died in Springfield, Missouri; he was 64. Long's song "That Silver Haired Daddy of Mine" was the record that made Gene Autry a recording star back in 1931–32. Long sang harmony on Autry's initial recording of that song, moved to Chicago with Autry and toured extensively with him in that area.

Jimmy Long became the first consistent source of hit song material for Gene Autry. Growing up "during an era in which sentimentality was not scorned, and many of the popular song hits featured plaintive, nostalgic lyrics," Long not only wrote original compositions but also gathered "old, forgotten songs which publishers dusted off and put forth with his name attached to them." Jon Guyot Smith points out "such novelty songs as 'I Was Born 4,000 Years Ago' and 'I Had But Fifty Cents' are among the latter group." Although Jimmy Long was credited with writing and first recording "That Silver-Haired Daddy of Mine," it is not certain he actually wrote the song. Dallas Burnette (wife of Smiley) once told Jon Guyot Smith that she recalled Smiley saying "Silver-Haired Daddy of Mine" was composed "by a convict."[7]

Songs that Long wrote for Autry included ""My Old Pal of Yesterday," "Mississippi Valley Blues," "The Crime I Didn't Do," "I'm Always Dreaming of You," "Have You Found Someone Else?," "In the Cradle of My Dreams," "The Old Folks Back Home," "Shine On, Pale Moon" "Gosh, I Miss You All the Time" and "Red River Lullaby." With Paul Dennis, he composed "Old Missouri Moon" and "Angel Boy."[8]

Autry's switch from the Jimmie Rodgers–type blue yodel to the 19th century type of sentimental ballads altered his career and put him on the path for his greatest stardom. But by mid–1937, Long was no longer part of Gene Autry's professional life. From that point forward, Jimmy Long played music as an avocation, not a profession. Long's wife, Jessie, had died in 1949; their two children, Jack and Beverly, survived.

The man who introduced Gene Autry to the young lady who became his wife was never interviewed by those writing about Autry during the 1940s or early 1950s. And Gene Autry rarely ever mentioned him in interviews.

****

Gene Autry's final movie, *Last of the Pony Riders*, was released in November 1953. Co-starring Smiley Burnette and Kathleen Case, it featured the songs "Sing Me a Song of the Saddle" and "Sugar Babe." According to the *Variety* review, "Gene Autry sings his swan song.... It is a regulation oater for a giddyap market that has dwindled sharply under the impact of television. Autry takes time out for only two oatunes during the 58 minutes of footage.... Autry's heroics are concerned with protecting the mail franchise, held by the Pony Express so he can set up a new stage line.... Autry's valiant heroics are mixed in with some Bible-reading by the star and a general 'right always triumphs' theme."[9]

In his last six movies, some filmed in 1952 and the rest in 1953, Autry came full-circle, reunited with Smiley Burnette. Over thirty years later, in his autobiography, Autry reflected on the end of his movie career and stated, "No one planned it that way, certainly not me, but that pretty well closed the pages on the series, or 'B' Western chapter of Hollywood history.... It just kind of slipped up on us. I don't remember ever saying that I had quit, or that I would never make another motion picture."[10]

"The fact is," wrote Autry, "I never really left the business. The business left me. Hollywood started turning out a new type of Western and half of the B theaters that had carried my films, and others like them, closed down. The other half started showing porno flicks. Meanwhile, television swallowed up the rest, the old Autry and Rogers and Hopalong Cassidy movies, and swamped our homes with the made-for-TV series: 'Gunsmoke,' 'The Virginian,' 'Have Gun, Will Travel,' 'Bonanza.'"[11]

"It may not stretch a point to say that we lost a little more of our innocence with the passing of the B Western," he continued. "Sportsmanship was the cloth we peddled. The good guy always won, but how he won and by what rules counted, too. Does memory trick us into thinking our way was better, and more fun? We thought so then.... And don't be misled by that B rating. Those movies were made and directed and produced by men who didn't think the work was unimportant."[12]

The year 1954 began with Gene Autry in the studio January 4 recording "Easter Mornin'," "The Horse with the Easter Bonnet" and two songs written by Smiley Burnette, "Closing the Book" and "It's My Lazy Day."

Around 9:30 in the evening of May 18 Don Law, head of the country division of Columbia Records, accompanied by Joe Johnson and Troy Martin from Autry's Golden West Melodies, was at the Nashville airport waiting for a private plane, Beechcraft number NC 830082, to arrive.

About ten minutes later the twin engine plane made a large circle over the field, landed and taxied to the hangar. The door opened and Gene Autry, Johnny Bond, Carl Cotner, Herb Green and Charlie Adams of Ridgeway Music Company all stepped out. It was an all-day flight from Los Angeles, and Gene was at the controls.

Don Law wanted Gene Autry to come to Nashville to record. "In Hollywood, he always has sixteen guys following him around and the phone is always ringing constantly," said Law. "Consequently, it was very difficult to get him to devote his undivided attention to the serious business of making phonograph records. I felt reasonably sure that if I could ever get Gene to myself in Nashville for a few days, we could make records every bit as good, or better, than the ones he made some years ago that were such fabulous sellers."[13]

Autry, Law and the others spent the next day in a hotel room, listening to songs. "He considered, literally, hundreds of songs and finally selected eight which we felt had good commercial possibilities," said Law. "That night, Gene and Johnny Bond carefully learned and rehearsed them. In the meantime, I had lined up a band consisting of the best country musicians in Nashville." The two recording sessions "went like clockwork. Gene was completely relaxed and had never sung better in his life," said Law.[14]

Don Law made those comments in July 1954, in the *Autry's Aces* newsletter. However, although eight songs are mentioned, session records show only six were recorded: "You're the Only Good Thing That's Happened to Me" b/w "20/20 Vision" was the first release, and the second release was "When He Grows Tired of You" b/w "It Just Don't Seem Like Home When You're Gone." The third release from that session was "You're an Angel" b/w "I'm Innocent."

Country music was popular in the early 1950s, but the 47-year-old Gene Autry had not kept up. The country charts were dominated by Webb Pierce, Eddy Arnold, Red Foley, Hank Williams, Jim Reeves, Hank Snow and Carl Smith. It was more "southern" than "western," although many of the performers wore western-themed outfits. The corporate center for country music had become Nashville, while the country music industry in Los Angeles, led by the singing cowboys, had been swallowed up by the movie industry, which increasingly produced adult westerns with psychological dramas.

Autry had found the song "You're the Only Good Thing That Happened to Me" in the Nashville prison where he had performed. Prisoner Jack Toombs gave the song to Autry, written on schoolbook paper, and he recorded it. Autry acquired the rights to the song "Just Walking in the Rain" from publisher Red Wortham. The song was written by Johnny Bragg and Robert Riley, two inmates at the Tennessee State Prison. Bragg was a member of the Prisonaires, whose recording of the song was a regional hit. Autry claimed to have recorded the song (although no records of the session or copies of the recording have been found) and felt it could be a big hit. Autry asked one of his employees, Joe Johnson, to approach publisher Wortham about buying the copyright. Wortham felt the song had run its course and sold it to Autry's publishing company, Golden West Melodies. Don Law took the song to Mitch Miller in New York who recorded it with Johnny Ray; Ray's version was a Top Five hit in 1956.[15]

At the Nashville recording session was Autry's old friend, Fred Rose, and the two reminisced. It would be one of their last meetings; on December 1, 1954, Fred Rose died.

That fall, Gene Autry made his first appearance on the Grand Ole Opry. He was one of the few country artists who had not appeared on the Opry. Autry flew his own plane into Nashville for the WSM National Disk Jockey Festival and then, on November 20, sang on the Opry.

Although he continued to draw large crowds to his shows, Gene Autry would never again be the dominant recording artist he had been during the 1930s and 1940s; a major reason was a new factor on the horizon. In 1954, Bill Haley recorded "Rock Around the Clock," and Elvis Presley made his first records for the Sun label, "That's All Right, Mama" b/w "Blue Moon of Kentucky." This would be the beginning of a rock and roll tidal wave that swept the music of Gene Autry and his generation off the radios and turntables of young Americans.

In September 1954, "The Gene Autry Show" switched to Saturday nights on CBS-TV. During 1955 the "Buffalo Bill, Jr." television show ran on Saturday mornings. Dick Jones played the fictional son of Buffalo Bill Cody with Harry Cheshire as Judge Ben Wiley and Nancy Gilbert as Calamity, his sister. The show was set in Wileyville, run by Judge Ben Wiley.

News that the "Annie Oakley" show had finally found a sponsor reached Autry and Gail Davis while they were in London in the summer of 1953. Filming began on October 26. The show was sponsored by Canada Dry and T.V. Time Popcorn. When the series was reviewed by *Variety* in January 1954, the publication expressed doubts a female could carry the lead in a weekly TV series. However, by the end of 1955, Annie Oakley merchandise sales topped the $10 million mark. It was sold in some 18,000 department and specialty stores and included items such as Annie Oakley dolls, lamps, comic books, puzzles, lunch boxes, records, and games.

Filming the show, Gail Davis remembered that "my routine consisted of getting up at 4 A.M., being in front of the cameras by 6 A.M. and filming until sundown. We were doing 3 shows a week to start with, and working 7 days straight to do it. We filmed at Vasquez Rocks (North of Hollywood), the Gene Autry Ranch (at Newhall), Apple Valley, and at Pioneer Town.[16]

"They just didn't have the money in those days! We didn't even have a 'honey wagon' up there in the middle of the desert. That was my biggest complaint to Mandy Schaefer.... I'd say, 'Mandy, the least you could do is get us a 'honey wagon.' We had to go to the bathroom behind a rock."

On the opening shot, Davis said, "I did the 'close-up' shot standing up in the saddle with the horse riding at a full gallop. My double, Donna Hall, who stayed on for the full-run of the series did the long-shot. Donna was absolutely wonderful."[17]

On September 30, 1955, "The Adventures of Champion," a half-hour TV show, premiered on Friday evenings on CBS. The show starred Barry Curtis as Ricky North, Jim Bannon as Sandy North, Francis McDonald as Will Calhoun and Ewing Mitchell as Sheriff Powers. Champion the Wonder Horse and a German shepherd named Rebel also starred. The show was set in the 1880s in the Southwest.

That same day Autry was in a recording studio doing Christmas songs and a duet with Cass County Boy member Bert Dodson on "You've Got to Take the Bitter with the Sweet." On October 4 he was back in the studio and did another song by Nashville prisoner Jack Toombs, "Two Cheaters in Love," as well as "If Today Were the End of the World."

The last program of "The Gene Autry Show" was shown on its regularly scheduled Saturday night slot at the end of 1955. On this last show, titled "Dynamite," Autry sang "Sierra Nevada." The previous three shows were a trilogy entitled "Code of the Flying A," designed to be shown as a movie. Directed by George Archainbaud, with screenplays by John K. Butler, the shows were titled "Saddle Up," "Ride, Ranchero!" and "The Rangerette." The cast included Pat Buttram, Sally Mansfield, Leonard Penn, the Cass County Boys, and songs on the program were "Gallivantin' Galveston Gal," "Pretty Mary," "Ridin' Down the Canyon," "Blue Montana Skies" and "Old MacDonald Had a Farm."

These shows were shown December 3, 10, and 17; the final show of the series was aired on Christmas Eve, although there would be reruns of past shows on CBS until the summer of 1956. The TV shows filmed in 1955 were all done in color, which meant those 13 shows cost about 30 percent more to film than the ones in black and white.

Autry wanted to continue the TV series, but when CBS requested that Wrigley undertake sponsorship of the series on a coast-to-coast basis, the chewing gum company said no. Apparently, the cost was too great and perhaps Wrigley felt that Autry's appeal to the youth was waning. Without a sponsor, the series died.[18]

25

THE SPOTLIGHT FADES

In 1956 it was the beginning of the end for Gene Autry as a star of stage, studio and screen. On February 27 he recorded "You Are My Sunshine" with Carl Smith, Rosemary Clooney, Don Cherry, and the Collins Kids; on April 23 he recorded "I Hang My Head and Cry" and "Be Honest with Me."

On May 13, 1956, the last "Melody Ranch" radio show was broadcast, but Gene Autry was not there. The announcement came from CBS radio and was a surprise to CBS president Arthur Hull Hayes, according to an article. A sticking point was that Autry wanted to record his shows while Wrigley preferred them live. But there was no doubt that other issues were involved.[1]

"We began to get the impression that the Boss had lost interest in the radio show," said Bond. "What with movie production already shut down, the TV films on their way out, maybe he felt that his radio years had had it."[2] On the last show, Charles Lyon, the announcer, pretended to be searching for Gene when a letter arrived which indicated he was tired and needed a rest. Some of his recordings were played.

The production of the show had been pared down, the orchestra gone due to the dwindling audience for national radio shows. The show had been moved out of the large studios at CBS, which were converted to TV studios. There was no longer a live audience, and the show had used some previous scripts instead of hiring writers for new, fresh material. On the last show only Carl Cotner, Pat Buttram, Johnny Bond and the other regulars appeared. There was a message from the sponsor that Autry "was always welcome back whenever he chose to return." Bond remembered Autry saying about the cancellation, "Well, that's the way the old ball bounces."[3]

After Autry's radio show ended, Johnny Bond decided to quit touring so he could perform on "Town Hall Party," a weekly TV show he co-hosted with Tex Ritter. Bond and Ritter also formed a publishing company. Autry hired Johnny Western to replace Bond on the tours. Their first date together was July 4 at the Colorado State Fair in Pueblo. "We had 12,000 people at each show for three straight days," said Western. "It was 103 degrees but we still had to do 'Rudolph.'"[4] Merle Travis, Gail Davis and the Cass County Boys were also on the show.

From Colorado the Autry troupe went to the Canadian National Exposition in

Toronto where "we played before three million people over 14 days," said Western. "Every show was a sell-out. Gene Autry was the biggest thing in the world then. It was Gene Autry and then everybody else."[5]

In December 1956, "The Annie Oakley Show" ended production after 81 black and white episodes. Gail Davis remembered that "Jimmy Hawkins grew up all of a sudden. In fact, the last year they would have to dig a hole for him to stand in and get a two-step for me to stand on. My 'little' brother that I used to pat on top of the head, was now almost 6 feet tall. He just outgrew the part. They talked about more episodes, but finally decided to let the series go. I kid Jimmy that it's all his fault. Look closely at some of the last 10 to 12 shows, and you may even catch me standing on a two-step!"[6]

On June 6, 1956, Gene Autry recorded his last session for Columbia, his label for the past 17 years and the company he recorded for — in one form or another — since 1929, or over 27 years. On that session, done in Hollywood, he recorded "Darlin' What More Can I Do" and "Half Your Heart." He had to form his own companies in order to record for the next several years. During that summer he recorded "No Back Door to Heaven" and "You're the Only Good Thing" for a *Melody Ranch* album.

During the fall he recorded a Christmas album, featuring "Jingle Bells," "Silver Bells," "Here Comes Santa Claus," "Up on the House Top," "Rudolph, the Red Nosed Reindeer," "Santa Claus Is Coming to Town," "Sleigh Bells," and a medley of "O Little Town of Bethlehem/Silent Night/Joy to the World" for his Challenge label. Autry wanted to name the label "Champion" but discovered that name was already registered with the musicians' union; he then wanted "Republic," but Herbert Yates would not allow him to use that name. Finally, he settled on Challenge.

After his radio and TV shows ended in 1956, Gene and Ina Mae "had a fine, long vacation in the Hawaiian Islands." In an interview he noted his seven nieces and nephews often visited him and Ina. His older sister's daughters, Giovanna and Nora Feriono, lived in North Hollywood, close to the Autrys, while his younger sister's children, Billy and Vicki Gleisnner, lived in San Diego. Glenda Spivey, daughter of Ina Mae's brother, lived with her family in Burbank while Ina Karns, daughter of Ina's sister, lived in Tulsa, Oklahoma. The youngest, the daughter of his youngest sister, was three years old while the others were teenagers.[7]

Autry told a reporter, "Baseball I never get enough of." But he added, "My hobby — if you can call it that — is writing songs.... The main reason I enjoy it is because song-writing is something I can do no matter where I am. I remember that 'Funny Little Bunny,' which did real well as an Easter song a couple of years back, was put together on a two-hour plane ride en route to a personal appearance date. 'Put together,' I say, because on that trip with me was my guitarist friend, Johnny Bond. We made the song up together. He composed the music and I made up the words."[8]

Autry told the interviewer "My dream for Melody Ranch ... is to set up a completely authentic Old West museum out there, which would be open to the public." He noted that when he bought Melody Ranch, included in the sale were "such things as old time printing presses, a dentist's drill operated by a foot pedal, blacksmith tools, branding irons — even old-fashioned mousetraps that our pioneer ancestors brought with them across the western plains! It was a real Old West treasure trove — and I've kept adding to it all along."[9]

In 1943, a year after he sold off his Flying A Ranch in Oklahoma, Gene Autry became a partner in the World Championship Rodeo Company, which furnished stock for many of the major rodeos of that era. In 1954, Autry purchased the stock of Leo J. Cremer, Sr., who died two years earlier.

Harry Knight managed the Cremer acquisition, which Autry operated as a separate entity until 1957, when he bought out his partners in the World Championship Rodeo Company and merged the two operations supplying rodeo stock. Autry set up headquarters for the operation on a 24,000 acre ranch near Fowler, Colorado. With Harry Knight as his working partner, Autry's company supplied stock for rodeos in Texas, Wyoming, Colorado, Montana and Nebraska. Managing director of the World Championship Rodeo Company was Everett Colburn.[10]

On Tuesday, April 15, 1958 at 2 P.M. Gene Autry sat in front of a Senate Subcommittee on Communications to testify in a bill ASCAP instigated which sought to prohibit a radio or television station from engaging in music publishing, manufacturing or recording. The bill was part of an on-going war between ASCAP and BMI, the two major American performing rights organizations in the United States. These organizations collect monies from radio and television and pass these monies on to publishers and songwriters. The war began when ASCAP (American Society of Composers, Authors and Publishers) increased its fees to radio stations in the late 1930s. The radio stations and networks (NBC and CBS) countered by forming their own organization, BMI (Broadcast Music, Inc.) in 1940, which provided competition and kept the fees down.

Songwriters who were not mainstream pop songwriters, connected to well-established New York and Los Angeles firms, could not obtain membership in ASCAP and thus could not collect performance royalties, or money from the airplay of their songs before BMI was formed. This affected those writing country, blues, rhythm and blues and Latin songs; as the rock and roll era began, this also affected songwriters writing rock and roll songs.

BMI instituted an "open door" policy for songwriters and publishers, which meant those writing and publishing country, blues, rhythm and blues, rock and roll and other non-mainstream pop fare could be represented and collect monies from radio and TV airplay.

ASCAP songwriters formed an organization, Songwriters of America, which protested the "leer-ics" and "filthy" music created by rhythm and blues and rock and roll artists and songwriters. They pushed for congressional hearings, argued the only reason radio played those rock and roll songs, instead of what they considered vastly superior pop songs, was because radio stations and labels were in cahoots via payola. It was alleged that radio stations and networks who owned BMI stock forced artists to only record BMI songs.

Gene Autry began his testimony by stating he had been involved in broadcasting since 1929 when he was on KVOO in Tulsa, Oklahoma. He told the subcommittee he owned two publishing companies, Western Music Publishing Company, which had been affiliated with ASCAP since 1940, and Golden West Melodies, which has been associated with BMI since 1945. Autry stated he owned controlling interest in KMPC, a 50,000 watt station in Los Angeles, which was acquired in 1956; KFSO, a 5,000 watt station in San Francisco; KOOL, a 5,000 watt station in Phoenix; KOOL-TV in Phoenix; KOLD, a 250 watt station; and KOLD-TV in Tucson. Autry told the senators that "in connection with our acquisition of KMPC, we acquired 103 shares of stock in BMI and in connection with our acquisition of KSFO in San Francisco, we acquired 273 shares of BMI stock."

Autry then told of his difficulties in becoming a member of ASCAP; he finally achieved active membership status in March 1939, after five years of writing successful songs for the movies and radio.

Countering the argument that, because his stations owned stock in BMI (which did not pay shareholder dividends), Autry preferred recording BMI songs, he stated, "I have always performed and recorded music on the basis of what would be best for my career as an artist." He emphasized this point by noting that the biggest hit of his career, "Rudolph, the Red-Nosed Reindeer," was a song licensed by ASCAP.[11]

Since he could not get into ASCAP until 1939, Autry formed his own publishing company because that was "the only way that I could get my songs before the public." Autry further stated that although ASCAP collected monies from airplay, "the writer that actually turned out the material got nothing" because the publisher received that money. Autry noted he started a record company in 1957 and he was "just as interested in songs published by persons other than myself because my recording company will succeed or fail based on our ability to furnish material that the public likes. No one has a monopoly on writing songs or picking hit records."

Confronting the campaign against rock and roll orchestrated by ASCAP writers, Autry stated, "Today there are many big records made of the so-called rock and roll or rockabillies or whatever you call it, and unfortunately, I cannot sing that type of song. I wish I could. I am sure the same thing is true with many writers. I am sure that a lot of them were writing stuff 20 years ago that they are still writing and that today it just simply does not fit the tastes of our new generation. Today you see, I do not know myself exactly what to write. I wish that I could find a big hit, and I think everybody does, but I just do not know what is right any more."[12]

That bill, after testimonies from artists, songwriters and publishers, was defeated in Congress. Autry had a vested interest in the issue of rock and roll; in addition to owning BMI publishing companies, Autry was part owner in a label that had a big rock and roll hit on the radio at the time of hearings.

Challenge Records was founded in January 1957. Autry owned 56 percent of the stock, while A&R head Joe Johnson and sales manager John Thompson each owned 20 percent. Another investor, Bernard Solomon, owned four percent. The first artist signed was Dave Burgess, who gathered some musicians in the studio and recorded an instrumental, "Tequila." The group named themselves the Champs after Autry's horse, Champion. The record entered the pop chart at the end of February 1958 and stayed Number One for five consecutive weeks.

In October 1958, Joe Johnson and John Thompson bought Challenge from Autry, who really wanted a label to release his own recordings. In November 1959 Autry started Republic Records.

In May 1958, Autry asked Merle Travis and Johnny Bond if they could get away from the popular TV and radio show "Town Hall Party," where they were regulars, to perform with him at a rodeo in Milwaukee. The rodeo was held May 27–June 1 and, as part of their agreement, Autry appeared on "Town Hall Party" twice. Tex Ritter introduced him. "The first time there he broke the house attendance record," remembered Bond.[13] But big moments in the spotlight came less often.

Still, he had a bright moment on television on a special, "The Western," on NBC when he and John Wayne did a 90 minute show, directed by John Ford and filmed at Melody Ranch on the history of the western movie. This was the first time Wayne and Autry had appeared on screen together, although the two had been the first contract players when Republic Pictures was formed.

Johnny Western toured with Autry for two years and often drove Autry "because his eyes were giving him some problems." Western remembered Autry "made it very clear that his business interests were taking over. He said they were taking a toll on his time, but they were very profitable. I saw a copy of Dun & Bradstreet in his station wagon one day just kind of lying open and I looked at it and it said his worth was in the neighborhood of $65 to $75 million. And they're always conservative...."

"Gene's thought processes were always toward business. But this was a man who genuinely loved every minute of being on that stage. I could see it in his eyes. He'd be champing at the bit, ready willing and able even under the worst of conditions to perform. I remember the announcer would say, 'And now here he is, ladies and gentlemen, boys and girls, America's favorite cowboy, make welcome Gene Autry and Champion!' and he was ready to spur that horse and jump into that arena. He loved it out there, loved that give and take on stage and giving an audience a thrill. When I did my song, 'Blue Shadows on the Trail,' he made me feel like a King out there — just with my one song...."

"Gene was good with numbers. He was always able to figure a deal and he had multiple businesses. He told me one time while riding along in the car, 'You know, the secret to this thing is to hire a good manager in each area where you're doing business. Then, know what he's doing with those dollars because the man and the dollars are real important. If the man at the top isn't producing the dollars, then he's got to go.

"Out on a tour, he would spent a certain amount of time each day checking with his radio, TV stations and newspapers and his general managers in each of those areas would have a report. He was like an octopus; he had his finger in a lot of enterprises. Gene kept a running tab of how everything was doing because if something started falling apart, he didn't want to be on the road for 45 days and not find out about it until he got home. He trusted his managers but he still wanted to know that everything was going well. That gave him confidence when he was on the road to go out and give a great performance. Gene did not like to have any project cost him money — he liked everything to have a positive cash flow."[14]

Western remembered that "Gene was a great audience for a joke and he was a great joke teller but he loved to be the straight man. All those skits with Pat Buttram and Johnny Bond and Smiley early on — he was the set-up guy for those jokes. And boy could he laugh! You could hear him get that high thing where he almost cackled because he laughed so hard. I saw him laugh a couple of times on tour where he had tears in his eyes. Then he became Mr. Businessman and I never saw anybody in my life so efficient with business. Everything was business down the line. He was a little more curt in his attitude to everybody on the show, not unfriendly, but more business-like all the way down. 'We're going to do such and such, let's change this part of the show, let's change this song, that one's not going over well enough' and then [snapping fingers] everything would come off like clockwork. He could run a show better than anybody I ever saw in my life. Top to bottom, he knew that show was his responsibility, even though he had a lot of pros with him like Carl Cotner, who had been with him 42 years.

"None of us ever had contracts with Gene. The loyalty factor with him was incredible. His handshake was his word, his bond, and it was better than anybody else's paper. I would rather have Gene Autry's handshake than the best contract ever made."[15]

By 1958, Gene Autry was no longer making movies, hosting a radio show or starring in a TV series. Although he spent a considerable amount of time on his business ventures, he continued to make personal appearances around the country. The Gene Autry Friendship Club still operated, although not at the level it once had.

In 1953 the club held its convention in New York and presented a birthday cake to Gene, who treated them to a special screening of *Saginaw Trail*. Shortly afterward, Autry made his last feature film, and Dot Crouse retired as president of the club. Beverly Kimball in Boston took over leadership, but in 1956 the club ceased operations for about a year. Autry then asked June Thornton of Tipton, Indiana, and Rose Marie Casten of St. Louis to take over the club. June and Rose (who became Rose Addison after her marriage) were faced with an immediate dilemma: how to keep up with Gene Autry's activities when there really wasn't much to report in his show business career. Still, the club struggled along under the leadership of Thornton and Addison through the rest of 1950s, continuing to put out *Autry's Aces* regularly.[16]

****

On July 1, 1959, Herbert J. Yates, beset with financial troubles, relinquished control of Republic Pictures and, after 1,000 films, including 386 westerns, Republic died. The company, which had once been a leading maker of B movies and a profitable enterprise for a number of years, was to be sold. Autry's films — as well as other Republic movies — were stored at the Consolidated Film Laboratories in Fort Lee, New Jersey, where they began to deteriorate.

In 1959 Gene Autry appeared in a number of small towns at county fairs before a grandstand crowd. Johnny Bond, who traveled with Autry, noted, "these are the hardest to play. The performers are stationed on a temporarily constructed stage in the center of a race track. The audience is so far away that the echo of the singer's voice bounces back from the loud speakers five or six seconds after the words have been sung or spoken. Plus there are outdoor noises. One finds himself in the middle of much confusion. We tried to do our comedy bit, but out there in the open, we found ourselves in competition with the peanut and popcorn salesmen, barkers, merry-go-round Calliopes.

"In order to offset the fact that we now were playing places beneath our dignity, we stopped off in New York City for a few days visiting with old business acquaintances just to get the feeling that we were still in the big time. We didn't have a full crew; it was Autry, Merle Travis, Carl Cotner, and me with a local band we'd hire, plus a few circus type acts brought in from other sources. It was mostly an outdoor affair, giving us all the feeling that we were now in a Carnival, sometimes considered to be a second rate class of show business. This smaller show coupled with the smaller crowds made it obvious to all that the end of the line was in sight."[17]

In Albany, New York, they performed August 21 and 22 in a baseball park on a crude stage built over the pitcher's mound. The only people who turned out were a few of his fan club members who were still around, remembered Bond. Autry commented, "Looks like we have them outnumbered," and laughed it off. "It's all a part of touring," he said. "Win a few, lose a few." The show ended when a heavy rain storm drenched everyone. Then it was on to Sedalia, Missouri, then Wichita. "Lots of people turned out for the Fair in those cities," said Bond, "but not everyone came into the Grandstand to see us."[18]

From Albany they went to Louisville and Nashville, where they performed September 21–26. On September 27, when they arrived in Richmond, the Los Angeles Dodgers were tied for first place, but there was no TV set at the fairgrounds so the crew bought Autry a portable television set as an early birthday present. During the tour Bond remembered Autry always watched the "Game of the Week" announced by Dizzy Dean every Saturday afternoon.

The Richmond date began on September 28 and the next day, Gene Autry's 52nd birthday, he watched the Dodgers beat the Milwaukee Braves in 12 innings to win the pennant. The Richmond dates were supposed to conclude on October 3 but on October 1, as the group sat in Autry's hotel suite watching the Dodgers play the Chicago White Sox in the first game of the World Series, Hurricane Grace blew in, hitting Richmond hard, and cancelled the rest of the tour. Autry caught a plane to Los Angeles where he sat in the stands and watched the rest of the Series.

During the tour, Bond remembered reading a headline in *Daily Variety*, "Autry sells TV re-runs for five million," but Autry never mentioned it to the crew.[19]

During 1958 there were no recordings released by Gene Autry. In the fall of 1959 he recorded "Buon Natale," "Nine Little Reindeer," and "Santa's Comin' in a Whirlybird" for his label. The last song was quite catchy but never became a national hit because of a lack of effective distribution.

During the late 1950s, Autry built his music holdings, added songs to his publishing companies and formed a label. He bought Pee Wee King's publishing company, and King remembered when he decided to sell his companies that "a fellow who was close to both me and Gene Autry said to me one day, 'Gene is a friend of yours, and I will be meeting with him on a business deal in a few days. Do you want me to tell him your publishing company is for sale?' I said, 'It's all right with me, but I don't think Gene will be interested. Anyway, I've already offered the company to Lawrence Welk.' He said, 'Well, don't expect to hear from Welk. He's awfully tight with money. He won't pay you what the company is worth.'"

King continued, "So he went ahead and talked with Gene and Gene called me on Thanksgiving night and said, 'Why in the hell didn't you ask me to buy your publishing company?' I said, 'Well, I didn't think you'd want it.' He said, 'What does it say on my stationery letterhead? *Gene Autry Music Group*.' Gene went ahead and made a deal with Charlie [Adams] and bought both of our companies, Ridgeway (BMI) and Longview

(ASCAP), and both the BMI and ASCAP song rights. He got the rights to our entire cat-alog of 470 songs, including 'You Belong to Me' and 'Slowpoke.' [When] Gene started a new record company called Republic Records [he] hired Charlie to run his recording studio until Charlie's death in 1982."[20]

26

A BASEBALL MAN

In June 1960, Gene Autry called Johnny Bond to accompany him on a show in Philadelphia. First they flew to Washington, where they met with congressmen and senators, including Speaker of the House Sam Rayburn. From Washington, Autry and Bond took the train to Philadelphia and checked into the Sheraton Hotel, where Bond and Autry roomed together. Bond called some local musicians and got a group together. The "Soldier's Field Thrill Show" occurred over three days, June 24–26. The show was held in Municipal Stadium, and Autry was the star attraction. There were 88,223 people in the audience during his performance, during which he sang five songs. In the midst of racing cars and trapeze acts, Autry did not perform with his horse. The show was brief, but went off fairly well. However, Gene Autry, now 53 years old, had grown tired of performing.

Back at the hotel, Autry watched a Phillies game on television and talked with Bond. About KMPC, the radio station he owned in Los Angeles, he said, "We don't play Country and we don't play rock.... You can't make a dime playing Country. We give 'em Pop music, news and sports and what's more, we're sold out twenty four hours a day. Can't do that with country."[1]

Talking about westerns, he said, "They're dead. Deader'n a door nail. Singing Westerns are through — finished — deader'n Kelsey's! And that's pretty damn dead.... Cost too much to make 'em anymore. In the silent days they could make a Western for practically nothing — very low budget. We made our pictures in the thirties. Even then they thought mine were costing too much, but hell, we had to have good songs. That's where most of them make their mistakes. They just won't pay for good songs. They think all you have to do is sing 'Red River Valley' in each picture and the fans will flood to the box office. And, they didn't have the unions then. Now production, music, musicians, everything costs more and I had to scrape up the money over at Columbia. To hell with it! They just don't pay off anymore. Can't even make back your nut."

Autry continued, "I got sore at old man Yates at Republic. I sued him for release. I sued to keep my films off TV. Rogers sued him. We called Yates every name we could think of, but I'm going to tell you one thing about that ole bald headed so-and so.... Every time we made a picture, he picked up the tab — every dime of it, and he didn't bat an eyelash. He put up the dough-ray-me!"

"Would you have been better off staying with Republic?" asked Bond.

"Hell, I don't know," replied Autry. "Who does know? They're not making any more either. The little 'B' Western, singing or otherwise, is dead. Only old Duke Wayne and some other of his type are doing Westerns. It's either a multi-million dollar budget, or nothing."

"When you have money, you're okay," continued Autry. "If you're broke, nobody loves you. It's that simple." Then he added, "I don't intend to die broke. I've got over $100,000 stashed away where nobody knows where it is. They can take everything I've got, but they won't know where to look for it."[2]

Gene Autry's last tour began in September 1960 at a fair in Knoxville, Tennessee. On the tour were Rufe Davis, Merle Travis, Johnny Bond and either Betty Johnson or Anita Bryant, depending on the date. Carl Cotner was not along; he operated a recording studio in LA on Sunset near Western. At each stop they hired some local musicians for added support.

"Gone were the huge crowds of old," remembered Bond. "Business was not good on these final tours. It is disheartening to look at a grandstand full of empty seats where once there were thousands of cheering fans."[3] Also on the tour was Ina Mae Autry, with Eddie Hogan taking care of logistics.

After Knoxville on September 12–14, the tour moved to a fair in Reading, Pennsylvania on September 16–17, then to Trenton, New Jersey on September 18–23. After finishing in Trenton, Bond and the Autrys flew on Autry's private plane to Detroit, where Autry met with business partner Bob Reynolds; they were interested in purchasing a radio station in the area. On October 17–21, the group was at the state fair in Columbia, South Carolina.

After Columbia, the troupe moved to Shreveport, Louisiana, and performed in a building instead of in front of the grandstand. There were some good crowds, and the next day they flew to New Orleans, where they visited the French Quarter and stayed at the Roosevelt Hotel. From New Orleans, they went to Baton Rouge, where they visited Governor Jimmie Davis in the governor's mansion.

"Most of the talk around the table was about Civil Rights," recalled Bond. "which was one of the Governor's most pressing problems at the moment. He was in his final months of his second term. He was glad to be getting out to let someone else tackle the problem." There was a good deal of discussion about the 1960 presidential campaign. Gene and Ina Mae Autry had watched the debates and were adamantly against John Kennedy, saying "how tragic it would be for the nation if Kennedy got elected." Both were staunch Nixon supporters.[4]

After their last date in Shreveport, Autry remarked, "Frankly, I think we've already had it." Back in Los Angeles, Autry regularly drove his Cadillac to the Brown Derby or Plaza Bar, where he hung out with friends.[5]

In many ways, the year 1960 was a bit of a nightmare for Gene Autry, but at the end of the year he achieved a lifelong dream when he became the owner of a major league baseball team.

Autry had always been a baseball fan. He owned part of the Hollywood Stars of the Pacific Coast League during the late 1930s and early 1940s and often attended games of the minor league Los Angeles Angels. When the Dodgers moved west from Brooklyn, he bought season tickets behind home plate. He was involved in baseball as the owner of KMPC in Los Angeles, which broadcast Dodgers games. For the 1961 season there would be two expansion teams in the American League — Los Angeles and Washington (the former Washington club had moved to Minnesota). Autry was active in those meetings, first trying to secure broadcast rights to the Dodgers games, then trying to own the California franchise.

According to Autry, his troubles began when the advertising agency for Walter O'Malley and the Dodgers called to cancel their contract with the 50,000-watt powerhouse KMPC in order to move over to the smaller KFI. Autry blamed this on O'Malley's purchase of a summer home in the hills above Lake Arrowood, which couldn't receive the broadcast from KMPC, but could from KFI.

In his autobiography, Autry related how he went to the owners' meeting to try to obtain broadcast rights to the new team Los Angeles would receive through expansion. The ownership for the new team couldn't strike a deal with O'Malley, which left ownership in the new team up for grabs, and Autry grabbed it.

But the issues — and the politicking — were much more complicated than that. It started when Baseball Commissioner Ford Frick opened Los Angeles to the American League and allowed the National League to return to New York by proclaiming them both open cities.[6] Since New York had only one club at this time (the American League Yankees) and Los Angeles had only one team (the National League Dodgers), the commissioner's ruling of both as an "open city" meant major league baseball needed a team from the opposite league in each city. The National League had already agreed, voting to expand to ten teams by adding New York and Houston for the 1962 season.

The issue was complicated because owner Calvin Griffith wanted to move his Washington Senators to Minneapolis, which left Washington, which had long had an American League team, without a franchise. The conflict with the American League owners was whether Washington would be allowed an expansion team if the Senators left for Minnesota and who would own the franchise. Finally, at an American League meeting, it was agreed that Cal Griffith could move his club to Minnesota, and General Elwood Quesada, a friend of Boston Red Sox owner Tom Yawkey, got the Washington franchise.

The question of who would receive the Los Angeles franchise looked like a done deal. There was only one candidate for this franchise: former major league star Hank Greenberg. Greenberg's prospective partner was C. Arnholt Smith, a Los Angeles banker who owned the San Diego Padres of the Pacific Coast League. Greenberg was a member of the committee organized to study the possibilities of expansion and was appointed by the committee to investigate Los Angeles; through this "investigation," Greenberg had basically locked up the option to own this franchise. But at a meeting of American League owners at the Plaza Hotel in New York in November 1960, the deal suffered a major setback.

The problem was Walter O'Malley, owner of the Los Angeles Dodgers, who did not want another major league baseball team in the city he considered his territory. It became obvious O'Malley was set to raise a long list of objections about an American League franchise in Los Angeles. Although O'Malley was an owner of a National League team and therefore had no jurisdiction over the issue of American League expansion, commissioner Ford Frick informed the American League team owners a settlement that was fair and equitable had to be made to O'Malley. This made Los Angeles an open city only under O'Malley's terms.

O'Malley wanted indemnifications, the right to dictate his opposition's television policy, and an agreement the American League team could not play in the Los Angeles Coliseum. (O'Malley's Dodgers played at the Los Angeles Coliseum, but O'Malley was building a new stadium at Chavez Ravine, set to open with the 1962 season.) In his investigation of the Los Angeles market, Hank Greenberg had reached an agreement for the new franchise to play at the Coliseum.

Greenberg met with Frick but was informed he would have to negotiate with O'Malley himself— the Commissioner would not step in to resolve the dispute nor use his power and authority to inform O'Malley the Dodger owner had no say in issues involving the American League franchise. Greenberg went to the American League owners, who could have simply voted a franchise in Los Angles despite O'Malley's objections and Frick's silence. Instead, the owners told Greenberg, "It's your problem. You have to solve it."[7]

Another problem confronted Greenberg, who operated under the understanding the new franchise would be able to purchase some experienced players. Under the original plan for expansion, each of the eight established teams would present their regular starting line-up, designating four of their regulars as "untouchables." The new clubs would each be allowed to purchase a remaining starter for $150,000. Under this plan, the new Washington and Los Angeles franchises would begin the season with four established players in their line-ups. However, the owners reneged on this original agreement; instead, they reserved all their top players, leaving only the second tier for the expansion teams.

Greenberg looked at this situation, knew he would lose money for the next several years, if not longer, and decided not to pursue the franchise. This left the issue of who would own the Los Angeles franchise wide open. That issue was tabled for the winter meeting of Major League Baseball scheduled in two weeks at St. Louis.

Charles O. Finley from Chicago, the wealthy owner of an insurance company, had long wanted to own a baseball franchise; he jumped in the fray. Finley had gone to see Kenyon Brown in Los Angeles to join the syndicate headed by Brown to obtain the franchise. Finley had offered Casey Stengel the job of managing the LA team — which didn't even exist — believing an agreement with Stengel would seal the deal for his franchise bid. Before the meetings began in St. Louis, a syndicate put together by Kenyon Brown seemed to have the inside track; Gene Autry was included in this group. Charles O. Finley, learning he was not to be in this group, countered by approaching Roy Rogers to join his syndicate; Rogers was not interested.

The owners of Major League Baseball gathered in St. Louis in December 1960 facing a difficult situation. First, the National League had agreed to expand to ten teams, beginning with the 1962 season, which gave them time to organize the new teams and set the schedules for the league. Next, the American League owners had agreed to let the Washington Senators move to Minneapolis for the 1961 season with a new franchise awarded to Washington for the 1961 season. This meant that, at this point, there were nine teams in the American League for the 1961 season, a difficult situation to schedule.

The other proposed franchise in Los Angeles did not have an owner and had to contend with a prickly, contentious, dictatorial Walter O'Malley. And it was December, with spring training set to begin in February!

The meeting began with Chicago White Sox owner Bill Veeck and Hank Greenberg pushing for New York to join the National League for the 1961 season, putting nine teams in each league. This would force owners to adopt inter-league play, which Veeck had long advocated and which many fans wanted because, unless there were two teams in a city, fans could never see the great players of the other league play. That idea was quickly voted down. (O'Malley supposedly liked this idea because it kept the American League out of Los Angeles for at least another year.)

In the early period of the St. Louis meeting the Kenyon Brown group had a re-shuffle, and Gene Autry, with his business partner Bob Reynolds, ended up on top. Part of the reason for this re-shuffle may have come because Autry, learning about the complications about the proposed new ownership, called Joe Cronin, president of the American League. Gene Autry was the singing cowboy hero who played the Boston Gardens back when Cronin was a star shortstop with the Red Sox, and Autry's dressing room was always open to major league players. Joe Cronin brought some kids by, and Autry gave them auto-graphed hats. Cronin told Autry he needed financial statements and a letter of credit for $1.5 million from a bank to make an offer for the franchise.

Among O'Malley's demands was he that had to approve who owned the Los Ange-les franchise, where the new team would play, how often the new team could play for the television audience. Plus, he would receive $350,000 for allowing the franchise to exist. Kenyon Brown was apparently not acceptable to O'Malley; Gene Autry was.

When it came to the TV package, O'Malley allowed eleven games to be broadcast from Wrigley Field, the minor league ballpark of the Los Angeles Angels of the Pacific Coast League. Further, beginning with the 1962 season, the new franchise was required to sign a contract with O'Malley to rent Chavez Ravine for their home games.

During the 1961 season the Dodgers would play at the Coliseum, which had a seat-ing capacity of a little under 100,000; the new franchise would play at Wrigley Field, which seated 20,500. This meant the new American League franchise was certain to lose money its first year; further, every American League team that played in Los Angeles would lose money on this road trip.

Los Angeles was the only American League franchise on the West Coast in 1961; it was costly to bring a team there. Also, even if there was a total sell-out in a stadium of 20,500 seats for every game, the revenue would not be enough to cover costs. As a result, it cost each team in the American League about $500,000 to play games in Los Angeles that season.

During the 1961 season, the Angels averaged less than 7,300 a game, finishing tenth in attendance in a ten team league, even though they resided in the second largest city in the United States. Even the Yankees, the top draw in the American League, could not sell out because fans did not believe they could get seats in a park which had such lim-ited seating. And so they did not try.

Although this situation does not shine a favorable light on Walter O'Malley or the American League owners at that time, the good news is that Gene Autry, lifelong baseball fanatic, became a baseball owner on December 7, 1960, at the winter meetings in St. Louis because he agreed to all of O'Malley's demands.

The deal stunk, but the other American League owners decided "it was none of our business what kind of a deal the new club made with O'Malley as long as the club itself was willing to make it."[8] The problem was that everyone liked the Autry group, and Gene Autry wanted to own a baseball club so badly that he was willing to do whatever he had to do to get one. Including kowtow to Walter O'Malley. Gene Autry came to regret some of the concessions he made, especially with O'Malley as his landlord and controller of the concessions at Chavez Ravine. But he never regretted becoming a baseball owner.

The new team would be called the Los Angeles Angels. As part of the agreement to obtain the team, Autry had to give $2.1 million to other owners in order to join "the club" of major league baseball owners in addition to the $350,000 he paid O'Malley for being in Los Angeles. The new team could choose 28 players from a list of players owned by other teams which the teams did not protect. In other words, according to Autry, "players nobody else wanted." That would cost him $75,000 per player.

Autry had breakfast with Red Schoendienst the morning after he and Bob Reynolds were awarded the franchise. Autry wanted to sign Schoendienst, who had been released by the Milwaukee Braves, but Schoendienst insisted he had to speak with the Cardinals first. When he did, Cardinals owner Bing Devine gave him a job as a player-coach. That meant the first player the Angels signed was catcher Del Rice.

In 1961, Gene Autry stopped doing concerts, although he continued to make appearances at luncheons, awards shows, and civic events. But his days as a performer were behind him. No longer was he a singing cowboy, now he had a new job and a new role: baseball man.

A "baseball man" is one who knows the inside of the game, who works in baseball, guiding the sport with an intimate knowledge of its history as well as current players. Gene Autry had long dreamed of being a baseball man, and for the rest of his life, that's what he would dedicate the bulk of his time being and doing.

The highlight of Gene Autry's years as a baseball man came on April 11, 1961, opening day, when the Los Angeles Angels played their first game in Baltimore against the Orioles. The Angels started Eli Grba at pitcher, while the Orioles had Milt Pappas on the mound. The game began with Angels lead-off hitter and centerfielder Albie Pearson hitting a single, then third baseman Eddie Yost walked. This was followed by a home run from first baseman "Big Klu" Ted Kluszewski. The next hitter, Bob Cerv, also walloped a home run, giving the Angels a 4–0 lead before the Orioles had a chance to bat.

A couple of innings later, Pearson singled, Yost was hit by the pitch, and Kluszewski homered again. The Angels won the first game in their history 7–2.

"That game remains my biggest thrill in baseball," remembered Autry years later. "The newness, the magic of opening day, fearing the worst and getting the best, there are just not many days that golden."[9] Indeed, Autry often remarked during the ensuing years that in the movies he never lost a fight but in baseball it seemed like he couldn't win one. Baseball gave him many thrills during the second half of his life, but it also broke his heart over and over again.

For that first season, Autry hired his old friend George Goodale as publicity director for the Angels. The Angels' general manager was Fred Haney, who had worked the "Game of the Week" for NBC before Autry asked him to help the team in the expansion draft and hire a staff to run the club. Autry talked him into becoming general manager, and they hired Bill Rigney as manager. Their first choice had been Casey Stengel, who had been fired by the New York Yankees at the end of the previous season "for turning 70." Said Casey, "I'll never do that again." But Stengel had a contract to serialize his life story for the *Saturday Evening Post* and, as part of that agreement, agreed to stay out of baseball for a year. Stengel also needed to devote time and attention to a bank in Glendale where he was a stockholder and director.

The 1961 baseball season is best remembered as the one in which Mickey Mantle and Roger Maris battled for the home run title during the season before Maris won it by breaking Babe Ruth's record when he hit his 61st in the 162-game season. The league had decided to expand from a 154-game season.

In the American League, both the Yankees and Tigers won more than 100 games, but New York took the title with a 109-53 record. Six teams had losing records, including the Angels at 70-91, but they finished ahead of the Kansas City Athletics, owned by Charles Finley, and the new Washington Senators, managed by Ted Williams.

In 1962 the Angels moved to Dodger Stadium, where they drew over a million fans and led the league on the Fourth of July. However, they slipped to third by the end of the season, although they remained in contention until the middle of September. Highlights for the year included a no-hitter thrown by rookie Bo Belinsky against Baltimore on May 5. Autry was so thrilled that he picked up the payments for Belinsky's Cadillac. Belinsky was a colorful character who dated a number of Hollywood actresses, including starlet Mamie Van Doren. After winning his first six games, Belinsky finished the season with a 10-11 record; at the end of the season Bill Rigney was named American League Manager of the Year.

The Angels finished next to last, or ninth, during the 1963 season in the American League with a 70-91 record. During the 1964 baseball season, the Angels finished fifth, with an 82-80 record under Bill Rigney. Twenty-three-year-old Dean Chance finished with a 20-9 record and 1.65 ERA and became the youngest pitcher to ever win the Cy Young Award. Chance led the American League in innings pitched, wins and ERA.

It was the era in baseball of "bonus babies," and the Angels paid over $200,000 to sign University of Wisconsin outfielder Rick Reichardt. The team signed a 35-year lease to play in a new stadium in the city of Anaheim, near Disneyland, in nearby Orange County. Autry and Reynolds made the decision after reading a report prepared by Stanford University that forecast Anaheim would become the geographical center for the Southern California population in the years ahead.

The Angels' crowds had been shrinking, and there were endless arguments with Dodgers owner O'Malley, who wanted to charge the Angels half the total cost for water and toilet paper, even though the Angels had drawn a fourth as many as the Dodgers.

During Angel home games, Gene Autry sat at a desk in his private box, with a telephone near, and kept meticulous score in a scorebook as he watched the game.

In spite of the good fortune Gene Autry enjoyed as a baseball man, major tragedies struck his life in the early 1960s. On April 28, 1961, Melody Ranch was destroyed by the

Southland Fire; Autry was in Vancouver at the time of the blaze. The fire destroyed over $1 million worth of movie sets, 54 buildings, stagecoaches, guns, Indian relics, his personal film wardrobe and about 75 percent of the ranch he purchased in 1952 from Monogram Studios.

In the fire "what I lost could not be replaced or even measured," said Autry.[10] The firestorm that raged through the San Gabriel Mountains scorched everything in its path, charring 17,000 acres and destroying three homes and portions of Olive View Hospital in addition to Melody Ranch. Over 1,300 men fought the blaze, whose damage estimate was $1,430,325.

The opening for "Gunsmoke" had been filmed on its main street. The "Wyatt Earp," "Death Valley Days" and "Bat Masterson" TV shows had also filmed there. Ina Mae Autry told reporters that Autry's valuable collection of antique guns and half his collection of Texas long horns were destroyed. His "dream of building a museum of western lore went up in smoke" she said.

"My husband has been collecting western antiques for years," said Ina Mae. "He planned to display his collection in a museum on the ranch. He was just waiting until he had time to get everything arranged." She noted, "Our horses were all in fireproof stables and all of them were rescued. And my husband's rodeo saddles all were stored in a fireproof tack room."[11] Firemen saved one of Autry's most precious collections — the films he'd made over his long career. Tragedy also struck the Autry family during the summer of 1962 when Gene's brother, Dudley "Doug" Autry, died on June 25.

****

During the winter of 1961 and 1962, Gene Autry did his last recording sessions at the International Sound Studios in Hollywood for an RCA album. He recorded past hits "You're the Only Star in My Blue Heaven," "Tweedle-O-Twill," "You Are My Sunshine," "Lonely River," "San Antonio Rose," "Trouble in Mind," "Hang Your Head in Shame," "Be Honest with Me," "Ages and Ages Ago," "Blues Stay Away from Me," "Tears on My Pillow," and "I Hang My Head and Cry," for the album, as well as four songs that were unissued, "Goodbye Little Darlin' Goodbye," "I'll Wait for You" and "Darlin' What More Can I Do." The album was released in 1962 as *Gene Autry's Golden Hits*. It seemed as if Gene Autry was back where he started, carving out a name for himself as a recording artist, albeit with a good number of past hits under his belt.

During the four-day session, "It was obvious that he was out of practice," remembered Bond. "We noticed that he perspired a lot, tiring out easily during each song." During the sessions, Jim Reeves stopped by to visit, and Autry observed "where once recording used to be a simple task, now it was a tougher job."[12]

In 1963 Autry was elected president of the Country Music Association, based in Nashville. "I don't mind doing the job," he remarked to a friend. "[But] they wanted to hold meetings all the time, in Nashville yet. Hell's fire, I can't go running down to Nashville every other day — or week. I let the Vice-President take over most of the time. You know the toughest part of that President's job? I had to sign all them damned membership cards. Have they got a lot of members!??!"[13]

At his final meeting as president, held at the Andrew Jackson hotel, Autry turned the reins over to Tex Ritter, who was elected president of the CMA for the next year.

The silver anniversary of *Autry's Aces* was in 1963, and Gene Autry Friendship Club co-presidents June Thornton and Rose Addison decided to end the club with this issue. However, at that time Smiley Burnette joined the CBS-TV show "Petticoat Junction," so the Smiley Burnette Fan Club was revitalized. Most of the early fans were not collectors, but Lillian Spencer started the Gene Autry Collectors' Club for those interested in collecting Autry memorabilia.[14]

In 1964 "Melody Ranch" became a television program on KTLA — Channel 5. Starring Carl Cotner, the Cass County Boys, Billy Mize and Johnny Bond, the one-hour show featured music and skits. Although Autry did not appear on the program, he sometimes dropped by rehearsals to watch. On May 10, 1965, he appeared on the television show with Smiley Burnette and Rufe Davis; it would be the last time they all appeared together.

Gene Autry's last recording session occurred in 1964, when he recorded two recitations, "One Solitary life" and "A Cowboy's Prayer," for Hilltop Records, a division of Starday.

On March 14, 1963, it was announced that Gene Autry with Bob Reynolds and Paul O'Bryan had purchased a chain of 20 hotels/motels for $20 million. The newly formed Gene Autry Hotel Company had Floyd Clodfelter as vice-president and Washington attorney Paul O'Bryan as secretary-treasurer and general counsel. The new hotels were in Seattle, Kennewick and Tacoma, Washington; Boise, Pocatello and Twin Falls, Idaho; Palm Springs, Hollywood and Oakland, California; and Portland, Oregon. Autry and Reynolds also owned the Continental Hotel in Los Angeles, the Mark Hopkins Hotel in San Francisco, as well as substantial holdings in the Los Angeles Angels, the Los Angeles Rams and the Los Angeles Blades ice hockey teams.

On October 29, 1963, it was announced that Golden West (Autry and Reynolds) had purchased KTLA-TV from Paramount Television Productions, beating out the *Chicago Tribune*, which was also negotiating to buy it. The sale of the TV station included the franchise, license and broadcasting facilities of the station, but not the real estate on Sunset Boulevard where it was located. The price was the highest ever paid for a TV station.

Golden West also owned KMPC, KSFO (San Francisco) KVI (in Seattle) and KEX (in Portland, Oregon). Autry also held major interests in television channels in Phoenix (KOOL) and Tucson (KOLD).

27

BUSINESSMAN

A long article in *LA Times West* magazine, headlined "It's Just Ol' Gene" by Mike Fessier, Jr., noted that each week day around nine A.M. "a pudgy, 59-year-old man in cowboy boots and conservative, Western-cut, dark brown suit" came into the Hotel Continental's coffee shop and sat at a table in the back, near the cash register. He ordered "four strips of very crisp bacon and a poached egg" and was "nervous as usual. From head to foot he is in motion — the eyes dart, the head jerks up towards a voice across the room, the hands fiddle compulsively with a spoon." There was a page over the loudspeaker: "Call for Number One." Autry took the phone from the back of the booth and talked "with an aide." People stopped by to chat, and he was friendly.[1]

When asked what kept him going, Autry replied, "I'll be damned if I know. It is not a matter of wanting to be the richest man in the graveyard, I know that. Maybe it's because I have worked all my life and don't know any other way to live. It drives me nuts to sit around. Maybe I'm a gypsy at heart."

Herb Green, his pilot, noted, "The same impetus that got him going initially keeps him going, but it's no longer for the money. It's a game." Armand Schaefer told the reporter, "I don't think anyone that busy is happy. You have to have a certain amount of tranquility, don't you think so?" Then Schaefer added, "Maybe his business is also his happiness."

Ina Mae commented, "I'm distressed that he can't let go. He hasn't learned how to let go. He's involved in so much. I try to get him to slow down, but I can't."

"I hate people to think I'm a millionaire tycoon," Autry told the reporter. "Actually, if I cashed everything in and paid everybody off I wouldn't have a hell of a lot left. People say I've made a lot of money, and I have, but I've always been the in-between guy."

Herb Green, who also worked for KMPC flying for traffic reports, remembered when they'd fly over a town, Autry not only remembered the town, but also the name of the theater and how many people came to the show. "He never forgot," said Green. Old friends and people who worked for him were quoted as saying, "I never heard a bad word about him," "the most honest," "the most humble," "the most real," and an "old friend." However, someone noted, "If somebody double-crosses him he's pretty unforgiving."[2]

During the 1964 election, Autry supported Barry Goldwater; he wanted nothing to

170

do with Lyndon Johnson because he disliked the Democrats' social programs. Johnson asked him to help in the campaign but Autry begged off, saying he had served under Goldwater in the Army Air Corps. However, after the election the Autrys accepted an invitation from Johnson to visit the Texas ranch. Always interested in politics, the Autrys were guests at the White House a number of times.

On June 14, 1965, Autry was given the Outstanding Humanitarian Services Award at an event co-hosted by Johnny Grant and Pat Buttram and attended by over 400 show business, sports and political figures. One of the dais guests was Herbert J. Yates, who made a rare public appearance, saying Autry "worked hard" and "earned his place" and was on his way to "his first billion."[3]

Autry was cited for his "selfless devotion" to the cause of underprivileged and handicapped children, exemplified by his donations to boys' clubs, anonymous gifts and underwriting an entire heart research wing at the City of Hope Hospital.

Telegrams of congratulations came from Roy Rogers, Walt Disney and U.S. Senator George Murphy. The Cass County Boys played western music at the Beverly Hilton luncheon. Co-host Johnny Grant called Autry "the John Wayne of the Stone Age." Pat Buttram noted, "If money is filthy lucre, we're here to honor one of the dirtiest old men I know. You've got to hand it to old Gene, otherwise he'll [do] you out of it," continued Buttram. "Maybe Autry couldn't act or sing, but he could add." Buttram added that one of the best things Autry did for moving pictures was "get out of them."[4]

Less than a year after this event — on February 4, 1966, Herbert Yates died in Sherman Oaks, California. He had suffered a stroke in 1965 while in Italy and had been retired since 1959, when he stepped down as the head of Republic. He was buried at Oakwood Cemetery, Long Island, New York.

In 1967, Golden West paid $6 million to purchase land on Sunset Boulevard between Van Ness and Bronson Avenues (once the home of Warner Brothers movie studio) where the KTLA studios were located. Golden West had leased the land from Paramount. Warner Brothers bought the lot in 1918 for $25,000; they paid nothing down and $1,000 a month. *The Jazz Singer* and *Rin Tin Tin* were both filmed there.

By 1968, KMPC, which had begun in 1928, was worth $15 million (Autry had purchased it for $800,000). The company opened a new facility at 5858 Sunset Boulevard. The station's annual operational budget was over $3,250,000. It had two helicopters, a vast mobile fleet, and a fixed-wing aircraft as part of its news organization.

In May, Autry sold KOCD-TV in Tucson to Universal Communications for $4.1 million. On August 1, it was announced the Signal Corporation had purchased 49.9 percent of Golden West Broadcasters, the company formed by Autry in 1952, for $25 million. Autry retained majority control of Golden West Broadcasters and continued as chief executive officer. After the sale, he assumed the office of president in addition to his chairman of the board title.

Signal was a multi-industry group that included Signal Oil and Gas Company, the Garret Corporation and Mack trucks, with interests in shipping, steel, banking and real estate. They purchased their stock from minority stockholders like Robert O. Reynolds, who became president of the newly formed sports division and remained president of the California Angels. Both Autry and Reynolds were vice presidents of the NFL Los Angeles Rams.

****

When Gene Autry finished his last feature in 1953, it effectively marked the end of Smiley Burnette's movie career as well. Smiley was 42 years old and, to make ends meet, went on a series of personal appearances where he was quite popular with children. However, as the years passed, and fewer and fewer children knew who Smiley Burnette — or his character Frog Millhouse — was because he was no longer in the public eye, it became more and more difficult to make a living.

By the 1960s, Burnette's personal appearances in the South were largely confined to shopping centers, where he tried to entertain a new generation of children unfamiliar with his film work. In 1962 he recorded an album for Starday Records that was soon deleted from the company's catalog. He moved to Missouri for a while and became acquainted with Paul Henning, producer of "The Beverly Hillbillies." Henning was planning another TV series, "Petticoat Junction," and cast Smiley as train engineer "Charley Pratt."[5]

In December 1966, Burnette, in his fourth season as Charley Pratt, was unwell, often short of breath. In February, he required oxygen between his scenes. Few knew this, but Smiley was suffering from acute leukemia. Burnette completed his last scene for "Petticoat Junction" on February 8, 1967; he was taken immediately to West Valley Hospital in Encino, where he died on February 17, 1967. Smiley Burnette was 55 years old.

Smiley and Gene Autry had lunch not long before his death and Autry was unaware that Smiley was sick. Autry did not attend the funeral at Forest Lawn. "I suppose some criticized me for it," he explained in his autobiography. "I can understand why they would. But I quit going to them over twenty years ago. The last funeral I went to, after my mother died, was my brother Doug's and I wouldn't go near the coffin."[6]

On September 26, 1967, Armand "Mandy" Schaefer died. The 69-year-old longtime friend of Autry was president of Gene Autry Productions and Flying A Pictures. Schaefer had joined Nat Levine back in 1935, then moved over to Republic, where he produced most of Autry's pictures. Later, he and Autry went into business together when Autry began producing his own movies with Columbia, then his television shows. Additionally, the Autrys and Schaefers were close personally.

On May 20, 1968, Mitch Hamilburg died at the age of 67 from cancer. He was a key person during Autry's long career, and Autry broke a longstanding tradition of not attending funerals to attend this one the next day at Hillside Memorial Chapel. On November 26 Delbert Autry, Gene's father, died in Bakersfield, California. He was 85 years old and had lived in Kern County for 28 years — since 1940. He left a wife (his fifth), 14 grandchildren, one great grandchild, and six daughters in addition to Gene.

Gene Autry was nominated for the Country Music Hall of Fame at the Country Music Association's annual awards show and telecast in 1969. At the induction, the five final nominees sat in the TV audience — not knowing who would be inducted — until their name was called. This was not the first time Autry had been nominated, but he vowed he would never again sit in the audience anxiously awaiting the name of the inductee, only to be embarrassed when someone else walked up in front of a national television audience. Autry decided he would not come to Nashville unless he was certain he was elected. The problem was that the name of the inductee was kept secret until the announcement on national television.

Autry was miffed that a number of people he helped — Fred Rose and Bob Wills — had already been inducted, in addition to those who followed in his footsteps after he spent years as a star — such as Hank Williams, Eddy Arnold and Ernest Tubb. A good case could be made that Gene Autry and Jimmie Rodgers should have been the very first inductees, instead of Rodgers, Fred Rose and Hank Williams.

There was some bitterness from Autry about the Country Music Association and the Hall of Fame. Talking about the Hall of Fame, Autry said, "I think from now on I'll leave all of my things to the Cowboy Hall of Fame in Oklahoma City. And what's more, I want my guitar back! If I have to, I'll go in there and get it myself."

Before the awards were held, Johnny Bond uncovered the name of the person who engraved the Hall of Fame plaque. Going to their shop, Bond managed to sneak a peak under the cloth covering the plaque and saw that Autry was the newest member of the Hall of Fame. He relayed this to Autry, who flew to Nashville for the honor and so, on October 12, 1969, Gene Autry was present when he was inducted into the Country Music Hall of Fame.[7]

That year, Johnny Cash was the big winner for the Country Music Association. The 3rd annual CMA Awards, presented as part of the "Kraft Music Hall," was running out of time for host Tex Ritter when Tennessee Ernie Ford broke in and announced Autry's honor. Taking the microphone, Autry said, "I don't deserve this. But then, I have arthritis, and I don't deserve that either."[8]

****

The Los Angeles Angels did not have a winning season in 1965; they finished seventh with a 75-87 record. The lineup did not contain a single .300 hitter. Their pitching ace was Dean Chance, who had a 15-10 record that year. During the 1966 baseball season, the Angels moved to Anaheim and became the California Angels. The park featured a million-dollar scoreboard and drew 1.5 million fans that season. The team finished sixth with an 80-82 record. When the season was over, Dean Chance was traded to Minnesota. During the 1967 baseball season, the Angels finished fifth with an 84-77 record. The team hosted the summer All-Star game that year.

In 1968, Autry ended his involvement in one sport when he got out of the rodeo business. He sold his World Championship Rodeo Company operation to Billy Minick of Fort Worth, Texas.[9] That year the Angels finished eighth in the American League under manager Bill Rigney with a 67-95 record.

The Angels underwent some changes in 1969. General manager Fred Haney retired and was replaced by Dick Walsh, hired from the Dodgers. While in New York on business, Autry received a call from Walsh saying there was a need to change managers — Bill Rigney had to go. Autry wanted to name Chuck Tanner, who managed their minor league club in Hawaii, but Walsh insisted on Lefty Phillips with the Dodgers. Walsh got his way and Phillips was hired. At the time of Rigney's dismissal, 39 games into the season, the club was 11-28; under Phillips their record was 60-63, and they finished third with an overall record of 71-91. The bright spot on the team was pitcher Andy Messersmith, whose record was 16-11 with a 2.52 ERA.

As an owner, Autry met all the players and tried to know something about them.

He liked to drop by the clubhouse after a game, or phone a player to congratulate him on a good game. He wrote notes to players who left the team after they were with the Angels for a long time. But Autry was not an owner who constantly called and badgered his managers, demanding to know why such and such a strategy was or was not used. He generally hired those he felt to be the best people and then let them do their job.

Gene Autry's great love was baseball and baseball players. He established a personal relationship with each Angels player, and those friendships caused problems when a player had to be cut. "I'm a lousy owner," said Autry. "I hate like hell to let anybody go. When a guy's a personal friend, you can't just treat him like *anybody*."[9]

During a typical night game Autry arrived an hour or two before game time, visited with publicity director George Goodale, then went to his office at the stadium (Autry maintained four offices for his various businesses). Autry would then "smile and nod his way through elevators and hallways of people up to the executive bar on press-box level." The bar had rich, candy-red carpets where Orange County dignitaries and their wives gathered. Autry kept "his amiability stoked up with a couple of quick snorts."

At the bar, Autry kept "flashing his marvelously ambiguous grin of good cheer, the one he has perfected in over 30 years of business socializing. And everybody keeps right on beaming back, because it is a fact that everyone gets along with the richest man in the room." Autry then found "someone to talk planes and pilots."

During the game, he kept a meticulous box score. A reporter noted, "At no time does that raw-nerve edginess leave him. It's as though there is a deal hatching someplace, and he senses it but can't get there and it hurts. Instead of revving down as his wife would like, he is forever revving up. He used to play some golf, 'but I don't have time to any more.' Some nights he can't sleep, and Ina Mae will find him on the couch the following morning surrounded by the many papers he reads: *The Wall Street Journal, Los Angeles Times* and *New Republic*."[10]

28

BASEBALL AND BUSINESS

During the 1960s, like so many from his era, Gene Autry was out of touch with the counterculture. He thought the young people with long hair were all hippies and all wrong. He instinctively supported the war in Vietnam and was against the "free love" movement and demonstrations for civil rights. He was planted firmly at the top of Richard Nixon's America, a prominent hero of the "silent majority" which was left behind when young people shifted over to rock and roll in the mid–1950s, then left further behind in the turbulent '60s.

Autry disliked Lyndon Johnson's liberal political policies and social welfare programs. He grew up a Democrat and supported Franklin Roosevelt and Harry Truman during their presidencies. Will Rogers, who said he'd "rather be right than Republican," was a major hero for Autry. He admired General Dwight Eisenhower and supported him for president; later he supported Ronald Reagan and Mike Curb when each ran for governor of California. Still, Autry would not call himself a Republican after years of being a staunch Democrat, so he claimed himself an independent, supporting the man over a party. But the men he supported in his later years were conservative Republicans — Richard Nixon, Barry Goldwater and Ronald Reagan — although he remained a registered Democrat his entire life.

Autry had moved to the right after Truman fired General Douglas MacArthur and continued moving further to the right through the civil rights struggles that began in the 1950s. Autry liked things the way they were — he would say he wasn't against change as long as it was done in a quiet, orderly manner. But the changes that rocked the nation during the '50s and '60s — civil rights, Vietnam — were wrenching changes, and he opposed them.

The era that Gene Autry had grown up and come of age in — when the United States was a rural nation, and the generation knew hardship and deprivation — had given way to a nation where the population increasingly settled in the suburbs and young people had no experience or memory of anything as harsh as the Great Depression. Autry, like most of his generation, did not adapt well to the rapid and wrenching changes during the 1960s.

In 1978 Gene Autry's autobiography, *Back in the Saddle Again* written with Mickey

175

Herskowitz, a sportswriter with a Houston newspaper, was published. In the book he observed, "It is risky, at any age, to reflect on how the times change. Times always do. But every turn in my career was dictated, or pushed along, by forces not always within my control."[1]

Autry noted, "Success is meant to be enjoyed, not analyzed." Performing "was a craft and I worked at it. You hear all the time about performers, whatever their personality, who were simply transformed when they hit that stage and felt the glow of the lights and the warmth of the crowd. But I never experienced that. So many singers would go on, like Jolson, and not only sing at the audience and down their throats, they had to have a runway so they could get closer. They overpowered you. I could never do that. I just laid back and let the audience come to me. It was like listening to the boy next door sing. I thought of myself as a showman, not a great entertainer. I never tried to be more or less than Gene Autry."[2]

Autry noted, "It has always amused me when people seem surprised by my success in business. Actually, working with numbers was what I did best. What I did less well was sing, act, and play the guitar."[3]

Although he was not active as an entertainer during the 1970s, Autry was still involved in show business. In the fall of 1970 Autry was inducted into the Nashville Songwriters Hall of Fame. In October 1971 Art Satherley, Autry's former record producer, was elected to the Country Music Hall of Fame.

In August 1972 Autry obtained ownership of his Republic films in a multi-million dollar deal; however, many had been seriously damaged during storage.

In 1974 Gene Autry sold his ranches in Oklahoma and Colorado, which raised stock for rodeos, but retained his interest in the music business through Republic Records which, in 1975, released Autry's recordings on a series of albums. Carl Cotner dropped one by the office of TV producer and host Dick Clark, who phoned over to Autry and asked if he could get another because former Beatle Ringo Starr was in Clark's office and wanted one. One of Ringo's boyhood heroes was Gene Autry, who was told that Ringo had a photograph of the singing cowboy over his mantle at home.

On August 25, 1975, Joseph Kane, who directed Autry and Roy Rogers in a number of movies, died in Santa Monica. The 81-year-old director began his career in 1920 as a musician. Later, he became a studio chauffeur, then wrote several scripts and became a film editor at Pathe. In 1935 he directed Autry's first film appearance *In Old Santa Fe.*

On April 1, 1973 — Gene and Ina Autry's 41st wedding anniversary — his first full-length movie, *Tumbling Tumbleweeds,* was shown over KTLA, Channel 5, the station he owned in Los Angeles. On October 25 he was on the cover of *Rolling Stone* magazine.

In the summer of 1976 the second of Autry's Champions died. Autry found out when Johnny Brousseau, manager of Melody Ranch and caretaker for Champion, called while Autry was in a hotel room in the East. Brousseau checked with a taxidermist, who could mount the horse for $1,500 so it could be put on display. He relayed this information to Autry, who replied, "Johnny, the horse had a good life. Let's not make him work for us now. Go ahead and bury him." Reflecting on the horses in his movies, Autry stated the "first was probably the best-tempered. He didn't act up even when the kids at a rodeo or a parade yanked hairs out of his tail for a souvenir."[4]

In 1977 Autry was elected president of the National Cowboy and Western Heritage Center (sometimes known as the Cowboy Hall of Fame) in Oklahoma City for the 1977–1978 year. Autry had served on the board for three years and most recently had served as vice president.

An article profiling Gene Autry as a chief executive ran in *Dun's Review* in the summer of 1975. The article noted, "The strong, sweet twang of the tenor voice has turned whispery; the tall, slim body has become corpulent; the sure-footed stride, exuding courage and righteousness, has slowed; the bright, steady eyes have dimmed." Autry was 67 at the time.[5]

The magazine noted Autry sat atop an empire worth an estimated $70 million with around 600 employees. Golden West Broadcasters owned four radio stations; KTLA in Los Angeles; a national radio time sales firm; a ten-acre movie and television production center; and the California Angels baseball club. Outside of Golden West, Autry himself owned a 118-room hotel in Palm Springs; a 20,000 acre cattle ranch in Colorado; a collection of old automobiles and locomotives; the 100-acre "Melody Ranch" movie lot; and the rights to his movies and TV shows.

The magazine estimated Autry's personal wealth at around $30 million and quoted former partner Bob Reynolds, who stated, "Gene is considered in his judgment. He's a good listener. He's an avid reader. He's a perceptive guy. He's got an inquisitive mind. He knows the bottom line. He's just got a lot of natural good business sense."

Golden West had been financed by Autry's movie, record and merchandising earnings and expansion had been financed through bank loans. Autry always refused to go public with his companies and Reynolds noted, "There were many approaches made to Gene to take the company public. But he felt that to go public would mean sacrificing a certain independence and ability to make decisions and he valued that independence more than he did the money he might make by going public. Gene was very adamant about it.

"Autry gets and keeps good people, say those closest to him, by giving them loyalty, operational freedom and money.... He leaves the day-to-day management of the company in the hands of others," said the article. Reynolds noted, "Gene expects loyalty and he gives loyalty, but he is never looking over anybody's shoulder and second-guessing. And he always prided himself on being willing to pay top money to get top people."

Autry paid ten people $100,000 or more a year. Autry defended those salaries, saying, "If a man does his job well, he is going to bring that money back to you and so you can afford to pay him well."[6]

The previous year, Golden West Broadcasters earned $40 million in revenues and $10 million from KMPC. The Angels lost around $300,000, but the club had shelled out big money to bring in Dick Williams as manager; Harry Dalton, director of player personnel during the Baltimore Orioles' three successful pennant drives, as general manager; and A. E. "Red" Patterson, former Dodger promotional whiz, as president.

The one big mistake Gene Autry the businessman made during his long, successful career was venturing into the hotel business. The Gene Autry Hotel Company, formed with Robert Reynolds and other investors, bought a number of hotels but, after several years, sold them. Reynolds stated, "We were not hotel people and we should not have been in the business. We just had to take our loss and get out." The last of their hotels was sold in 1967, although Autry purchased the former Holiday Inn in Palm Springs and renamed it the Gene Autry Hotel.

Autry's routine was to rise at seven each morning, read the newspapers and then drive from his home to the Lakeside Golf Club for a game with his adviser and attorney, Clair Stout. He usually arrived in his office around 11 and left by five.

Although he was in "fairly good health," the magazine noted he "walks with difficulty as a result of two foot injuries and reluctantly wears glasses for distance viewing since he had an operation to repair a detached retina several years ago."[7]

****

During the 1970s the Angels had only two winning seasons. In the 1970 season, with Lefty Phillips as manager, the Angels finished third with an 86-76 record. Left fielder Alex Johnson led the American League in hitting with a .329 average, while pitcher Clyde Wright had a 22-12 record with 2.93 ERA. Wright pitched a no-hitter against Oakland. The Angels finished fourth in the 1971 season with a 76-86 record under manager Lefty Phillips. At the end of the season, the Angels traded shortstop Jim Fregosi to the Mets for several players, including Nolan Ryan.

Del Rice, the first player the Angels ever signed, became their manager in 1972. The Angels finished fifth in the American League West under Rice. Nolan Ryan was 19-16 with a 2.28 ERA and led the league in strikeouts, but the Angels finished next to last in their division and only drew 800,000 fans. Nolan Ryan pitched two no-hitters during the 1973 season — the first on May 15 at Kansas City and the second at Detroit on July 15 — and led the league in strikeouts with a record-setting 383. The club finished fourth under manager Bobby Winkles with a 79-83 record. Ryan was 21-16 with a 2.87 ERA.

Winkles had not been the first choice as manager for the 1973 season; Dick Williams was. Williams had just won the World Series for Oakland but couldn't get along with owner Charles Finley. Williams stayed with the A's for the 1973 season then left because he wanted to manage the Yankees. Finley stopped that move; the A's then hired Alvin Dark, and the Yankees hired Bill Virdon.

Williams was sitting out the 1974 season, working for a building contractor in Florida, when Autry called Finley, then met with him at a hotel in Oakland to discuss the Angels hiring Williams as manager. The Angels had problems with managers during this season; Winkles started the season and compiled a 30-44 record, then Whitey Herzog took over and went 2-2.

Autry had supported Charlie Finley when Finley wanted to move the A's from Kansas City to Oakland. Autry called in that favor and received permission to sign Williams as manager. The favor did not come cheap; Autry had to give Finley a check for $50,000 for the right to sign Williams.

The Angels compiled a 36-48 record under Williams for the rest of the '74 season. The Angels finished last but drew almost one million fans. Nolan Ryan struck out a record 367 batters that year, 19 in one game against Boston, and threw his third no-hitter on September 28 against Minnesota.

At the end of the season, Jim "Catfish" Hunter, an outstanding pitcher for the A's, was declared a free agent after a breach of contract by A's owner Finley, and teams began bidding on the pitcher. Autry, with manager Dick Williams and general manager Harry Dalton, visited Hunter at his home in North Carolina and discussed a deal with Hunter's attorney. Autry offered a contract for $1 million a year over five years, half of it deferred, but the pitcher elected to sign with the Yankees for a record amount. When the other baseball players heard about this lucrative contract, the old "reserve clause" was dead and the doors of free agency were blown wide open. From this point forward teams engaged in bidding wars for players, and players acquired riches they never before imagined.

The Angels finished last in the American League West during the 1975 season with a record of 72-89 under manager Williams. Pitcher Frank Tanana had a good year with a 16-9 record and 2.62 ERA, while Nolan Ryan was 14-12 with a 3.45 ERA. Tanana led the American League in strikeouts with 269. The highlight of the year came on June 1 when Nolan Ryan threw his fourth no-hitter against Baltimore, winning 1–0.

In 1976 the Angels finished fourth in the American League West with a 76-86 record. Manager Dick Williams was 39-57 before he was replaced by Norm Sherry, who went 37-29 the rest of the season. Nolan Ryan had a losing record that year — 17-18 with a 3.36 ERA but led the league in shutouts with seven and strikeouts with 327. Second in strikeouts was fellow Angel Frank Tanana with 261, whose record was 19-10 with a 2.44 ERA. At the end of the season, the Angels went into the free agent market and signed three players — Joe Rudi, Don Baylor and Bobby Grich — to contracts worth $5 million.

The Angels finished fifth in the American League West in 1977 with a 74-88 record. During the season manager Norm Sherry was replaced by Dave Garcia. Nolan Ryan was 19-16 with a 2.77 ERA and led the league in strikeouts with 341; Frank Tanana was 15-9 with a league leading 2.54 ERA and finished third in strikeouts with 205.

On August 26, 1977, in Detroit, Gene Autry became so frustrated with the team that he went to their dressing room and chewed them out. He told the team there was a lack of incentive and motivation, that they were content with their mediocrity and that there would be wholesale changes by next summer. Outfielder Bobby Bonds said afterward, "He didn't say anything that particularly upset me. Besides, he's the owner.... He has the right to say what he thinks. We did have a bad home stand. It was embarrassing for me and the whole club. We didn't try to make asses of ourselves but that's the way it turned out. All in all, it's been a very disappointing year."[8]

It was even more disappointing for Autry, since he spent $5 million signing Don Baylor, Bobby Grich and Joe Rudi as free agents. After the tongue lashing the team beat the Tigers 7–4.

During the 1978 season the California Angels finished second in the American League West with an 87-75 record. Manager Dave Garcia was replaced by Jim Fregosi, taking on his first managerial job. Once again Nolan Ryan led the league in strikeouts with 260 as he compiled a 10-13 record; Frank Tanana notched an 18-12 record.

Autry noted, "I had long contended that winning teams had to be grown. You could not buy them. But now I felt compelled to try. My attitude had not changed since the Catfish Hunter auction, but the system had. As a result of a series of court decisions, we had moved into a nearly open marketplace. While the players are clearly elated, deliriously so, I believe the changes are not healthy for baseball and I am not happy about them. But these are the new facts of life and we have to adjust. We have a commitment to our fans, to our sponsors, and to the players who went through lean years with us. We had to improve the club. The Angels never had a player with a $100,000 contract until Frank Robinson in 1973. Now we have seven and in 1978 our average salary was about $75,000.... Gone forever, I fear, is the sense of family that many teams once felt. Some critics say that attitude was paternalistic and demeaning. I never thought so."[9]

Angel Don Baylor was the America League Most Valuable Player in 1979 as the Angels finished first in their division under Jim Fregosi with an 88-74 record. Rod Carew hit .318 while Brian Downing hit .326. Nolan Ryan went 16-14.

During the playoffs, the Angels suffered a crushing loss to Baltimore. At the end of the season, Nolan Ryan left the club for a $1 million salary with the Houston Astros.

29

GOLDEN YEARS

On May 19, 1980, Ina Mae Autry died in her sleep in Palm Springs. She was 69 years old, had been married to Gene Autry for 48 years and was a director in many of his businesses. Her death was sudden and unexpected; ironically, an article in *People* magazine was published on Gene Autry the week she died.

The article noted the 72-year-old Autry never worried about the past. "It's kind of a crime to go back and daydream," he said. "You can't make yourself young again." He admitted: "I honestly never considered myself an actor. An actor would be someone like Paul Muni or Spencer Tracy. I was more of a personality."

Reflecting on his life, Autry said, "I've never feared growing old or death.... It's something every person has to face. The worst thing a person can do in this world is to quit on life. We're here such a short time as it is."[1]

Autry spent most of his time at a bungalow in Palm Springs on the grounds of the Gene Autry Hotel. "I've got a real good staff," said Autry. "So I don't put in that much time in the office. I'm in contact with the television and radio stations every day, but I spend about 25 percent of my day on the team."

When the Angels played at home, Autry and his bodyguard, Les Bagwell, drove from Palm Springs to the ballpark — about a two hour drive — in a Mercedes. Autry noted, "I get threats all the time so I carry someone with me who has a gun. There are a lot of crackpots out there." Bagwell never let his boss out of his sight and carried a .38 Smith & Wesson.[2]

The Angels went from first in 1979 to worst in 1980. They finished sixth in the American League West with a 65-95 record. Rod Carew hit .331, and designated hitter Jason Thompson hit .317 after spending the first part of the season with Detroit, while Frank Tanana compiled a 11-12 record with a 4.15 ERA.

Discussing his ball team, Autry said he was "frustrated disappointed, disgusted and ashamed. Not to mention angry. Some of our pitchers don't have any guts. Some of our players have given up. They've quit. Not all of them. A lot still have pride. But too many have just folded up. We've had all those injuries and they've hurt us plenty, but the problem goes deeper.... Not doing your best is a disgrace. It concerns me a great deal."[3]

The problems for Autry and the Angels began the previous fall, when they lost to the Orioles in the American League playoff. Then Nolan Ryan left for a $1 million contract with the Houston Astros. To replace him the Angels signed Pittsburgh pitcher Bruce Kison for $2.4 million.

The labor dispute in baseball resulted in the abolishment of the old free-agent clause, replaced by a new rule that said players could sell their services to any team after they had been in the majors for six years; the players demanded that be lowered to four years while the owners wanted to retain the existing rule. The owners also wanted compensation from any club that signed one of their free agents. A strike deadline was set for May 22, 1980.

"I don't blame the players," said Autry. "Some of them have no idea of business, of what it takes to field a club. But if they don't wake up, it may be the last roundup. I think we ought to lock them out." An article in *People* noted, "Such harshness is uncharacteristic of Autry. During an earlier player walkout this spring his team sent a letter assuring him it was nothing personal. Ordinarily, he is one of the most generous owners in baseball."[4]

On August 4, the *Los Angeles Times* reported that Autry was in Palm Springs, recuperating from cataract surgery on both of his eyes. "I haven't been reading much about the Angels lately," he said. "I have to use a magnifying glass to read. Actually, I haven't been reading much of anything. I guess that's my lucky break."[5]

During Christmas 1980, Autry led the Hollywood Christmas parade and reflected that in 1946, when he led the parade, he got the idea for the song "Here Comes Santa Claus." On New Year's Eve, he began courting a young lady who became his second wife. Jackie Ellam, born October 2, 1941, left her home in northern New Jersey in 1959 at the age of 17 and moved to California to attend the University of California at Berkeley. Instead, she landed a job as switchboard operator at Security First National Bank in Palm Springs for $225 a month. Ellam decided she made too much money to quit, so she stayed at the bank and rose quickly through the ranks. At 24 she was assistant bank manager, at 30 bank manager and at 32 a vice president who handled Gene Autry's financial affairs with his hotels. At the end of 1980 she was vice president of the Cathedral City branch of Security Pacific.

Autry first met Ellam in 1964 when he went into her bank in Palm Springs to arrange a loan to purchase the Holiday Inn, which he renamed the Gene Autry Hotel. Autry dealt with her regularly through the years and during the Christmas season of 1980, the first he faced without his wife in 48 years, debated calling her. He didn't want to look foolish; he had too much dignity and pride to be viewed as chasing a younger woman, but he finally called and invited her and a companion — if she chose — to come to the New Year's Eve party he was hosting in Palm Springs. She accepted — after turning down two other dinner dates — and the two talked throughout the evening, beginning a courtship that blossomed into a romance.

On July 19, 1981, 72-year-old Gene Autry married 39-year-old Jackie Elam at the First Methodist Church in Burbank. The Angels had been scheduled to play the Yankees at home that day, but the 1981 baseball strike meant that Autry had that day — and a number of others — off.

Reflecting on her marriage, Jackie Autry told the *Los Angeles Times* in April 1982,

"My lifestyle has changed, I don't really feel that I have as much time to myself as I usually have. But as far as my disposition or personality, I'm a pretty stubborn person. The funny thing about my relationship with my husband is we have so many interests that are very similar. We like the same people, we like to do the same things, but he's such a well known person that there are occasions when I feel like I'm starting to lose my own identity because he is a very overwhelming person."[6]

****

The Angels finished the abbreviated 1981 season with a 51-59 record, fifth in their division. Jim Fregosi managed during the first half of the season, Gene Mauch during the second half. The Angels finished fourth in the first half, then seventh in the second half of the split season. Rod Carew hit .305; Bobby Grich hit .304 and led the American League in home runs with 22.

In 1982 the California Angels broke Gene Autry's heart as it had never been broken before. Under manager Gene Mauch, the Angels finished first in the American League West with a 93-69 record. During the five game playoff against Milwaukee, the Angels won the first two games, then came close to winning the deciding third game before a last inning home run defeated them. The Milwaukee club won the next two to claim the crown and go to the World Series. It was the closest Gene Autry and the Angels ever came to a World Series during his lifetime.

During the season, to show how much the support of Autry meant to the team, number 26 — because Autry was the "26th man" on the roster — was retired.

After the playoffs, the *Los Angeles Herald* reported that Autry sat in his private booth at the restaurant in the Gene Autry Hotel and, while trying to eat scrambled eggs and a hamburger patty, accommodated a string of patrons filing by and offering their condolences. "Thanks ... we'll just get 'em next year," Autry replied over and over.

"I've been in the entertainment field too long to get depressed about failure," said Autry. "I learned when I was touring the country putting on shows that some nights things go well and other nights they don't. If you let every failure in life get you down, you might as well stop living."

Autry confessed, "I've had two great ambitions in life — to win an Oscar and to go to the World Series. I know I'll never win an Oscar, so that leaves the World Series."

In spite of Autry's watchword to "wait till next year," the Angeles slumped to fifth in the AL West during the 1983 season under manager John McNamara. Rod Carew hit .339, while pitchers Tommy John and Bruce Kison went 11-13 and 11-5, respectively. The Angels' record that year was 70-92.

****

On October 27, 1982, it was announced that Gene Autry had struck a deal to sell KTLA to the Signal Corporation so he could obtain sole ownership of the California Angels. KTLA was the top-rated independent TV station in Los Angeles. The investment group also purchased other TV holdings of KTLA's parent company, Golden West Broadcasters. In the deal, Autry purchased the 49.9 percent interest in Golden West held by the Signal Company; he paid Signal $225 million for the Angels.

Autry had acquired KTLA from Paramount Picture Corp for $12 million in 1964. Signal had bought 49.9 percent in Golden West Broadcasting in 1968 for $25 million and agreed to pay $250,000 a year for the option to buy the rest of Golden West when Autry died; however, that option ended with this agreement. Autry had put KTLA on the block in 1969 and 1971 but could never agree on a selling price.

The buyer of KTLA was a new company formed by Kohlberg, Kravis and Roberts, an investment firm specializing in management buyouts. It was reported that Autry would not sign any contract until all employees of KTLA and its divisions were taken care of by the new owner.

A number of awards came Gene Autry's way during the 1980s. On April 6, 1987, Gene Autry was honored with his fifth star in the Hollywood Walk of Fame in front of the Roosevelt Hotel. This made Autry the only person with five stars: for movies, radio, TV, recordings and live appearances. The star was the 1,845th in the Walk. A personal highlight occurred when Gene Autry received an honorary Doctor of Laws degree from Pepperdine University in Malibu.

In the summer of 1986, Gene Autry signed an agreement with The Nashville Network to host "Melody Ranch Theater," a daily 90-minute show that aired his old movies. Co-hosting with the 79-year-old Autry was his old sidekick Pat Buttram. Autry and Buttram taped "wrap-arounds" at the beginning and end of each movie in which they commented on the film and aspects related to it. These were filmed in Knoxville.

In October 1987 Roy Rogers joined Gene Autry on TNN's "Melody Ranch Theater," then Gene returned the favor and appeared with Roy in "Happy Trails," the TNN series that showcased the movies of Roy Rogers.

In August 1985 Autry purchased the FM radio station KUTE from Inner City Broadcasting for an estimated $10–16 million. KUTE was a pop/jazz station. In April 1987 Autry sold the 12.4 acres he had leased, and where KTLA was situated, to the Tribune Company of Chicago. The property held the offices of KTLA, Golden West Broadcasters, KMPC-FM and KUTE-FM.

When Gene Autry sold KTLA to raise $245 million in order to buy out the minority interests in the Angels, the sale triggered a divestiture clause in Ina Mae Autry's will that gave Autry five years to sell off all Golden West broadcast properties they had jointly owned. According to the will, all proceeds from the sales were to go into a nonprofit charitable foundation named for her.

During a dinner with Monte and Joanne Hale, Gene and Jackie Autry brought up the idea of a museum of the West to be named after Autry and funded by him. Joanne Hale was named the first executive director and set about finding a site. The city of Burbank offered a site at Buena Vista Park, but the Los Angeles Recreation and Park Commission vetoed it in February 1985.

Political problems caused the Autrys to withdraw their offer of a museum in Burbank in May, but in October a Griffith Park site was selected for the Autry Museum. The city agreed to lease 13.2 acres for $1 a year for 50 years as part of the deal. On November 12, 1986, the beginning of a dream came true for Gene Autry when the ground breaking for the Autry Museum was held.

In February 1987, a black tie benefit to raise money for the Autry Museum was held at the Century Plaza Hotel. With tickets priced from $25 to $2500, 1,055 attended and $790,000 was raised. Among guests at the dinner were James Arness, Roy Rogers and Dale Evans. The entertainment was provided by Frank Sinatra, Dean Martin, Sammy Davis and Rosemary Clooney.

On November 21, 1988, Gene Autry used a bowie knife to cut the lariat ribbon which officially opened the Autry Western Museum. The $54 million museum had a bronze statue of Autry and Champion out front and more than 16,000 items inside, including Teddy Roosevelt's Colt revolver, Buffalo Bill Cody's saddle, and Annie Oakley's gold-plated guns. There were seven permanent galleries and the Wells Fargo theater, which showed Autry's old movies.

During the 1960s, '70s and '80s Johnny Western occasionally got in touch with his old boss, "but he was always so busy with business," said Western. "He had a wonderful office staff: Karla, Maxine and Alex Gordon. He had a great gal named Pat who was with him for years and years. He had an accounting staff and there were always people coming in who just had to have his attention, papers to sign, a financial problem — those kinds of things. But as soon as that was over, he'd always find time to sit and talk about old times.

"He'd talk about the shows. He could talk about them from fifty or sixty years back. He could remember them like they were yesterday. I don't think people think of a cowboy star as being charming, but Gene Autry in a personal setting was charming. He was a great guy with the guys and extremely charming with the ladies and everybody walked out of the room just loving Gene Autry. Everyone felt wonderfully warmed just by being in his presence. He could regale you with stories, talk about your home town like it was his home town 'cause he'd played every place in the world. Because he was such a big star, people didn't realize how many small, little rinky-dink theaters he'd played in his life. The little rodeos and small ventures; he'd played everywhere. He was so charming and it made you feel so wonderful. It was not a put-on; that's just the way he was."[7]

The years took their toll on Autry, with old friends passing away and his health deteriorating. On February 10, 1986, Art Satherley died in Los Angeles. On November 14, 70-year-old Carl Cotner died in Buena Park. On August 6, 1989, Nat Levine, the founder of Mascot Pictures and the man who signed Gene Autry to his first movie contract, died in Los Angeles at the age of 89.

By the middle of 1989, Gene Autry was legally blind; he had corneal transplants to rectify this.

The California Angels bounced back to finish second in the AL West during the 1984 season under manager John McNamara. During the season, Reggie Jackson hit his 500th home run, Rod Carew collected his 3,000th hit, and Mike Witt pitched a perfect game on the last day of the season.

The Angels finished first in the American League West in the 1986 season with a 92-70 record under Gene Mauch. It was a bittersweet year for Gene Autry and the Angels; they lost the playoff to the Boston Red Sox, managed by John McNamara.

In 1987 the Angels finished sixth in their division under manager Gene Mauch. In 1988 Gene Autry did not go into the office every day at 5858 Sunset Boulevard, but Jackie did. However, Gene went to every baseball game, and watched the Angels finish fourth, compiling a 75-87 record under Cookie Rojas.

On July 7, 1989, the California Angels hosted "Western Heritage Night" before they played the Texas Rangers. In attendance as honorees were Clayton Moore, Buddy Ebsen, Pat Buttram, Richard Farnsworth, Cameron Mitchell, Glen Campbell, Rex Allen, George Montgomery, Eddie Dean, Cliffie Stone, Monte Hale, and Casey Tibbs.

Replicas of Autry's five stars on the Hollywood Walk of Fame on the sidewalk in front of the Angels' stadium were unveiled by Autry during All Star Week, July 4–11. The Angels finished third that year in their division under manager Doug Rader. Pitcher Bert Blyleven compiled a 17-5 record and 2.73 ERA, while Kirk McCaskill was 15-10, Chuck Finley was 16-9 and one-armed pitcher Jim Abbott, the hottest story in baseball that year, was 12-12.

During the 1980s and 1990s, there was a new interest in Gene Autry's singing cowboy career. In England, Alf Hill started the Gene Autry International Fan Club during the 1980s. During the 1990s, inspired by Autry's appearances on TNN's "Melody Ranch Theatre," Rose Marie Addison rekindled the Gene Autry Friendship Club; she and Jon Guyot Smith edited the newsletter.[8]

On May 9, 1990, Henry Crowell, manager of Melody Ranch, put the last Champion to sleep. It was "one of the hardest things I ever had to do," said Crowell. The manager had been with Autry at Melody Ranch for 28 years at the time.[9] After the death of his final Champ, Autry sold off the last ten acres of Melody Ranch.

He didn't need the money; in 1990 Autry was listed as one of the 400 richest Americans by *Forbes*—the only entertainer on the list.

In July 1991 Autry was given a "Lifetime Achievement Award" by the Songwriter's Hall of Fame at the New York Hilton; the award was presented by Morton Gould. "This is really one of the happiest evenings that I have had in a long, long time," said Autry. "In my early days of coming to New York, I used to look forward to putting on my rodeo at Madison Square Garden and to my friendship with so many fine fans."[10] He told the *New Yorker* magazine he liked to listen to songs by Irving Berlin, Walter Donaldson and Hoagy Carmichael.

In January 1992, Autry was honored at the Doheny Eye Institute. The popular western group Riders in the Sky entertained, and group member Fred LaBour ("Too Slim") remembered that Autry came by their table and spoke with them, a friendly, affable man who was good at meeting people and making them feel at ease.[11] That gesture summed up Gene Autry, a genial people-person who loved working a crowd, who was comfortable with his fame and gracious to everyone who wanted to meet him.

In 1993 Gene Autry was heard singing "Back in the Saddle" in the popular movie, *Sleepless in Seattle*. During the fall of 1994, a documentary, "Gene Autry: Melody of the West," narrated by Johnny Cash, was shown on the American Movie Classics (AMC) cable channel. Autry's recording career was rejuvenated through re-issues. In 1992 *The Essential Gene Autry: 1933–1946* CD was released by Columbia. In 1994, the *Gene Autry Christmas* CD was released. The early years of Gene Autry's recording career were documented in 1996 when the CD *Gene Autry: Blues Singer*, compiled from his days before he was a movie star, was released. During 1997 a three CD set, *Gene Autry: Sing Cowboy Sing*, was released. Consisting mostly of outtakes from his radio show, the collection was released on Rhino and sold approximately 15,000 copies — not bad for a boxed set of a man who had not been active in the music business since 1960 — and won a Grammy.

During the 1990s, some of Autry's leading ladies died: June Storey passed away on December 18, 1991; Mary Lee Wooters died June 6, 1996; and on March 15, 1997, 71-year-old Gail Davis died.

During the 1990 season, the Angels finished fourth with an 80-82 record under manager Doug Rader. During the season, Mark Langston and Mike Witt combined to pitch a no-hitter against Seattle, with Langston throwing the first seven innings and Witt the last two.

In 1991 Anaheim named the street leading to the stadium Gene Autry Way. For the 1991 season, Autry handed the control of the Angels to his wife, Jackie. She noted the ball club had lost $25–$30 million during the past five years. During 1991, *Forbes* listed Autry's worth at $300 million. That season the Angels finished seventh — last — with a 81-81 record. There were two managers — Doug Rader began the season but was replaced by Buck Rodgers for the last 38 games. That same year the Angels retired Nolan Ryan's number 30; Ryan had posted a 138-121 overall record with the Angels.

The Angels began their 1992 season under Buck Rogers, then had John Wathen manage before finishing under Marcel Lachemann. They finished fifth with a 72-90. Near disaster struck early in the season when they were involved in a bus crash, but all team members survived. In 1993, the Angels had a 71-91 record. Their big hitter was Tim Salmon with 31 home runs and 95 RBIs; the right fielder won American League Rookie of the Year honors. In 1994 the Angels had a 47-68 record during the strike season when there was no World Series played.

In 1995, Autry sold 25 percent of the Angels to the Disney Corporation, which assumed controlling interest; the agreement stated that Disney would purchase the rest when he died. The team was then valued at $120 million; he had bought the club for $2.5 million.

That season, the Angels lost a one-game playoff to the Seattle Mariners after both had finished in a tie for first. During the playoff, pitcher Randy Johnson hurled the Mariners to their win. Tim Salmon hit .330 with 34 home runs and 105 RBIs; relief pitcher Lee Smith had 37 saves.

In 1997, the Angels, under manager Terry Collins, finished second. They changed their name to the Anaheim Angels for this season; renovations were underway at Anaheim Stadium. The club had a 66-50 record by early August and led their division by a half game, but season-ending injuries to pitcher Chuck Finley and catcher Todd Green were major factors in the Angels going 18-28 the rest of the way and finishing six games behind the Mariners.

30

INTO THE SUNSET

Gene Autry wore a smile in his heart wherever he went. Fans of the Angels saw that smile at the Angels' home opener in 1998. The crowd in the stands was surprised to see Gene Autry suddenly appear in left field in a golf cart before the game started. As he was driven in, everything at the stadium stopped, and the entire crowd rose to their feet and cheered. It seemed time was running out to "Win One for the Cowboy," but that was certainly the emotion of those in attendance that day.

The revival of western heritage through the increased popularity of western music, cowboy poetry and western festivals led to a new awareness of Gene Autry for the generations who had not grown up watching him on Saturday afternoons on the movie screen during the 1930s and 1940s. The World War II generation had no problem remembering Gene Autry; now they had the time to enjoy his old movies and recordings again.

By this point, the Autry office in California owned most of Autry's movies and radio shows, and played an active role — originally led by Gene himself — in keeping the singing cowboy in the spotlight. There were reissues of his old movies on video, then DVD; there were releases of a wide variety of his recorded material, everything from old recordings on Columbia, to performances pulled from his movies and radio shows. Computers and the digital era made it easier to restore, reissue and keep track of the wealth of Gene Autry material.

In time, the Autry Museum of the West in Burbank proved itself to be one of the great museums in the United States. Visiting it, young school children were exposed to the western experience in America — as well as the West in entertainment. It is fitting that Gene Autry built a lasting legacy of his life's work for all to appreciate — and that he lived long enough to know that.

There were several strong indications the end was near in 1998. On July 6 Roy Rogers died in Apple Valley, California. Autry continued to attend Angels games, but the rest of the time he was mostly confined to his home where age was taking its toll on his body, although his mind stayed relatively sharp.

On September 5 Gene Autry attended his last Angels game and watched them beat the Kansas City Royals 2–1. He told a reporter that night, "I loved everything I did." Earlier in the year he sold his home in the Autry Hotel in Palm Springs to Merv Griffin.

On September 29, 1998, Gene Autry celebrated his 91st birthday; a few days later, on October 2 — his wife, Jackie's 57th birthday — he died at his home in Studio City, California.

The death of Gene Autry made front page news all over the world. An article in the *Los Angeles Times* noted that perhaps Autry's closest companion during his final days was a UPS worker who moonlighted at the stadium as a press-box usher. "John Moynihan, 65, would accompany Autry around the country ... or pick him up in Studio City for breakfast in Toluca Lake," wrote Bill Plaschke. Moynihan related that Autry "would always say, 'Hi, howarya,' and we just became friends. Soon he started calling me, asking if I could go with him here or there, and I said sure."

Moynihan was with Autry during his last visit to the ballpark. Autry required a wheelchair but "hated being seen in it but loved seeing his players. So Moynihan wheeled him into the clubhouse for a pregame visit...."

"He met with Gary DiSarcina, Chuck Finley, some guys he felt close with," Moynihan said. "He told stories, we had some good laughs." After the game Moynihan was wheeling Autry toward the exit when the owner told him to stop. "I want to walk out," he said, pulling himself to his feet. And so on his last departure from his beloved team, Gene Autry walked, proudly, along the crowded concourse to the curb, through packs of fans who stared, whispered and admired."[1]

In an article in Nashville's *Tennessean* newspaper, long-time Autry friend Ed Gregory recalled he set up a meeting between President Clinton and Autry so the president could give him the Medal of Freedom award in February.

"The President walks in, and Gene is sitting in this big armchair," said Gregory. "He starts to get up. The President said, 'You sit right there.' President Clinton then sat on a coffee table next to the great cowboy. Gene looks at him, and just as straight as can be, says: 'Now, son, where do you live now?' The President told Autry he lived in Washington, D.C. Gene says to the President: 'Great town. I've played there many times.'"[2]

People who knew Gene had insightful stories about him. "Some of those old cowboy stars didn't save their money and ended up on hard times," remembered Johnny Western. "Ken Maynard was living in a trailer in the San Fernando Valley and was completely broke. I know Gene had given him several handouts, had taken care of him several times and one day at Gene's office on Sunset, Ken came in with a plastic bag carrying a white hat of his in mint condition. He asked Gene to buy the hat for $500 because he was desperate. Gene immediately gave him the $500 and then gave him the hat back. Gene would not take the hat under those conditions."

"I also remember something Earl Lindsay, the road manager for Gene when I toured with him, told me" continued Western. "He told me that Gene totally supported a boy's home down in Texas. Gene and Ina Mae never had any kids but he always felt that since kids loved him so much, he should give something back. He didn't want that publicized but that home had about 40 or 50 needy kids and he sent them a check every year which basically covered all their expenses."[3]

On October 27, 1998, the Angels hosted a public tribute to Autry at Edison Field. The speakers included Buck Rogers, Clyde Wright, Don Baylor, Rod Carew, Dick Enberg (MC), John Hall (*Times* writer), and Ross Newham (sportswriter).

In a special issue of *American Cowboy* devoted to Gene Autry, writer Robert W. Phillips noted, "Autry did not single-handedly popularize the cowboy image, per se. But he did perfect one version of it, that of the 'Singing Cowboy.' And he did more than anyone else to advance the cowboy image during this century. What he did was keep the good guy image of the cowboy before the masses. At his height, Autry was the idol of red-blooded American youth. His like cannot be found today."

The article concluded, "With his passing, we're reminded of how important were the values he represented. This nation, and especially its youth, has never been in greater need of cowboy heroes. Autry's 'Cowboy Code' tells one story of why he was so great, and why we need those with the moral courage to follow in his footsteps, to lead by example as Gene Autry led us for so many decades."[4]

What made Gene Autry's movies so successful? The obvious answer is Gene Autry. He had a musical background, was young, handsome and, after each movie was released, he went out and promoted the movie on a singing tour. But the true answer is much more elusive, as elusive as the concept of stardom. Simply put, Gene Autry had the magic. This magic is an indefinable characteristic which stars have and others don't. Many have argued — and Autry even conceded — that he was not a great singer and not a great actor, yet he became a big star.

However, the fact is that Autry was a very good singer; his voice had a clear resonance and warmth to it that conveyed his songs well. It was distinctive and yet an everyman's voice; he did not have a great range or timbre to overpower a listener, but instead made a listener feel comfortable. Ann Rutherford related that her mother always said Gene Autry had a "come out of the kitchen voice," meaning that when you heard it, you stopped what you were doing, came out of the kitchen, and paid close attention to the radio. Eddy Arnold said, "There was something about Gene Autry's voice" that captured him. Something that made him stop and take notice. That was Gene Autry's singing talent — not the notes he could hit or how far away someone could hear him without a microphone.

And as for acting, the simple fact is that Gene Autry played Gene Autry better than anyone else. That may sound like an obvious statement, but it isn't. A lot of actors and singers tried to play a singing cowboy, but they couldn't do it like Gene Autry. The closest was Roy Rogers, but even he never had that broad appeal as both a singer and actor that Autry did.

Gene Autry was handsome, with a look of youthful innocence and sincerity. He was also an extremely hard worker. He took the talent he had and multiplied it through his relentless touring, promotion and dedication to his career. When some part of his career needed improvement, he worked at it; when it needed time, he gave it.

How can you sum up Gene Autry in a sentence, a paragraph or even a book? How do you explain his success? How can you communicate to those who did not grow up with Gene Autry as a hero just how and why he became a hero? Maybe Marty Stuart's experience having dinner with Gene Autry at the legendary cowboy's home captures it. "Marty could never understand why Johnny Cash was so enamored with Gene Autry," said Johnny Western. "Other than Gene Autry was just a monster big name. But in fifteen minutes of being in Gene Autry's presence, Marty realized he was in the presence of greatness, and that's when he realized how everyone was so captured by the magic of Gene Autry. You just felt so honored to be around him for a little while and absorb part of that aura that was Gene Autry."[5]

For those who did not grow up watching Gene Autry on the silver screen or seeing him in person on one of his tours it is difficult to convey how your heart would jump into your throat when you saw this cowboy. Watching Gene Autry meant having the experience of being transported to a better place and time, where good was rewarded, evil was punished, and the good guys won.

Gene Autry showed us what a hero looks like.

CONCLUSION

It's a long, long way from Tioga, Texas, to Hollywood, measured by more than just the miles. Sometimes it feels a bit stunning to see a small, humble town where such a great man came from.

Tioga is a still a small town, located along Highway 377 in north Texas. A sign there advertises its population as 754, adding that it was the birthplace of Gene Autry. Train tracks run parallel to the highway, and trains roll by several times a day. It's easy to imagine a young boy, watching a train and dreaming about where it had been and where it was going and wanting to be part of that railroad, which was much bigger than himself and which linked the country.

Turning east off 377 is Gene Autry Drive, site of the annual Gene Autry Festival since 2002. There is a small museum at the back of the empty lot where the festival is held. The building is home to the Tioga Chamber of Commerce but the Tioga Chamber is not a full time job. There is a sign in the window with several phone numbers to call if you'd like to visit the museum. The museum is one room filled with pictures, articles and a few items of memorabilia of Gene Autry.

The place where Gene Autry was born is under water now, covered by a man-made lake where tree trunks rise above the water. Down a gravel road west of Highway 377 is the Indian Creek Baptist Church, newly refurbished and painted, where Gene Autry's grandfather preached and where the young Gene first sang. In the northeast corner of the graveyard is a section where the Autrys are located. Buried in the red Texas clay is the grave of Gene Autry's mother, whose tombstone states simply "Elnora Ozment Autry, 1882–1932."

The museum in Gene Autry, Oklahoma, close to Ardmore, sits near the railroad depot where Autry appeared when the town changed its name from Berwyn. The museum is filled with Gene Autry pictures, posters and other memorabilia. If you want to get a good dose of just how big Gene Autry was in the 1930s and 1940s, this is a good place to do it. More than any other place, this will give a visitor an idea of the excitement created by Gene Autry when he was starring in his singing cowboy pictures.

The Autry Museum of the West in Los Angeles is not a museum of Gene Autry; instead it is one of the finest museums of the West — its history, image, romance and legacy — in the world today. This museum is truly an American treasure, and this entire country, especially the city of Los Angeles, is incredibly fortunate that Gene Autry provided the money and endowment that created this timeless legacy.

And, well, wouldn't you know it!

In 2002 the Anaheim Angels defeated the New York Yankees three games to two in the American League Division series, then beat the Minnesota Twins four games to one in the American League Championship Series. In the World Series, they beat the San Francisco Giants in a thrilling seven game series.

But the Cowboy did not see it, at least not sitting in the earthly stands. And yet everyone there remembered him. TV cameras showed Jackie Autry, and the announcers talked about the dream that Gene Autry never saw come true during his own lifetime.

Gene Autry was disappointed but took it all in stride, just as he took the fame and acclaim of his singing cowboy days in stride. Autry once said to Johnny Western: "When a crowd applauds you, let it go to your heart, but don't let it go to your head."[1] He never won an Oscar, and the Angels never won a World Series during his lifetime. It almost seems unfair that the man who made dreams come true for so many others was denied two of his own most cherished dreams.

Gene Autry was not one to let that get him down. He always knew, as his wife once told him when he talked to her about visiting children in hospitals, that he was a man who was more blessed than most.

More blessed than most — that could also be said of all of us who were captured by the presence of Gene Autry as a hero when we were young and have never stopped carrying the warm memory of that magical moment in our hearts.

CHAPTER NOTES

Introduction

1. Douglas B. Green, "Gene Autry." In *Stars of Country Music*, edited by Bill C. Malone and Judith McCulloh (Urbana: University of Illinois Press, 1975), 167.

2. Johnny Western, telephone interview by author, 31 August 2005.

3. Jon Guyot Smith, e-mail to author, 20 March 2005.

Chapter 1

1. Jon Guyot Smith, e-mail to author, 12 April 2005

2. Ibid.

3. www.autrynationalcenter.org

4. Gene Autry, interview by Mike Oatman, Palm Springs, California, 14 February 1983.

5. Wayne W. Daniel, "Gene Autry: America's Number 1 Singing Cowboy," *Nostalgia Digest*, February/March 2003, 7.

6. Glenn White, telephone interview by author, 2 May 2005.

7. Information on Otto Gray came from William W. Savage, Jr., *Singing Cowboys and All That Jazz: A Short History of Popular Music in Oklahoma* (Norman: University of Oklahoma Press, 1983, 34–36; and by Douglas B. Green, *Singing in the Saddle: The History of the Singing Cowboy* (Nashville: Country Music Foundation Press and Vanderbilt University Press, 2002), 35–36.

8. Autry, interview by Mike Oatman.

9. "Fame Hasn't Spoiled Autry Says 'Key Punching' Tutor." This article was a clipping obtained from Glenn White's files.

10. Maxine Arnold, "Maxine in Movieland." This article was a clipping obtained from Glenn White's files.

11. Gene Autry, with Mickey Herskowitz, *Back in the Saddle Again* (Garden City, N.Y: Doubleday, 1976), 167.

12. Larry Hopper, e-mail to author, 12 March 2005.

13. Jon Tuska, *The Vanishing Legion: A History of Mascot Pictures 1927–1935* (Jefferson, N.C.: McFarland, 1982), 163.

14. Steve Gragert of the Will Rogers Memorial Museum, e-mail to author, 4 May 2005. The telegram may be found in James M. Smallwood and Steven K. Gragert, eds., *Will Rogers' Daily Telegrams, Vol. 1, The Coolidge Years, 1926–1929* (Stillwater: Oklahoma State University Press, 1978), 207–208.

15. Glenn White, telephone interview by author.

16. William Strauss and Neil Howe, *Generations: The History of America's Future, 1584 to 2069* (New York: Quill/William Morrow, 1991).

Chapter 2

1. Frankie Marvin, interview at Country Music Hall of Fame & Museum, Oral History Project, n.d.

2. The information about the early recording sessions by Gene Autry, Frankie Marvin, Jimmy Long, and others can be found in Tony Russell, *Country Music Records: A Discography, 1921–1942* (New York: Oxford University Press, 2004).

3. Frankie Marvin, interview.

4. Ibid.

5. Nolan Porterfield, *Jimmie Rodgers: The Life and Times of America's Blue Yodeler* (Urbana: University of Illinois Press, 1979), 5.

6. Ibid., p. 237.

7. Nolan Porterfield, "Jimmie Rodgers — The Discography," recording notes to *Jimmie Rodgers: The Singing Brakeman* (Bear Family Records BCD 15540 FI, 1992), compact disc boxed set.

8. Walter Darrell Haden, "Vernon Dalhart." In *The Stars of Country Music*, edited by Bill C. Malone and Judith McCulloh (Urbana: University of Illinois Press, 1975), 84.

9. "The Catfish Band," n.p., n.d. This is a photocopied article from Glenn White.

10. Johnny Western, interview by Douglas B. Green, Nashville, Tennessee, 17 December 1997.

11. Autry with Herskowitz, *Back in the Saddle*, 12.

12. The information on Art Satherley comes from

the interview with him at the Country Music Hall of Fame & Museum for the museum's Oral History Project, n.d.

13. Ibid.

14. Autry, with Herskowitz, *Back in the Saddle*, 15.

Chapter 3

1. Satherley, interview.

2. Laurence Bergreen, *Louis Armstrong: An Extravagant Life* (New York: Broadway Books, 1997), 216–217.

3. Information on Herbert Yates and Republic Pictures comes from Richard Maurice, *Republic Studios: Between Poverty Row and the Majors* (Metuchen, N.J.: Scarecrow Press, 1979); *The* Jon Tuska, *Vanishing Legion: A History of Mascot Pictures, 1927–1935* (Jefferson, N.C.: McFarland, 1982); and Alex Ben Block, "Salute to Republic Entertainment," *The Hollywood Reporter*, 24 October 1995.

Chapter 4

1. Eddy Arnold, interview with the author, 18 March 2005. I am the biographer of Eddy Arnold, and we get together regularly and have lunch. During the writing of this book I often asked him questions about Gene Autry — who was a personal friend — and some of the other acts that Arnold knew in the past.

2. Russell, *Country Music Records,* 510–512.

3. Gene Autry, letter to Callie Jean Autry. I received a copy of this letter from Glenn White in Oklahoma City.

4. Jon Guyot Smith, "Some Thoughts Regarding the Evolution of Gene Autry's Recording Career." This was originally published in a *Gene Autry's Friends* newsletter and copied for the author.

5. Satherley, interview.

6. Gene Autry, "3 Pals," *Country Song Roundup*, 1950 (?). This article was found in a scrapbook at the Gene Autry Oklahoma Museum.

7. Esther Carlin, "The Cowboy and His Lady," *TV Stage*, n.d. This article was in a scrapbook at the Gene Autry Oklahoma Museum.

Chapter 5

1. Marie Frank, interview, Country Music Hall of Fame & Museum, Oral History Project, n.d.

2. Ibid.

3. Ivan Tribe, "Brother Gene Autry: The Original Singing Cowboy," *Knight Templar* 44, no. 1 (January 1998), 21.

4. Carlin, "The Cowboy and His Lady."

5. Laurence Bergreen, *Capone: The Man and the Era* (New York: Touchstone/Simon & Schuster, 1994), 85.

6. An excellent overview of Chicago in the era of Al Capone may be found in Bergreen, *Capone.*

7. James Evans, *Prairie Farmer and W.L.S.: The Burridge D. Butler Years* (Urbana: University of Illinois Press, 1969), 229.

8. Gene Autry, as told to Morris Gelman, "Gene Autry Recalls 53 Mostly Golden Years," *Daily Variety*, 28 October 1980, 202.

9. Henry Bentinck, "The Nation's Barn Dance," *Radio Guide* 4, no. 2 (11 November 1934).

10. Ibid.

11. Gene Autry, interview by Kenneth E. Baughman, Los Angeles, California, 5 July 1990.

12. Ibid.

13. Carlin, "The Cowboy and His Lady."

14. Russell, *Country Music Records,* 510–512.

15. Carlin, "The Cowboy and His Lady."

16. Marriage license for Orvon Autry and Ina Mae Spivey, Office of Recorder of Deeds, City of St. Louis, Missouri, 1 April 1932.

17. "List'ning in with Prairie Farmer. WLS: The Voice of Agriculture," *Prairie Farmer* magazine, 16 April 1932, 16.

18. "List'ning in," 14 May 1932, 18.

19. "List'ning in," 11 June 1932, 22.

20. Russell, *Country Music Records,* 71–87.

21. "List'ning in," 25 June 1932, 18.

22. *Variety*, 1 November 1932, 48.

23. "List'ning in," 26 November 1932, 12.

Chapter 6

1. Russell, *Country Music Records*, 71–87.

2. Jon Guyot Smith, "Gene Autry on Victor Records." This was originally published in a *Gene Autry's Friends* newsletter and copied for the author.

3. "List'ning in," 15 April 1933, 8.

4. "List'ning in," 29 April 1933, 5.

5. "List'ning in," 13 May 1933, 8.

6. "List'ning in," 27 May 1933, 12.

7. *Variety*, 1 November 1932, 48.

8. *Variety*, 2 May 1933, 36.

9. *Variety*, 6 June 1933, 41.

10. Jon Guyot Smith, e-mail to author, 13 April 2005.

11. Porterfield, *Jimmie Rodgers: The Life and Times of America's Blue Yodeler.*

12. Russell, *Country Music Records*, 71–87.

13. Green, *Singing in the Saddle,* 71.

14. Advertisement, *Billboard*, 9 December 1933, 13.

15. Jonathan Guyot Smith, "Smiley Burnette: It's Nice to Be Important, but More Important to Be Nice," *DISCoveries*, April 1994, 26–30.

16. Ibid.

17. Autry, interview by Kenneth E. Baughman.

18. *WLS Family Album: 1933* (Chicago: WLS, 1933).

Chapter 7

1. *Billboard*, 21 April 1934, 14.

2. Autry, interview by Kenneth E. Baughman.

3. Autry, with Herskowitz, *Back in the Saddle*, 117.

4. "Gene Autry," *People* magazine, 26 May 1980.

5. Autry, interview by Kenneth E. Baughman.

Chapter 8

1. Tuska, *The Vanishing Legion*, 8–23.
2. Ibid., 184.
3. Satherley, interview.
4. Haynes, Dick, Interview with Gene Autry, broadcast on KLAC, February 20, 1974.
5. Autry, as told to Gelman, "Gene Autry Recalls 53 Mostly Golden Years," op. cit.
6. Satherley, interview.
7. Autry, with Herskowitz, *Back in the Saddle*, 33
8. Ibid.
9. Tuska, *The Vanishing Legion*, 156.
10. Ibid., 132–133.
11. *Billboard*, 14 July 1934, 7.
12. Wesley Tuttle, interview by author, Los Angeles, California, 3 January 2001.
13. Tuska, *The Vanishing Legion*, 136.
14. Ibid., 133.
15. Ibid., 136.
16. Thomas Doherty, *Pre-Code Hollywood: Sex, Immorality, and Insurrection in American Cinema 1930–1934* (New York: Columbia University Press, 1999), 326–327.

Chapter 9

1. *Billboard*, 9 March 1935, 2, 6.
2. Marie Frank, interview, Country Music Hall of Fame & Museum, Oral History Project, n.d.
3. Tuska, *The Vanishing Legion*, 156.
4. Goodale's version of being hired by Autry was found in an article, "Angels PR in Good Hands," in the files at either the Academy of Motion Picture Archives or the Baseball Hall of Fame.
5. Mayme Ober Peak, "Encouraged Him to Go into Movies," *Boston Globe*, 11 June 1939.
6. This information was found in Ben Yagoda, *Will Rogers: A Life* (New York: Knopf, 1993) and corroborated in an e-mail from the Will Rogers Museum and Archive in Claremore, Oklahoma.
7. Tuska, *The Vanishing Legion*, 182–186; Alex Ben Block, "Salute to Republic Entertainment," *The Hollywood Reporter*, 24 October 1995.
8. Autry, with Herskowitz, *Back in the Saddle*, 35.
9. *Westward Ho!* is available on home video.

Chapter 10

1. Russell, *Country Music Records*, 71–87.
2. Jon Guyot Smith, "The Wonderful Ann Rutherford," originally published in *Gene Autry's Friends* and copied for the author.
3. Johnny Bond, "Gene Autry: Champion," unpublished manuscript in the Country Music Hall of Fame & Museum archives. n.d.
4. "Cowboy Sings for Admirers," *The Daily Oklahoman*, 12 November 1935.
5. Review of movie *Oh, Susannah, Variety*, 24 March 1937, 21.
6. Jon Guyot Smith, "The Wonderful Ann Rutherford."

7. Review of movie *The Big Show, Variety*, 3 March 1937, 15.
8. Robert J. Duncan, "Oldtimer Recalls Colorful Past of Town That Will Be Auctioned," *Dallas Times-Herald*, 26 September 1982, 83A.
9. Sam Blair, "Tall Tales from Tioga: How a Hollywood Cowboy Left His Mark on This Grayson County Town," *Dallas Morning News*, 20 October 1993, C1, C2.

Chapter 11

1. Review of movie *Roundup Time in Texas, Variety*, 7 July 1937, 25.

Chapter 12

1. The best source for information on Bing Crosby is Gary Giddins, *Bing Crosby: A Pocketful of Dreams: The Early Years, 1903–1940* (Boston: Little, Brown, 2001).

Chapter 13

1. "Autry Held by Republic," *Variety*, 13 October 1937, 25.
2. "Balladeering Mustang Stars OK B.O.; Autry Started It, Others Now Click," *Variety*, 13 October 1937, 25.
3. Suze Hamblen, interviewed by author, Santa Clarita, California, 23 March 2001.
4. Robert W. Phillips, *Roy Rogers* (Jefferson, N.C.: McFarland, 1995), 15–16.
5. Ken Griffis, *Hear My Song: The Story of the Celebrated Sons of the Pioneers* (Northglenn, Colorado: Norken, 2001), 21–29.
6. Review of movie *Manhattan Merry-Go-Round, Variety*, November 1937.
7. Autry, with Herskowitz, *Back in the Saddle*, 58.
8. "The Year in Pictures: A Review of 1937," *Variety*, 7 January 1938, 12.
9. "Autry Demands More Money from Republic," *Variety*, 19 January 1938.
10. "Yates' $902,100 More in Republic in 1937," *Variety*, 13 April 1938, 17.
11. "Republic Counting on Autry's Peaceful Return Despite Walk," *Variety*, 26 January 1938, 4.
12. "Hero of Horse Operas Summons Aid for Legal thriller Here," *Nashville Banner*, 30 January 1938, 4.
13. "Autry Says Rep Using His Pix as Club on Exhibs; Defends Coin Demand," *Variety*, 2 February 1938, 11.
14. Ibid.
15. Ibid.
16. Ibid.
17. Ibid.
18. Ibid.
19. "Autry Demands More Money from Republic," op. cit.
20. Autry, with Herskowitz, *Back in the Saddle*, 61.
21. "Rep Hustling Prod. with Grainger in as Headman; Await Autry Move," *Variety*, 9 February 1938.
22. "Autry Denies He's Settled Troubles: Film

Cowboy Here Going to Chicago to Visit Friends," *The Nashville Tennessean*, 4 February 1938.

23. "Rep Hustling Prod. with Grainger in as Headman," op. cit.

24. "Rep — Autry in Stymie; New Mustanger," *Variety*, 16 February 1938, 5.

25. Ibid.

26. "20th After Autry," *Variety*, 16 March 1938.

27. "Autry on S.A. Tour Unless Rep. Kicks in with 25G Per Pic," *Variety*, 23 March 1938, 4.

28. "456 Pictures for 1938–1939," *Variety*, 6 April 1938, 1.

29. "Republic Sales Meet Draws 200 to Coast," *Variety*, 20 April 1938.

30. "Rogers' P.A. Tour Routed Over Autry Strongholds," *Variety*, 13 April 1938, 7.

31. Review of movie *Under Western Stars*, *Variety*, 20 April 1938, 15.

32. "Autry's Song Warning," *Variety*, 4 May 1938.

33. "Autry Yipees Again for Republic; Peace Terms in His Favor," *Variety*, 14 May 1938.

34. "Inside Stuff—Pictures, *Variety*, 18 May 1938, 10.

35. "Autry Draws 10G Per Pic as Rep Settler," *Variety*, 18 May 1938, 4.

Chapter 14

1. Ronald L. Davis, *Duke: The Life and Image of John Wayne* (Norman: University of Oklahoma Press, 1998), 71.

2. Information on Fred Rose comes from John Woodruff Rumble, "Fred Rose and the Development of the Nashville Music Industry, 1942–1954," Ph.D. diss., Vanderbilt University, 1980.

3. Ibid.

4. Wade Hall, *Hell-Bent for Music: The Life of Pee Wee King* (Lexington, Ky.: The University Press of Kentucky, 1996), 194.

5. Ibid., 195.

6. Ibid., 194.

7. Ibid., 194

8. Hall, *Hell-Bent for Music*, 196.

9. Ibid., 197.

10. Ibid., 175.

11. Ibid., 35–36.

12. The information on Mitch Hamilburg comes from the *Variety* obituary of 22 May 1958 and an interview with Mitch Hamilburg, Jr., on the telephone, 3 March 2002.

13. Review of movie *Prairie Moon*, *Variety*, 19 October 1938, 27.

Chapter 15

1. Dorothy Horstman, *Sing Your Heart Out, Country Boy: Classic Country Songs and Their Inside Stories by the People Who Wrote Them* (New York: E. P. Dutton, 1975), 291; and an e-mail from O. J. Sikes, 16 April 2005.

2. Ray Whitley, interview by Douglas B. Green, Country Music Hall of Fame & Museum, Oral History Project, 30 March 1975.

3. Mayme Ober Peak, "Encouraged Him to Go into Movies," *Boston Globe*, 11 June 1939.

4. Gene Autry, testimony at the Hearings Before the Subcommittee on Communications of the Committee on Interstate and Foreign Commerce: United States Senate, Eighty-Fifth Congress, Second Session on S.2834: Amendment to Communications Act of 1934, 15 April 1958, 446–456.

5. Ibid.

6. M. M. Cole, letter to the Hearings Before the Subcommittee on Communications of the Committee on Interstate and Foreign Commerce: United States Senate, Eighty-Fifth Congress, Second Session on S.2834: Amendment to Communications Act of 1934, 972–973.

7. Autry, Senate testimony.

8. Autry, with Herskowitz, *Back in the Saddle*, 72.

9. Ibid.

10. Ibid., 73.

11. Ibid.

12. Jim Bob Tinsley, *For a Cowboy Has to Sing* (Orlando: University of Central Florida Press, 1991), 211–212.

13. "Mex Bans Autry Pic on Oil-Revolution," *Variety*, 7 August 1940, 1.

Chapter 16

1. Autry, with Herskowitz, *Back in the Saddle*, 75.

2. Review of radio program *Melody Ranch*, *Variety*, 10 January 1940, 36.

3. Autry told this story during his testimony at the Hearings before the Subcommittee on Communications of the Committee on Interstate and Foreign Commerce.

4. Linda Lee Wakely, *See Ya Up There, Baby: The Jimmy Wakely Story* (Canoga Park, Calif.: Shasta Records, 1992), 11–12.

5. Ibid., 10.

6. Johnny Bond, *Reflections: The Autobiography of Johnny Bond* (Los Angeles: The John Edwards Memorial Foundation, 1976).

7. Linda Lee Wakely, *See Ya Up There, Baby*, 15.

8. Review of movie, *Gaucho Serenade*, *Variety*, 15 May 1940, 16.

9. Hedda Hopper, "Gene Autry," *Chicago Sunday Times*, 31 July 1949.

10. Johnny Bond, "Gene Autry: Champion," op. cit.

11. Ibid.

12. Ibid.

13. Linda Lee Wakely, *See Ya Up There, Baby*, 17.

14. Ibid., 19.

15. Review of movie *Melody Ranch*, *Variety*, 1 January 1941, 14.

16. "Autry Leads the Herd in Rep's Western Pix," *Variety*, 18 December 1940, 22.

17. Ibid.

Chapter 17

1. Johnny Bond, "Gene Autry: Champion," op. cit.

2. "Autry Guaranteed 100G for Rodeo Appearances," *Variety*, 29 January 1941, 2.

3. This was found in an article from the Gene Autry, Oklahoma Museum; unfortunately, the article's title, date, and publication were missing.

4. "Local Rancher Once Headed Autry's Rodeo Show, Ranch," n.p., n.d., in files at Gene Autry Oklahoma Museum.

5. Johnny Bond, "Gene Autry: Champion," op. cit.

6. Autry, with Herskowitz, *Back in the Saddle*, 79–80.

7. Johnny Bond, "Gene Autry: Champion," op. cit.

Chapter 18

1. Percy Knauth, "Gene Autry, Inc.," *Life*, 28 April 1948, 88–100.

2. Johnny Bond, "Gene Autry: Champion," op. cit.

3. Review of movie *Heart of the Rio Grande*, *Variety*, 11 March 1942, 20.

4. Autry, with Herskowitz, *Back in the Saddle*, 85.

5. "Eight Autry Pix Halted by Enlistment in Air Force: Western Star Joins Army Next Week," *The Hollywood Reporter*, 9 July 1942.

6. Ibid.

7. Garry Wills, *John Wayne's America: The Politics of Celebrity* (New York: Simon & Schuster, 1997), 108.

8. Randy Roberts and James S. Olson, *John Wayne: American* (New York: Free Press, 1995), 220–221.

9. Ibid.

10. "Local Rancher Once Headed Autry's Rodeo Show, Ranch," n.p., n.d., in files at Gene Autry Oklahoma Museum.

11. Autry, with Herskowitz, *Back in the Saddle*, 82–83.

12. Satherley, interview.

13. Johnny Bond, "Gene Autry: Champion," op. cit.

14. Ibid.

15. Autry, with Herskowitz, *Back in the Saddle*, 85.

16. The threats to ruin Autry's career made by Herbert Yates (according to Autry) may be found in the court case *Gene Autry v. Republic Productions, Inc., et al.*, Supreme Court of California, No. 19381; and in Autry, with Herskowitz, *Back in the Saddle*, 61.

17. Review of movie *Bells of Capistrano*, *Variety*, 16 September 1942, 8.

Chapter 19

1. Jon Guyot Smith, "An Informal History of the Gene Autry Friendship Club (And Its Successors). Originally published in *Gene Autry's Friends* and copied for the author.

2. Joel Whitburn, *Top Country Singles, 1944–1988*. (Menomonee Falls, Wisc.: Record Research, 1989), 17.

3. Jon Guyot Smith, "Gene Autry's Best-Selling Records: A Guide for Identifying Them." Originally published in *Gene Autry's Friends* and copied for the author by Smith.

4. Ibid.

5. Autry, with Herskowitz, *Back in the Saddle*, 27.

6. Donovan Webster, *The Burma Road: The Epic Story of the China-Burma-India Theater in World War II* (New York: Farrar, Straus and Giroux, 2003), 69–70.

7. "Autry Home After Tour of GI Camps," *Los Angeles Citizen-News*, 6 September 1945.

8. Autry, with Herskowitz, *Back in the Saddle*, 92.

9. Ibid., 93.

Chapter 20

1. *Gene Autry v. Republic Productions, Inc., et al.*, Supreme Court of California, No. 19381.

2. Whitburn, *Top Country Singles,* 17.

3. "Autry and Hoss Thrill Moppetts," *Variety*, 11 November 1946, 17.

4. Autry, with Herskowitz, *Back in the Saddle*, 137.

5. Whitburn, *Top Country Singles,* 17.

6. This came up during several conversations with Eddy Arnold while I was doing Arnold's biography.

7. This draft of the studio bio was found in the Academy of Motion Picture Archive.

8. "Gene Autry Is Back at the Ranch," *Movie Review*, April 1946.

9. Ibid.

Chapter 21

1. Review of movie *Trail to San Antone, Variety*, 29 January 1947, 8.

2. This press release was found in the Academy of Motion Picture Archive.

3. Autry, with Herskowitz, *Back in the Saddle*, 97.

4. Draft of studio bio in Academy of Motion Picture archive.

5. B. Arentz, "Gene Autry: Businessman, Pilot," *Flying*, December 1949, 30–31, 62.

6. Johnny Bond, "Gene Autry: Champion," op. cit.

7. Jon Guyot Smith, "Some Thoughts Regarding the Evolution of Gene Autry's Recording Career." Originally published in *Gene Autry's Friends* and copied for the author.

8. Russell, *Country Music Records.*

9. Jon Guyot Smith, "Some Thoughts Regarding the Evolution of Gene Autry's Recording Career."

10. Review of movie *The Last Round-Up, Variety*, 8 October 1947, 8.

11. Jon Guyot Smith, "An Informal History of the Gene Autry Friendship Club (And Its Successors)."

12. "Oater Stars in Autry Production," *Variety*, 7 April 1948, 10.

13. Review of movie *The Strawberry Roan, Variety*, 28 April 1948, 8.

14. "Autry's Champion," *Nashville Tennessean*, 4 February 1949.

15. Whitburn, *Top Country Singles,* 17.

16. Review of movie *Loaded Pistols, Variety*, 22 December 1948, 6.

17. Autry, with Herskowitz, *Back in the Saddle*, 101.

18. Robert Cromie, "Cromie Looks at Authors and Books," *Chicago Tribune*, 7 December 1965.

19. Johnny Bond, "Gene Autry: Champion," op. cit.
20. Hopper, "Gene Autry," op. cit.
21. Ibid.
22. Whitburn, *Top Country Singles*, 17.

Chapter 22

1. Jack Wade, "Why Autry Can't Quit," n.d., in files at National Cowboy and Western Heritage Museum.
2. Ibid.
3. "Gene Autry, Dempsey Strike Oil in Oklahoma," *Chicago Tribune*, 22 February 1950.
4. Wade, "Why Autry Can't Quit."
5. Jon Guyot Smith, "'The Gene Autry Show': The Greatest Western Series in Television History." Originally published in *Gene Autry's Friends* and copied for the author.
6. "Petrillo OK on Autry Cracking AFM TV Hold," *Variety*, 19 April 1950, 1.
7. Jon Guyot Smith, "'The Gene Autry Show,'" op. cit.
8. "Autry Aims Six-Shooter at Theatre Owners," *Motion Picture Herald*, 12 August 1950.
9. Ibid.
10. "Autry States His Case for TV Pix at Allied Parley," *Variety*, 4 October 1950.
11. "Autry Pitching Strong Sales Talk on Pix Going to His Radio Listeners," *Variety*, 25 October 1950, 3.
12. "Autry and Burnette Continue to Wax Fat on Road Trek," *Billboard*, 10 February 1951, 41.
13. "Autry Grosses 20G at Baltimore P.A.," *Billboard*, 24 February 1951.
14. Howard C. Heyn, "Autry Owns 4 Planes Now," n.p., n.d., in files at Gene Autry Oklahoma Museum.
15. Johnny Bond, "Gene Autry: Champion," op. cit.
16. Ibid.
17. Jon Guyot Smith, "Gene Autry's Best-Selling Records: A Guide for Identifying Them." Originally published in *Gene Autry's Friends*.
18. Johnny Bond, "Gene Autry: Champion," op. cit.
19. "Harpo on a Horse — Chi Rodeo to 'Break' Marx As Autry Replacement," *Variety*, 26 September 1951, 137.
20. "Autry Trades Vittles Line to New Corp," *Billboard*, 10 February 1951, 5.
21. "Gene Autry Rides Range on Clothing," *Billboard*, 24 November 1951, 1.
22. William Lynce Vallee, "If You Were Gene Autry," n.p., n.d., in files at the National Cowboy and Western Heritage Museum.
23. Ina Mae Autry, "My Husband, Gene Autry," *Radio Best*, n.d., in files at the National Cowboy and Western Heritage Museum.
24. Mrs. Gene Autry, "Marry Your Man for Keeps," n.p., n.d., in files at the Gene Autry Oklahoma museum.
25. Mrs. Gene Autry, "An Open Letter to Gene Autry," n.p., n.d., in the Gene Autry Oklahoma Museum.
26. Ibid.

27. Carlin, "The Cowboy and His Lady."
28. Ibid.
29. Ibid.
30. "Gene Autry at Home," n.p., n.d., in files at the Gene Autry Oklahoma Museum.
31. Viola Moore, The Gene Autrys' Design for Living." n.p., n.d., in files at the Gene Autry Oklahoma Museum.
32. Louise Heising, "Life in a Ten Gallon Hat," n.p., n.d., in files at National Cowboy and Western Heritage Museum.
33. "Horray for Gene!" TV *Radio Mirror*, n.d., in files at the Gene Autry Oklahoma Museum

Chapter 23

1. "Autry Tour of 1-Day Stands Drew 243,844," *Billboard*, 8 March 1952.
2. Norman Weiser, "New Autry Act, Capsule Version of Arena Show, Is Solid Combo Fare," *Billboard*, 7 June 1952, 3, 14.
3. Ibid.
4. Ian Irving, "Gene Autry," *TV Radio Mirror*, n.d. in files at the Gene Autry Oklahoma Museum.
5. Johnny Bond, "Gene Autry: Champion," op. cit.
6. Ibid.
7. Ibid.
8. "Gail Davis," n.p., n.d., article in scrapbook at Gene Autry, Oklahoma Museum.
9. Ibid.
10. "Autry to Ride Italian Video," *Billboard*, 21 June 1952, 1.
11. "Autry Adds Booking Firm," *Billboard*, 8 November 1952, 1.
12. "Autry's Super Sked," *Variety*, 17 September 1952, 58.

Chapter 24

1. "Autry Going Thataway?" *Variety*, 27 May 1953, 2.
2. "FCC Nod to Autry's Two Radio Stations," *Variety*, 7 January 1953, 1.
3. "TV Aids Autry on 585G Tour," *Billboard*, 28 March 1953, 1, 48.
4. "Owe $142,400 in Back Taxes, 'Cowboy' Told: Gene Autry Gets a Bill from U.S.," *Chicago Tribune*, 4 April 1953.
5. Johnny Bond, "Gene Autry: Champion," op. cit.
6. Review of movie *Pack Train*, *Variety*, 1 July 1953, 6.
7. Jon Guyot Smith, e-mail to author, 29 March 2005.
8. Jon Guyot Smith, "Gene Autry: Brilliant Judge of Songs and Songwriters." Originally published in *Gene Autry's Friends*, copied for author.
9. Review of movie *Last of the Pony Riders*, *Variety*, 4 November 1953, 6.
10. Autry, with Herskowitz, *Back in the Saddle*, 103.
11. Ibid.
12. Ibid., 104.

13. Jon Guyot Smith, "Treasure Chest: Unissued Gene Autry Recordings Reportedly Located." Originally published in *Gene Autry's Friends*, copied for author.

14. Ibid.

15. Jay Warner, *Just Walkin' in the Rain* (Los Angeles: Renaissance Books, 2001), 124 163.

16. "Gail Davis," n.p., n.d., article in scrapbook at Gene Autry, Oklahoma Museum.

17. Ibid.

18. Jon Guyot Smith, "'The Gene Autry Show': The Greatest Western Series in Television History."

Chapter 25

1. "Autry to Drop Radio Tie-Up with Wrigley," *Chicago Tribune*, 12 May 1956, F 3.

2. Johnny Bond, "Gene Autry: Champion," op. cit.

3. Johnny Bond, "Gene Autry: Champion," op. cit.

4. Johnny Western, telephone interview by author, 31 August 2005.

5. Ibid.

6. "Gail Davis," n.p., n.d., article in scrapbook at Gene Autry, Oklahoma Museum.

7. Gene Autry, "The Way I Live," *TV and Movie Screen*, 1957. In files at the Gene Autry Oklahoma Museum.

8. Ibid.

9. Ibid.

10. "Stock Contractors," *ProRodeo Sports News* 27, no. 23 (1979), 57.

11. Autry, testimony at the Hearings.

12. Ibid.

13. Johnny Bond, "Gene Autry: Champion," op. cit.

14. Johnny Western, interview by Douglas B. Green, Nashville, Tennessee, 17 December 1997.

15. Ibid.

16. Jon Guyot Smith, "An Informal History of the Gene Autry Friendship Club (And Its Successors)."

17. Johnny Bond, "Gene Autry: Champion," op. cit.

18. Ibid.

19. Ibid.

20. Hall, *Hell-Bent for Music*.

Chapter 26

1. Johnny Bond, "Gene Autry: Champion," op. cit.

2. Ibid.

3. Ibid.

4. Ibid.

5. Ibid.

6. Bill Veeck, with Ed Linn, *Veeck as in Wreck: The Autobiography of Bill Veeck* (Chicago: University of Chicago Press, 1962, 1973), 360.

7. Ibid., 361.

8. Ibid., 366.

9. Autry, with Herskowitz, *Back in the Saddle*, 153.

10. Ibid., 188.

11. Jim Bennett, "Autry's 'Old West' Destroyed," *Los Angeles Herald-Examiner*, 29 August 1962, A1, 22.

12. Johnny Bond, "Gene Autry: Champion," op. cit.

13. Ibid.

14. Jon Guyot Smith, "An Informal History of the Gene Autry Friendship Club (And Its Successors)."

Chapter 27

1. Mike, Fessier, Jr., "It's Just Ol' Gene," *LA Times West Magazine*, 19 February 1967.

2. Ibid.

3. "Gene Autry given 'Outstanding Humanitarian Services Award,'" *Variety*, 14 June 1965.

4. Ibid.

5. Jon Guyot Smith, "Smiley Burnette: Gentle Genius Who Was Gene Autry's Pal." Originally published in *Gene Autry's Friends* and copied for author.

6. Autry, with Herskowitz, *Back in the Saddle*, 115.

7. Johnny Bond, "Gene Autry: Champion," op. cit.

8. Ibid.

9. Fessier, "It's Just Ol' Gene," op. cit.

10. Ibid.

Chapter 28

1. Autry, with Herskowitz, *Back in the Saddle*, 30.

2. Ibid., 21.

3. Ibid., 167.

4. Ibid., 126.

5. "A Chief Exec Named Gene Autry," *Dun's Review*, August 1975. In the files at the National Cowboy and Western Heritage Museum.

6. Ibid.

7. Ibid.

8. Don Merry, "Autry Gets Hot as Angels Catch Fire in Detroit," *Los Angeles Times*, 27 August 1977.

9. Autry, with Herskowitz, *Back in the Saddle*, 164–165.

Chapter 29

1. Doug Krikorian, "Still a Man Without a World Series," *Los Angeles Herald Examiner*, 15 October 1982, B1–2.

2. "Gene Autry," *People* magazine, 26 May 1980.

3. Ibid.

4. Ibid.

5. John Hall, "Autry Speaks," *Los Angeles Times*, 4 August 1980.

6. Grahamel Jones, "Jackie Autry: Angels Owner Banks on Her," *Los Angeles Times*, 14 April 1982, Part III, 3.

7. Johnny Western, interview by Douglas B. Green.

8. Jon Guyot Smith, "An Informal History of the Gene Autry Friendship Club."

9. Henry Crowell, "My Years with Mr. Autry and Melody Ranch," *Old Town Newhall Gazette*, 27–29 May 1997.

10. *New Yorker*, July 1991.

11. Fred LaBour told me this story while I was working on *It's the Cowboy Way: The Amazing, True Adventures of Riders in the Sky* (Lexington: University Press of Kentucky, 2003).

Chapter 30

1. Bill Plaschke, "Forget Record: Autry Was a Real Winner. The Cowboy's Last Roundup," *Los Angeles Times*, 3 October 1998, C 1, 6.

2. Tim Ghianni, "Friend Mourns Autry: Singing Cowboy Was 'Most Loving' Man," *The Tennessean*, 3 October 1998, 2.

3. Johnny Western, interview by Douglas B. Green.

4. Robert W. Phillips, "Remembering an American Cowboy: Gene Autry Gave His Nation Hope and Inspiration," *American Cowboy Magazine*, February 1999, 18–22.

5. Johnny Western, interview by Douglas B. Green.

Conclusion

1. Johnny Western, interview by author.

BIBLIOGRAPHY

Adams, Les, and Buck Rainey. *Shoot-Em-Ups: The Complete Reference Guide to Westerns of the Sound Era*. Waynesville, N.C.: World of Yesterday, 1978.

Advertisement. *Billboard*. 9 December 1933: 13.

Advertisement. *Billboard*. 9 March 1935: 2

Advertisement. *Nashville Banner*. 26 January 1938.

Advertisement. *Variety*. 4 May 1938.

Altman, Rick. *The American Film Musical*. Bloomington and Indianapolis: Indiana University Press, 1989.

"Angels Back in Town." *Los Angeles Times*. 4 August 1980.

Antczak, John. "Star of Westerns, Business, Gene Autry Dies." *The Tennessean*. 3 October 1998: 1.

Aquila, Richard, ed. *Wanted Dead or Alive: The American West in Popular Culture*. Urbana, Illinois and Chicago: University of Chicago Press, 1996.

Arentz, B. "Gene Autry: Businessman, Pilot." *Flying*. December 1949: 30–31, 62.

Arnold, Eddy. Conversations with the author (unpublished). 13 April 1999, and 18 March 2005.

"At Home with Gene Autry." *TV Close-ups*. n.d. Scrapbook in Gene Autry Oklahoma Museum.

"Autry Adds Booking Firm." *Billboard*. 8 November 1952: 1.

"Autry Aims Six-Shooter at Theatre Owners." *Motion Picture Herald*. 12 August 1950.

"Autry and Burnette Continue to Wax Fat on Road Trek." *Billboard*. 10 February 1951: 41.

"Autry and Hoss Thrill Moppetts." *Variety*. 11 November 1946: 17.

"Autry at WHAS." *Variety*. 3 April 1935: 45.

"Autry Buys KTLA for $12 million." *Los Angeles Times*. 29 October 1963.

"Autry Demands More Money from Republic." *Variety*. 19 January 1938.

"Autry Denies He's Settled Troubles: Film Cowboy Here Going to Chicago to Visit Friends." *Nashville Banner*. 1 February 1938.

"Autry Draws 10G Per Pic as Rep Settler." *Variety*. 18 May 1938.

"Autry Gallops Thru Allied Ambuscade With Well-Aimed Shots." *Variety*. 3 October 1950.

"Autry Going Thataway?" *Variety*. 27 May 1953: 2.

"Autry Grosses 20G at Baltimore P.A." *Billboard*. 24 February 1951.

"Autry Held by Republic." *Variety*. 13 October 1937: 25.

"Autry Home After Tour of GI Camps." *Los Angeles Citizen-News*. 6 September 1945.

"Autry Hypes Rodeo in Pitt to $38,000, More Than Doubling '39 Take." *Variety*. 8 May 1940: 2.

"Autry in Nashville: Stopped by WSM on Saturday." *Nashville Banner*. 17 January 1938.

"Autry in Rep.'s Lineup of 55 Pix for '38–'39 Season." *Variety*. 4 May 1938.

"Autry Lawyers to Appeal Ruling on Republic Deal." *Billboard*. 24 May 1952: 3, 44.

"Autry Leads the Herd in Rep's Western Pix." *Variety*. 18 December 1940: 22.

"Autry on S.A. Tour Unless Rep. Kicks in with 25G Per Pic." *Variety*. 23 March 1938: 4.

"Autry Rodeo Opens 26-Day Run at Garden." *Variety*. 9 October 1948: 3.

"Autry Says Rep Using His Pix as Club on Exhibs; Defends Coin Demand." *Variety*. 2 February 1938: 11.

"Autry Set for WSM Debut." *Variety*. 13 November 1954: 1.

"Autry States His Case for TV Pix at Allied Parley." *Variety*. 4 October 1950.

"Autry Still Tied to Rep." *Variety*. 6 February 1946: 2.

"Autry to Drop Radio Tie-Up with Wrigley." *Chicago Tribune*. 12 May 1956: F 3.

"Autry to Head Own Rodeo; Pic Unit Waits." *Variety*. 14 November 1945: 9.

"Autry to Ride Italian Video." *Billboard*. 21 June 1952: 1.

"Autry to Sell KTLA." *Los Angeles Herald-Examiner*. 27 October 1982.

"Autry to Sue Rep." *Variety*. 24 October 1951: 60.

"Autry Tour of 1-Day Stands Drew 243,844. *Billboard*. 8 March 1952.

"Autry Trades Vittles Line to New Corp." *Billboard*. 10 February 1951: 5.

"Autry vs. Republic Hearings Concluded; Summations Next." *Billboard*. 22 March 1952.

"Autry Yippees Again for Republic; Peace Terms in His Favor." *Variety*. 14 May 1938.

"Autry's Boston Party." *Variety*. 6 November 1940: 8.

"Autry's OK 10½G, Pitt." *Variety*. 6 February 1952: 53.

"Autry's Song Waning." *Variety*. 4 May 1958.

"Autry's Troy Benefit." *Variety*. 31 January 1953: 43.

Autry, Gene. "52 Days We Look Forward to All Year." n.p., n.d. In files at the Gene Autry Oklahoma Museum.

_____. "3 Pals." *Country Song Roundup*. 1950 (?). In files at the Gene Autry Oklahoma Museum.

_____. "I Doff My Stetson to Will Rogers." *Movie Thrills*. 1950. In files at the National Cowboy & Western Heritage Museum.

_____. Interview by Kenneth E. Bauthman. Los Angeles, California. 5 July 1990.

_____. Interview by Mike Oatman. Palm Springs, California. February 14, 1983.

_____. Interview by Mr. Higham. Los Angeles, California. Columbia University Oral History Research Office. July 22, 1971

_____. "Memories of the Place I Called Melody Ranch." *Old Town Newhall Gazette*. November–December 1995.

_____. "My Biggest Thrills." n.p., n.d. Gene Autry Oklahoma Museum.

_____. Radio interview by Dick Haynes. KLAC, Los Angeles, California. 20 February 1974.

_____. Testimony at the Hearings Before the Subcommittee on Communications of the Committee on Interstate and Foreign Commerce: United States Senate, Eighty-Fifth Congress, Second Session on S.2834: Amendment to Communications Act of 1934. 15 April 1958: 446–456.

_____. "The Way I Live." *TV and Movie Screen*. 1957. Gene Autry Oklahoma Museum.

Autry, Gene, as told to Morris Gelman. "Gene Autry Recalls 53 Mostly Golden Years. *Daily Variety*. 28 October 1980: 202.

Autry, Gene, with Mickey Herskowitz. *Back in the Saddle Again*. Garden City, N.Y.: Doubleday, 1976.

Autry, Ina Mae. "My Husband, Gene Autry." *Radio Best*. 1950 (?). Gene Autry Oklahoma Museum.

Autry, Mrs. Gene. "Marry Your Man for Keeps": 59, 87. National Cowboy & Western Heritage Museum.

_____. "An Open Letter to Gene Autry." n.p., n.d.

"Balladeering Mustang Stars OK B.O.; Autry Started It, Others Now Click." *Variety*. 13 October 1937.

Barbour, Alan. *The Thrill of It All: A Pictorial History of the B Western from the Great Train Robbery and Other Silent Classics to the Color Films of the Genre's Last Days of Glory in the '50s*. New York: Macmillan, 1971.

Barfield, Ray. *Listening to Radio, 1920–1950*. Westport, Conn.: Praeger, 1996.

Barrios, Richard. *A Song in the Dark: The Birth of the Musical Film*. New York: Oxford University Press, 1995

Baseball Encyclopedia: The Complete and Definitive Record of Major League Baseball. 10th Edition. New York: Macmillan, 1996.

"Baseball: It's a Tough Business." *The Palm Springs Desert Sun*. 16 January 1987.

Beard, Tyler. *100 Years of Western Wear*. Salt Lake City: Gibbs-Smith, 1993.

Bebb, Bruce. "Gene Autry: The Trail to the Golden West." *Hollywood Reporter*. 23 November 1987.

Beck, Ken. "Autry Good Wright Stuff: The Collectors." *The Tennessean*. 22 May 1991: D1.

Bennett, Jim. "Autry's 'Old West' Destroyed." *Los Angeles Herald-Examiner*. 29 August 1962: A1, 22.

Bennett, Joseph E. "Gene Autry: Tioga Tumbleweed." *Texas Mason*. Fall 1992: 7–9.

Bentinck, Henry. "The Nation's Barn Dance." *Radio Guide* IV, no. 2 (11 November 1934).

Bentley, William. "Rudolph, the Red Nosed Reindeer: Surprised Chicagoan Sees His Christmas Poem Become a Legend — and a Gold Mine." *Chicago Tribune*. 17 December 1950.

Bergreen, Laurence. *Capone: The Man and the Era*. New York: Touchstone/Simon & Schuster, 1994.

_____. *Louis Armstrong: An Extravagant Life*. New York: Broadway Books, 1997.

Biggar, George C. "The National Barn Dance." In *Country Music Who's Who*: 17–18.

Blair, Sam. "Tall Tales from Tioga: How a Hollywood Cowboy Left His Mark on This Grayson County Town." *Dallas Morning News*. 20 October 1993: C1, C2.

Block, Alex Ben. "Salute to Republic Entertainment." *The Hollywood Reporter*. 24 October 1995.

Bond, Johnny. "Gene Autry: Champion." Unpublished manuscript in the Country Music Hall of Fame & Museum archives. n.d.

_____. Interview. Country Music Hall of Fame & Museum, Oral History Project. n.d.

_____. *Reflections: The Autobiography of Johnny Bond*. Los Angeles: John Edwards Memorial Foundation, 1976.

"Boy Wins 40G Suit vs. Autry & Firms Over Cowboy Outfit." *Billboard*. 25 December 1948: 51.

Brooks, Tim, and Earle Marsh. *The Complete Directory to Prime Time Network TV Shows 1946–Present*. New York: Ballantine Books, 1988.

Buscombe, Richard. *The BFI Companion to the Western*. New York: Atheneum, 1988.

"Buttram and Johnny Grant Rib Autry as He Receives Variety Club Plaque." *Variety*. 14 June 1965.

Byworth, Tony. *The History of Country & Western Music*. New York: Exeter Books, 1984.

Cameron, Ian, and Douglas Pye, eds. *The Book of Westerns*. New York: Continuum, 1996.

"Campaign to Make Big Cities Autry-Minded." *Variety*. 23 October 1940: 2.

Canutt, Yakima, with Oliver Drake. *Stunt Man: The Autobiography of Yakima Canutt*. Norman: University of Oklahoma Press, 1979.

Carlin, Esther. "The Cowboy and His Lady." *TV Stage*. n.d.

Carr, Patrick, ed. *The Illustrated History of Country Music*. New York: Dolphin, 1980.

Cary, Diana Serra. *The Hollywood Posse: The Story of the Gallant Band of Horsemen Who Made Movie History*. Boston: Houghton Mifflin, 1975.

Cawelti, John. *The Six-Gun Mystique*. Bowling Green, Ohio: Bowling Green University Popular Press, 1971.

"A Chief Exec Named Gene Autry: The One Time Western Star Has Had an Even Bigger Success Running His Own Company." *Dun's Review*. August 1975: 57–59.

Cole, M. M. Letter to the Hearings Before the Subcommittee on Communications of the Committee on Interstate and Foreign Commerce: United States Senate, Eighty-Fifth Congress, Second Session on S.2834: Amendment to Communications Act of 1934: 972–973.

"Columbia Phonograph Label Acquired by Columbia System; Deny J. C. Stein or Concert Ties." *Variety*. 16 November 1938: 25.

"Consolidated Film's $605,755 Net for 1937." *Variety*. 16 March 1938: 6.

"Cowboy Sings for Admirers." *The Daily Oklahoman*. 12 November 1935.

"Cowboy Vogue Going Co-Ed? Gene Thinks So." *Billboard*. 19 April 1952.

Coyne, Michael. *The Crowded Prairie: American National Identity in the Hollywood Western*. London and New York: I. B. Tauris, Publisher, 1997.

Crafton, Donald. *The Talkies: American Cinema's Transition to Sound, 1926–1931*. New York: Scribner's, 1996.

Cromie, Robert. "Cromie Looks at Authors and Books." *Chicago Tribune*. 7 December 1965.

Crowell, Henry. "My Years with Mr. Autry and Melody Ranch." *Old Town Newhall Gazette*. 27–29 May 1997.

Cunningham, Dave. "Museum Finished, the Cowboy Has One Last Dream." *Los Angeles Press-Telegram*. 20 January 1989.

Cusic, Don. *Baseball and Country Music*. Madison: University of Wisconsin Press, 2004.

_____. *Cowboys and the Wild West: An A to Z Guide from the Chisholm Trail to the Silver Screen*. New York: Facts on File, 1994.

_____. *The Cowboy Way: The Amazing True Adventures of Riders in the Sky*. Lexington: University Press of Kentucky, 2003.

_____. *Eddy Arnold: I'll Hold You in My Heart*. Nashville: Rutledge Hill, 1997.

Daniel, Wayne W. "Gene Autry: America's Number 1 Singing Cowboy." *Nostalgia Digest*. February/March 2003: 6–14.

David, W. B. "Greatest Cowboy Star to Build Film Around South of the Border." n.d.

Davis, Robert Murray. *Playing Cowboys: Low Culture and High Art in the Western*. Norman: University of Oklahoma Press, 1992.

Davis, Ronald. L. *Duke: The Life and Image of John Wayne*. Norman: University of Oklahoma Press, 1998.

Dellar, Fred, and Roy Thompson. *The Illustrated Encyclopedia of Country Music*. New York: Harmony Books, 1977.

Dick, Bernard F. *The Merchant Prince of Poverty Row: Harry Cohn of Columbia Pictures*. Lexington: University Press of Kentucky, 1993.

Dobbins, Dick. *The Grand Minor League: An Oral History of the Old Pacific Coast League*. Emeryville, Calif.: Woodford Press, 1999.

Doherty, Thomas. *Pre-Code Hollywood: Sex, Immorality, and Insurrection in American Cinema 1930–1934*. New York: Columbia University Press, 1999.

Duncan, Robert J. "Oldtimer Recalls Colorful Past of Town That Will Be Auctioned." *Dallas Times-Herald*. 26 September 1982: 83A.

Dunning, John. *On the Air: The Encyclopedia of Old-Time Radio*. New York: Oxford University Press, 1998.

The Editors of *Country Music* magazine. *The Comprehensive Country Music Encyclopedia*. New York: Times Books, 1994.

"Eight Autry Pix Halted by Enlistment in Air Force: Western Star Joins Army Next Week." *The Hollywood Reporter*. 9 July 1942.

"Eight Tunes for Autry Pic; Off for Sagebrush." *Variety*. 25 May 1938: 7.

Elley, Derek, ed. *The Chronicle of the Movies: A Year-By-Year History from* The Jazz Singer *to Today*. New York: Crescent Books, 1991.

Emmons, Steve. "Green Sunset: Autry Hanging Up Spurs with Cash Register Jinglin.'" *Los Angeles Times*. 20 May 1995.

Evans, James. *Prairie Farmer and W.L.S.: The Burridge D. Butler Years*. Urbana: University of Illinois Press, 1969.

Everson, William K. *History of the Western Film*. Secaucus, N.J.: Citadel Press, 1969.

Eyles, Allen. *The Western*. Cranbury, N.J.: A. S. Barnes, 1975.

"FCC Nod to Autry's Two Radio Stations." *Variety*. 7 January 1953: 1.

Fenin, George N., and William K. Everson. *The Western from Silents to the Seventies*. New York: Penguin, 1977.

Fernett, Gene. *Hollywood's Poverty Row: 1930–1950*. Hollywood: Coral Reef Productions, 1973.

Fessier, Mike, Jr. "It's Just Ol' Gene." *LA Times West Magazine*. 19 February 1967.

"Film Cowboys, Yodelers to Air Four-Hour Show for British War Kids." *Variety*. 4 December 1940.

Fimrite, Ron. "Whitey, Buck and the Singing Cowboy." *Sports Illustrated*. 13 April 1992.

Finigan, Joe. "Gene Sneers at TV Cowboys." *Chicago Sunday Tribune*. 6 December 1959.

Finler, Joel W. *The Hollywood Story*. New York: Crown, 1988.

"49.9 Percent of Golden West Broadcasters Sold to Signal Companies, Inc. for $25 million." *Hollywood Citizen-News*. 1 August 1968.

"456 Pictures for 1938–39: Not Counting 74 Westerns." *Variety*. 6 April 1938: 1.

Frank, Marie. Interview. Country Music Hall of Fame & Museum, Oral History Project. n.d.

Freidel, Frank. *Franklin D. Roosevelt: A Rendezvous with Destiny*. Boston: Little, Brown, 1990.

"Gail Davis." *The Pioneers*. n.d. National Cowboy & Western Heritage Museum.

"Gail Davis: I Was Annie Oakley." *Western Women*. n.d. National Cowboy & Western Heritage Museum.

Garfield, Brian. *Western Films: A Complete Guide*. New York: Rawson Associates, 1982.

"Gene Autry at Home. n.d. In files at the Gene Autry Oklahoma Museum.

Gene Autry bio. Columbia Pictures. n.d. Motion Picture Archive.

"Gene Autry Buys KMPC." *Los Angeles Times*. 20 November 1952.

"Gene Autry, Dempsey Strike Oil in Oklahoma." *Chicago Tribune*. 22 February 1950.

"Gene Autry Elected President of Cowboy Hall Board." Press Release from National Cowboy Hall of Fame and Western Heritage Center. 6 May 1977.

"Gene Autry Ends Radio Show." *Variety*. 11 May 1956.

"Gene Autry Enters Pact to Sell KTLA." *Los Angeles Times*. 27 October 1982.

"Gene Autry Given 'Outstanding Humanitarian Services Award.'" *Variety*. 14 June 1965.

"Gene Autry Home." *Los Angeles Citizen-News*. 6 September 1945.

"Gene Autry Is Back at the Ranch." *Movie Review*. April 1946.

"Gene Autry Lauded at Award Ceremony. *Hollywood Reporter*. 14 June 1965.

Gene Autry obituary. *Country Music*. January/February 1999: 14–15.

"Gene Autry Rides Range on Clothing." *Billboard*. 24 November 1951: 1.

"Gene Autry Signs for New AMA Rodeo." *Variety*. 6 March 1946: 56.

"Gene Autry Sued for $2 million." *Los Angeles Times*. 8 May 1963.

"Gene Autry Twirled a Mighty Fetching Lariat." *Variety*. 4 October 1950.

Gene Autry's Hometown Missed a Bet: Name Change May Have Brought Fame and Fortune to Tiny Tioga, Texas." *The Atlanta Journal/The Atlanta Constitution*. 24 October 1993: A4–5.

"Gene Autry's Hoss by Plane Costs Rodeo Star $3,400." *Variety*. 9 October 1940.

"Gene Autry." *People*. 26 May 1980.

"General Features Signs Autry for Comics." *Billboard*. 29 March 1952.

George-Warren, Holly. *Cowboy: How Hollywood Invented the Wild West*. Pleasantville, N.Y.: Reader's Digest Books, 2002.

_____. "The Singing Cowboy as Everlasting Everyman." *New York Times*. 25 January 1998.

George-Warren, Holly, and Michelle Freedman. *How the West Was Worn*. New York: Harry N. Abrams, 2001.

Ghianni, Tim. "Friend Mourns Autry: Singing Cowboy Was 'Most Loving' Man." *The Tennessean*. 3 October 1998: 2.

Giddins, Gary. *Bing Crosby: A Pocketful of Dreams: The Early Years, 1903–1940*. Boston: Little, Brown, 2001.

"Globe Trotters, Autry Up Gate at Waterloo." *Billboard*. 8 March 1952.

Goldman, Herbert G. *Jolson: The Legend Comes to Life*. New York: Oxford, 1988.

Goldstein, Norm. *The History of Television*. New York: Portland House, 1991.

Goodwin, Doris Kearns. *No Ordinary Time: Franklin and Eleanor Roosevelt: The Home Front in World War II*. New York: Touchstone, 1994.

Gordon, Alex. Recording notes. *Gene Autry: The Singing Cowboy, Chapter 2*. Varese Sarabande, 1998. Compact disc.

Graebner, William S. *The Age of Doubt: American Thought and Culture in the 1940s*. Boston: Twayne, 1991.

Green, Douglas B. "Gene Autry." In *Stars of Country Music*, edited by Bill C. Malone and Judith McCulloh. Urbana: University of Illinois Press, 1975.

_____. *Singing in the Saddle: The History of the Singing Cowboy*. Nashville: The Country Music Foundation Press and Vanderbilt University Press, 2002.

Greenberg, Hank. Edited by Ira Berkow. *The Story of My Life*. New York: Times Book, 1989.

Griffis, Ken. *Hear My Song: The Story of the Celebrated Sons of the Pioneers*. Northglenn, Colorado: Norken, 2000.

Grossman, Gary H. *Saturday Morning TV: Thirty Years of the Shows You Waited All Week to Watch*. New Rochelle, N.Y.: Arlington House, 1981.

Haden, Walter Darrell. "Vernon Dalhart." In *Stars of Country Music*, edited by Bill C. Malone and Judith McCulloh. Urbana: University of Illinois Press, 1975.

Hake, Ted. *Hake's Guide to Cowboy Character Collectibles*. Radnor, Pa.: Wallace-Homestead, 1994.

Hall, John. "Autry Speaks." *Los Angeles Times*. 4 August 1980.

Hall, Wade. *Hell-Bent for Music: The Life of Pee Wee King*. Lexington: The University Press of Kentucky, 1996.

Hamblen, Suze. Interview by author. Santa Clarita, California. 23 March 2001.

Hamilburg, Mitch. Obituary. *Variety*. 22 May 1968.

Hamilburg, Mitchell, Jr. Interview by author. 3 March 2002.

Hardy, Phil, and Dave Laing, eds. *The Faber Companion to 20th Century Popular Music*. London: Faber and Faber, 1990.

"Harpo on a Horse—Chi Rodeo to 'Break' Marx As Autry Replacement." *Variety*. 26 September 1951: 137.

Harris, Beth. "Only Baseball Success Eluded Versatile Celebrity." *The Tennessean*. 3 October 1998: 2.

Harris, Charles W., ed. *Six-Shooters, Songs and Sex*. Norman: University of Oklahoma Press, 1976.

Harrison, Nigel. *Songwriters: A Biographical Dictionary with Discographies*. Jefferson, N.C.: McFarland, 1998.

Haslam, Gerald W. *Workin' Man Blues: Country Music in California*. Berkeley and Los Angeles: University of California Press, 1999.

"Hearing on Autry Writ Set Today." *Nashville Banner*. 3 February 1938.

Heide, Robert, and John Gilman. *Box-Office Buckaroos: The Cowboy Hero from the Wild West Show to the Silver Screen*. New York: Abbeville Press, 1989.

Heising, Louise. "Life in a Ten Gallon Hat." n.p. 1950 (?). National Cowboy & Western Heritage Museum.

Hemming, Roy. *The Melody Lingers On: The Great Songwriters and Their Movie Musicals*. New York: Newmarket Press, 1986.

"Hero of Horse Operas Summons Aid for Legal Thriller Here." *Nashville Tennessean*. 30 January 1938.

Heyn, Howard C. "Autry Owns 4 Planes Now." n.p., n.d. Gene Autry Oklahoma Museum.

Hill, Dick. "Gene Autry." *Joslin's Jazz Journal.* February 1983.

Holland, Jack. "Gail Davis: I Want to Get Married." *TV and Movie Screen.* n.d.

Holland, Ted. *B Western Actors Encyclopedia: Facts, Photos, and Filmographies for More Than 250 Familiar Faces.* Jefferson, N.C.: McFarland, 1989.

"Hollywood Flocks into Arizona Radio through Caldwell, Autry, Webb." *Variety.* 17 July 1946: 30.

"Hollywood Takes Its Ranching Seriously Nowadays; Strictly a For-Revenue-Only Standard." *Variety.* 11 May 1938.

"Hood Manny Skar Slain, Shot Outside Lake Shore Apartment: Assailants Flee in Auto." *Chicago Tribune.* 11 September 1965.

"Hope, Autry Hit Road to Cash in On Arena Shows." *Variety.* 11 January 1950: 2.

Hopper, Hedda. "Gene Autry." *Chicago Sunday Times.* 31 July 1949.

Hopper, Lawrence. *Bob Nolan: A Biographical Guide and Annotations to the Lyric Archive* at the University of North Carolina, Chapel Hill. Limited publication by Paul Lawrence Hopper, 2000.

Horowitz, James. *They Went Thataway.* New York: E. P. Dutton, 1976.

Horstman, Dorothy. *Sing Your Heart Out, Country Boy: Classic Country Songs and Their Inside Stories by the People Who Wrote Them.* New York: E. P. Dutton, 1975.

Horwitz, James. "In Search of the Original Singing Cowboy." *Rolling Stone.* 25 October 1973: 32–34, 36, 38.

Hurst, Richard Maurice. *Republic Studios: Between Poverty Row and the Majors.* Metuchen, N.J.: Scarecrow Press, 1979.

Hurst, Tricia. "How Popular Can You Get?" *Screenland.* n.d. Gene Autry Oklahoma Museum.

Hussar, John. "Jackie Autry Rides Herd on Museum Project." *The Palm Springs Desert Sun.* 16 January 1987.

_____. "Jackie Autry Shares Spotlight." *The Palm Springs Desert Sun.* 16 January 1987.

Huston, Sue. "At Americana Ball, Cowboy Autry Definitely the Good Guy." *Palm Springs Desert Sun.* 28 March 1987.

Hyams, Jay. *The Life and Times of the Western Movie.* New York: Gallery, 1983.

"In Memoriam: Gene Autry." *American Cowboy Magazine.* February 1999: 17.

Irving, Ian. "Horray for Gene!" *TV Radio Mirror.* n.d. Gene Autry Oklahoma Museum.

Ivey, Bill. "The Bottom Line: Business Practices That Shaped Country Music." In *Country: The Music and the Musicians,* edited by Paul Kingsbury and Alan Axelrod. New York: Abbeville Press, 1988.

"Jackie Autry." *Los Angeles Times.* 14 April 1982.

"Jackie Autry Profile." *The Palm Springs Desert Sun.* 16 January 1987.

Jackson, Carlton. *Zane Grey.* New York: Twayne, 1973.

Jones, Grahamel. "Jackie Autry: Angels Owner Banks on Her. *Los Angeles Times.* 14 April 1982: III, 3.

Kaye, Joseph. "Gene Autry Tells His Own Story." *True Story.* 1950. National Cowboy & Western Heritage Museum.

Kenney, William H. *Recorded Music in American Life.* New York: Oxford University Press, 1999.

Ketchum, Richard M. *Will Rogers: The Man and His Times.* New York: Touchstone, 1973.

Kingsbury, Paul, ed. *The Country Reader: 25 Years of the* Journal of Country Music. Nashville: Country Music Foundation Press and Vanderbilt University Press, 1996.

_____, ed. *The Encyclopedia of Country Music.* New York: Oxford University Press, 1998.

Kingsbury, Paul, and Alan Axelrod, eds. *Country: The Music and the Musicians.* New York: Abbeville Press, 1988.

Kitsinger, Otto. Recording notes. *Pee Wee King & His Golden West Cowboys.* Bear Family Records, 1994. Compact disc boxed set.

"KMPC Began in 1928; Now Worth $15 m." *Los Angeles Times.* 19 June 1986.

Knauth, Percy. "Gene Autry, Inc." *Life.* 28 June 1948: 88–100.

Krikorian, Doug. "Still a Man Without a World Series." *Los Angeles Herald Examiner.* 15 October 1982: B1–2.

Lackmann, Ron. *Same Time ... Same Station: An A–Z Guide to Radio from Jack Benny to Howard Stern.* New York: Facts on File, 1996.

Lahue, Kelton C. *Riders of the Range: The Sagebrush Heroes of the Sound Screen.* New York: Castle Books, 1973.

"Lamour, Autry, Audie in Dallas Benefit for Texas Tornado Victims." *Variety.* 20 May 1952: 2.

Let's Shoot Straight!: They Say Autry Can't Ride, Has Wife Trouble, Hates His Fans, Loves Publicity But..." *Modern Screen.* 1950: 63, 63, 92, 93.

Lewis, Tom. *Empire of the Air: The Men Who Made Radio.* New York: HarperCollins, 1991.

Lightfoot, William E. "Belle of the Barn Dance: Reminiscing with Lulu Belle Wiseman Stamey." *The Journal of Country Music* 12, no. 1: 2–15.

_____. "From Radio Queen to Raleigh: Conversations with Lulu Belle: Part I." *Old Time Country* 6, no. 2 (Summer 1989): 4–10.

_____. "From Radio Queen to Raleigh: Conversations with Lulu Belle: Part II." *Old Time Country* 6, no. 3 (Fall 1989): 3–11.

"List'ning in with Prairie Farmer. WLS: The Voice of Agriculture." *Prairie Farmer.* Various issues, 1931–1935.

"Local Rancher Once Headed Autry's Rodeo Show, Ranch." n.d. Gene Autry Oklahoma Museum.

Logsdon, Guy, William Jacobson, and Mary Rogers. *Saddle Serenaders.* Salt Lake City: Gibbs-Smith, 1995.

Loy, R. Philip. *Westerns and American Culture, 1930–1955.* Jefferson, N.C.: McFarland, 2001.

Malone, Bill C. *Country Music U.S.A.* Austin: University of Texas Press, 1968.

_____. *Don't Get Above Your Raisin': Country Music and the Southern Working Class.* Urbana: University of Illinois Press, 2002.

_____. *Singing Cowboys and Musical Mountaineers: Southern Culture and the Roots of Country Music.* Athens, Ga.: University of Georgia Press, 1993.

Malone Bill C., and Judith McCullough eds. *Stars of*

Country Music. Urbana: University of Illinois Press, 1975.

Maltin, Leonard. *The Great American Broadcast.* New York: E. P. Dutton, 1997.

Manchel, Frank. *Film Study: A Resource Guide.* Rutherford, N.J.: Fairleigh Dickinson University Press, 1973.

Manhattan Merry-Go-Round. Movie review. *Variety.* November 1937.

Martin, Chuck. "The Top Hand of Melody Ranch." *Hoofs and Horns* 11, no. 10 (April 1942).

Marvin, Frankie. Interview. Country Music Hall of Fame & Museum, Oral History Project. n.d.

Marvin, Johnny. Obituary. *Variety.* 27 December 1944.

McCloud, Barry, ed. *Definitive Country: The Ultimate Encyclopedia of Country Music and Its Performers.* New York: Perigee, 1995.

McClure, Arthur F., and Ken D. Jones. *Heroes, Heavies and Sagebrush: A Pictorial History of the "B" Western Players.* Secaucus, N.J.: A. S. Barnes, 1972.

McDonald, Archie. *Shooting Stars: Heroes and Heroines of Western Films.* Bloomington: Indiana University Press, 1987.

McDougal, Dennis. "FM Radio: Real Sound Investment." *Los Angeles Times.* 27 December 1985.

McElvaine, Robert S. *The Great Depression: America, 1929–1941.* New York: Times Books, 1984.

McReynolds, Edwin C. *Oklahoma: A History of the Sooner State.* Norman: University of Oklahoma Press, 1954.

Merry, Don. "Autry Gets Hot and Angels Catch Fire in Detroit." *Los Angeles Times.* 27 August 1977.

"Mex Bans Autry Pic on Oil-Revolution." *Variety.* 7 August 1940: 1.

Meyer, William R. *The Making of the Great Western.* New Rochelle, N.Y.: Arlington House, 1979

Miller, Don. *The Hollywood Corral.* New York: Popular Library, 1976.

Miller, Nathan. *Theodore Roosevelt: A Life.* New York: Morrow, 1992.

Monaco, James, and the editors of *Baseline. The Encyclopedia of Film.* New York: Perigee, 1991.

Montana, Patsy, with Jane Frost. *Patsy Montana: The Cowboy's Sweetheart.* Jefferson, N.C.: McFarland, 2002.

Moore, Viola. "The Gene Autrys' Design for Living." n.p., n.d. Gene Autry Oklahoma Museum.

Morris, Edmund. *The Rise of Teddy Roosevelt.* New York: Ballantine, 1979.

_____. *Theodore Rex.* New York: Random House, 2001.

Morris, Edward. "New, Improved, Homogenized: Country Radio Since 1950." In *Country: The Music and the Musicians,* edited by Paul Kingsbury and Alan Axelrod. New York: Abbeville Press, 1988.

Nachbar, Jack, ed. *Focus on the Western.* Englewood Cliffs, N.J.: Prentice-Hall, 1974.

Nachman, Gerald. *Raised on Radio.* New York: Pantheon, 1998.

Newhan, Ross. "At 80, Autry Is Still Chasing Champion." *Los Angeles Times.* 29 September 1987: 1, 5.

_____. "No. 26 on Wall, No. 1 in Their Hearts. The Cowboy's Last Roundup." *Los Angeles Times.* 3 October 1998: C1, 6,

Night Stage to Galveston. Movie review. *Variety.* 19 March 1952: 6.

Nightengale, Bob. "It's the Straw That Breaks Autry's Back." *Los Angeles Times.* 15 September 1994.

O'Neal, Bill. *Tex Ritter: America's Most Beloved Cowboy.* Austin: Eakin Press, 1998.

O'Neal, Bill, and Fred Goodwin. *The Sons of the Pioneers.* Austin: Eakin Press, 2001.

Oermann, Robert K. *America's Music: The Roots of Country.* Atlanta: Turner Publishing, 1996.

Oliver, Myrna. "Cowboy Tycoon Gene Autry Dies." *Los Angeles Times.* 3 October 1998: A1, A24.

Orr, Jay. "'Riders in the Sky' Singer Recalls Visit." *The Tennessean.* 3 October 1998: 2.

Osborne, Jerry. *55 Years of Recorded Country/Western Music.* Phoenix: O'Sullivan & Woodside, 1976: viii–xii.

"Owe $142,400 in Back Taxes, 'Cowboy' Told: Gene Autry Gets a Bill from U.S." *Chicago Tribune.* 4 April 1953.

Page, Don. "Sagebrush Saga: Gene Autry — From Nags to Riches." *Los Angeles Times.* n.d. Gene Autry Oklahoma Museum

Paris, Mike. "Gene Autry, the Singing Cowboy." *Country Music People.* December 1976: 38.

Parks, Jack. "Hollywood's Singing Cowboys: They Packed Guitars as Well as Six Shooters." *Country Music.* July 1973: 24, 32.

Peak, Mayme Ober. "Encouraged Him to Go into Movies." *Boston Globe.* 11 June 1939.

"Petrillo OK on Autry Cracking AFM TV Hold." *Variety.* 19 April 1950: 1.

Phillips, Robert W. "Remembering an American Cowboy: Gene Autry Gave His Nation Hope and Inspiration." *American Cowboy Magazine.* February 1999:18–22.

Phillips, Robert W. *Roy Rogers.* Jefferson, N.C.: McFarland, 1995.

_____. *Singing Cowboy Stars.* Salt Lake City: Gibbs-Smith, 1994.

Pitts, Michael R. *Western Movies.* Jefferson, N.C.: McFarland, 1986.

Plaschke, Bill. "Forget Record: Autry Was a Real Winner. The Cowboy's Last Roundup." *Los Angeles Times.* October 3, 1998: C1, 6,

Porterfield, Nolan. "Jimmie Rodgers — The Discography." Recording notes. *Jimmie Rodgers: The Singing Brakeman.* Bear Family, 1992. Compact disc boxed set.

_____. *Jimmie Rodgers: The Life and Times of America's Blue Yodeler.* Urbana: University of Illinois Press, 1979.

Pucin, Diane. "Autry's Code As Owner Was Class." *Los Angeles Times.* 28 October 1998.

Ragan, David. *Who's Who in Hollywood, 1900–1976.* New Rochelle, N.Y.: Arlington House, 1976.

Rainey, Buck. *The Shoot-Em-Ups Ride Again.* Waynesville, N.C.: World of Yesterday, 1990.

Rambeck, Richard. *The History of the Angels.* Mankato, Minn.: Creative Education, 2000.

Randall, Stephen, and Carole Knaul. "Gene Autry: Still Riding High in Golden West's Saddle." *Los Angeles Magazine.* February 1977: 54, 59, 62, 65, 66, 68.

"Regan Follows Autry in Break with Rep, Wants Pact Release." *Variety.* 23 February 1938: 6.

"Rep Hustling Prod. with Grainger in As Headman; Await Autry Move." *Variety.* 9 February 1938.

"Rep — Autry in Stymie; New Mustanger." *Variety.* 16 February 1938: 5.

"Republic Counting on Autry's Peaceful Return Despite Walk. *Variety.* 26 January 1938: 4.

"Republic Not to Expand — Yates." *Variety.* 26 January 1938: 2.

"Republic Sales Meet Draws 200 to Coast." *Variety.* 20 April 1938.

Review of movie *Apache Country. Variety.* 21 May 1952: 6.

Review of movie *Back in the Saddle. Variety.* 26 March 1941: 18.

Review of movie *Barbed Wire. Variety.* 2 July 1952: 20.

Review of movie *Bells of Capistrano. Variety.* 16 September 1942: 8.

Review of movie *Beyond the Purple Hills. Variety.* 19 July 1950: 6.

Review of movie *The Big Show. Variety.* 3 March 1937: 15.

Review of movie *The Big Sombrero. Variety.* 13 April 1949: 11.

Review of movie *The Big Sombrero. Variety.* 2 February 1949: 12.

Review of movie *The Blazing Sun. Variety.* 8 November 1950: 18.

Review of movie *Boots and Saddle. Variety.* 13 October 1937: 16.

Review of movie *Call of the Canyon. Variety.* 19 August 1942: 8.

Review of movie *Carolina Moon. Variety.* 17 July 1940: 18.

Review of movie *Colorado Sunset. Variety.* 2 August 1939: 25.

Review of movie *Comin' Round the Mountain. Variety.* 29 April 1936: 36.

Review of movie *Cow Town. Variety.* 10 May 1950: 6.

Review of movie *The Cowboy and the Indians. Variety.* 2 November 1949: 22.

Review of movie *Cowboy Serenade. Variety.* 1 April 1942: 8.

Review of movie *Down Mexico Way. Variety.* 29 October 1941: 9.

Review of movie *Gaucho Serenade. Variety.* 15 May 1940: 16.

Review of movie *Gene Autry and the Mounties. Variety.* 24 January 1951: 6.

Review of movie *Git Along, Little Dogies. Variety.* 8 December 1937: 17.

Review of movie *Gold Mine in the Sky. Variety.* 6 June 1938: 15.

Review of movie *Goldtown Ghost. Variety.* 20 May 1953: 6.

Review of movie *Guns and Guitars. Variety.* 13 January 1937: 30.

Review of movie *Heart of the Rio Grande. Variety.* 11 March 1942: 20.

Review of movie *Hills of Utah. Variety.* 12 September 1951: 18.

Review of movie *Home in Wyomin.' Variety.* 29 April 1942: 8.

Review of movie *Home on the Prairie. Variety.* 22 March 1939: 20.

Review of movie *In Old Monterey. Variety.* 9 August 1939: 14.

Review of movie *In Old Santa Fe. Variety.* 20 March 1935: 17.

Review of movie *Indian Territory. Variety.* 3 January 1951: 67.

Review of movie *Indian Territory. Variety.* 6 September 1950: 8.

Review of movie *Last of the Pony Riders. Variety.* 4 November 1953: 6.

Review of movie *The Last Round-Up. Variety.* 8 October 1947: 8.

Review of movie *Loaded Pistols. Variety.* 22 December 1948: 6.

Review of movie *Man from Music Mountain. Variety.* 17 August 1938: 17.

Review of movie *Man from Music Mountain. Variety.* 22 September 1943: 43.

Review of movie *Melody Ranch. Variety.* 1 January 1941: 14.

Review of movie *Melody Trail. Variety.* 11 December 1935: 34.

Review of movie *Mexicali Rose. Variety.* 21 June 1939: 16.

Review of movie *Mountain Rhythm. Variety.* 12 July 1939: 12.

Review of movie *Mule Train. Variety.* 26 July 1950: 10.

Review of movie *Oh, Susannah. Variety.* 24 March 1937: 21.

Review of movie *Old Barn Dance. Variety.* 12 January 1938: 15.

Review of movie *The Old Corral. Variety.* 4 August 1937: 19.

Review of movie *The Old West. Variety.* 9 January 1952: 6.

Review of movie *Pack Train. Variety.* 1 July 1953: 6.

Review of movie *Prairie Moon. Variety.* 19 October 1938: 27.

Review of movie *Public Cowboy No. 1. Variety.* 22 September 1937: 18.

Review of movie *Rancho Grande. Variety.* 7 December 1938: 13.

Review of movie *Rancho Grande. Variety.* 27 March 1940: 17.

Review of movie *Red River Valley. Variety.* 11 November 1936: 15.

Review of movie *Rhythm of the Saddle. Variety.* 9 November 1938.

Review of movie *Ride, Ranger, Ride. Variety.* 21 April 1937: 15.

Review of movie *Ride, Tenderfoot, Ride. Variety.* 21 August 1940: 18.

Review of movie *Riders in the Sky. Variety.* 7 December 1949: 6.

Review of movie *Riders of the Whistling Pines. Variety.* 23 March 1949: 20.

Review of movie *Ridin' on a Rainbow. Variety.* 29 January 1941: 18.

Review of movie *Rim of the Canyon. Variety.* 7 September 1949: 11.

Review of movie *Robin Hood of Texas. Variety.* 10 September 1947: 17.

Review of movie *Rootin' Tootin' Rhythm*. *Variety*. 4 August 1937: 25.

Review of movie *Roundup Time in Texas*. *Variety*. 7 July 1937: 25.

Review of movie *Rovin' Tumbleweeds*. *Variety*. 10 January 1940: 16.

Review of movie *Saddle Pals*. *Variety*. 18 June 1947: 8.

Review of movie *Sagebrush Troubadour*. *Variety*. 9 September 1936: 17.

Review of movie *Saginaw Trail*. *Variety*. 26 August 1953: 6.

Review of movie *Shooting High*. *Variety*. 6 March 1940: 16.

Review of movie *Sierra Sue*. *Variety*. 12 November 1941: 9.

Review of movie *Silver Canyon*. *Variety*. 13 June 1951: 6.

Review of movie *The Singing Cowboy*. *Variety*. 26 November 1936: 19.

Review of movie *Singing Vagabond*. *Variety*. 29 July 1936: 15.

Review of movie *Sioux City Sue*. *Variety*. 27 November 1946: 28.

Review of movie *Sons of New Mexico*. *Variety*. 28 December 1949: 6.

Review of movie *South of the Border*. *Variety*. 13 December 1939: 11.

Review of movie *Springtime in the Rockies*. *Variety*. 24 November 1937.

Review of movie *Springtime in the Rockies*. *Variety*. 23 September 1942: 8.

Review of movie *Stardust on the Trail*. *Variety*. 27 May 1942: 8.

Review of movie *The Strawberry Roan*. *Variety*. 28 April 1948: 8.

Review of movie *Sunset in Wyoming*. *Variety*. 13 August 1941: 12.

Review of movie *Texans Never Cry*. *Variety*. 7 March 1951: 18.

Review of movie *Trail to San Antone*. *Variety*. 29 January 1947: 8.

Review of movie *Tumbling Tumbleweeds*. *Variety*. 5 February 1936: 33.

Review of movie *Twilight on the Rio Grande*. *Variety*. 16 April 1947: 20.

Review of movie *Under Fiesta Stars*. *Variety*. 31 December 1941: 8.

Review of movie *Under Western Stars*. *Variety*. 20 April 1938: 15.

Review of movie *Valley of Fire*. *Variety*. 7 November 1951: 18.

Review of movie *Wagon Team*. *Variety*. 10 September 1952: 6.

Review of movie *Western Jamboree*. *Variety*. 21 December 1938: 15.

Review of movie *Whirlwind*. *Variety*. 4 April 1951: 6.

Review of movie *Yodelin' Kid from Pine Ridge*. *Variety*. 13 October 1937: 17.

Review of radio program "The Eddie Cantor Show." *Variety*. 1 June 1938.

Review of radio program "Melody Ranch." *Variety*. 10 January 1940: 36.

Riders in the Sky, with Texas Bix Bender. *Riders in the Sky: The Book*. Salt Lake City: Gibbs-Smith/Peregrine Smith Books, 1992.

Roberts, Randy, and James S. Olson. *John Wayne: American*. New York: Free Press, 1995.

Robinson, Francis. "Gene Autry Tells of His Movie Start During Stop in Nashville." *Nashville Banner*. January 17, 1938.

Robinson, Ray. *American Original: A Life of Will Rogers*. New York: Oxford University Press, 1996.

"Rogers' P.A. Tour Routed Over Autry Strongholds." *Variety*. 13 April 1938: 7.

Rogers, Roy, and Dale Evans, with Carlton Stowers. *Happy Trails: The Story of Roy Rogers and Dale Evans*. Waco, Texas: Word Books, 1979.

Rogers, Roy, and Dale Evans, with Jane and Michael Stern. *Happy Trails: Our Life Story*. New York: Simon & Schuster, 1994.

Rosebrook, Jeb J. "Gene Autry in Arizona." *Arizona Highways* 75 (December 1999): 12.

Rothel, David. *The Gene Autry Book*. Madison, N.C.: Empire Publishing, 1988.

_____. *The Roy Rogers Book*. Madison, N.C.: Empire Publishing, 1996.

_____. *The Singing Cowboys*. Cranbury, N.J.: A. S. Barnes, 1978.

_____. *Those Great Cowboy Sidekicks*. Waynesville, N.C.: WOY Publications, 1984.

Rovin, Jeff. *The Great Television Series*. Cranbury, N.J.: A. S. Barnes, 1977.

"Roy and Gene Play Golf." *Life Magazine*. April 1950.

Rumble, John Woodruff. "Fred Rose and the Development of the Nashville Music Industry, 1942–1954." Ph.D. diss., Vanderbilt University, 1980.

Russell, Tony. *Country Music Records: A Discography, 1921–1942*. New York: Oxford University Press, 2004.

Rust, Brian. *The American Record Label Book*. New Rochelle, N.Y.: Arlington House, 1978.

"S-Q Rodeo Act Proves Gene Autry's Gun-Grip on Kids Undimmed by Army." *Variety*. 1 May 1946: 56.

"Salute to Autry!" *Western Stars*. Winter 1950.

Satherley, Art. Interview. Country Music Hall of Fame & Museum, Oral History Project. 1974.

Savage, William K., Jr. *The Cowboy Hero: His Image in American History and Culture*. Norman: University of Oklahoma Press, 1979.

_____. *Singing Cowboys and All That Jazz: A Short History of Popular Music in Oklahoma*. Norman: University of Oklahoma Press, 1983.

Scott, Vernon. "Fiasco at Brussels' Fair." *The Detroit News*. 25 June 1958: 12.

Seemann, Charles. Recording notes. *Back in the Saddle Again: American Cowboy Songs*. New World Records, 1983. LP record album.

Seemann, Charlie. "Gene Autry." *The Journal of the American Academy for the Preservation of Old-Time Country Music*, no. 22 (August 1994).

"See Oldies in Continued Sale to TV Despite Rogers' Win Over Republic." *Variety*. 24 October 1951: 2.

Sennett, Ted. *Hollywood Musicals*. New York: Harry N. Abrams, 1981.

Shaikin, Bill. "The Cowboy's Last Roundup." *Los Angeles Times*. 3 October 1998: C1, 6,

Shelton, Robert, and Burt Goldblatt. *The Country Music Story: A Picture History of Country & Western Music*. New York: Bobbs-Merrill, 1966.

Simon, Richard, and Susan King. "Friends and Fans Recall an American Icon." *Los Angeles Times*. 3 October 1998: A25.

Smallwood, James M., and Steven K. Gragert, eds. *Will Rogers' Daily Telegrams, Vol. 1: The Coolidge Years, 1926–1929*. Stillwater: Oklahoma State University Press, 1978.

Smith, John M., and Tim Cawkwell, eds. *The World Encyclopedia of the Film*. New York: World Publishing, 1972.

Smith, Jon Guyot. "A Brief Assessment of Gene Autry's Role in the Development of Country Music. *Gene Autry's Friends*. n.d.

_____. "Gene Autry: Brilliant Judge of Songs and Songwriters." *Gene Autry's Friends*. n.d.

_____. "Gene Autry on Victor Records: Elusive Collector's Items Throughout the Years." *Gene Autry's Friends*. n.d.

_____. "Gene Autry Recordings We All Want to Hear — For the First Time." *Gene Autry's Friends*. n.d.

_____. "Gene Autry: The Important Place He Has Occupied in Our Lives for So Long." *Gene Autry's Friends*. n.d.

_____. "The Gene Autry Show": The Greatest Western Series in Television History." *Gene Autry's Friends*. n.d.

_____. "Gene Autry's Best-Selling Records: A Guide for Identifying Them." *Gene Autry's Friends*. n.d.

_____. "An Informal History of the Gene Autry Friendship Club (And Its Successors)." *Gene Autry's Friends*. n.d.

_____. Recording notes. *Gene Autry with the Legendary Singing Groups of the West*. Varese Sarabande, 1997. Compact disc.

_____. Recording notes. *Sing, Cowboy, Sing*. Rhino Records, 1997. Compact disc boxed set.

_____. "Smiley Burnette: Gentle Genius Who Was Gene Autry's Pal." *Gene Autry's Friends*. n.d.

_____. "Some Thoughts Regarding the Evolution of Gene Autry's Recording Career." *Gene Autry's Friends*. n.d.

_____. "'This Is Gene Autry, for Doublemint Askin' You to Keep Thinkin' of Us.' A Brief Review of Our Favorite Radio Program, 'Gene Autry's Melody Ranch.'" *Gene's Autry's Friends*. n.d.

_____. "Treasure Chest: Unissued Gene Autry Recordings Reportedly Located." *Gene Autry's Friends*. n.d.

_____. "The Wonderful Ann Rutherford." *Gene Autry's Friends*. n.d.

Smith, Jonathan Guyot. "The Brilliant Artistry of Gene Autry." *Movie Collector's World*. n.d.

_____. "Smiley Burnette: A Career Appreciation." *Movie Collector's World*. n.d.

Smith, Jonathan Guyot. "Smiley Burnette: It's Nice to Be Important, but More Important to Be Nice." *DISCoveries*. April 1994: 26–30.

Smith, Packy. Recording notes. *Gene Autry: That Silver Haired Daddy of Mine*. Bear Family Records, 2006. Compact disc boxed set.

Smith, Packy, and Ed Husle, eds. *Don Miller's Hollywood Corral: A Comprehensive B Western Roundup*. Burbank, Calif.: Riverwood Press, 1993.

Smith, Richard Norton. *The Colonel: The Life and Legend of Robert R. McCormick, 1880–1955*. Evanston, Ill.: Northwestern University Press, 1997.

Stambler, Irwin, and Grelun Landon. *Country Music: The Encyclopedia*. New York: St. Martin's Press, 1997.

Stamper, Pete. *It All Happened in Renfro Valley*. Lexington, Ky.: University Press of Kentucky, 1999.

Steckmesser, Kent Ladd. *The Western Hero in History and Legend*. Norman: University of Oklahoma Press, 1965.

Stedman, Raymond William. *The Serials: Suspense and Drama by Installment*. Norman: University of Oklahoma Press, 1977.

Steinberg, Cobbett. *TV Facts*. New York: Facts on File, 1980.

"Stock Contractors." *ProRodeo Sports News* 27, no. 23 (1979): 57.

Strauss, William, and Neil Howe. *Generations: The History of America's Future, 1584 to 2069*. New York: Quill/William Morrow, 1991.

Summers, Neil. *The First Official TV Western Book*. Vienna, W.V.: Old West Shop Publishing, 1987.

_____. *The Official TV Western Book, Vol. 2*. Vienna, W.V.: Old West Shop Publishing, 1989.

_____. *The Official TV Western Book, Vol. 3*. Vienna, W.V.: Old West Shop Publishing, 1991.

Teaford, Elliott. "Late-Inning Bid by Disney Won the Angels." *Los Angeles Times*. 20 May 1995.

Terrace, Vincent. *Radio's Golden Years: The Encyclopedia of Radio Programs, 1930–1960*. San Diego: A. S. Barnes, 1981.

Tinsley, Jim Bob. *For a Cowboy Has to Sing*. Orlando, Fla.: University of Central Florida Press, 1991.

_____. *He Was Singin' This Song*. Orlando, Fla.: University of Central Florida Press, 1981.

Townsend, Charles R. *San Antonio Rose: The Life and Music of Bob Wills*. Urbana: University of Illinois Press, 1976.

Tribe, Ivan. "Brother Gene Autry: The Original Singing Cowboy." *Knight Templar* 44, no. 1 (January 1998): 21.

Tuska, Jon. *The American West in Film: Critical Approaches to the Western*. Westport, Conn.: Greenwood Press, 1985.

_____. *The Filming of the West*. New York: Doubleday, 1976.

_____. *The Vanishing Legion: A History of Mascot Pictures, 1927–1935*. Jefferson, N.C.: McFarland, 1982.

Tuttle, Wesley. Interview by author. 3 January 2001.

"TV Aids Autry on 585G Tour." *Billboard*. 28 March 1953: 1, 48.

"20th After Autry." *Variety*. 16 March 1938.

"Under Western Lies, or a Plea for More Realism in Mustang Films." *Variety*. 11 May 1938.

Vallee, William Lynce. "If You Were Gene Autry." n.p., n.d. In files at the National Cowboy & Western Heritage Museum.

Vasey, Ruth. *The World According to Hollywood, 1918–1939*. Madison: University of Wisconsin Press, 1997.

Vaughn, Gerald F. *Ray Whitley: Country-Western Music Master and Film Star*. Newark, Del.: Privately published by author, 1973.

Veeck, Bill, with Ed Linn. *Veeck As in Wreck: The Autobiography of Bill Veeck.* Chicago: University of Chicago Press, 1962, 2001.

"Ventura Blvd. Plant Completes Mascot Commitments." *Variety.* 18 September 1935.

Wade, Jack. "Why Autry Can't Quit." n.p. 1949. Gene Autry Oklahoma Museum

Wakely, Linda Lee. *See Ya Up There, Baby: The Jimmy Wakely Story.* Canoga Park, Calif.: Shasta Records, 1992.

Walker, John, ed. *Halliwell's Who's Who in the Movies.* 13th edition. New York: HarperPerennial, 1999.

Wallis, Michael. *The Real Wild West: The 101 Ranch and the Creation of the American West.* New York: St. Martin's, 1999.

Warner, Jay. *Just Walkin' in the Rain: The True Story of a Convict Quintet, a Liberal Governor, and How They Changed Southern History Through Rhythm and Blues.* Los Angeles: Renaissance Books, 2001.

Webster, Donovan. *The Burma Road: The Epic Story of the China-Burma-India Theater in World War II.* New York: Farrar, Straus and Giroux, 2003.

Weiser, Norman. "New Autry Act, Capsule Version of Arena Show, Is Solid Combo Fare." *Billboard.* 7 June 1952: 3, 14.

Western, Johnny. Telephone interview by author. 31 August 2005.

_____. Interview by Douglas B. Green. Nashville, Tennessee. 17 December 1997

Whitburn, Joel. *Top Country Albums, 1964–1997.* Menomonee Falls, Wisc.: Record Research, 1997.

_____. *Top Country Singles, 1944–1988.* Menomonee Falls, Wisc.: Record Research, 1989.

_____. *Top 40 Country Hits: 1944–Present.* New York: Billboard Books, 1996.

_____. *Top Pop Singles: 1955–1990.* Menomonee Falls, Wisc.: Record Research, 1991.

White, Glenn. Telephone interview by author. 2 May 2005.

Whitley, Ray. Interview by Douglas B. Green. Country Music Hall of Fame & Museum, Oral History Project. 1 July 1974.

_____. Interview by Douglas B. Green. Country Music Hall of Fame & Museum, Oral History Project. 30 March 1975.

_____. Interview by Murray Nash. Country Music Hall of Fame & Museum, Oral History Project. 8 June 1978.

Wiener, Allen J. "Gene Autry: America's Singing Cowboy." *DISCoveries.* November 1997.

Wills, Garry. *John Wayne's America: The Politics of Celebrity.* New York: Simon & Schuster, 1997.

The Winning of the West. Movie review. *Variety.* 21 January 1953: 18.

WLS Family Album, 1933. Chicago: WLS, The Prairie Farmer Station, 1933.

Wolfe, Charles K. *Classic Country: Legends of Country Music.* New York: Routledge, 2001.

_____. "The Triumph of the Hills: Country Radio, 1920–1950." In *Country: The Music and the Musicians,* edited by Paul Kingsbury and Alan Axelrod. New York: Abbeville Press, 1988.

Yagoda, Ben. *Will Rogers: A Life.* New York: Knopf, 1993.

"Yates' $902,100 More in Republic in 1937." *Variety.* 13 April 1938: 17.

"Yates Reappointed President of Republic." *Variety.* 15 November 1950.

"The Year in Pictures: Review of 1937." *Variety.* 7 January 1938: 12.

Yoggy, Gary. *Riding the Western Range: The Rise and Fall of the Western on Television.* Jefferson, N.C.: McFarland, 1995.

_____, ed. *Back in the Saddle: Essays on Western Film and Television Actors.* Jefferson, N.C.: McFarland, 1998.

Zimmerman, David. "Now, He's Mostly Ropin' in Business." *USA Today.* n.d. Gene Autry Oklahoma Museum.

Zingg, Paul J., and Mark D. Medeiros. *Runs, Hits, and an Era: The Pacific Coast League, 1903–58.* Urbana and Chicago: University of Illinois Press, 1994.

Zinman, David H. *Saturday Afternoon at the Bijou: A Nostalgic Look at Charlie Chan, Andy Hardy, and Other Movie Heroes We Have Grown to Love.* New Rochelle, N.Y.: Arlington House, 1973.

Zwonitzer, Mark, with Charles Hirshberg. *Will You Miss Me When I'm Gone? The Carter Family & Their Legacy in American Music.* New York: Simon & Schuster, 2002.

INDEX

Pat + Gene
on Melody Ranch 1978